A New Testament Journey

May We Serve
Christ!

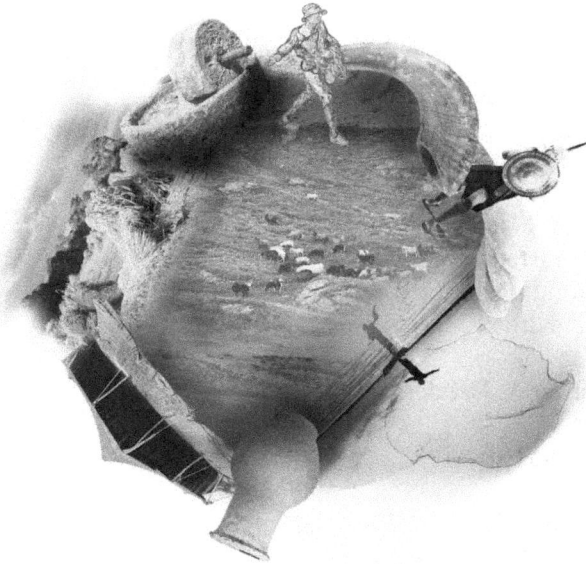

WARREN HENDERSON

May We Serve Christ! – A New Testament Journey

By Warren Henderson
Copyright © 2022

Cover Design: Ben Bredeweg
Editing/Proofreading: Dan Macy
    and David Lindstrom

Published by Warren A. Henderson Publishing
1025 Iron Cap Dr.
Stevensville, MT 59870

Perfect Bound ISBN: 978-1-939770-68-4
eBook ISBN: 978-1-939770-69-1

Copies of *May We Serve Christ! – A New Testament Journey* are available through various online retailers worldwide. Our website address is: warrenahendersonpublishing.com

Daily Devotions

January 1 – A New Year
Introduction

One day near the end of Christ's earthly pilgrimage, certain Greeks arrived at Jerusalem to observe the Passover and to worship God. But their souls were yearning for something beyond religious formality; they asked Philip, *"Sir, we wish to see Jesus"* (John 12:21). *May We See Christ? – An Old Testament Journey* was previously published to fill the believer's eyes with prophetic allegories, types, and shadows of Christ from the Old Testament. Through New Testament truth we are able to appreciate how God the Father has portrayed His Son in Scripture. Spiritual growth begins when we are in awe of Jesus Christ; otherwise, we will have no appetite for His Word or to obey what He says. The *May We Serve Christ?* series is provided to better equip believers to trust and obey Christ, and to serve Him as He deems best.

After the Greeks asked Philip "to see Jesus," Philip discussed the matter with Andrew and then both men conveyed the request to the Lord Jesus. The Lord responded to their sincere appeal by saying that He must die soon to be able to share eternal life with them. Those who would receive Him for salvation and then live in obedience to Him would experience the fruitful benefits of His resurrection life. True submission to God's will and faithful service to God are only possible through resurrection power. Because believers are positionally dead to themselves and to the world, each of us has an opportunity to live out what we possess, Christ's life. The lost must see Christ in His Church.

At this moment, each of us is as close to the Lord Jesus Christ as we desire to be. Our patient Savior is always ready to assist anyone genuinely seeking Him and desiring to serve Him in his or her appointed capacity and calling. Through His Word and His Spirit, God aids a true seeker every step of the way into a deeper knowledge of Himself and His purposes. *May We Serve Christ? – A New Testament Journey* draws practical application from Scripture to convict, to confront, and to encourage us to *"press toward the goal for the prize of the upward call of God in Christ Jesus"* (Phil. 3:14). There is a Savior to know, a work to do, a calling to be fulfilled, and a race to run! As you begin this new year, my prayer is that your daily meditations will draw you into a higher personal experience with our great God and Savior.

January 2 – Bear Fruit Worthy of Repentance!
Matthew 3:6-10

When he saw many of the Pharisees and Sadducees coming to his baptism, he said to them, "Brood of vipers! Who warned you to flee from the wrath to come? Therefore bear fruits worthy of repentance, and do not think to say to yourselves, 'We have Abraham as our father.' For I say to you that God is able to raise up children to Abraham from these stones. And even now the ax is laid to the root of the trees. Therefore every tree which does not bear good fruit is cut down and thrown into the fire."

The Pharisees and Sadducees, and indeed much of the Jewish nation, believed that being children of Abraham uniquely qualified them to receive God's blessing above any other people group. The divine token given to Abraham to remind him and his descendants of God's covenant (i.e., male circumcision) had become a badge of elitism, instead of prompting the Jews to be a consecrated people having no confidence in their flesh. Consequently, John did not mince words with these self-righteous hypocrites, who in their own estimation did not need to repent of anything. They were immersed in the rabbinical traditions and therefore were in good standing with God. John warned them that there was only one way to avoid God's forthcoming wrath on the wicked: they must humble themselves before God and confess their sins to God. Ultimately, forgiveness for their sins would come through Christ, the One John was foretelling of.

John's message to these religious zealots was forthright: Your religiosity does not impress God; you need to experience a spiritual transformation, which begins with repentance. True repentance is more than lip service to God; it has tangible evidence of a changed heart. This includes a deep conviction that I have nothing within myself but sin and if God judges me in accordance with what He finds in me, I stand condemned before Him. The Word of God and Spirit of God put such a soul under a deep moral conviction of guiltiness and therefore is brought to God by the necessity of repentance. Repentance permits us to stand with God against ourselves and believes that God alone can make us right in His presence. The necessity of repentance is essential to gospel preaching and we do well to not neglect it (Luke 13:3).

January 3 – Baptism of the Holy Spirit and of Fire
Matthew 3:11-12

I indeed baptize you with water unto repentance, but He who is coming after me is mightier than I, whose sandals I am not worthy to carry. He will baptize you with the Holy Spirit and fire. His winnowing fan is in His hand, and He will thoroughly clean out His threshing floor, and gather His wheat into the barn; but He will burn up the chaff with unquenchable fire.

Some in Christendom have equated the baptism of the Holy Spirit and of fire as being the same thing and also as being a desirable blessing from God. But careful examination of four pertinent passages will reveal quite a different understanding. First, when used metaphorically in Scripture, "fire" speaks of various forms of divine judgment (Gen. 19:24; Num. 16:35; Matt. 13:39-40). This means that God's fire is not desirable, with the only exception being that the Lord permits His people to pass through refining trials to better them (Job 23:10; Mal. 3:2-3). But this is obviously not Matthew's meaning as he further clarifies that the baptism of fire is of an unquenchable nature that completely devours the chaff (unbelievers), in contrast to the wheat (true believers) which is gathered safely into God's barn (heaven).

Next, notice that in Matthew's account John is speaking to a mixed audience of believers and rebels, so he mentions both baptisms. In a future day, believers would be baptized by the Holy Spirit, while those rejecting Christ would be cast into the eternal Lake of Fire. Likewise, Luke records John speaking to a mixed group and also promises both baptisms will come upon those listening to him (Luke 3:16). Yet, Mark records a different scene in which John is only speaking to those who had repented and were baptized by him. To these he promises only the baptism of the Holy Spirit; there is no mention of fire (Mark 1:8).

Lastly, just before the Lord's ascension to heaven, He refers to John's promise: *"For John truly baptized with water, but you shall be baptized with the Holy Spirit not many days from now"* (Acts 1:5). The Lord is speaking to His disciples and there is no mention of fire. Dear believer, the Holy Spirit is not given in measure (John 3:34). If you have been born again, you have all of Him that you will ever get and all that you will ever need to achieve whatever God has for you to do.

January 4 – The Lord's Patience in Calling His Disciples
Matthew 4:18-22

And Jesus, walking by the Sea of Galilee, saw two brothers, Simon called Peter, and Andrew his brother, casting a net into the sea; for they were fishermen. Then He said to them, "Follow Me, and I will make you fishers of men." They immediately left their nets and followed Him. Going on from there, He saw two other brothers, James the son of Zebedee, and John his brother, in the boat with Zebedee their father, mending their nets. He called them, and immediately they left the boat and their father, and followed Him.

The Lord Jesus exhibited tremendous patience in calling His disciples. Initially, He invited two of John's disciples, including Andrew (Peter's brother), to His home to spend some time with Him, but at the end of the day they departed (John 1:39). Andrew then told Peter that he had found the Messiah, but Peter did not come to Christ on his own. The Lord had to repeatedly call Peter to follow Him, but after each time, Peter dedicated more of himself to Christ.

First, Peter forsook his fishing nets to follow Christ at His bidding in Mark 1:18. Later, Peter forsook all to pursue the Savior (Luke 5:11). After Christ's resurrection, the Lord again called Peter to follow Him with the understanding that it would cost Peter his life (John 21:15-19). A few days earlier Peter had vehemently denied the Lord to protect himself from harm, but it is at this juncture that Peter settled "the death question" once and for all. He had learned that it was harder to live daily for the Lord than to die for Him once. In Acts 2 we do not see a shrinking, denying Peter, but a fully restored, Spirit-filled apostle preaching Christ to the saving of 3,000 souls.

The Lord's patience with Peter is an encouragement to all those who are involved in training others. Those who mentor younger believers must be patient and tender. New believers need "breathing room" – we should not attempt to conform them to our pattern of Christianity before the Holy Spirit works in their hearts or they might turn into religious legalists instead of disciples of Christ. Prioritize needful exhortations; not everything needs to be corrected all at once, and often the less serious matters will resolve themselves as the young believer submits to the leading and conviction of God in his or her life.

January 5 – Blessed Are the Poor in Spirit
Matthew 5:1-3

And seeing the multitudes, He went up on a mountain, and when He was seated His disciples came to Him. Then He opened His mouth and taught them, saying: "Blessed are the poor in spirit, for theirs is the kingdom of heaven."

The Sermon on the Mount is the manifesto of the King, literally the constitution of the millennial kingdom, once Christ returns to earth to establish it. Although it is true that those in the Church Age who have the Holy Spirit indwelling them should be exhibiting behavior consistent with the Kingdom Constitution, the kingdom exists now in only that spiritual sense. The literal sense is yet future.

The Lord pronounces a blessing on those who are "poor in spirit." But what kind of disposition is the Lord speaking of? W. T. P Wolston answers the question, "What does it mean to be poor in spirit?"

Exactly the reverse of what you find in the world. In the world people stick up for themselves, stand for their rights. A person who does that is not in the kingdom of heaven at all, that is, is not in it in spirit. One who is poor in spirit, is self-emptied, self is out of sight. ... It is a blessed thing to be self-emptied (poor-spirited the world would call you); that is it, but the Lord reckons such "blessed." May the Lord give us to know in our hearts the meaning of it.[1]

The Lord wants all believers to learn what Paul learned, *"My grace is sufficient for you, for My strength is made perfect in weakness"* (2 Cor. 12:9). The Lord does not need our wealth, natural abilities, or religious feats; He simply wants our hearts soft, pliable, and beating for Him. To be poor implies a situation where there is a legitimate lack, but to be *poor in spirit* is a self-imposed disposition of helplessness – a willful discipline of emptiness. Paul warns, *"If anyone thinks himself to be something, when he is nothing, he deceives himself"* (Gal. 6:3). Those who talk about themselves and vaunt of their talents and accomplishments are not poor in spirit and therefore lose out on the Lord's blessing for being so inclined. Let us remember that the Lord is our all in all and without Him we are completely helpless!

January 6 – Blessed Are Those Who Mourn
Matthew 5:4

Blessed are those who mourn, for they shall be comforted.

On one particular day, early in His ministry, the Lord Jesus ventured into a synagogue in His hometown of Nazareth. He was handed a scroll of Isaiah to read from. After announcing that the Spirit of the Lord was upon Him, He read Isaiah 61 verse 1 and half of verse 2 and then closed the book, returned it to the attendant and sat down. With every eye in the synagogue fixed on Him, the Lord then declared, *"Today this Scripture is fulfilled in your hearing"* (Luke 4:21).

The Jews understood that the Lord was claiming to be the One Isaiah was prophesying of, that is, the Messiah. They became so enraged by His claim that they sought to push Him over a cliff. The Lord did not read the remaining portion of verse 2 or verse 3, as that content pertained to His second advent, when He will return to judge the nations and restore Israel to a proper place of honor: *"And the day of vengeance of our God; to comfort all who mourn, to console those who mourn in Zion..."* (Isa. 61:2-3). For Israel, the Lord's promise to comfort those who mourn will be realized after the Tribulation Period. Obviously, believers in the Church Age can always approach the throne of grace for help when needed (Heb. 4:16), but this prophecy confirms the type of special comfort God provides for particular mourners.

While there are many hardships in life that may cause us to mourn, the idea of Isaiah's prophecy is that Christ will be a special solace for all those who have suffered the contradiction of sinners, the sorrow of a God-hating world, or for upholding matters of righteousness or for identifying with Christ in His rejection. Our English word "comfort" is derived from two Latin roots, *con*, "to be with," and *fortis*, "strong." Literally "comfort" means "to strengthen by companionship."[2] God's infinitely strong arms fully embrace us with His tender mercies!

Like Israel, some of our sorrows may be caused by God's chastening hand over sin, but much suffering today results from those resisting God's rule for their lives. Godly comfort is the lasting remedy for life's sorrows. In a coming day, God Himself will wipe away every tear of those who mourn and they will be eternally comforted.

January 7 – Blessed Are the Meek
Matthew 5:5

Blessed are the meek, for they shall inherit the earth.

By nature none of us are meek, but rather we are temperamental, often volatile; if we have the means of getting our own way, we will do so. However, being spiritually bonded with Christ provides a different disposition towards what is important to God and what is self-seeking. A meek person is not self-willed, self-promoting and does not force his or her way on others even when there is the ability to do so. Meekness is power in control and is not to be confused with weakness. Weakness means that one does not have the capacity to right a wrong, but in meekness, one chooses not to right the wrong even if there were an opportunity to do so. Meekness exercises restraint and self-control to do what is best for others and to honor the Lord.

The ultimate example of meekness is when the Lord laid aside His glory and position in heaven to become a man in order to be a humble substitute for us at Calvary (Phil. 2:6-8). At His crucifixion, He reminded His disciples that He could call twelve legions of angels to His rescue if He thought it was necessary, but He never summoned them (Matt. 26:53). The Lord Jesus was doing the will of His Father, in being His Lamb which would take away the sin of the world – He could not be rescued from doing the Father's will.

> Christ is the humility of God embodied in human nature; the Eternal Love humbling itself, clothing itself in the garb of meekness and gentleness, to win and serve and save us (Andrew Murray).

Meekness accepts a lowly position to extend mercy for the good of others. The Lord desires us to learn this aspect of His character: *"Take My yoke upon you and learn from Me, for I am gentle and lowly in heart, and you will find rest for your souls"* (Matt. 11:29). By being yoked with Him, believers learn of the Lord's gentle and humble spirit, enjoy fruitfulness, and gain His peace. Representing Christ to others in this way ensures that the meek will inherit disdain, injustice, and abuse presently. However, the Lord promises that when He returns to set up His kingdom, the meek will inherit the earth with Him!

January 8 – Blessed Are Those Yearning for Uprightness
Matthew 5:6

Blessed are those who hunger and thirst for righteousness, for they shall be filled.

Naturally speaking, we are born going our own way and seeking our own things and morality does not control our decision making. But after being confronted with the gospel message and trusting in Christ alone for salvation, we receive a new nature from God that longs for righteousness. This is accomplished through an act of the Holy Spirit called regeneration: *"But when the kindness and the love of God our Savior toward man appeared, not by works of righteousness which we have done, but according to His mercy He saved us, through the washing of regeneration and renewing of the Holy Spirit"* (Tit. 3:4-5). The Holy Spirit washes us by bringing us to see the wrong in our sinful attitudes and desires. He makes us feel their uncleanness, and leads us to repent of and repudiate them.

Peter refers to the new nature received as a divine nature: *"By which have been given to us exceedingly great and precious promises, that through these you may be partakers of the divine nature, having escaped the corruption that is in the world through lust"* (2 Pet. 1:4). Regeneration is the implantation of a new life and a new order of living. This is why a regenerated person is referred to as a "new man" in Colossians 3:10; he or she received a new disposition which is to govern his or her thinking and behavior. This new disposition is God's own nature, which cannot sin (1 Jn. 3:9), though the believer may still sin by ignoring its moral reckoning (1 Jn. 1:9-2:1).

Having God's own nature within prompts every believer to pursue personal holiness and to yearn for God's righteousness to be evident everywhere. Only those who have a passion for holiness in their own lives will hunger and thirst for honesty, integrity, virtue, and justice in society also. When the Lord Jesus returns to establish His kingdom on earth, those yearning for righteousness will be completely satisfied, for Christ shall reign over the world with justice and in righteousness. Given God's great salvation to come, the prophet Isaiah exhorted his countrymen: *"Keep justice, and do righteousness, for My salvation is about to come, and My righteousness to be revealed"* (Isa. 56:1).

January 9 – Blessed Are the Merciful
Matthew 5:7

Blessed are the merciful, for they shall obtain mercy.

So rend your heart, and not your garments; return to the Lord your God, for He is gracious and merciful, slow to anger, and of great kindness; and He relents from doing harm (Joel 2:13).

Mercy and grace are complementary aspects of God's character. It has been said that *mercy* is not getting what you do deserve, while *grace* is getting what you don't deserve. As sinners we deserved to spend eternity in the Lake of Fire, but God's mercy intervened on our behalf. As rebels opposing God, we certainly did not merit heaven, but by God's grace we gain entrance into God's marvelous abode.

Paul acknowledges that it is only through the finished work of Christ that sinners can experience God's mercy: *"Not by works of righteousness which we have done, but according to His mercy He saved us"* (Tit. 3:5). In the Old Testament, God's prophets often threatened God's retribution for waywardness, but did not often speak of God's good character as a motivation for repentance. But Scripture reveals that God is gracious, merciful, slow to anger, and full of kindness and hence longs to forgive those who confess their sin!

God's holy character and attributes are perfectly and consistently demonstrated in all that He does; He can do nothing against His holy nature. Hence, God is completely satisfied with all that He does. His love does not overpower His holiness. His mercy does not ignore justice. His grace is not prompted by mere sympathy, but by what is best for those in need. Scripture tells us that God is good and does good (Ps. 119:68). God's holy character ensures that He must judge sin (Ex. 34:7). God would be unjust if He did not prosecute that which opposes His nature, as a lack of action against sin endorses wickedness. Yet, His mercy tempers such judgments to permit every opportunity for the wicked and the wayward to repent that they might be blessed. We also should mimic God's character by showing mercy to others for this same purpose. Mercy does not forget sin or ignore offenses, but rather it chooses not to act immediately so that grace might abound. Those who show mercy in this manner will have God's mercy also.

11

January 10 – Blessed Are the Pure in Heart
Matthew 5:8

Blessed are the pure in heart, for they shall see God.

Those with pure hearts are assured of enjoying God's presence. For Israel this will be in the Kingdom Age, but for believers in the Church Age, we continue to enjoy intimate communion with God by maintaining a pure heart. In Psalm 24, David affirms that the Lord, as Creator, reigns supreme over all His creation from His holy hill. He then asks the questions: *"Who may ascend into the hill of the Lord? Or who may stand in His holy place?"* (Ps. 24:3). The answer to both questions is the same: *"He who has clean hands and a pure heart, who has not lifted up his soul to an idol, nor sworn deceitfully"* (Ps. 24:4).

Although Satan wanted to *ascend to the hill of the Lord* and reign as God, his pride was judged and he lost his privileged status as a covering cherub and was cast off God's holy mountain (Isa. 14:12-15; Ezek. 28:12-17). Only those whom God has cleansed within through the regeneration of His Spirit have the capacity to have clean hands and a pure heart; these alone are permitted to be with the Lord in His holy dwelling place.

Israel will enjoy this blessing later, but believers today can enjoy God's presence to the degree that they strive to remain in fellowship with Him. We are able to enjoy God through His Word and by the illumination and communion of His Spirit. But this wonderful privilege requires maintaining short-accounts with Him on the matter of sin. Sinful behavior, ungodly thoughts, and sins of omission must be confessed and forsaken immediately once we realize their true nature. The Lord promises, that *"if we confess our sins, He is faithful and just to forgive us our sins and to cleanse us from all unrighteousness"* (1 Jn. 1:9). By the blood of Christ, God cleanses us to a condition of pureness so that we can again enjoy His intimate fellowship.

What the psalmist Asaph said long ago is still accurate today: *"Truly God is good to Israel, to such as are pure in heart"* (Ps. 73:1). God is good and does good to the pure in heart. Such upright souls are promised that they shall see God. This includes spiritual communion with God presently, but also the opportunity to bask in His glory forever in a coming day.

January 11– Blessed Are the Peacemakers
Matthew 5:9

Blessed are the peacemakers, for they shall be called sons of God.

The main Greek word rendered "peace" in the New Testament is *eirene,* which means to be "at one with." *Eirene* is used to describe the effort of Moses to bring two of his striving brethren into peace; he sought *"to set them at one again"* (Acts 7:26; KJV) or *"to reconcile them"* (NKJV). This is what Christ accomplished for us. We were once enemies of God, but through His finished work at Calvary, Christ has reconciled us with a holy God to become His children with the privilege of a full inheritance. Positionally speaking we have peace with God through Christ (Phil. 1:2). Practically speaking we have the peace of God when we adopt the mind of Christ in our thinking (Phil. 4:7-8). When believers have God's perspective on their circumstances, they will cease to be anxious over what is beyond their control.

We learn from Paul's opening salutations in many of his epistles that grace is the forerunner of peace: *"Grace to you and peace from God"* (Eph. 1:2). We cannot enjoy God's peace without the work of His grace in our lives. Peace in our hearts is positive proof that God's grace has been at work in our lives. He cannot give peace unto those who have not given over their lives to Him (John 14:27). This means there are two components to being a God-honoring *peacemaker*:

First, we must be faithful to share the good news message of Jesus Christ, so that those who are dead in their trespasses and sins can be forgiven and thereby reconciled with God. These receive the peace of God and become one with Him. This mimics the ministry of God's own Son, thus, such peacemakers *shall be called sons of God.*

Second, we must be faithful to uphold the mind of Christ in all conversations to pursue peace. Paul writes: *"If it is possible, as much as depends on you, live peaceably with all men"* (Rom. 12:18). Because the fountainhead of strife is pride, it is not always possible to come into oneness if the flesh has any part in the reconciliation effort. At such times it is good to remember that the promised blessing is for those who humble themselves and genuinely labor for peace; it is not contingent on bringing one or more antagonists into peace, as only the Spirit of God can accomplish true and lasting peace.

January 12 – Blessed Are the Persecuted
Matthew 5:10

Blessed are those who are persecuted for righteousness' sake, for theirs is the kingdom of heaven.

Previously, the Lord promised a blessing for those who hungered and thirsted after righteousness. These individuals desire to know what God determines is right and proper. Furthermore, they yearn to see such a standard of morality upheld by everyone, everywhere. The blessing of this beatitude is for those who not only yearn for righteousness, but are determined to live righteously despite the personal repercussion of doing so. This blessing is afforded to those who suffer, not for their own wrongdoings, but because others condemned their right conduct.

The kingdom of God is pledged to those who suffer for doing what is right. William MacDonald explains the hostility: "Their integrity condemns the ungodly world and brings out its hostility. People hate a righteous life because it exposes their own unrighteousness.[3] The Lord later reminded His disciples to expect this type of hatred from those who do not appreciate having their sin exposed:

All these things they will do to you for My name's sake, because they do not know Him who sent Me. If I had not come and spoken to them, they would have no sin, but now they have no excuse for their sin. He who hates Me hates My Father also. If I had not done among them the works which no one else did, they would have no sin; but now they have seen and also hated both Me and My Father (John 15:21-25).

The unregenerate do not appreciate having their sin exposed by the validity of a righteous life. Yet, we may be encouraged that their displayed anger is proof that the Lord is speaking to the conscience of the oppressors. Expressed anger of this fashion reveals insecurity in their flawed belief-system and worldview. Paul puts the matter this way: *"Only let your conduct be worthy of the gospel of Christ ... with one mind striving together for the faith of the gospel, and not in any way terrified by your adversaries, which is to them a proof of perdition, but to you of salvation, and that from God"* (Phil. 1:27-28). Suffering for righteousness is a powerful testimony to the lost of what is real.

January 13 – Blessed Are "You"
Matthew 5:11-12

Blessed are you when they revile and persecute you, and say all kinds of evil against you falsely for My sake. Rejoice and be exceedingly glad, for great is your reward in heaven, for so they persecuted the prophets who were before you.

The parallel passage in the Gospel of Luke provides some additional information:

Blessed are you when men hate you, and when they exclude you, and revile you, and cast out your name as evil, for the Son of Man's sake. Rejoice in that day and leap for joy! For indeed your reward is great in heaven, for in like manner their fathers did to the prophets (Luke 6:22-23).

First, notice that the Lord switches from announcing general beatitudes to addressing the disciples personally, *"blessed are you"* instead of "blessed are those." In the original language the "you" is plural, so no doubt the disciples perked up a bit to hear what the Lord was directly promising them, and by implication to succeeding generations of disciples in the Church Age.

Second, at first glance this beatitude may seem redundant to the one in verse 10, *"blessed are those who are persecuted for righteousness' sake."* While the outcome of suffering persecution is consistent, the reason for it is different. Verse 10 speaks of those who suffer for doing what is right and just. Their integrity rebuffs the wicked and condemns ungodliness. However, verse 11 addresses believers who are persecuted for Christ's sake. Because the world hates Christ, it also will hate those who identify with His name and live for Him (John 15:19-20).

Where the former group was persecuted for their righteous living, the latter group is simply hated for associating with Christ's name. Clearly then, believers should expect worldlings to isolate from them, revile them, and speak evil of them, even when nothing was done to deserve such disdain. Yet, the Lord told His disciples to rejoice greatly in their afflictions at such times, for their reward was waiting for them at the Judgment Seat of Christ (in heaven). It is waiting there for us too.

January 14 – They Persecuted the Prophets Before You
Matthew 5:12

Rejoice and be exceedingly glad, for great is your reward in heaven, for so they persecuted the prophets who were before you.

Besides promising His disciples a heavenly reward for suffering persecution as a result of identifying with His name, He also reminded them that they would be treated no differently than God's previous messengers of truth – His holy prophets.

The Old Testament prophets often drank of their own ministries to further substantiate God's message to His wayward people. Hosea was permitted to feel the pain of a lascivious wife (Hos. 1). Daniel and his friends were likely made eunuchs (Isa. 20:18, 39:7). God told Ezekiel that the death of his beloved wife would be an object lesson to motivate exiled Jewish captives (Ezek. 24:18). Jeremiah was thrown in a deep, muddy pit and left to die (Jer. 37:11-38:13). Isaiah was commanded to publicly strip off his prophet's attire to demonstrate how Assyria would shame their captives (Isa. 20). These servants of the Lord suffered daily hardships, threats against their lives, and the loss of loved ones to remain faithful to their God-ordained calling.

Indeed the disciples did follow the example of the prophets before them. In his autumn years, John was banished and imprisoned on the Isle of Patmos. James was executed by Herod. Nero crucified Peter upside down. Andrew was crucified in Greece. Thomas was pierced by the spear. Philip was put to death for converting the wife of a Roman proconsul. Matthew was stabbed to death in Ethiopia. Simon was killed in Persia for refusing to sacrifice to the sun god. James, the half-brother of Christ, was stoned and then clubbed to death at the temple. Paul, a prominent Jewish leader who came to Christ on the road to Damascus (Acts 9), faithfully preached Christ until finishing his course; then, he was beheaded by Nero.

If your Christian ministry ever seems too arduous to endure, remember the previous example of the prophets and the apostles has been given to us as a pattern to follow. They were God's servants doing God's will and were thus invincible until God's mission for their lives was complete. May we learn from their example – lest we ever think that the Lord asks more from us than what He deserves (Luke 17:10).

January 15 – Salt and Light
Matthew 5:13-16

You are the salt of the earth; but if the salt loses its flavor, how shall it be seasoned? It is then good for nothing but to be thrown out and trampled underfoot by men. You are the light of the world. A city that is set on a hill cannot be hidden. Nor do they light a lamp and put it under a basket, but on a lampstand, and it gives light to all who are in the house. Let your light so shine before men, that they may see your good works and glorify your Father in heaven.

A brief review of how salt was used in the Old Testament sacrifices will increase our appreciation of what the Lord was implying by this similitude. Salt is a symbol of purification in Scripture (Num. 18:19) and was thus required to be added to the various burnt offerings on the Bronze Altar. Salt stands in sharp contrast with leaven, which corrupts and, accordingly, was never permitted on the Bronze Altar. When the salt put on the Levitical offerings was burned, it created billowing white smoke. It was unnoticed until tested by fire and then the evidence of its presence was unmistakable. In this sense, salt speaks of pure, uncompromised truth. This is why Paul exhorts believers to *"Let your speech always be with grace, seasoned with salt* [the pure truth], *that you may know how you ought to answer each one"* (Col. 4:6).

Salt also enhances the flavor of what we eat and serves as a food preservative. Combining all these useful facets of salt we can understand why the Lord Jesus exhorted His disciples to have a "salty" testimony – declaring preserved truth enhances our testimony. Like salt, light also portrays a meaning of undefiled truth in Scripture: *"God is light and in Him is no darkness at all"* (1 Jn. 1:5). Salt that is no longer salty and a lamp that is hidden under a basket have no value. A believer who no longer lives to declare the goodness of Christ in word and by deed is become "good for nothing" and his or her testimony will be happily trampled under as meaningless by the children of the devil.

The cross of Christ has carved believers out of the world (Gal 2:20). We are the Church – God's *called-out company* of blood-bought, born again, Spirit-equipped people that have died to self and are alive in Christ. How can we not represent Christ in a dark world that desperately needs to see and to taste His goodness?

January 16 – Murder Begins in the Heart
Matthew 5:21-22

You have heard that it was said to those of old, "You shall not murder, and whoever murders will be in danger of the judgment." But I say to you that whoever is angry with his brother without a cause shall be in danger of the judgment ....

Anger is a powerful emotion that heightens the body's physical capability to respond in a way it would not normally be able. However, righteous anger must serve God and others and be quickly extinguished after accomplishing its work or it will lead us into sin. Hence, the Lord warns us against harboring congealed anger in our hearts towards others; such resentment will ultimately result in bitterness. Bitterness negatively affects all relationships of the person willfully swallowing such poison. One believer internalizing, instead of releasing his or her anger feelings to the Lord, can destroy a marriage, an assembly, etc. Bitterness is like a virus that spreads among God's people.

Believers must learn the characteristics of God's anger and pray for grace to conform the outworking of our anger to His. When we are in close fellowship with the Lord, the power of the Holy Spirit will effectively control and mold our anger so that we behave in a God-like way. For example, God is slow to anger (Ps. 145:8). Anger should not be a quickly-triggered emotion that abruptly enters and exits our daily routine. God desires that we have a long-suffering attitude, which allows anger to deliver a calculated response at the most advantageous time. Additionally, God is provoked to anger (Deut. 4:25). Likewise, we should not be an angry people, but rather be provoked to anger by some appalling event in order to equip the body to act in an extraordinary way to face the challenge. When we first sense a surge of anger, we should ask ourselves if we have a present righteous cause for being angry. If we act in anger when the situation does not call for such measures, we have been wrongly provoked to anger (Eph. 4:26-27).

God is not only slow to become angry, but even when provoked He takes time to fully develop His anger before rendering any action. He is also a God that is quick to forgive those willing to confess their sin (Ps. 86:5). Anger is an emotion, not a behavior. May we learn to control our anger in such a way that what we do has God's approval.

18

January 17 – Adultery in the Heart
Matthew 5:27-28

You have heard that it was said to those of old, "You shall not commit adultery." But I say to you that whoever looks at a woman to lust for her has already committed adultery with her in his heart.

The Lord begins by affirming the authority of the seventh of the Ten Commandments: *"You shalt not commit adultery"* (Ex. 20:14). While the word *fornication* encompasses a broader range of sexual sins, including those outside of marriage (e.g., Mark 7:21; 1 Cor. 6:13), *adultery* occurs when the sexual sanctity of a marriage covenant has been violated. When a married person has intercourse with someone other than his or her spouse, this is the sin of adultery (Rom. 7:3). While all immorality is an abomination to God, the willful desecration of one's marriage vows is particularly grievous. Adultery is rebellion against God's original design for marriage (Gen. 2:22-24). This commandment secures and protects the sexual union of a husband (a biological male) with his own wife (a biological female; Matt. 19:4-6). God created male and female and thereby He designed the sexual union to be an enjoyable experience within the bounds of marriage and for the purpose of procreation.

Regrettably, divorce had become rampant in the Jewish society and God hated that reality (Mal. 2:14-16). So when the Lord affirmed God's original design for marriage to His audience, that would have been received as a stern rebuke to what had become common behavior. But the Lord did not stop there; He went beyond the actual act of sin to the source of the sin – unchecked lusting in the heart. Subjects of the kingdom must be committed to holiness and it is impossible to control one's behavior, until one's thoughts and desires are brought under God's control. To look at a woman for the purpose of lusting after her is to commit adultery in the heart. To admire a woman's qualities and beauty is one thing, but it is quite another to imagine satisfying lustful desires with her. A sanctified sex-life begins when our inner desires have been yielded to God's will for marriage. If not, then seeing will lead to touching, and touching to immorality. We must realize that lusting in our hearts for what God hates is no less offensive to Him than actually engaging in it.

January 18 – Let Your "Yes" Be "Yes"
Matthew 5:37

But let your "Yes" be "Yes," and your "No," "No." For whatever is more than these is from the evil one.

In the Old Testament, swearing (i.e., the taking of an oath) to validate a promise was quite common among the Jews. It was done to strongly affirm a promise or statement by using the Lord's name. In the New Testament, however, the Lord Jesus traversed the high moral ground on the subject of swearing. The Lord reminded His audience that what they said should always be accurate. If they promised to do something, their words should stand alone without trying to reinforce their validity by swearing.

Believers should not swear to increase the credence of what they say; the merit of everything said should be consistently wholesome and truthful without adding God's name to it. We should never think that somehow by starting a statement with the words, "To be honest..." somehow strengthens the worth of what we are about to say. Later, the Lord issued another warning concerning the importance of our speech:

But I say to you that for every idle word men may speak, they will give account of it in the day of judgment. For by your words you will be justified, and by your words you will be condemned (Matt. 12:36-37).

Not only will our ungodly speech be judged in a coming day, but we will have to give account of all our idle chit-chat also (i.e., words having no value for eternity). Swearing involves tying God's name to our statements in an attempt to better validate what we say – to heighten the credibility of our words. The believer should not engage in such practices, for to do so would certainly bring low the name of God. James likewise warns against such behavior: *"But above all, my brethren, do not swear, either by heaven or by earth or with any other oath. But let your 'Yes' be 'Yes,' and your 'No,' 'No,' lest you fall into judgment"* (Jas. 5:12). Demeaning the name of the Lord by swearing falsely is a terrible thing. As we are forgetful creatures and are rarely perfect in our speech, it behooves us to refrain from doing so.

January 19 – Turn the Other Cheek
Matthew 5:38-41

You have heard that it was said, "An eye for an eye and a tooth for a tooth." But I tell you not to resist an evil person. But whoever slaps you on your right cheek, turn the other to him also. If anyone wants to sue you and take away your tunic, let him have your cloak also. And whoever compels you to go one mile, go with him two.

In this portion of the Sermon on the Mount we find the Lord declaring the true nature of the Law, where grace is all but absent: *An eye for an eye and a tooth for a tooth.* If someone intentionally or unintentionally caused you harm, the exact equivalent retribution was demanded by the Law – no more, and no less. But the Lord was introducing His Jewish audience to the concept of extending unmerited favor; He wanted them to realize that grace had the power to remit every claim of retribution. But such thinking is difficult to receive unless one has first experienced God's abounding grace, has received a full pardon, and has been forgiven all debt.

The Law taught stringent justice for crimes and offenses, even if they were unintentionally committed. Its tit-for-tat restitution would satisfy the injured party's desire for vengeance, but it did not teach man how the divine qualities of love, grace, and mercy should govern one's behavior. Certainly, the lack of these in resolving life's offenses would cause man to be more appreciative of God's ultimate means of making restitution for our intentional and unintentional offenses against Him – the giving and judging of His Son in our place.

The Lord Jesus Christ would be, and indeed was, the sin-sacrifice for all humanity. Through Christ we don't get what we do deserve (all the horrors of hell) and we do receive what we don't deserve (all the blessings of heaven); the former is God's mercy to us and the latter is His grace. Consequently, every aspect of our salvation is permeated by the sweet aroma of Christ's love. May we never get over the love of Christ and may we long for others to know it too! This is the motivation for enduring social injustice and persecutions related to the cause of Christ. When viciously struck in the face by an ignorant, self-righteous worldling, the only motivation for turning the other cheek and enduring more hardship is to declare the power of Christ's grace.

January 20 – Love Your Enemies
Matthew 5:43-44

You have heard that it was said, "You shall love your neighbor and hate your enemy." But I say to you, love your enemies, bless those who curse you, do good to those who hate you, and pray for those who spitefully use you and persecute you.

Following the "Turn the Other Cheek" challenge, the Lord offered a second contrast between the life-styles of rigid Law-keeping and of yearning to extend grace. The latter ideology would not only be possible but expected conduct during the Church Age. The "eye for an eye" doctrine of the Law taught the Jews that disobedience must be punished, whereas the "love your enemies" exhortation reflected a much deeper truth pertaining to the New Testament: Believers in the Church Age would come to realize that no one could earn heaven by Law-keeping and therefore must trust in Christ alone for salvation. After Christ's resurrection, believers would receive the Holy Spirit and then have the wherewithal to both *keep* the Law (i.e. sin is a conscious choice for a true Christian), and *fulfill* the Law (which would actively demonstrate both God's character and the outworking of His grace).

We do not naturally want to bless our enemies, so the Lord offers us the means of transforming our selfish thinking into actually wanting to do what He asks – we are to pray for our enemies. Have you ever tried to pray to God while you were angry with someone? It doesn't work. As we pour our hearts out to the infinite Creator, our hearts become humbled and softened. Prayer is transforming! We may start by asking the Lord to "smash 'em," but as we continue to pray, we are overtaken by the hurt and pain that the offending party is inflicting on themselves, their family, the Church, and Christ. Suddenly, our pain does not seem so great when looking at the big picture. Next time you are offended by someone, try praying for them – prayer really softens the vindictive heart and refreshes our soul.

How much less contention would there be in the Church today if believers permitted the Lord to judge all the injustices, false gossip, and slander amongst us? How much more powerfully would Christ be displayed to the lost through genuine acts of self-sacrifice? The love of Christ can soften the hardest of hearts to consider the truth.

January 21– When You Do Charitable Deeds
Matthew 6:1-4

Take heed that you do not do your charitable deeds before men, to be seen by them. Otherwise you have no reward from your Father in heaven. Therefore, when you do a charitable deed, do not sound a trumpet before you as the hypocrites do in the synagogues and in the streets, that they may have glory from men. Assuredly, I say to you, they have their reward. But when you do a charitable deed, do not let your left hand know what your right hand is doing, that your charitable deed may be in secret; and your Father who sees in secret will Himself reward you openly.

In contrast with showing love and doing acts of kindness to those who are lovable and then expecting the same in return (Matt. 5:46-48), the Lord challenged His audience to selflessly love those who were undeserving and to do so without any expectations of thanks or a return favor. Such conduct was beyond anything the Law demanded, but would mark those who had truly experienced grace in Christ.

The Lord then reminded everyone that when people do good deeds to be seen and to be praised by others, they have their reward, but regrettably they do not have God's approval. Therefore, He stresses three times with different verbiage the "secret" nature the true giving must have to receive God's appreciation: First, Christ spoke of doing deeds before men to be seen. Second, He addressed those doing good deeds and then sought others to notice what they had done. Third, the Savior reproved those doing good deeds without keeping the matter completely secret. His main point being, that if we want an eternal reward for our service, we must seek God's approval alone. Wanting to be seen by others for the purpose of acknowledgment and praise when we do something is a warning to us that our hearts are not right before the Lord.

The Lord is still on the mount, and still declaring the manifesto of His coming Kingdom. During the Church Age, the outworking of this constitution would be evident in only a hidden spiritual sense (the fruit of the Spirit in Christians). Regardless, the Kingdom reality cannot be measured by the external doings, but rather hidden power. Hence, doing to be seen by men is an evidence of poor spirituality in any age.

January 22 – When You Pray
Matthew 6:5-8

And when you pray, you shall not be like the hypocrites. For they love to pray standing in the synagogues and on the corners of the streets, that they may be seen by men. Assuredly, I say to you, they have their reward. But you, when you pray, go into your room, and when you have shut your door, pray to your Father who is in the secret place; and your Father who sees in secret will reward you openly. And when you pray, do not use vain repetitions as the heathen do. For they think that they will be heard for their many words. Therefore do not be like them. For your Father knows the things you have need of before you ask Him.

The Lord Jesus carried the "in secret" motivation into the matter of prayer. Obviously, there are times believers should meet corporately to pray together (Acts 4:24-31, 12:12), but here the Lord is addressing our personal prayer-life. The Lord wanted the subjects of His kingdom to follow His example of spending much time in seeking the face of His Father in prayer. The Lord would often rise early in the morning in order to be able to pray without distraction or without observation. If people pray aloud in public to be heard by men, their prayers never reach heaven. They demonstrate through their actions that they value the esteem and praise of men more than receiving God's blessing and appreciation – *"they have their reward."*

The Lord employed the expression "when you pray" three times to uphold the type of attitude God did appreciate while praying: First, do not seek to be noticed by men. Second, go to a private place free of distractions and the temptation of showing off. Third, pray from the heart, not by rote. It is not our many words that God appreciates, but rather our meaningful communication which shows Him that we value who He is, not just what He can do.

Lawrence Richards summarizes Christ's "in secret" message:

In this age, before Jesus comes in power, the kingdom and the Father exist "in secret." But the God who sees us in secret does reward us. The God who sees us *is*, and He does act in the world of here and now. If we seek the kingdom, we dare not let the traditions of the men of our age draw us away from the God who *is*. It is our secret life with Him which is the key to our experience of the kingdom.[4]

24

January 23 – When You Fast
Matthew 6:16-18

Moreover, when you fast, do not be like the hypocrites, with a sad countenance. For they disfigure their faces that they may appear to men to be fasting. Assuredly, I say to you, they have their reward. But you, when you fast, anoint your head and wash your face, so that you do not appear to men to be fasting, but to your Father who is in the secret place; and your Father who sees in secret will reward you openly.

The Lord Jesus affirms again that believers have the wonderful privilege of entering their own secret place to speak to their heavenly Father in His secret place. The Lord had already spoken against vain prayers; now He addresses another self-exalting behavior – vain fasting. Fasting to appear humble or spiritual was putrid to God.

First, notice that the Lord said, *"when you fast,"* to affirm that fasting should be a normal part of the believer's life. Second, fasting is not simply debasing one's self and appearing sad for sadistic reasons, but rather is a time for intense inner reflection and focused listening. Fasting for public display is contrary to its purpose and therefore negates its benefit. Hunger pangs remind us of our dependence on the Lord and lengthy times of introspection result in mental clarity to see things as God does. Third, Isaiah reminds us that heartfelt affliction of the soul would result in just and good conduct: the oppressed would be freed, those who were hungry would be fed, and the poor would be clothed (Isa. 58:6-7). The prophet firsts asks, *"Is your fasting what God has chosen?"* And then Isaiah indicates the type of fasting that would be acceptable to God – that which emphasizes moral transformation rather than ceremonial fanfare.

Fasting should result in our greater awareness of God's will and in our desire to be in the center of His will. If our fasting does not lead to changed attitudes and behavior, then it did not achieve God's intended outcome. Let us be careful of entering into any programs or gimmicks in which fasting is touted as a means of obtaining God's blessing. Anything of humanistic origin or with vain intentions is not going to impress God. But, to enter into our secret place to be alone with our Father who desires to more fully reveal Himself to us – that is a worthwhile spiritual undertaking.

January 24 – What Do You Treasure?
Matthew 6:19-21

Do not lay up for yourselves treasures on earth, where moth and rust destroy and where thieves break in and steal; but lay up for yourselves treasures in heaven, where neither moth nor rust destroys and where thieves do not break in and steal. For where your treasure is, there your heart will be also.

Worldliness and materialism walk hand in hand with spiritual complacency. Materialism is an ideology that has plagued God's people through the ages. Love for the Lord and His Word are supplanted by materialism and other worldly ambitions. Little in one's life has value to God after a man or a woman has become mesmerized by earthly things!

What or who we love is demonstrated by what we spend our time thinking about, talking about, and how we spend our money. This is what the Lord meant by *"For where your treasure is, there your heart will be also."* The world offers many tantalizing thrills in an attempt to sequester the believer's affection. Participating in or watching sporting events, educational pursuits, acquiring wealth, seeking fame, political ambitions, professional growth, and talent competitions are only a few of the entrapments that cause us to treasure what we ought not. If Christ is truly the Lord of our lives, then He must have first place in our thinking; every activity, every relationship, and every conversation much have His approval.

Other than our children, everything else that the Lord bestows to us in grace is going to eventually rot, disintegrate, corrode, or burn. The Lord was asserting that it did not make much sense to stockpile earthly things which one could not take to the grave; rather, it would be better to invest what one has for eternity and be rewarded by God for doing so. Only what is invested for eternity has value to the Lord. On judgment day all else will be shown to be worthless and will be incinerated by the brilliance of God's holy presence (1 Cor. 3:11-15). May we all live for eternity and not passing things.

He is no fool who gives what he cannot keep to gain what he cannot lose.

— Jim Elliot

January 25 – Why Worry?
Matthew 6:25-27

Therefore I say to you, do not worry about your life, what you will eat or what you will drink; nor about your body, what you will put on. Is not life more than food and the body more than clothing? Look at the birds of the air, for they neither sow nor reap nor gather into barns; yet your heavenly Father feeds them. Are you not of more value than they? Which of you by worrying can add one cubit to his stature?

In teaching His disciples how to pray, the Lord had emphasized their needed daily dependency on God: *"Give us this day our daily bread"* (Matt. 6:11). If they were truly trusting God to provide their daily necessities (food, water, clothing, etc.), then there would be no room for worry in their hearts. If they were anxious, that meant that their faith was deficient. Furthermore, who can add anything to what is lacking through the act of worrying about it? Worry cannot change the reality of things, but God can, so commit your needs to Him in prayer! We cannot serve the Lord faithfully if we are given over to anxiety; we waste time fretting about things we cannot change anyway. Worrying robs us of our peace and is a poor testimony of Christ to the world.

To illustrate the point, the Lord reminded them that His Father took wonderful care of the birds of the air. Yet, the birds did not spend time sowing seed or reaping a harvest for later use – they were dependent on their Creator every day for their food.

For those of us who live within the affluent Western culture, the idea of trusting the Lord for our daily bread is mostly an untested theoretical concept. Little of our abundance is needed to supply our actual daily necessities and even less of it is used to feed and clothe the poor. Rather, our vast wealth is used to insulate ourselves against any conceivable mishap, to collect stuff we really don't need, and to indulge or pamper our flesh with thrills and creature comforts that last only a moment and waste valuable time. There is certainly nothing wrong with planning ahead; the point is this: few Christians in our post-modern society actually rely on God for their necessities, let alone everything. No wonder the Western world has become a God-denying, self-centered culture; the cosmopolitan man has no need that he cannot provide for himself; he therefore surmises that he has no need for God.

January 26 – Judge Not
Matthew 7:1-2

Judge not, that you be not judged. For with what judgment you judge, you will be judged; and with the measure you use, it will be measured back to you.

Often it is the wayward that quote Matthew 7:1 in an attempt to avoid personal accountability for their sin, especially public reproof or Church discipline. However, as the verses that follow explain, the context of what the Lord is saying is not that God's people should not judge each other in matters of sin, but rather we should not do so with unChrist-like attitudes and we should not judge a person's motives. We cannot help others until we think and speak as Christ would (this is the plank in Matt. 7:3-5). The fact that the Lord goes on to say that believers should "beware of" false teachers clearly shows that there are things that must be judged (evaluated), namely, sinful behavior and doctrine. On this point, C. H. Mackintosh writes:

> God's assembly is responsible to judge the doctrine and morals of all who claim entrance at the door. And why, we may ask, was this separation demanded? Was it to uphold the reputation or respectability of the people? Nothing of the sort. …We do not judge and put away bad doctrine in order to maintain *our* orthodoxy; neither do we judge and put away moral evil in order to maintain our reputation and respectability. The only ground of judgment and putting away is this, *"Holiness becomes Thine house, O Lord, forever."*[5]

Scripture commands Christians to judge each other in the areas of life and doctrine. Paul instructed the assembly at Corinth to put out a man from the assembly fellowship who was committing blatant acts of immorality and then bragging about it. When someone is in unrepentant sin, he or she cannot be in fellowship with God, nor His people – believers can only enjoy Christ's fellowship with each other while being in unbroken communion with Him. Paul instructed the believers at Thessalonica not to have close association with those claiming to be Christians, but that were not holding to the apostles' teaching (2 Thess. 3:6, 14). Believers are required to judge others identifying with Christ in the area of life and doctrine to determine whether association is permitted.

January 27 – Remove the Plank
Matthew 7:3-5

And why do you look at the speck in your brother's eye, but do not consider the plank in your own eye? Or how can you say to your brother, "Let me remove the speck from your eye"; and look, a plank is in your own eye? Hypocrite! First remove the plank from your own eye, and then you will see clearly to remove the speck from your brother's eye.

While believers are to judge each other to confirm soundness of doctrine and life, the Lord issued a warning in how this was to be accomplished. For example, we cannot properly see to pull a speck from our brother's eye, if we have a plank in our own eye. The plank may be unconfessed sin, but more often it is simply unChrist-like attitudes and motives that keep us from responding as Christ would in the situation. It is often those initial thoughts that come to mind, when someone abruptly intrudes into our day with their problems that give evidence of the plank: "Why is she calling me again with the same old issue?" "I wish he would get his act together and quit bothering me." "I hope that he will tell others how I helped him." If we are not motivated by selfless love for the good of others, we are not going to skillfully remove the speck as Christ would. We need to first confess our own failures, wrong motives, and bad attitudes before we can help others.

It is also good for us to remember that, though we are to judge the behavior and doctrine of others, we are not to judge fellow believers in the following areas: their personal liberty (Rom. 14:1-3), their motivation for service (Matt. 7:1-5), their ministry's profitability (1 Cor. 4:1-4) or their salvation in Christ – only the Lord knows for sure who are His sheep and who are not (John 5:21-24). Concerning the matters of Christian liberty, someone's motives, the value of someone's ministry, and the validity of salvation – only the Lord knows what is in our hearts and why we do what we do, so let us be careful judging such things.

For this reason Paul warns fellow servants of Christ not to judge each other, for only the master will judge his own servants: *"Who are you to judge another's servant? To his own master he stands or falls"* (Rom. 14:4). If we have the opportunity to help others, let us behave as Christ would and let us not intrude in matters that only He can judge properly.

January 28 – Ask, Seek, and Knock
Matthew 7:7-8

Ask, and it will be given to you; seek, and you will find; knock, and it will be opened to you. For everyone who asks receives, and he who seeks finds, and to him who knocks it will be opened.

The Lord has spent two chapters identifying the high character and virtuous behavior of individuals enjoying His future kingdom on earth. Those receiving the Holy Spirit during the Church Age would be equipped to exemplify such traits before the Kingdom Age but not without receiving wisdom and power from above. So the Lord next spoke of the type of praying that believers were to be engaged in – ASK: keep *asking*, keep *seeking*, and keep *knocking*. The idea being that persistent praying in the Spirit prepares us to gratefully receive God's answer. What may seem like unanswered prayers are really just inopportune timing for God to bring about the best outcome of our prayers for everyone involved.

The Lord Jesus desires us to obtain all that is necessary to serve and honor Him. For this reason He instructed His disciples to petition His Father in His name for that which was lacking or needful:

Therefore I say to you, whatever things you ask when you pray, believe that you receive them, and you will have them (Mark 11:24).

Most assuredly, I say to you, whatever you ask the Father in My name He will give you. Until now you have asked nothing in My name. Ask, and you will receive, that your joy may be full (John 16:23-24).

James puts the matter this way: *"The effective, fervent prayer of a righteous man avails much"* (Jas. 5:16). When believers walk in integrity with God and are burdened over what concerns Him, God is inclined to honor their prayers for the honor of His own name: *"Now this is the confidence that we have in Him, that if we ask anything according to His will, He hears us"* (1 Jn. 5:14). Not only does James tell us about effectual praying, but he also speaks to how we must approach God in prayer: *"If any of you lacks wisdom, let him ask of God, who gives to all liberally and without reproach, and it will be given to him. But let him ask in faith, with no doubting"* (Jas. 1:5-6). In faith, let us keep asking, seeking, and knocking at the throne of grace!

January 29 – Do Unto Others
Matthew 7:12

Therefore, whatever you want men to do to you, do also to them, for this is the Law and the Prophets.

This axiom is often referred to as the "Golden Rule." Here, it directly follows the Lord's teaching on prayer and the opportunity to receive all good things from our heavenly Father. He desires to bountifully provide all our legitimate needs. Some have put a negative spin on the Golden Rule to infer that if someone treats you poorly, then that is how he or she desires you to treat them in return. But that type of thinking reflects the Law's "eye for an eye" mentality, not the idea of grace stewardship that God wants His people to both experience and to exercise towards others:

Every good gift and every perfect gift is from above, and comes down from the Father of lights, with whom there is no variation or shadow of turning. Of His own will He brought us forth by the word of truth, that we might be a kind of firstfruits of His creatures (Jas. 1:17-18).

What should the proper conduct of believers be when treated poorly by others: *"Repay no one evil for evil"* (Rom. 12:17) and *"Do not be overcome by evil, but overcome evil with good"* (Rom. 12:21). Those infused with God's grace are able to rise above temporal offenses knowing that God will accomplish eternal good in every situation.

What did the Lord mean by the expression, *"for this is the Law and the Prophets"*? To do good to others even when it is not deserved fulfills the moral teaching of the Law of Moses (the Pentateuch) and the writings of the prophets (speaking of the prophetic books of the Old Testament). William MacDonald explains that this is a summary statement of God's greatest intention of Old Testament Scripture:

The righteousness demanded by the OT is fulfilled in converted believers who thus walk according to the Spirit (Rom. 8:4). If this verse were universally obeyed, it would transform all areas of international relationships, national politics, family life, and church life.[6]

Souls transformed by grace desire others to be changed also.

January 30 – Be Fruit Inspectors
Matthew 7:18-20

*A good tree cannot bear bad fruit, nor can a bad tree bear good fruit.
Every tree that does not bear good fruit is cut down and thrown into
the fire. Therefore by their fruits you will know them.*

As in the Old Testament, false prophets and teachers were a
constant ongoing threat to Israel's spiritual vitality. The Lord did not
want His disciples fooled by high-sounding speech or humanized
religiosity. The virtue of one's character will normally validate the
source of the message. Like a bad tree, an unregenerate person cannot
produce spiritual fruit pleasing to God; only someone that has been
born again (a good tree) can bear such good fruit. As we do not know
an individual's heart, we cannot judge his or her salvation, but we can
be fruit inspectors. If a person's life is not consistent with sound
doctrine, we are to ignore that individual's influences; he or she is not
going to bring us closer to God. With that said, it also possible to be
fooled by someone that carefully conveys themselves as a Christian in
outward appearance and through service who is not, but time and
hardship always reveal the truth of the matter eventually.

Consider the individual illustrated by the shallow soil in the first of
seven kingdom parables of Matthew 13. The Word of God prompted a
guilty conscience to self-reformation, but without the individual
coming to true repentance and experiencing rebirth. The plant we see
above the ground may look genuine for a time, but eventually trials
(exposure to the hot sun) prove what is actually in the human heart (i.e.,
what is below the ground and we do not see). Only God knows if there
is really a root of faith there or not, which means what we see above
ground may be misleading. Time will eventually prove the reality of a
true believer, for a real plant cannot exist long without a true root. "No
root" means that there never was true faith resulting in regeneration.
God's truth had an effect on the person, but repentance resulting in
spiritual rejuvenation, as evidenced by spiritual fruitfulness, never
happened.

All this to say that it is possible to be fooled for a while; however,
eventually, the reality of the root and of the tree is observed in the fruit
that appears on the branches. A good tree consistently bears good fruit!

January 31 – Not Everyone Who Says "Lord, Lord"
Matthew 7:21-23

Not everyone who says to Me, "Lord, Lord," shall enter the kingdom of heaven, but he who does the will of My Father in heaven. Many will say to Me in that day, "Lord, Lord, have we not prophesied in Your name, cast out demons in Your name, and done many wonders in Your name?" And then I will declare to them, "I never knew you; depart from Me, you who practice lawlessness!"

The Lord said many will know who He is without trusting Him for salvation and making Him Lord of their lives. Many who identify with Him and do things in His name are not saved. Clearly, it is possible for people to know a lot about the Lord and serve Him without ever being born again. The Lord knows who are truly His and who the counterfeits are. Having information about the Lord and doing ministry in His name does not necessarily equate to loving Him. Many identifying with Christ, even calling Him Lord, are not actually saved. The true test of knowing and serving the Lord is found in our desire to do God's will.

Just believing that some *higher power* exists, or even in the one true God, does not save anyone; James warns, *"You believe that there is one God. You do well. Even the demons believe – and tremble!"* (Jas. 2:19). Clearly the demons believe in God, but are still condemned to the Lake of Fire because of their past rebellion against God (Matt. 25:41).

At the Great White Throne Judgment, which occurs just prior to the Eternal State, everyone who has not experienced bodily resurrection will. Hades, the holding place of disembodied souls of the wicked, will be cleared out and these individuals, in resurrected bodies, will stand before the Lord Jesus to be judged. Some think that religion will save them and earn them an eternal place in the *Book of Life*; this will be the moment that they will learn otherwise. There are many mysterious aspects about this book, but there really is only one question which each of us should be concerned with: "Is my name written in God's registry of the redeemed?" If your name is not written in *The Lamb's Book of Life*, you will not spend eternity with God in heaven; rather, you will make your eternal abode with Satan and his angels in the Lake of Fire: *"And anyone not found written in the Book of Life was cast into the lake of fire"* (Rev. 20:15). Is your name written in God's book?

February 1 – Building on the Rock, Not the Sand
Matthew 7:24-27

Therefore whoever hears these sayings of Mine, and does them, I will liken him to a wise man who built his house on the rock: and the rain descended, the floods came, and the winds blew and beat on that house; and it did not fall, for it was founded on the rock. But everyone who hears these sayings of Mine, and does not do them, will be like a foolish man who built his house on the sand: and the rain descended, the floods came, and the winds blew and beat on that house; and it fell. And great was its fall.

The Lord introduces this house-building parable at the end of His Sermon on the Mount message to appeal to His audience to make a choice. What does a house and the two foundations of rock and sand represent in this parable? A true believer's faith must be based in Christ's teaching (or more generally speaking, in Scripture); it is a trustworthy foundation (a solid rock) to build one's life upon. The house (a life) built on this foundation can weather the storms of adversity, and the battering winds of humanism. A house built on a rock foundation is a permanent structure. The life built on Christ and His teachings is an eternal abode for God to dwell in.

However, the house that is built on a foundation of sand represents a life lived according to secular philosophies and the world's religion of thinking apart from Christ. Such a structure is temporary and the shallow footings of humanism provide not lasting stability when life's storms (hardships) buffet its walls. This represents someone living for the present, for self, by sight and is easily swayed by emotional appeals and relative thinking.

True believers must build a *fact – faith – feelings* style of belief-system to interpret the issues of life accurately and safeguard their souls against satanic attack. The *fact* of God's Word is accepted as the only foundation to build on. We then develop our *faith*, what we believe God's Word means. From our established *faith*, we are then able to judge our *feelings* properly. If we flip the building program upside down, then we will allow our feelings to determine our faith, which then will cause us to interpret God's Word erroneously. May we choose to build our lives on the solid Rock – Christ!

February 2 – Must Be Under Authority
Matthew 8:7-10

And Jesus said to him, "I will come and heal him." The centurion answered and said, "Lord, I am not worthy that You should come under my roof. But only speak a word, and my servant will be healed. For I also am a man under authority, having soldiers under me. And I say to this one, 'Go,' and he goes; and to another, 'Come,' and he comes; and to my servant, 'Do this,' and he does it." When Jesus heard it, He marveled, and said to those who followed, "Assuredly, I say to you, I have not found such great faith, not even in Israel!

Hearing of the Lord's arrival at Capernaum, a Roman centurion sent Jewish elders to ask Him for assistance. The centurion had a faithful servant that was suffering from severe paralysis and was near death (Luke 7:2). This scene is ironic, as we have Jewish leaders that did not believe that Jesus was the Christ being constrained to beseech Him for Messianic power on behalf of a Gentile they esteemed more important. The elders told the Lord that the centurion loved the Jewish people and was kind to them; he had even built them a synagogue. This was to convince the Lord that the centurion was worthy of His help.

The Lord agreed to go, but before arriving at the centurion's home the officer sent messengers to tell the Lord not to trouble Himself any further, but just say the word and his servant would be healed. The messengers then explained that as an officer in authority, the centurion commanded the affairs of his soldiers; he understood that one must be under authority to have authority. Since the Lord Jesus had authority over diseases, the centurion knew that He was under authority and could therefore heal his servant. Furthermore, the honorable centurion did not feel that he was worthy enough for the Lord to come under his roof. The Lord was astonished by the officer's response. The centurion possessed little truth, but enough to exercise tremendous faith, which the Lord praised. The Lord honored his faith by healing his servant.

There are only two authority structures in the universe: God-ordained and Satanic-controlled. Remaining under God's authority enables us to exercise His authority and bless others. But those who reject His authority do not escape authority, but rather find themselves under Satan's authority, and there is only misery to be found there.

35

February 3 – Let the Dead Bury Their Dead
Matthew 8:19-22

Then a certain scribe came and said to Him, "Teacher, I will follow You wherever You go." And Jesus said to him, "Foxes have holes and birds of the air have nests, but the Son of Man has nowhere to lay His head." Then another of His disciples said to Him, "Lord, let me first go and bury my father." But Jesus said to him, "Follow Me, and let the dead bury their own dead."

In Luke 9, three men desiring to be Christ's disciples are identified. Before the third man would follow Christ, he first wanted to bid his family farewell. The Lord responded to him, *"No one, having put his hand to the plow, and looking back, is fit for the kingdom of God"* (Luke 9:62). This is a remarkable illustration of three would-be disciples who allowed something to hinder their dedication to Christ.

The first man is enthusiastic and volunteered to follow the Lord anywhere, no matter what the cost might be. But the Lord reminded him that He was a homeless wanderer; He did not even have a pillow to lay His head on at night. The implication being, "Are you really ready to give up all the material comforts of life to follow me?" Apparently, not, as we hear no more from him.

The second man did not volunteer, as the first man did, but rather the Lord called him to be His follower. This man was interested, but he had something he wanted to do first. Burying one's father is an important task, but certainly the Lord would have known all about it, yet, He still called the man. Anytime we say, "Lord, let me first," we have sinned against Him. He is never to have second place in anything.

The third man resembled the first in that he volunteered to follow the Lord. Yet, he is like the second in that he used those same contradictory words, "Lord, let me first...." There is certainly nothing wrong with showing love to one's family by bidding them farewell, but the man permitted his family ties to supersede the place of Christ. The Lord's illustrative response concerning the hard and focused work of plowing indicated that His disciples could not be self-centered in following Him; rather, they must remain fully focused on the tasks He gives them. Earthly comforts, jobs and important doings, and tender relationships still hinder people from following the Lord today.

February 4 – The Harvest Is Plentiful
Matthew 9:35-38

But when He saw the multitudes, He was moved with compassion for them, because they were weary and scattered, like sheep having no shepherd. Then He said to His disciples, "The harvest truly is plentiful, but the laborers are few. Therefore pray the Lord of the harvest to send out laborers into His harvest."

The Lord spent about two years with His disciples preaching the kingdom good news message to the lost sheep of Israel; Capernaum became His central base of operation during this time. During this era, the Lord demonstrated His compassion for His fellow countrymen by not only sharing His message, but healing them of their infirmities and disabilities. The Lord could not casually stroll by those in need and not be prompted to act. Oh, that all believers would have such a burden for the spiritual welfare of those lost in trespasses and sins.

While looking over the masses that were wandering aimlessly without a shepherd, the Lord told His disciples that there was a great harvest of souls that needed to be reaped and gathered into God's barn, but there were few willing to labor with God to do it. With this incredible need identified, He instructed His disciples to pray that *the Lord of the harvest would send out laborers into His Harvest."*

Interestingly in the next verse we read:

And when He had called His twelve disciples to Him, He gave them power over unclean spirits, to cast them out, and to heal all kinds of sickness and all kinds of disease (Matt. 10:1).

This verse reveals two important truths for us to consider: First, the Lord Jesus is the Lord of the harvest, for He is the one sending and equipping laborers for the work of harvesting souls. Second, that prayer was used to both burden and prepare the disciples to answer the call for needed laborers. They, themselves, were the answer to their own prayers concerning the need for laborers. This shows the transforming power of prayer and that we should be willing to simply pray for what needs we are made aware of without presupposing what God's solution might be. We just might be God's answer to our own prayers also.

37

February 5 – Freely Give What You Freely Receive
Matthew 10:8-10

Heal the sick, cleanse the lepers, raise the dead, cast out demons. Freely you have received, freely give. Provide neither gold nor silver nor copper in your money belts, nor bag for your journey, nor two tunics, nor sandals, nor staffs; for a worker is worthy of his food.

The disciples had been uniquely equipped by the Lord to be His workers in the harvest. Believers today should not think that they have been given the same credentials or calling that the twelve were in the scene before us. Their equipping for the work was unique and their calling was to a specific audience, the lost sheep of Israel.

The Lord told His disciples that their ministry was to be free of charge. This would demonstrate that the nature of the kingdom message itself was founded in grace and not the Law. Isaiah foretold the nature of Messiah's message centuries earlier: *"Everyone who thirsts, come to the waters; and you who have no money, come, buy and eat. Yes, come, buy wine and milk without money and without price"* (Isa. 55:1). While it is true that God does supply the physical needs of those who trust in Him, the primary focus of this invitation is the spiritual satisfaction of individuals in the Jewish nation. Why spend money on bread which cannot satisfy one's true need? It would be wise to receive from God that which abundantly delights the soul forever.

God promises to satisfy our spirit's deepest need without any human compensation (i.e., no one can buy or earn His forgiveness through payment or doing "good works"). For this reason the disciples were to freely receive from those responding to their no-cost message. They were not to worry about where their next meal would come from. Neither were they to hoard funds and store up provisions for their journey; these would only encumber them in performing the task that they had been assigned. Storing up what might be needed would also hinder them from seeing God's hand in providing for their daily needs.

The disciples were to go forth into the harvest being completely dependent on the Lord to direct their way, to empower their ministry, and to provide whatever they needed in shelter, clothing, and food. They would learn of Christ's sufficiency in all matters of life as they shared His message of life with others. We too learn of Christ as we go!

February 6– Do Not Worry About What to Say
Matthew 10:18-20

You will be brought before governors and kings for My sake, as a testimony to them and to the Gentiles. But when they deliver you up, do not worry about how or what you should speak. For it will be given to you in that hour what you should speak; for it is not you who speak, but the Spirit of your Father who speaks in you.

The Lord told His disciples they would have the opportunity to testify of His name before kings. When a believer chooses to obey God's calling for his or her life, God will equip and enable that individual to successfully answer every difficulty associated with fulfilling that call. The disciples did not need to worry about what to say or how to say it; the Holy Spirit would enable them to speak the truth that God wanted them to convey.

Hudson Taylor, a pioneer missionary into China in the mid-nineteenth century, had two important sayings on the matter of spiritual resources in God's work. First, "God always gives his very best to those who leave the choice with him."[7] Second, quoting the missionary Anthony Norris Groves, Taylor said, "When God's work is done in God's way for God's glory, it will not lack for God's supply."[8] This is especially true in times of ministry crisis.

Later in his ministry, Taylor noted that every time there had been a wonderful expansion of the missionary work in China, it had been preceded by a time of deep trial. This had required the missionaries to cast themselves on the Lord afresh and to look to Him alone for the Lord's help. The Lord enables His people both to suffer for Him and to serve Him, if they will remain faithful to Him. Faith forged in fiery trials is made stronger than it was before.

When a ministry is a true work of God and its minister is truly doing the work of God, there will be no lack of God's enablement for both. The believer must be faithful to his or her calling and must learn to trust the Lord for wisdom and grace in every situation. Faith that is not tested will not be trusted; trials, therefore, become a necessary part of any ministry. The good news is that because believers are one in Christ, everything that comes into our lives also comes into His, and He is able to rise above every perceived obstacle and hardship.

February 7 – A Disciple Learns to Be Like His Teacher
Matthew 10:24-25

A disciple is not above his teacher, nor a servant above his master. It is enough for a disciple that he be like his teacher, and a servant like his master. If they have called the master of the house Beelzebub, how much more will they call those of his household!

A few verses later, the Lord invited all those who wanted to follow Him to take His yoke in order to learn of Him:

Come to Me, all you who labor and are heavy laden, and I will give you rest. Take My yoke upon you and learn from Me, for I am gentle and lowly in heart, and you will find rest for your souls. For My yoke is easy and My burden is light (Matt. 11:28-30).

The main objective of discipleship is to learn Christ and to become like Him (Matt. 10:25). This is accomplished by yielding to His yoke (His Lordship). True disciples of Christ never gain disciples to themselves – they point others to Christ. As Amos Alcott has said, "The true teacher defends his pupils against his own personal influence."[9] George MacDonald warns, "No teacher should strive to make men think as he thinks, but to lead them to the living Truth, to the Master Himself, of whom alone they can learn anything."[10]

Mentoring those younger in the faith is not a process of making clones of oneself; rather, it is a ministry that selflessly encourages others to forsake all and follow after the Lord Jesus Christ. The Greek word for "disciple" is *mathetes*, which literally means "a learner." Again, the pursuit of the disciple is to learn Christ and to be like Him. Guilt trips and accountability may work for a short time, but only love for Christ will propel the new believer onward in growth and service.

Every discipler must implant the vision of spiritual duplication and growth into those they disciple. The truth must be passed on. Paul told Timothy, *"The things that you have heard from me ... commit these to faithful men who will be able to teach others also"* (2 Tim. 2:2). The Greek word *anthropos* rendered "men" in this verse means human beings; it is not gender specific both men and women are to be trained to teach others. Making and training disciples is Christ's plan for building His Church; may we learn from Him and follow His example.

February 8 – Finding a Life That Counts
Matthew 10:37-38

*He who loves father or mother more than Me is not worthy of Me.
And he who loves son or daughter more than Me is not worthy of Me.
And he who does not take his cross and follow after Me is not worthy
of Me. He who finds his life will lose it, and he who loses his life for
My sake will find it.*

The Lord candidly conveys the type of allegiance He expected from those saying they would be willing to follow Him. Luke records the parallel account of the Lord's statement in a slightly different way: *"If anyone comes to Me and does not hate his father and mother, wife and children, brothers and sisters, yes, and his own life also, he cannot be My disciple"* (Luke 14:26). By comparing the narratives of Matthew and Luke, we understand that the word for "hate" expresses a comparison: our love for the Lord should be so great that any natural affection would, comparatively, seem like hate. The Lord was weary of shallow followers; He wanted true disciples. He desired quality in consecration, not a large quantity of half-hearted patriots.

When it comes to misplaced affection and devotion, there is no middle ground with the Lord. The Lord expects our love for Him to be so astounding that by comparison our affections for anyone else would seem like hate! To love anyone or anything more than the Lord is a form of idolatry and proves we are not worthy of Him. God desires His people to be totally committed to Him and to love Him above all else. Commitment is being given over to a cause without reservation, even if death is required. This means that we are willing to set aside our personal agendas and our own expectations in order to live for Christ and gain a life that has value to God. It is only by losing ourselves for the cause of Christ that we find a life worth living.

True discipleship requires each believer to settle the death question, as the Lord forced Peter to do in John 21: "Do I love the Lord enough to be willing to live for Him no matter the personal cost?" Only by affirming "yes" to this question will a believer have the unwavering obedience and devotion that the Lord demands of us. The cross is a symbol of shame and of death, but we gladly take up our cross for the Lord, because He bore His cross to save our souls from hell.

February 9 – Tolerance on the Day of Judgment
Matthew 11:21-24

Then He began to rebuke the cities in which most of His mighty works had been done, because they did not repent: "Woe to you, Chorazin! Woe to you, Bethsaida! For if the mighty works which were done in you had been done in Tyre and Sidon, they would have repented long ago in sackcloth and ashes. But I say to you, it will be more tolerable for Tyre and Sidon in the day of judgment than for you. And you, Capernaum, who are exalted to heaven, will be brought down to Hades; for if the mighty works which were done in you had been done in Sodom, it would have remained until this day. But I say to you that it shall be more tolerable for the land of Sodom in the day of judgment than for you."

How is it possible for the Lord to be more tolerant of wicked cities such as Tyre, Sidon, and Sodom in the day of judgment than the Jewish cities such as Chorazin, Bethsaida, and Capernaum? Because where God permits greater responsibility there will always be greater accountability. The former cities had little revelation of truth to reject (Sodom only had the half-hearted testimony of one carnal believer named Lot), but the latter cities had the Son of God standing in their midst and they rejected His message. Just as there are different rewards in heaven for faithfulness, there are differing degrees of eternal judgment depending on how much truth was rejected (Luke 10:11-16, 12:41-48, 20:47). Everyone is given some divine truth to consider (e.g., creation demands a Creator, and the human conscience contains moral reckoning), but some receive more evidence and truth to consider; thus they have more accountability with God.

The prophet Ezekiel foretold that many of the Jewish cities destroyed by Gentile rulers would be rebuilt and resettled in exactly the same locations after God gathers His covenant people back to their homeland in the Kingdom Age (Ezek. 36:11, 24). Today, there are many cities in Israel that bear the ancient names of previous biblical cities: Cana, Nazareth, Jericho, Nain, Bethany, Bethlehem, Hebron, Gaza, etc. This is a testimony that God has honored part of Ezekiel's prophecy. However, only a few ruins remain of those cities which the Lord Jesus cursed, Capernaum, Bethsaida, and Chorazin, for their rejection of His message. No one can escape His righteous judgments.

February 10 – Take My Yoke and Learn of Me
Matthew 11:28-30

*Come to Me, all you who labor and are heavy laden, and I will give
you rest. Take My yoke upon you and learn from Me, for I am gentle
and lowly in heart, and you will find rest for your souls. For My yoke
is easy and My burden is light.*

The Lord conveys a two-part message in these verses. First, there is
an invitation in verse 28 for all those who are burdened by the weight
of their own sin. Anyone desiring to be liberated from their ongoing
guilt must come to Christ; hence, He implores His audience, "Come to
Me." Christ is the object of our faith and God's only solution for our
sin. Once forgiven by Him, we experience God's peace and enter into
His rest. The blood of Christ cleanses the guilty conscience and we
have a new beginning with God (Heb. 9:14).

The remainder of the Lord's message pertains to discipleship. As
previously discussed, the main objective of discipleship is to learn of
Christ and to become like Him (Matt. 10:25). His means of achieving
rest in our souls is quite unusual – we must be willing to take His yoke
about our necks and then go on with Him. A yoke was used to harness
two or more animals together for the purpose of getting more pulling
power for transportation or agricultural purposes.

A yoke is normally connected with slavery or laboring in Scripture,
but the Lord promises that His yoke is easy. Those who choose to walk
in step with Him will not be burdened, because He would be the One
pulling the load that He has assigned us to bear (Gal. 6:5). However, if
we attempt to walk ahead or behind the Lord while being yoked with
Him, we create work and stress in our lives. He is not the source of it –
we are, because we are attempting to walk outside of His will for us.
This is why learning the Lord's character, His mind, and His desire for
our lives is an essential part of being one with Him in service.

This is the only passage in the New Testament where the Lord
Jesus personally informs His disciples of what He is like and tells them
that they should learn of Him. May we learn of Him and be like Him,
for He is meek and lowly in heart. Believers learn of the Lord's gentle
and humble spirit when yoked with Him in service, and they enjoy the
peace of His presence when they rest in Him.

February 11 – Tares Among the Wheat
Matthew 13:24-25

Another parable He put forth to them, saying: "The kingdom of heaven is like a man who sowed good seed in his field; but while men slept, his enemy came and sowed tares among the wheat and went his way."

In the eight *Mystery of the Kingdom* parables of Matthew 13, the Lord reveals a chronology of events that would characterize the "kingdom of heaven" from His first advent (a seed-sowing mission) until His return to rule the world in peace. Satan is busy in the first four parables undermining the kingdom of heaven (the realm of human profession of God's sovereignty). In these parables, Satan is seen attacking the gospel message, trying to neutralize the influence of believers on earth, corrupting church leadership, order, and structure, and finally, promoting the corruption of God's Word and spreading false doctrine within the Church. However, in the last three parables, Satan is absent, and God demonstrates His fathomless grace in saving sinners. Christ paid the great price to redeem the hidden treasure (yet unrestored Israel), the pearl (the Church), and those Gentiles who would not bow to the Antichrist (the good catch found in the net).

In the second of the eight parables, the Lord tells of an enemy sneaking in at night and planting tares alongside the wheat the master of the field had sown previously. The tares, or darnel (*Lolium temulentum*), is a prolific weed that looks much like wheat until harvest time. When wheat matures, it develops a fruit-laden head of grain that bows down before its Creator as it ripens. The darnel has no such fruit-laden head of grain and thereby maintains a haughty disposition before God. The master told his servants not to uproot the darnel, as that would also damage the wheat. Rather, the matter would be settled at harvest time. The wheat (i.e., God's children) would be gathered into God's heavenly barn, while the darnel, the children of the devil, would be gathered up by holy angels and cast into eternal fire.

If you are doing anything for the Lord, expect the devil to notice and sow his workers right next to you in order to try to neutralize your testimony for Christ or to negate your ministry for Christ. God has you right where He wants you in the world (His field), so expect opposition from the enemy until such time that the Lord takes you home.

February 12 – Beware of the Doctrines of Men
Matthew 15:7-9

Hypocrites! Well did Isaiah prophesy about you, saying: "These people draw near to Me with their mouth, and honor Me with their lips, but their heart is far from Me. And in vain they worship Me, teaching as doctrines the commandments of men."

Much of the Old Testament contains the sad history of God's people languishing under human traditions instead of being taught Scripture. Whether in Israel previously, or in the Church today, there are always consequences when men lord themselves over God's people and burden them with their own rules. Approaching God in other manner than humble sincerity and in obedience to His revealed will is utter vanity. He is not pleased with such religiosity; rather, His wrath is invoked against those offering to Him what He considers putrid.

When believers embrace human traditions as a measure of spirituality, a number of negative outcomes can be expected. First, a loss of God's blessing occurs as His people suffer reduced agility and power through grieving the Holy Spirit. Second, man-made rules eventually displace the importance of observing God's Law, thus leading God's people into sin. Third, human pride judges those acting in the liberty and power of the Holy Spirit. Those who enforce their own foolish rules will do whatever it takes to save face, even to wallowing in utter stupidity, rather than humbly acknowledging their error. Fourth, because these human traditions are void of God's endorsement, they ultimately put divinely-ordained authority to public shame. Accordingly, we should not be surprised when those who are spiritually-minded rise up and speak out against their carnal leaders, and rightly so (1 Sam. 14:45; Acts 5:29; 1 Tim. 5:20)!

One of the strongest statements of God's disgust over His people's vain religiosity was in Isaiah's first message to idolatrous Israel: *"Wickedness and the solemn meeting I cannot bear"* (Isa. 1:13; JND). He utterly despised their sacrifices, offerings, prayers, and observances! The seriousness of Israel's offense is bluntly expressed by the phrase *"My soul hates"* in the next verse, which literally means, "I hate with all my heart!" God keenly feels the offense of exchanging His commandments for the traditions of men – He utterly hates it!

February 13 – Beware of the Leaven
Matthew 16:6

Then Jesus said to them, "Take heed and beware of the leaven of the Pharisees and the Sadducees."

Leaven, in Scripture, speaks of sin, corruption, or evil doctrine (Matt. 13:33; 1 Cor. 5:8). Because leaven (yeast) is used in the fermentation process, it is a perfect symbol of decay and corruption, which is why, spiritually speaking, we should not be contaminated by it.

The leaven to be avoided in the believer's life comes in diverse varieties. The Lord Jesus warned His disciples against the influence of humanized traditions that oppose sound doctrine: *"Beware of the leaven of the Pharisees, which is hypocrisy"* (Luke 12:1). Church traditions have caused many professing Christians to ignore Christ's command to remember Him often through the Lord's Supper or to transform the memorial feast into some unscriptural practice. Some, for example, associate the eating of the bread and the drinking of the wine in the Lord's Supper with receiving or maintaining their salvation. This kind of leaven (i.e., false teachings) undermines the gospel message of grace declared repeatedly in the New Testament (e.g., Gal. 1:6-9).

The Lord spoke about the leaven of the Sadducees. The Sadducees were materialists who denied the existence of the supernatural, the spiritual nature of man, and the idea of a future resurrection. In our present day, the ideologies of the Sadducees live on in intellectualism, humanism, higher criticism, post-modernism, and naturalism.

Lastly, the Lord Jesus warned His disciples not to be influenced by *"the leaven of Herod"* (Mark 8:15). Herod, a Jew, was in cahoots with the Romans, and was, therefore, a friend of the world (Jas. 4:4). In the case of Herod, and those like him, love for God and His Word had been supplanted by the love for materialism, fame, and political ambition.

Paul mentions another kind of leaven to be avoided. He warned the Corinthians not to fellowship with someone identifying with Christ but continuing in sin: *"Do you not know that a little leaven leavens the whole lump? Therefore purge out the old leaven, that you may be a new lump, since you truly are unleavened"* (1 Cor. 5:6-7). If sin in the Church is not dealt a deadly blow, it will thoroughly corrupt all who do not esteem holiness as a necessity for maintaining Christ's fellowship.

February 14 – Deny Himself and Take Up His Cross
Matthew 16:24-26

Then Jesus said to His disciples, "If anyone desires to come after Me, let him deny himself, and take up his cross, and follow Me. For whoever desires to save his life will lose it, but whoever loses his life for My sake will find it. For what profit is it to a man if he gains the whole world, and loses his own soul? Or what will a man give in exchange for his soul?"

Many come to Christ's cross for salvation but then neglect to go on with Him and bear their own cross; this is an affront to the discipleship message He taught. The believer was never to flee the cross, but rather is to die daily upon it – only then does his or her life count for eternity.

This was the lesson Peter learned; he found that it was harder to live for Christ and die daily, than to just die once as a martyr. The believer must, practically speaking, die for the life of Christ to be lived out, as A. W. Tozer explains:

If we are wise, we will do what Jesus said: endure the cross and despise its shame for the joy that is set before us. To do this is to submit the whole pattern of our life to be destroyed and built again in the power of an endless life. And we shall find that it is more than poetry, more than sweet hymnody and elevated feeling. The cross will cut into our lives where it hurts worst, sparing neither us nor our carefully cultivated reputation. It will defeat us and bring our selfish life to an end.[11]

The man with a cross no longer controls his destiny; he lost control when he picked up his cross. That cross immediately became to him an all-absorbing interest, an overwhelming interference. No matter what he may desire to do, there is but one thing he can do; that is, move on toward the place of crucifixion.[12]

Taking up one's cross means that we will follow Christ no matter the personal cost. The Lord Jesus is a perfect gentleman; He will not force us to bear our cross or obey His calling for our lives. However, to ignore His calling is to pursue an existence which has no meaning or no eternal value. May each of us learn the necessity of denying ourselves, taking up our cross, and following the Lord with all our heart.

February 15 – Personal Offense Resolution
Matthew 18:15-18

Moreover if your brother sins against you, go and tell him his fault between you and him alone. If he hears you, you have gained your brother. But if he will not hear, take with you one or two more, that "by the mouth of two or three witnesses every word may be established." And if he refuses to hear them, tell it to the church. But if he refuses even to hear the church, let him be to you like a heathen and a tax collector.

The Lord provides some timeless instruction in how to resolve personal offenses. If an offense is taken, be sure to gather all the facts before you respond. Often the first appearance of a situation is not correct. Additionally, our minds tend to fill in missing information with negative thoughts, so train yourself to stay positive or at least give the benefit of the doubt until you know the facts.

Once the facts are known, you need to decide if this is a releasable offense or something that would benefit the offender by bringing it to his or her attention. If the latter course of action is determined, then you must "go and tell" the person what the "fault" is between you. "Go and tell" means no letters, text messages, emails, or even phone calls. Face-to-face communication is the best means of resolving conflict. "Fault" is singular so never take a list of grievances to someone and expect a favorable outcome. The Lord's people need to keep short accounts with the Lord and with each other; work problems one at a time.

If the offending party accepts your claim and asks for forgiveness, then you should declare your forgiveness (Luke 17:3) and the matter should be forgotten. If your claim is rejected, then you can decide if you want to pursue the matter further or not. Ask yourself if doing so would benefit the other person by correcting a sin or bent? Be sure to take one or two trusted persons with you as witnesses if you decide to pursue the matter further. If the issue is still not resolved, then decide if you should take the matter to the elders or release it? Realize that you are asking for a church decision for a one-time offense between two people. The "you" is singular; you are not forcing uninvolved people to have an issue with someone else because you do. This cannot be a matter of Church discipline unless there is ongoing sin by the offender.

February 16 – Where Two or Three Are Gathered
Matthew 18:19-20

Again I say to you that if two of you agree on earth concerning anything that they ask, it will be done for them by My Father in heaven. For where two or three are gathered together in My name, I am there in the midst of them.

The power of believers collectively praying in unity is witnessed several times in the book of Acts (e.g., 1:14, 4:24-31, 12:6-11). In each case there was a wonderful work of God in response to the prayers of the saints. In response to the corporate prayers in Acts 1, the Holy Spirit came in Acts 2, and the Church Age began with spectacular signs and miracles. The result was 3,000 souls were won to Christ.

In Acts 4, the believers with one accord exalted the Lord and prayed for boldness to preach the Word of God. What was the result of their praying? *"And when they had prayed, the place where they were assembled together was shaken; and they were all filled with the Holy Spirit, and they spoke the word of God with boldness"* (Acts 4:31).

Then, in Acts 12, we read of another situation prompting the Church to gather for corporate prayer:

Peter was therefore kept in prison, but constant prayer was offered to God for him by the church. ... So, when he had considered this, he came to the house of Mary, the mother of John whose surname was Mark, where many were gathered together praying (Acts 12:5, 12).

Herod intended to have the apostle publicly executed the next day, but the Lord had different plans and sent an angel to rescue Peter from prison. He then went to a house where he knew the saints would be gathered to pray and indeed they were. The apostle was then able to inform everyone how God had wonderfully answered their prayers.

The Lord promises to answer those prayers asked of the Father in His name (John 14:13, 15:16, 16:23). Additionally, He promises that when two or more are in agreement on requests, He will honor His name by answering them (Matt. 18:19-20). Having immediate access to God should prompt Christians to labor together in prayer, wherever and whenever they can (Heb. 4:14-16). Never resist the urge to pray!

February 17 – Why Do You Call Me Good?
Matthew 19:16-17

Now behold, one came and said to Him, "Good Teacher, what good thing shall I do that I may have eternal life?" So He said to him, "Why do you call Me good? No one is good but one, that is, God. But if you want to enter into life, keep the commandments."

Matthew records the dialogue of a rich young man who wanted to be justified before God and thereby be assured of heaven. Many think that they are good by their own standards of evaluation, but since only God is *good*, the Lord Jesus challenged the young man to think of goodness according to *divine standards*. The Lord then used God's commandments to bypass the intellect to speak to the inquirer's conscience. The purpose of the Law is to show us our sin and that we might understand that only God is good (Rom. 3:9-12).

Sadly, the Law did not achieve its intended purpose in the rich young ruler's heart. Instead of feeling guilt and impending judgment, he pompously declared that he had kept all of the Law, which he ironically broke by that false assertion. Our gracious Lord did not rebuke the young man for his audacious statement, but instead set about to show him who his god really was:

Jesus said to him, "If you want to be perfect, go, sell what you have and give to the poor, and you will have treasure in heaven; and come, follow Me." But when the young man heard that saying, he went away sorrowful, for he had great possessions (Matt. 19:21-22).

After being told that he needed to sell his possessions, give the proceeds to the poor, and follow Christ, the young man departed in sorrow, for he was wealthy. Money was his god; he valued it more than treasure in heaven and following the Lord.

Using the Law to speak to the human conscience is a necessary step in pointing people to Christ. One cannot be found until they understand that they are hopelessly lost. A cure for a deadly disease is appreciated only after a person knows that they have been infected. Hence, quoting John 3:16 to someone who does not understand that they are dead in sin will not make sense to them – it is a cure without a diagnosis. The Law cannot save, but when used properly, it does point people to the Savior.

February 18 – Rewards Now and Later
Matthew 19:27-30

Then Peter answered and said to Him, "See, we have left all and followed You. Therefore what shall we have?" So Jesus said to them, "Assuredly I say to you, that in the regeneration, when the Son of Man sits on the throne of His glory, you who have followed Me will also sit on twelve thrones, judging the twelve tribes of Israel. And everyone who has left houses or brothers or sisters or father or mother or wife or children or lands, for My name's sake, shall receive a hundredfold, and inherit eternal life. But many who are first will be last, and the last first."

The Lord Jesus had previously told His disciples of the divisive outcome of gospel preaching: *"Do not think that I came to bring peace on earth. I did not come to bring peace but a sword. For I have come to 'set a man against his father, a daughter against her mother, and a daughter-in-law against her mother-in-law'; and 'a man's enemies will be those of his own household'"* (Matt. 10:34-37). Those who freely chose Christ as Lord and Savior would be isolated and persecuted by those who had not chosen Him. This dynamic was exceptionally painful when the division happened within a family. It is evident from Paul's instructions to the saints at Corinth that even marriages were being split apart by the gospel message (1 Cor. 7:12-16).

The rich young ruler had departed the Lord's presence sorrowfully because he was not willing to part with his wealth to follow Christ. This was the opposite response of the disciples, who had identified with Christ and had been willing to forsake all to follow Him. This prompted Peter to ask the Lord what type of reward they might expect for doing so. The Lord then affirmed that they would be highly honored and given authority in His coming kingdom. Additionally, they would possess eternal life and even now could expect a hundred fold increase for every relationship severed by the gospel.

It is the same for believers today. For every person who persecutes a believer, there will be a hundred more believers to lend him or her a helping hand. Christian love is a powerful weapon against the enemy, for it conveys the reality of the gospel message to the lost. May we all give thanks to the Lord for all the gracious benefits of a loving community of saints during our earthly sojourn.

February 19 – Lead by Serving Others
Matthew 20:25-28

But Jesus called them to Himself and said, "You know that the rulers of the Gentiles lord it over them, and those who are great exercise authority over them. Yet it shall not be so among you; but whoever desires to become great among you, let him be your servant. And whoever desires to be first among you, let him be your slave – just as the Son of Man did not come to be served, but to serve, and to give His life a ransom for many."

What the Lord taught in word and deed was counter to the world's philosophies of success. Worldlings will say "save your life at all costs," but the Lord taught "lose your life to gain one worth living." The world exclaims "live for the moment," but Christians are to "live for eternity." Worldlings want to be served by others, but Christ taught His disciples to humble themselves and serve others, for that was the true path to greatness in His kingdom.

Biblical leadership is not one of lordship or heavy-handed tactics of control, but rather is a style that serves God's sheep and upholds them so that they flourish. The Gentile kings were often dictators, who oppressed their subjects, but those who would lead God's people must not do so. Those who love Christ must follow His sacrificial example. Christ stated that He had not come into the world to be served, but rather to die – to give His life as a ransom for those who did not deserve God's favor in any way, shape, or form. If the Lord of Glory can do that for others, should not we be able to serve those who are difficult to serve?

One must be a submitted servant before he or she can be a true leader of others. The Lord Jesus humbled Himself to serve and develop others into profitable leaders. He devoted three-plus years of His life to train twelve men, one of which was a traitor. A true mark of Christlike leadership is the ability to develop greatness in others by serving them.

The Lord's meek and humble character, His compassion for the suffering, and His resolute spirit in the face of opposition invite us to follow His example – He was a true Servant of God. Christ's selfless ministry shows us that true love needs no title to serve, just the power to do so, which is supplied by Him alone. Those who follow His example of selfless service will have the appreciation of the saints now, and will be joyfully honored by the Lord Jesus in the future.

February 20 – You Are All Brethren
Matthew 23:8-12

But you, do not be called "Rabbi"; for one is your Teacher, the Christ, and you are all brethren. Do not call anyone on earth your father; for one is your Father, He who is in heaven. And do not be called teachers; for one is your Teacher, the Christ. But he who is greatest among you shall be your servant. And whoever exalts himself will be humbled, and he who humbles himself will be exalted.

Interestingly, no title of position can be found before the name of any disciple of Christ anywhere in Scripture. In fact, the Lord here forbids His disciples from adopting such nomenclature as "Teacher" or "Father." We understand that the Lord is referring to titles that should be reserved for the Godhead. These are spiritual designations which rise above natural, professional, or academic associations. There is nothing wrong with a child calling out to his daddy for help. Or a patient referring to his or her physician as "Doctor …".

However, the Lord was prohibiting the use of titles which exalted man at God's expense. He was their Teacher and taught them nothing but the truth; there was no one else that they could better learn God's will from than Him. They also only had one spiritual Father, His Father, God the Father who was in heaven; therefore, why revere an imperfect man on earth with a title that belongs to God the Father?

Titles of status and honor in Scripture belong to God, with most titles of honor being reserved for Christ. This helps ensure that we continue to regard Him as the only Lord of the Church, and ourselves as merely brethren. Men covet titles so that they might be honored by others – it is natural to our fallen nature. But those who worship Christ must not dishonor Him by stealing His glory. The believer's allegiance is to Him alone: we are His priests, His brethren, His friends, and His bond-servants. The Lord Jesus said that He alone was Master of all believers, who formed one class of people called "brethren."

Let me not, I pray you, accept any man's person, neither let me give flattering titles unto man. For I know not to give flattering titles; in so doing my Maker would soon take me away (Job 32:21-22; KJV).

February 21 – The Temple Sanctifies the Gold
Matthew 23:16-17

Woe to you, blind guides, who say, "Whoever swears by the temple, it is nothing; but whoever swears by the gold of the temple, he is obliged to perform it." Fools and blind! For which is greater, the gold or the temple that sanctifies the gold?

In His pungent "Woe" message to the Pharisees, the Lord Jesus addressed the hypocritical act of swearing in a way which degraded the name of the Lord. In esteeming the gold band that adorned the pinnacle of the temple more than the temple itself, the Pharisees were demonstrating disdain for God. Where is the value? In the gold or the temple? In the offering or the altar? The Lord bluntly told them that the altar gave value to the sacrifice, and that the temple bestowed the honor to the gold. The altar and the temple were patterned after holy heavenly realities (Heb. 9:23); each was directly connected to God. In placing the value on the offering and the gold, the Pharisees had disassociated themselves from God, but the Lord was telling them that only that which is connected with God has value; their traditions and swearing were just human nonsense and an insult to God.

The highest honor for gold would have been to be used in the house of God. The highest honor of a lamb was to be used as a sacrifice on the bronze altar. If gold and sheep had ambition, this would have been their highest calling. Christ was teaching that man apart from his connection with God is nothing; ambition apart from God is nothing; abilities apart from God are nothing! The only reason believers can be honored before God is because of their association with Christ.

Christ wants our motives, our abilities and our entire life to be connected with Him. It is possible for us to ignorantly commit the same form of blasphemy that the Pharisees did (i.e., undervaluing our association with Christ). For example, the reader might have a brilliant mind and be prompted to think, "The Lord would be fortunate to have a mind like mine in His service." Wrong! That which is in association with Christ is what has the value. The right thinking is: "My greatest privilege in life is to use my talents for the Lord." Your intellect does not sanctify Jesus Christ, but He sanctifies your mind for His purpose and glory. Likewise, all of our abilities must be submitted to Him.

February 22 – The Sacrifice Sanctifies the Altar
Matthew 23:18-22

And, "Whoever swears by the altar, it is nothing; but whoever swears by the gift that is on it, he is obliged to perform it." Fools and blind! For which is greater, the gift or the altar that sanctifies the gift? Therefore he who swears by the altar, swears by it and by all things on it. He who swears by the temple, swears by it and by Him who dwells in it. And he who swears by heaven, swears by the throne of God and by Him who sits on it.

I once heard William MacDonald tell the following story; I share it with you to illustrate what we should apply from the Lord's message to the Pharisees:

A number of years ago, while touring Paris, an American found an amber necklace in a secondhand street shop. It was marked with a low price, so he bought it. However, the customs officials really socked it to him with a duty tax when he reentered the U.S., which aroused his suspicion. He went to a jeweler who estimated its worth to be $25,000. He went to a second gemologist who said the necklace was worth $30,000. The man, being astounded, asked why it was worth so much. The jeweler handed him the magnifying glass and told him where to look on the necklace, where he read the inscription: "To Josephine from Napoleon." The necklace was not worth $30,000 in itself, but its association with Josephine and Napoleon made it valuable.

The same is true of you, dear believer. You only have value because of your association with Christ. We should not mock His Lordship and defame His name by thinking we have some ability or talent that He would do well to value and use. Such thinking is nothing less than hypocrisy and a pharisaical expression of pride – a form of blasphemy! Our highest service to the Lord is to be a living sacrifice, an emptied vessel of honor (2 Tim. 2:21) fitted for His sovereign use. If we live a holy, consecrated life, He will honor Himself; we need not presuppose our profitability to God.

May we all repent of such wrong attitudes and again esteem Christ above all things, *"that in all things He may have the preeminence"* (Col. 1:18). Without Him we are and have nothing of value to God!

February 23 – While You Are Going (Part 1)
Matthew 28:18-19

And Jesus came and spoke to them, saying, "All authority has been given to Me in heaven and on earth. Go therefore and make disciples of all the nations, baptizing them in the name of the Father and of the Son and of the Holy Spirit."

The Church is to engage in the upward ministry of *exalting* God, the inward ministry of *edifying* the Church and the outward ministry of *evangelizing* all nations. Literally, the Lord was commanding His disciples "as you are going ... make disciples of all nations."

Two separate images are used in Scripture to speak of this ministry. First, the fisherman ventures to the water (where the fish are) and casts in a line and works to catch a fish, which are landed one at a time. Fish rarely jump into the boat; rather, a fisherman must cast a line into the water and entice them to take the bait. This pictures one-on-one evangelism, such as employed by Philip when he explained the gospel message in private conversation with the Ethiopian eunuch in Acts 8, by Peter to Cornelius in Acts 10, by Paul to Lydia and later to the Philippian jailer in Acts 16, and by Paul before King Agrippa in Acts 26. Paul reminded the elders from Ephesus that he had ventured house to house with the gospel message while there (Acts 20:20). The Lord Jesus demonstrated the effectiveness of one-to-one evangelism; eleven such encounters are recorded in John's gospel account.

Second, Acts 20:20 informs us that Paul preached the gospel publicly also. In fact, he declared its message in schools (Acts 19:9), in synagogues (Acts 19:8), and wherever else he could (Acts 20:25). This is a different type of evangelistic ministry than "fishing" one-to-one; Scripture uses the image of a farmer sowing seed in a field to picture this type of evangelism (Matt. 13:1-23). Like the fisherman who goes to the water to catch fish, the farmer must journey to the field (where the people are) to sow seed. The seed represents the Word of God, and the various soils into which it is cast symbolize the different hearts of men in whom the Word is sown. Some will reject it flatly, some will be influenced by it but not unto salvation, and others will receive it and trust it – these alone bear fruit to God. Both fishing for men and seed-sowing are important ministries that must not be neglected today.

February 24 – While You Are Going (Part 2)
Matthew 28:19

Go therefore and make disciples of all the nations, baptizing them in the name of the Father and of the Son and of the Holy Spirit.

Believers are to be witnesses for Christ in the world and the Church is to send out workers to do the same. The book of Acts shows us that these workers were sent out by local churches, not by mission boards or parachurch organizations. Each church was responsible for overseeing their missionaries. The missionaries identified in Acts did not raise funds in order to be sent; rather, they *were* sent and the Lord provided for them as they went (Acts 13:1-5, 14:26, 15:40). They were to live by faith and, when necessary, to work with their own hands so that their motives for service would not be questioned by the people they were trying to reach (Acts 18:3; 2 Cor. 11:7-9). The Great Commission demonstrates God's great love for the lost and the fact that He wants to see as many as possible redeemed by the blood of His Son (2 Pet. 3:9).

Sadly, there are many ways in which God's desire to reach the world with the gospel has been distorted. One of these is the popular idea that only those with the gift of evangelism are responsible for the Great Commission. Others teach that a person is not saved until he or she becomes a member of their local church. The call, then, is "Come to a church meeting to hear the gospel and get saved"; the attitude is "you come" instead of "we go." Consequently, a significant portion of the world's population is not being reached for Christ. The Great Commission does not center in inviting people to a meeting, but rather imploring them to repent of their sins and receive Christ as their Lord and Savior. Inviting the lost to come to a future meeting does not convey to them the urgency of their need; today is the day of salvation!

Church meetings should be composed of believers who gather for the purpose of worship, prayer, teaching, and fellowship (Acts 2:42); although ministry from the pulpit should not be void of the gospel message, it is not the food needed to stimulate spiritual growth in believers (1 Pet. 2:2; Heb. 5:11-6:1). The meetings of the Church are for the Church, not for the lost (1 Cor. 14:22), and sharing the gospel with the lost, wherever they may be, is true evangelism.

February 25 – While You Are Going (Part 3)
Matthew 28:19-20

Go therefore and make disciples of all the nations, baptizing them in the name of the Father and of the Son and of the Holy Spirit, teaching them to observe all things that I have commanded you; and lo, I am with you always, even to the end of the age.

The Lord Jesus instructed His disciples to teach new converts to observe all the things that He had commanded them, as well as those things which the Holy Spirit would teach them after Christ's ascension into heaven (John 16:13-15). Scriptural doctrines and practices are to be the illumination of Christ's glory in the life of the believer.

Just as we do not expect a newborn to be earning income for the family two weeks after birth, spiritual growth in new converts requires time and care. Paul gives us a good pattern to follow in discipling those who profess Christ: consistent tender care but also only committing to reliable people who will be faithful with what they are taught:

But we were gentle among you, just as a nursing mother cherishes her own children. So, affectionately longing for you, we were well pleased to impart to you not only the gospel of God, but also our own lives, because you had become dear to us (1 Thess. 2:7-8). *And the things that you have heard from me among many witnesses, commit these to faithful men who will be able to teach others also* (2 Tim. 2:2).

Paul had a nurturing ministry with the Thessalonian believers, but yet he exhorts Timothy to invest only in those who would be faithful to the truth. Striking the balance between these two bookends is one of the difficult tasks of discipleship. Those who profess Christ as Savior will require tender care and regular feedings of the sincere milk of the Word (i.e., the rudiments of the Christian faith; 1 Pet. 2:2; Heb. 5:12) to encourage their growth, yet maturity must be realized. Maturity is evidenced by a deepening devotion to Christ, being a witness for Him, spending time in Bible study and prayer, repenting and forsaking sin, and faithfully attending church meetings. False professors or the apathetic can absorb our time and distract us from fulfilling the Great Commission. At some point, it would be appropriate to commit these to the Lord (with an open invitation for renewed interest), and move on.

February 26 – Let Us Go Into the Next Towns
Mark 1:36-38

And Simon and those who were with Him searched for Him. When they found Him, they said to Him, "Everyone is looking for You." But He said to them, "Let us go into the next towns, that I may preach there also, because for this purpose I have come forth."

It is evident from Mark's account that the Lord Jesus served the people tenaciously and compassionately; He did not seek to be popular. What was the Lord's response when His disciples informed Him that *"everyone is looking for You"*? The Lord replied, *"Let us go into the next towns."* He could have used the opportunity to promote Himself and gain a fan club, but as Arthur Pink notes that was not His way: "We like to boast of the crowds that attend our ministry. But the perfect Servant of God never courted popularity, He shunned it. And when His disciples came and told Him – no doubt with pleasurable pride – *'All men seek for Thee,'* His immediate response was, *'Let us go!'*"[13]

Mark shows the progressive attitude of humility by the Lord in response to His instant fame. At first, He tolerated the popularity, then He shunned it, and finally He avoided it altogether:

And immediately His fame spread throughout all the region around Galilee (Mark 1:28).

But Jesus withdrew with His disciples to the sea. And a great multitude from Galilee followed Him, and from Judea (Mark 3:7).

Immediately his ears were opened, and the impediment of his tongue was loosed, and he spoke plainly. Then He commanded them that they should tell no one; but the more He commanded them, the more widely they proclaimed it (Mark 7:35-36, see also 8:25-26).

Then they departed from there and passed through Galilee, and He did not want anyone to know it (Mark 9:30).

It is evident from these accounts that the Lord did not desire fame for helping others, though He deserved it. Rather, He showed through a selfless example that genuine service for others is veiled in secrecy. The Lord had the approval of His Father and that was all that mattered. May each of us keep small and keep hidden as we follow His example.

February 27 – Come Out of the Man
Mark 5:7-9

And he cried out with a loud voice and said, "What have I to do with You, Jesus, Son of the Most High God? I implore You by God that You do not torment me." For He said to him, "Come out of the man, unclean spirit!" Then He asked him, "What is your name?" And he answered, saying, "My name is Legion; for we are many."

The Lord Jesus often cast out demons to heal the populace of their physical and mental infirmities, and spiritual oppression. In this story, our Lord was willing to sail to the southeast shore of the Sea of Galilee with His disciples to meet one demon-possessed man in much turmoil. The region was known as the Gadarenes (Gerasenes). The town of Gadara was about seven miles southeast of the seashore. The Lord teaches us to go the extra mile to assist those suffering affliction.

The possessed man immediately came out of tombs to meet the Lord. He had often been shackled and chained but broke his bonds. Day and night he was screaming and cutting himself with stones. His condition was one of utter misery. After seeing the Lord, he fell down before Him and acknowledged His authority as the Son of God. The demons speaking through the man were afraid that Christ had come early to render final judgment on them, but that was not the case.

Notice that it is the demons that ramble on in the dialogue; the Lord spoke few words: "What is your name?" "Come out of the man." The demons answered the Lord, and yielded to His authority by coming out of the man, then entered a large herd of swine, which ran violently off a cliff and perished in the sea. The enemy often will use the tactic of verbal fogging to avoid accountability, but it does not work with the Lord. An entire legion of demons was cast out of the man.

When the townsfolk heard of what happened, they found the previously possessed man sitting, clothed, and in his right mind. This meant that the one who had accomplished this miracle was more powerful than a multitude of demons and they were afraid; they even asked the Lord to leave the region. Notice that the man was clothed. Perhaps a disciple donated clothing, but it seems more likely that Christ crossed the sea with every provision to resolve this man's pain and shame. If we decide to help someone, let us do our best to do the same.

February 28 – A Time to Grieve and a Time to Work
Mark 6:30-32

Then the apostles gathered to Jesus and told Him all things, both what they had done and what they had taught. And He said to them, "Come aside by yourselves to a deserted place and rest a while." For there were many coming and going, and they did not even have time to eat. So they departed to a deserted place in the boat by themselves.

We have the story of John the Baptizer's murder in Mark 6:14-29. Herod Antipas had illegally married his brother Philip's wife, Herodias (she had divorced her husband, which the Law did not permit), and John rebuked their adultery publicly, which got him arrested. Herod feared John, because he was a just and holy man and therefore sought to protect him (Mark 6:20). However, Herodias loathed John and schemed with her young daughter to trick Herod into granting her request of John's head on a platter. The pompous king fell into the feminine trap and to save face Herod had John executed.

After hearing of the news, the Lord told His disciples that it was time to come aside (i.e., time to separate themselves from the crowds and daily ministry) to rest for a while. The Lord teaches us that there should be a legitimate time to grieve the loss of a loved one. Proper grieving requires time away from life's normal responsibilities in order to reflect and settle one's soul in prayer and reading His Word. The disciples departed in a boat *together* to journey to a deserted place to achieve solitude. Notice that they did not isolate from each other during this time. To be free from responsibilities and distractions during the grieving process is important, but isolating from friends and family is dangerous. It is at such times as this that we need our closest friends and family members nearby to anchor our minds in the truth and to weep with us. To give a grieving person a hug from the Lord when the bottom has dropped out of their world is a tremendous blessing.

After an unknown time of solitude, the crowds became aware of their location and sought them. When the Lord saw the multitude, He was moved with compassion for them (Mark 6:36). He ministered to them and also fed them by multiplying five loaves of bread and two fish. Indeed, we should take time to mourn the death of a loved one, but the Lord shows us that there is also a time to get back to serving others.

February 29 – Would Have Passed Them By
Mark 6:45-50

Immediately He made His disciples get into the boat and go before Him to the other side, to Bethsaida, while He sent the multitude away. And when He had sent them away, He departed to the mountain to pray. Now when evening came, the boat was in the middle of the sea; and He was alone on the land. Then He saw them straining at rowing, for the wind was against them. Now about the fourth watch of the night He came to them, walking on the sea, and would have passed them by. And when they saw Him walking on the sea, they supposed it was a ghost, and cried out; for they all saw Him and were troubled.

After a long day of ministry, which included feeding perhaps twenty thousand people from a lad's sack lunch, it was time for the crowds to disperse. The Lord desired to be alone with His Father, so He told His disciples to enter a boat and cross the sea back to Capernaum without Him. Just before dark, the Lord saw His disciples in the midst of the sea and struggling to row against a contrary north wind. The Lord continued praying throughout the night and in the early dawn hours (i.e., the fourth watch was between 3 and 6 a.m.) the Lord came towards them walking on the rough sea. John notes that they had only rowed three or four miles total since entering the boat (John 6:19).

Although it was not the Lord's intention, it seemed to the disciples that the Lord was going to pass them by, so they cried out to Him. At first they were terrified by His presence, thinking He was a ghost, but He comforted them with these words, *"Be of good cheer! It is I; do not be afraid."* The Lord entered the boat and the impeding wind ceased and the boat was instantly moved across the sea to Capernaum, its intended destination (John 6:21). Their half-day arduous trial was over.

This text reminds us that the Lord is completely cognizant of where we are at and what we are going through. The disciples were safer in that boat in a raging sea than anywhere else on earth because they were in the will of God. In fact, what they feared most, the sea, is what brought the Lord nearer to them. This is often the case in our own difficulties. The Lord did not force Himself into their hardship until they called out for Him; when they did, they were comforted by His presence and their exhausting trial was over. The Lord longs to show Himself strong in our lives, but He will wait to be invited to do so.

March 1 – Those Not Against Us Are for Us
Mark 9:38-40

Now John answered Him, saying, "Teacher, we saw someone who does not follow us casting out demons in Your name, and we forbade him because he does not follow us." But Jesus said, "Do not forbid him, for no one who works a miracle in My name can soon afterward speak evil of Me. For he who is not against us is on our side."

In this narrative the Lord corrects the sectarian spirit of His disciples. They had witnessed someone casting out demons in the Lord's name, because they were not specifically associated with the disciples. The man was not teaching false doctrine or doing anything immoral; he just sought to help others and further the cause of Christ.

The Lord told His disciples not to hinder the man, for if he had enough truth and faith in Christ to cast out demons, he was on His side. This meant that the man was confronting Satan and therefore would not be speaking ill of Christ. Anyone believing that Christ was the Son of God was on the right side; they were not working against the Lord.

It is easy for us to think of other believers as "us" and "them" because they do not associate with us or they think differently than we do. Yet, the Lord affirmed the oneness and equal-standing of all believers when He told His disciples, *"For one is your Teacher, the Christ, and you are all brethren"* (Matt. 23:8). Christians are identified by biblical names such as Christians, believers, saints, and brethren. No denominations, cliques, or separate followings should be found in the Body of Christ. Paul asked the Corinthians, who were bestowing special honors to particular preachers instead of following Christ, *"Is Christ divided?"* (1 Cor. 1:13). The act of identifying with anyone or any organization instead of Christ is completely unbiblical. Rather, we should identify with David's thinking, *"I am a companion of all who fear You, and of those who keep Your precepts"* (Ps. 119:63).

In the practical sense, Christian fellowship (i.e., what we share together in the commonwealth of Christ) is dependent on how much we determine we have in common with other believers. While it is true that we will not be able to have the same degree of fellowship with all believers, we should strive to walk as far as we can with all those who have been redeemed by the precious blood of Christ.

March 2 – Depart From Me
Luke 5:8-11

When Simon Peter saw it, he fell down at Jesus' knees, saying, "Depart from me, for I am a sinful man, O Lord!" For he and all who were with him were astonished at the catch of fish which they had taken; and so also were James and John, the sons of Zebedee, who were partners with Simon. And Jesus said to Simon, "Do not be afraid. From now on you will catch men." So when they had brought their boats to land, they forsook all and followed Him.

Apparently, Peter and Andrew and their partners James and John had been fishing all night without catching a single fish. They were out of their boats and cleaning their nets along the shore as a crowd gathered to listen to the Lord Jesus. In order to be heard better, the Lord entered into Simon's boat and asked him to push out a little from the shore. The Lord then sat down and taught the multitude.

Afterwards the Lord commanded Simon Peter to launch out into the deep and to let down his *nets* for a catch. Peter balked at this idea because of their long, weary night of catching nothing. Furthermore, a line and hook were normally used to catch fish during daytime hours and a net in deep water at night, so what the Lord was asking Peter, an experienced fisherman, to do was not sensible. But Peter relented saying that because He had requested him to do it, he would let down "the net." The net quickly filled with a great number of fish and Peter signaled to his partners for assistance. There were so many fish that the net tore and some fish escaped, but the catch was so significant that both boats began to sink from the fish that had been harvested.

When Peter saw what had happened, he fell on his knees before the Lord and said, *"Depart from me, I am a sinful man, O Lord."* There were at least two things on Peter's mind. First, the Lord had said to let down his nets and Peter had let down only one net which tore under the strain of the catch. His partial obedience had limited Christ's blessing to him. May we remember that partial obedience is still disobedience. Second, the Lord had called Peter to follow Him previously and Peter responded by forsaking his fishing nets, but then he returned to fishing (Mark 1:18). Now, Peter would forsake all and follow the Lord. He received a new occupation: He would fish for men instead of fish!

March 3 – If I Am Lord, Do What I Say
Luke 6:46

But why do you call Me "Lord, Lord," and not do the things which I say?

The Lord Jesus warned His audience not to enthrone themselves and reject Him as their Lord: *"But why do you call Me 'Lord, Lord,' and not do the things which I say?"* or to put it in the modern vernacular, "Don't call Me Lord if you are not going to do what I say." It is mockery to refer to Jesus Christ as Lord, but then do what we want to regardless of what He commands.

Normally, when Scripture speaks of the will of God, it explicitly states what it is. There is no mystery about it; God has declared to us His general will for our lives. Consequently, the more pertinent question becomes, not what the will of God is for my life, but will I obey the revealed will of God for my life? The Lord Jesus told His disciples, *"If you love Me, keep My commandments"* (John 14:15). Obedience to the Lord Jesus practically proves our love for Him. A lack of love for the Lord will be shown through an unyielded spirit and through disobedience. There is such an intimate tie between genuine love for the Lord and obedience to the Lord that Paul bluntly states, *"If any man love not the Lord Jesus Christ, let him be Anathema* [eternally condemned]" (1 Cor. 16:22).

The Lord commands those identifying with Him in a profession of faith to be publicly baptized in His name (Matt. 28:19-20). Yet, many who say that they have trusted Christ as Savior flaunt various reasons for not being baptized. The Lord commanded His disciples to often remember Him by keeping the Lord's Supper (Luke 22:19-20). The New Testament Church met weekly on Sunday to obey this command (Acts 20:7). Regrettably, many believers disobey the Lord's command for the most superfluous reasons. Believers are also commanded not to forsake the assembling of themselves together for meetings of the Church (Heb. 10:25). The assembly is simply a gathering of believers in one locale under the oversight of God's under-shepherds. Any time a believer willingly chooses to miss meetings of the church for illegitimate reasons, he or she casts a vote to close down the church. If Christ is Lord, let us honor Him with our obedience.

March 4 – There Is Not a Greater Prophet
Luke 7:28

For I say to you, among those born of women there is not a greater prophet than John the Baptist; but he who is least in the kingdom of God is greater than he.

Because John was chosen by God from the womb to be Christ's forerunner and to prepare the Jewish nation for Messiah's coming, the Lord referred to him as the greatest of the prophets. This high status did not relate to John's personal character or even to the quality of his service, but rather to the important role that was assigned him. There were many Old Testament prophets that were bold and zealous messengers for God, even losing their lives to complete their assigned callings, but only John was given the honor of pointing Israel to *"the Lamb of God who takes away the sin of the world!"* (John 1:29). This was why the Lord gave John such a high accolade.

Building on this realization, the Lord then taught His disciples about positional greatness: he who is least in the kingdom is greater than John. In other words, the blessings of Christ's kingdom are greater than just being the forerunner of the King. Although John had a prominent and esteemed ministry in pointing his countrymen to Christ, those actually becoming one with Christ through the new covenant secured by Christ at Calvary would be greater positionally.

The Lord's statement reminds us that our positional greatness in Christ overshadows anything that we can do for Him. This realization highlights the importance of understanding who we are in Christ and what we have in Him: redemption (Rom. 3:24), no condemnation (Rom. 8:1), power over sin (Rom. 8:2), the love of God (Rom. 8:39), oneness with Christ (Rom. 12:5), sanctification (1 Cor. 1:2), hope (1 Cor. 15:19), eternal life (1 Cor. 15:22), victory by God's grace (2 Cor. 2:14), being made a new creation (2 Cor. 5:17), liberty (Gal. 2:4), being made a child of God (Gal. 3:26), having all spiritual blessings in heavenly places (Eph. 1:3), being created to good works (Eph. 2:10), complete salvation (2 Tim. 2:10), and preservation from wrath (Jude 1).

John had a spectacular ministry and did great things for the Lord, but those things are not even comparable with all that believers in the Church Age have in Christ and the eternal inheritance secured in Him.

March 5 – Those Forgiven Much Love Much
Luke 7:47-50

Therefore I say to you, her sins, which are many, are forgiven, for she loved much. But to whom little is forgiven, the same loves little. Then He said to her, "Your sins are forgiven." And those who sat at the table with Him began to say to themselves, "Who is this who even forgives sins?" Then He said to the woman, "Your faith has saved you. Go in peace."

A Pharisee named Simon invited the Lord to his home for a meal and the Lord accepted the invitation. While they were eating, a woman of ill repute came into the house with an alabaster flask of fragrant oil. What she did next to the Lord Jesus was astounding: *"she began to wash His feet with her tears, and wiped them with the hair of her head; and she kissed His feet and anointed them with the fragrant oil"* (Luke 7:38). The woman was publicly showing her appreciation for Christ and His message. However, because of her sinful background (being a prostitute), Simon thought less of the Lord for willfully receiving her expression of kindness: *"This Man, if He were a prophet, would know who and what manner of woman this is who is touching Him, for she is a sinner"* (Luke 7:39).

The Lord overheard Simon's thought and told him a story to rebuke his cold-hearted attitude. The woman, an outcast of society with fewer resources, had done much more to refresh Him than Simon, an esteemed and wealthy religious figure, had done. The Lord called Simon's attention to her good works, *"Do you see this woman?"* He then told the woman that though her sins were many, they had been forgiven. *"Your faith has saved you. Go in peace."*

The woman's testimony was used to rebuke Simon in two ways. First, James tells us that *"Faith by itself, if it does not have works, is dead"* (Jas. 2:17). Simon may have been curious about what Jesus was teaching, but his actions showed that he had not trusted in His message or he would be demonstrating his appreciation for being forgiven also. Second, the Lord affirmed *"to whom little is forgiven, the same loves little"* (Luke 7:47)! The portion that we return of what we have received from the Lord directly reflects how much we believe we have been forgiven and how much we love Christ. Those forgiven much love much and therefore give much!

67

March 6 – What Is Written in the Law?
Luke 10:25-29

And behold, a certain lawyer stood up and tested Him, saying, "Teacher, what shall I do to inherit eternal life?" He said to him, "What is written in the law? What is your reading of it?" So he answered and said, "'You shall love the Lord your God with all your heart, with all your soul, with all your strength, and with all your mind,' and 'your neighbor as yourself.'" And He said to him, "You have answered rightly; do this and you will live." But he, wanting to justify himself, said to Jesus, "And who is my neighbor?"

A lawyer engaged the Lord in a conversation about how to obtain eternal life. The lawyer was not serious about the subject matter, but rather was hoping to somehow trip the Lord up in His words through probing questions. He had come to test the Lord rather than to consider His message with an open heart. The Lord answered the lawyer's question about how to obtain eternal life with two of His own: *"What is written in the law?"* and *"What is your reading of it?"* First, the Lord caused the man to consider what the Word of God stated about the matter of salvation. An individual cannot repent and receive Christ as Savior without first understanding the Word of God; *"faith comes by hearing, and hearing by the word of God"* (Rom. 10:17).

Second, conversion is impossible without the work of the Holy Spirit to convince the sinner of his or her sin, the need for a righteous standing before God, and of forthcoming judgment for those who rebel (John 16:7-11; 1 Cor. 2:8-15). If Christians would follow the Lord's example of asking questions and referring their listeners to God's Word for the answers, they would avoid almost all arguments. It is the injection of our words, feelings, traditions, and methods into conversations which hinder the work of God on the unregenerate.

The lawyer answered the Lord's questions correctly. He had upheld the Law's righteousness, so the Lord replied, *"Do this and you will live."* Obviously, this was impossible, for no one can keep the Law. In saying this, the Lord was affirming the need to declare one's sin as the first step in receiving salvation. But instead of allowing the Law to condemn his behavior, the Lawyer sought to justify himself, by asking the Lord another question, "Who is my neighbor?" The Lord's response reveals His desire to convert testy lawyer-types into good neighbors.

March 7 – Sitting at the Lord's Feet
Luke 10:38-42

Now it happened as they went that He entered a certain village; and a certain woman named Martha welcomed Him into her house. And she had a sister called Mary, who also sat at Jesus' feet and heard His word. But Martha was distracted with much serving, and she approached Him and said, "Lord, do You not care that my sister has left me to serve alone? Therefore tell her to help me." And Jesus answered and said to her, "Martha, Martha, you are worried and troubled about many things. But one thing is needed, and Mary has chosen that good part, which will not be taken away from her."

The home of two sisters, Mary and Martha (and perhaps of their brother Lazarus), became a frequent resting place for the Lord. They lived in Bethany, which was located only two miles east of Jerusalem (John 11:1). During one such visit, the Lord took the opportunity to teach those who had gathered in their home to hear Him. Mary chose to sit at the Lord's feet and listen to Him, which frustrated her sister Martha, who was encumbered with much serving. She even asked the Lord to rebuke her sister so that she would rise and help her.

The Lord gently corrected Martha by saying that Mary had chosen what was best and would be blessed for doing so. Obviously, serving the Lord as He has called us to do is expected, but what we see others doing, or not doing, should not make us anxious (they are accountable to the Lord for their own actions) and our ministry should never replace having spiritual intimacy with the Lord. Certainly, what Martha was doing would benefit others, but fretting about what does not matter robs our joy in serving and keeps others from appreciating it too.

There are at least two things that we can glean from Mary's behavior: First, she had to say "no" to some legitimate activities in order to have time to sit at the Lord's feet and learn from Him. Second, after doing so, she was misunderstood by someone that did not have the same conviction. Regardless, Mary was complimented by the Lord in front of everyone for making the best choice. If we feel ourselves getting anxious or judgmental of others while engaged in ministry, it is time to come aside and sit at the Lord's feet and be refreshed by Him. This is the "good part" for our souls, although others may not agree.

March 8 – Neglecting Weightier Matters
Luke 11:42

But woe to you Pharisees! For you tithe mint and rue and all manner of herbs, and pass by justice and the love of God. These you ought to have done, without leaving the others undone.

Our natural tendency is to develop routine patterns and traditions that often result in unscriptural or unbalanced behavior over time. As an example, the Lord rebuked the Pharisees for neglecting *"the weightier matters of the law: justice and mercy and faith"* (Matt. 23:23). Although no teaching in Scripture should be neglected or ignored, the Lord did affirm that there were weightier matters of doctrine to consider first. It would be good for us to weigh out what we believe Scripture is teaching in doctrine and in pattern and categorize each aspect under what is essential, what is important, and what is a preference. It is important to discern between what is commanded in Scripture and also what was merely a pattern of the early Church.

For example, the Lord said to remember him often by keeping the Lord's Supper (Luke 22:19-20). The early Church settled on a practice of remembering the Lord each Sunday by breaking bread. Because this was the practice of the apostles, we may consider this a safe form to follow, but there is nothing wrong with meeting on other days of the week or more or less often to break bread.

What are some essential doctrines that cannot be compromised?
Doctrines of Salvation: the gospel message (the death and resurrection of Christ), salvation is in Christ alone, justification by grace through faith, the three tenses of salvation (regeneration, sanctification and glorification), eternal security (assurance of salvation), the difference between relationship and fellowship (position and practice), spiritual baptism, identification truth, and judicial and parental forgiveness.

The Study of God: only one God, the Trinity, the deity of Christ, the deity and personage of the Holy Spirit, the biblical attributes and character of God, the incarnation and humanity of Christ, the substitutionary death of Christ, and the Lordship of Christ.

Scripture: the inspiration and authority of Scripture, the Bible is God's timeless Word to humanity (holy books of world religions are not).

March 9 – Making Excuses
Luke 14:18-20

But they all with one accord began to make excuses. The first said to him, "I have bought a piece of ground, and I must go and see it. I ask you to have me excused." And another said, "I have bought five yoke of oxen, and I am going to test them. I ask you to have me excused." Still another said, "I have married a wife, and therefore I cannot come."

The Lord told *The Great Supper* parable to express God's desire for heaven to be full of redeemed sinners, but sadly most snub His kind offer to feast with Him. A certain man (representing the Lord) sent out his servants (picturing the Lord's disciples) with invitations to a great feast to be held at his home. The invites went to *the many* (Jewish leaders), to *the people in the streets* (common Jews), to *the people on the highways* traveling through the land (the Gentiles), and lastly to anyone in need (the poor, the blind, the crippled, the lame, etc.).

Many made excuses for not attending the great feast. Only a wealthy person buys property before looking at it first. Materialism and wealth (speaking of self-sufficiency) are often a hindrance for considering the gospel message of Christ. The excuse of testing five yoke of oxen just purchased pictures how jobs, careers, and business affairs often impede people from heeding Christ's invitation. A husband spending time with his new wife would be a proper expectation, but no natural relationships should keep us from seeking the only One who will satisfy the longing in our souls – Christ.

After hearing *The Great Supper* parable, a crowd began following Christ, but knowing that many just desired a good meal and not spiritual transformation, He turned towards them and taught them about the cost of following Him. The Lord was much more interested in the commitment of His disciples to Him than in the crowd of people merely following Him. The Lord longs for quality, not just quantity.

In secular movements, numbers are everything, but rarely do vast hordes of people represent God's will. This anomaly is quite evident in the modern Church movement, which equates church attendance with church success. The mindset is that big church meetings are obviously evidence of divine blessing. However, it is making true disciples of Christ that is the key to Church growth and vitality (Matt. 28:19-20).

March 10 – Faithfulness in Little Things
Luke 16:9-10

And I say to you, make friends for yourselves by unrighteous mammon, that when you fail, they may receive you into an everlasting home. He who is faithful in what is least is faithful also in much; and he who is unjust in what is least is unjust also in much.

What was the application of the *Parable of the Unjust Steward?* The Lord Jesus told His disciples to use their money wisely to further His cause in the world before their money inevitably lost its value. If they chose not to obey this command, it would indicate that they were mastered by money and not by Him. The Lord then reminded His disciples that the test of faithfulness begins in "what is least" (i.e., in small things). The Lord puts value on those seemingly obscure tasks that often have no visible honor. None of us was born with discipline, but we learn discipline by doing what we know we should even when we do not feel like it. This type of learned discipline accomplishes what good intentions cannot and continues to serve when all motivation fails, because we know the Lord is watching and we want His approval in the least of things. May we keep busy, even in mundane tasks of life, wherever the Lord has us in training for reigning. Relish every occasion to please the Lord and to show Him to others in what we do.

The daily matters of life matter as long as we do everything for the Lord and for the honor of His name. The Lord provides greater opportunities for service as His people are faithful to what they have already been asked to do (Luke 16:10-11). There is no example in Scripture where the Lord called a lazy person to serve Him. Elisha was plowing behind twelve yoke of oxen when he received his call from Elijah. Moses and David were shepherding sheep when God beckoned them to service. Gideon was summoned while threshing wheat. Four of the disciples were fishing when they were told by the Lord Jesus, "Follow Me." The Lord calls working people to serve Him.

A good many are kept out of the service of Christ, deprived of the luxury of working for God, because they are trying to do some great thing. Let us be willing to do little things. And let us remember that nothing is small in which God is the source.

— D. L. Moody

March 11 – Remember Lot's Wife
Luke 17:32-33

Remember Lot's wife. Whoever seeks to save his life will lose it, and whoever loses his life will preserve it.

Abraham's nephew, Lot, and his family lived in the wicked city of Sodom, which pictures worldliness of a sensual nature in Scripture. He and his family had become so infatuated with worldliness that the two angels God sent to rescue them literally had to lay hold of them to pry them from the city, so God could destroy it (Gen. 19:16).

Even after Lot understood that righteous souls must be separated from ungodly living, he still longed to have a bit of the world in his life. The angel told him to separate and to flee to the mountains for safety, but Lot begged him to allow him to dwell in a "little" city (Zoar) that he not die. This was clearly the issue: Lot was not willing to die to self and live for God. It is a testimony of God's grace that the selfish request of carnal Lot saved the city of Zoar from God's wrath! Lot, a ruined man, eventually found out that the world offered nothing substantial. He was estranged from God, and in the end, he was deserted by the world also. The world had exacted its price and proven its hatred for all that have been declared righteous; thus, Lot is driven by his own fears into further isolation.

The angels had commanded that they not look back towards Sodom – they were to make a "clean break" from the world. But, the heart of Lot's wife was still in Sodom, and as God rained down fire and brimstone upon the city, she either stole a glance at her old life or was lagging far enough behind that she instantly experienced the judgment of God. She either instantaneously became a pillar of salt or perhaps was buried by tons of salt when the catastrophic upheaval destroyed all the cities of the plain. The Hebrew word translated "looked back" is *nabat* which means "to look intently" or "to regard with pleasure." Christian discipleship requires forsaking the pleasures of the world and following Christ unhindered.

Lot's wife was used as an example by the Lord in Luke 17:32 to warn those listening not to think lightly about His offer of salvation. During His entire ministry the Lord told His listeners to remember only two people – Himself and Lot's wife. The choice He gave to His listeners was Himself or the world; the consequences of this choice would be life or death, blessing or judgment. We are given the same choice!

March 12 – Well Done, Good Servant
Luke 19:15-17

And so it was that when he returned, having received the kingdom, he then commanded these servants, to whom he had given the money, to be called to him, that he might know how much every man had gained by trading. Then came the first, saying, "Master, your mina has earned ten minas." And he said to him, "Well done, good servant; because you were faithful in a very little, have authority over ten cities."

In the parable of *The Ten Minas*, the master gave each of his ten servants one mina (worth about 100 denarii) to invest while he was on a long journey. The disciples believed that Christ's earthly kingdom would be soon, but this parable was to teach them that there would be a long interim between His first and second advents. During this time believers in the Church Age would have the opportunity to invest into Christ's future kingdom. When He does return, each servant will give an account of their stewardship to Him. This will occur at the Judgment Seat of Christ directly after the rapture of the Church, but before the Tribulation Period and Christ's second coming to the earth.

In the story, all servants were given the same amount to invest during the interim that the master was away. Yet, the servants had varying success depending on their degree of faithfulness. In the Church Age, all believers receive differing spiritual gifts and abilities, and prospects to serve, but this parable deals with those things we are all given equal *availability* to. For example, all believers are given the gospel message to share, the same amount of time each day to work, access to God through prayer, the benefit of knowing God's Word, to show hospitality, etc. However, not all believers will use what God has made available to them for serving Him in the same way.

One servant made ten pounds and was rewarded with ten cities to rule, while a second servant made five pounds and was given five cities. One unfaithful servant, who did not rightly know the character of his master, lost his reward through slothfulness. A person may be a Christian and waste his or her life – living a life without any concern for what God wants. Those believers will lose what they have, which will be given to the faithful person with proven devotion. Let us be found faithful to what the Lord has graciously entrusted us with.

March 13 – The Widow's Two Mites
Luke 21:1-3

And He looked up and saw the rich putting their gifts into the treasury, and He saw also a certain poor widow putting in two mites. So He said, "Truly I say to you that this poor widow has put in more than all, for all these out of their abundance have put in offerings for God, but she out of her poverty put in all the livelihood that she had."

Voluntary gifts were collected at the temple and placed in the temple treasury. As the Lord was observing individuals putting their gifts into the treasury, He was mindful of the stark contrast between the hearts of those who gave. The rich had not given sacrificially to the Lord, but out of their abundance – what they did not need. He called His disciples' attention to a poor widow who had put two mites into the collection. Although the rich had contributed more monetarily, the Lord declared that she had actually given more from God's perspective because her contribution was from her livelihood.

In the Lord's day, it was common for boys to go out and catch sparrows and then sell them to the poor who would make a little pie out of them. Two sparrows were sold for a farthing (Matt. 10:29), which was the equivalent of the two mites. This is the amount that the poor widow cast into the temple treasury (Mark 12:42). She basically gave her last meal to the Lord and was trusting in Him to supply her needs. God puts a premium on such sacrifices, because such show the giver's faith and confidence in His character. Likewise, when we give to God and share with others what we have and leave the implications with God, He is able to bless our generosity and cause us to flourish: *"The generous soul will be made rich, and he who waters will also be watered himself"* (Prov. 11:25). *"Cast your bread upon the waters, for you will find it after many days"* (Eccl. 11:1).

Because God controls all things, He alone is able to satisfy all our needs, even after we have been His instrument to bless others. The more God enables us to help others, the more we will be blessed. If someone really has a heart to give to the Lord, He will provide a way for that person to do so. Not giving to the Lord is the consequence of a spiritual problem, not finances as demonstrated by the widow who gave two mites. She gave what she had and was blessed by God for doing so.

March 14 – When You Have Returned to Me
Luke 22:31-32

And the Lord said, "Simon, Simon! Indeed, Satan has asked for you, that he may sift you as wheat. But I have prayed for you, that your faith should not fail; and when you have returned to Me, strengthen your brethren."

The Lord foretold that Peter would soon deny Him. Peter immediately rejected this statement and replied, *"Lord, I am ready to go with You, both to prison and to death."* The Lord then informed Peter that though Satan desired to sift the disciples like wheat (the "you" is plural), He had already prayed that Peter's faith would not fail. The devil wanted to remove Peter's faith, but the Lord wanted to use the harsh trial to rid the chaff of self-confidence from Peter's character.

Any of us would be stunned to learn that Satan, perhaps the most powerful being ever created and the arch-enemy of God, desired to bring us down in defeat. What a comfort for Peter to also be informed that the Lord had already prayed for him: *"that your faith should not fail."* As Paul explains, we have the same provision of mercy from the Lord Jesus: *"Who is he who condemns? It is Christ who died, and furthermore is also risen, who is even at the right hand of God, who also makes intercession for us"* (Rom. 8:34).

Peter's courage did fail him, for a few hours later he did deny the Lord three times, exactly as the Lord said he would. But thankfully his faith was refined and strengthened through the failure. This is the tenacious nature of true faith – what is not perfect is not destroyed but made stronger through suffering and hardships. We are to learn from our mistakes, rise up in grace, and go on with the Lord.

Through Peter's refining process, he would gain a greater capacity to encourage and bless others. Foreknowing this, the Lord Jesus instructed him that after he was restored to Him again he was to strengthen his brethren. The Lord was speaking of a future day when Peter would repent of his failure (sin) and be brought back into fellowship with Him. Our fellowship with Christ is based on our behavior, but our position in Christ is based on His ability to secure what is His. A. W. Tozer suggests, "It is doubtful whether God can bless a man greatly until He has hurt him deeply."

March 15 – Reason, but Do Not Retaliate
Luke 22:52-53

Then Jesus said to the chief priests, captains of the temple, and the elders who had come to Him, "Have you come out, as against a robber, with swords and clubs? When I was with you daily in the temple, you did not try to seize Me. But this is your hour, and the power of darkness."

This is one of many examples in Scripture where Satan attacks proper authority (God-ordained authority) and tries to replace it with weaker authority (those under Satan's authority). Absalom's revolt against the rightful king of Judah – David – is a good example of this tactic. The Pharisees were now directly attacking the Lord's authority and message to replace it with human traditions and legalism. The Lord Jesus already knew what was going to happen to Him at Calvary and did not resist being arrested though He had the power to do so.

The Lord's response to those arresting Him was noteworthy. He clearly states the facts in order to appeal directly to the consciences of those arresting Him: "I was with you daily in the temple without any expression of hostility; why then are you coming against Me now with clubs and swords?" "What have I done that now justifies you treating Me like a robber?" The Lord does not try to escape what He knows is necessary, but He still has a compassionate heart towards those under the enemy's control. He chooses to reason with them, not attack or retaliate against them in anyway. Indeed the situation was being incited by wickedness in high places, yet the Lord's compassion for those individuals under its influence is paramount.

Just moments earlier, Judas led a mob to the location in the Garden of Gethsemane where he knew the Lord often resided. He told the mob, *"Whomever I kiss, He is the one; seize Him"* (Matt. 26:48). He then immediately went up to the Lord and said, *"Greetings, Rabbi!"* and kissed Him. But the Lord responded to his betrayal with these words: *"Friend, why have you come?"* (Matt. 26:50). Fully knowing what Judas was doing, our Savior still extended kindness to Judas. Although under Satan's control, the Lord still felt it was necessary to appeal to Judas' conscience one last time. When it seems like everything around you is dark and evil, remember individual souls still need to be reached.

March 16 – Did Not Our Heart Burn Within Us?
Luke 24:30-32

Now it came to pass, as He sat at the table with them, that He took bread, blessed and broke it, and gave it to them. Then their eyes were opened and they knew Him; and He vanished from their sight. And they said to one another, "Did not our heart burn within us while He talked with us on the road, and while He opened the Scriptures to us?"

It was Sunday, the day of the Lord's resurrection. Mary Magdalene was the first to see Him alive near His tomb, and then the Lord Jesus appeared to other women who were returning home after being at the tomb. He had also met with Peter privately (Luke 24:34). There were two disciples, who were walking from Jerusalem to Emmaus (a village about seven miles northwest of Jerusalem). They were talking together about all that had transpired in recent days when the Lord joined their company. The two disciples did not recognize the Lord, for *"their eyes were restrained so that they did not know Him."* When the Lord inquired about what they were talking about, one of the disciples named Cleopas expressed his surprise that their new companion was not informed about how the priests and rulers had crucified Jesus of Nazareth. This implied that the entire nation was familiar with Christ's ministry. The two dismayed travelers believed that Jesus was a Prophet of God and perhaps the Messiah, but now doubts filled their minds.

The Lord chided them for not believing what the Old Testament had revealed about Messiah's coming. He then supplied them a thorough survey of what Moses and the prophets had foretold of Himself. But it was not until they reached Emmaus and the Lord gave thanks and broke bread with the disciples that they understood who He was. The Lord then instantly vanished. As the Lord had expounded Scripture to them on the road, they admitted to each other that their hearts surged with excitement. The two disciples then decided to return to Jerusalem and tell the eleven that *"the Lord is risen indeed."*

No one can breathe in the atmosphere of the risen Savior and remain in an isolated, independent condition. The news of Christ must be shared and enjoyed with others. Furthermore, like the two disciples in the story, the more we receive God's Word, the more fellowship with Christ we will desire, for all Scripture speaks of Him.

March 17 – Began With Prayer – Finished With Praise
Luke 24:50-53

And He led them out as far as Bethany, and He lifted up His hands and blessed them. Now it came to pass, while He blessed them, that He was parted from them and carried up into heaven. And they worshiped Him, and returned to Jerusalem with great joy, and were continually in the temple praising and blessing God. Amen.

Luke began his account with people praying at the temple, for they were longing for Messiah's coming. He closes his record with Messiah praying for His people, His newly created temple – the Church. The Lord lifted His hands to bless His disciples before returning back to heaven, thereby identifying with them and showing His divine care of them. In Luke's Gospel, the hands of the Lord are repeatedly touching and blessing those in need. Luke often refers to the Lord's prayer-life, which is in keeping with his presentation of Christ's humanity. Especially in Luke's Gospel, the Lord shows us the importance of prayer from the beginning to the end of our ambassadorship for Christ.

How often do we surge ahead of God's perfect plan? Waiting is often harder than working, for we feel compelled to do something, but often it is not to pray. Prayer demonstrates complete faith in the Lord to initiate, direct, and complete each matter of our lives according to His will (1 Jn. 5:14). Besides moving the hand of God, prayer transforms our hearts by conforming our thinking to the mind of Christ.

Before choosing His disciples, the Lord spent an entire night in prayer (Luke 6:12). The Lord prayed before feeding the 5000, just prior to Peter's pronouncement that He was *"the Christ, the Son of the living God,"* and before raising Lazarus from the dead. The Lord's final hours before Calvary were spent in prayer. The prayer life of the Lord Jesus was so intense and so fruitful that on one occasion the disciples asked the Savior to teach them how to pray. They wanted in on the blessings of prayer. How about you? How is your prayer life? We should follow the Lord's wonderful example: prayer preceded service and followed accomplishments – prayer preceded crisis and followed achievements. It is the Lord's desire that we be a dependent people given to prayer so that we faint not while serving Him: *"Then He spoke a parable to them, that men always ought to pray and not lose heart"* (Luke 18:1).

March 18 – He Must Increase, but I Must Decrease
John 3:26-30

And they came to John and said to him, "Rabbi, He who was with you beyond the Jordan, to whom you have testified – behold, He is baptizing, and all are coming to Him!" John answered and said, "A man can receive nothing unless it has been given to him from heaven. You yourselves bear me witness, that I said, 'I am not the Christ,' but, 'I have been sent before Him.' He who has the bride is the bridegroom; but the friend of the bridegroom, who stands and hears him, rejoices greatly because of the bridegroom's voice. Therefore this joy of mine is fulfilled. He must increase, but I must decrease."

The Pharisees were trying to make John jealous by calling his attention to the fact that his disciples were leaving him to follow Jesus Christ. Yet, John turned their words around on them, by declaring that this dynamic was proof that his ministry was approved by God. He was Christ's forerunner and his divinely appointed mission was to call his countrymen to repentance and point them to the Savior – Jesus Christ.

In application, if a so-called Christian ministry or particular preacher is gathering people to themselves and not pointing those they have influence with to Christ, then that activity or person must be rejected. Disciples of Christ should not seek the praise of men, high positions, or honorable titles – all epithets and all praise are reserved for the Lord Jesus Christ.

John had already told the Pharisees that he was not the Christ, that he was not Elijah, and that he was not the esteemed prophet foretold by Moses. John was merely the friend of the Bridegroom who rejoiced greatly because the Bridegroom was nearby and John could still hear His voice. John's declaration should be the motto of every servant of Christ: *"He* [the Lord Jesus] *must increase, but I must decrease"* (John 3:30).

Until self-effacing men return again to spiritual leadership, we may expect a progressive deterioration in the quality of popular Christianity year after year till we reach the point where the grieved Holy Spirit withdraws – like the Shekinah from the Temple.

— A. W. Tozer

March 19 – Must Worship In Spirit and Truth
John 4:23-24

But the hour is coming, and now is, when the true worshipers will worship the Father in spirit and truth; for the Father is seeking such to worship Him. God is Spirit, and those who worship Him must worship in spirit and truth.

The Lord Jesus desired to travel through Samaria to meet privately with a distraught woman who had come to draw water from Jacob's well. The woman had been married five times and was now living in sin with a sixth man. The Lord knew all about her past, which He revealed to her after offering her living water for her soul. The woman, being uncomfortable with her sin being exposed, tried to divert the conversation into a religious-ethnic discussion, but the Lord quickly refocused her attention on the key matter – salvation through Messiah.

The Lord informed the Samaritan woman that there was a time coming in which those who would worship God would be able to do so in spirit and truth. The Lord was speaking of the Church Age. Those who had been born again through the gospel message would have the Holy Spirit within them and be able to worship God through their human spirit in scriptural truth. Thankfully, the woman found a seventh man that day, the perfect Man, who gave her eternal life and she responded by gladly telling everyone she could that Messiah had come.

As promised, today the Holy Spirit guides believers into a deeper understanding of truth concerning the Lord Jesus and the overall greatness and goodness of God (John 16:13-14). Only through Spirit-led worship, which will be completely founded in divine truth, can the believer offer any acceptable sacrifice of praise to God. Thus, the words of John the baptizer ring true: *"A man can receive nothing, except it be given him from heaven"* (John 3:27). Many continue this practice today by identifying with Christ through religious rote without knowing Him personally as Savior (Matt. 7:21-23). Worship that pleases God must emerge from a willing heart that is illuminated by the Holy Spirit in accordance with revealed truth: *"God is Spirit, and those who worship Him must worship in spirit and truth."* If what we say or do is not true or Spirit-led, it does not honor God; it is mere form, religious fanfare, and has no eternal value.

March 20 – Do Not Judge According to Appearance
John 7:24

Do not judge according to appearance, but judge with righteous judgment.

We have a propensity to judge matters after hearing or seeing only part of the story (especially if presented by a friend or loved one). The Lord warned His disciples not to permit their feelings or a superficial examination of the facts to guide their decisions. In the book of Proverbs, King Solomon likewise warned:

He who answers a matter before he hears it, it is folly and shame to him (Prov. 18:13).

The first one to plead his cause seems right, until his neighbor comes and examines him (Prov. 18:17).

If someone is asking us for counsel, or to help resolve an offense, it behooves us to listen carefully to what is said, to ask questions, and to gather available information before rendering a decision. Moreover, we must realize that it would be normal for those in sin to try to deceive us by providing inaccurate information or by spinning the truth. Someone desiring to hide the truth from us will flavor the events of what really happened in order to win us to their side. But in such matters there is only one side that matters – that the Lord is honored by the truth.

Furthermore, the first appearance of things is usually not the reality of the matter and a wise person does not grip a one-sided story. If the first party does not want us to talk to the other party in a disagreement, that is usually a good indication of some level of guilt. A believer should always desire that the truth be revealed in a situation, which will require investigating the facts, praying for wisdom, and maintaining an unbiased perspective. James reminds us that if we lack wisdom, we have an opportunity to receive what we need: *"If any of you lacks wisdom, let him ask of God, who gives to all liberally and without reproach, and it will be given to him"* (Jas. 1:5). Paul encourages believers to go to wise brethren in the Church for judgments on unresolvable personal disagreements (1 Cor. 6:5). May we all remember that deception is of the devil and that God's nature is truth.

March 21 – Abide in My Word
John 8:31-32

Then Jesus said to those Jews who believed Him, "If you abide in My word, you are My disciples indeed. And you shall know the truth, and the truth shall make you free."

For anyone to have an effective ministry, he or she must first personally know the Lord, and then discern and yield to God's revealed Word. Whatever we pursue outside the will of God is meaningless to Him and usually results in the disdain of His name. Because a true servant of God knows and loves the Lord, he or she is determined to abide in His Word. The Lord Jesus told His disciples that continuing to do what He had told them to do was proof that they were His disciples: *"If you abide in My word, you are My disciples indeed"* (John 8:31).

The Lord Jesus also promised that those who keep His commandments will bask in His love and be entrusted with more illumination: *"He who has My commandments and keeps them, it is he who loves Me. And he who loves Me will be loved by My Father, and I will love him and manifest Myself to him"* (John 14:21). Those demonstrating their love for the Lord through obedience will be blessed with an enhanced understanding of God and of things important to Him. Hence, the obedient servant is continually drawn into deeper communion with God and is permitted to increasingly experience God's security, peace, power, and love.

Today, through the means of technology, Christians have more opportunities to hear good preaching than at any other time in the Church Age. Besides being able to gather to hear the Word of God expounded during meetings of the Church and at conferences, audio and video messages can be downloaded and streamed endlessly. But God's people are not promised to be blessed by merely hearing Scripture taught – the blessing comes by obeying what we hear: *"Blessed are those who hear the word of God and keep it!"* (Luke 11:28). The Lord told His disciples that only those who were truly His would obey His commands. May we prove our devotion to the Lord by searching out the will of God as revealed in Scripture and then obey what we understand to be true. We can only experience God and have His blessing in our lives when we yield to what He says.

March 22 – Praying at the Lord's Feet
John 11:32-33

When Mary came where Jesus was, and saw Him, she fell down at His feet, saying to Him, "Lord, if You had been here, my brother would not have died." Therefore, when Jesus saw her weeping, and the Jews who came with her weeping, He groaned in the spirit and was troubled.

The Lord had been summoned four days previous to come quickly, for the one that He loved (Lazarus, the brother of Mary and Martha) was severely ill. It would have taken a day for Mary and Martha's message, originating in Bethany, to reach the Lord and His disciples who were at Bethabara at this time (John 1:28, 10:40). The Lord already knew about the situation and after hearing the passionate summons told His disciples that Lazarus was already dead. He also said that Lazarus' death would be used to glorify God and to honor His Son, speaking of Himself. The Lord tarried at Bethabara for two more days before informing His disciples that it was time for them to journey to Judea. Their destination was troubling to some of the disciples, for they knew that the Jewish religious leaders were plotting to kill their Master.

Many Jews were gathered at the home of Mary and Martha to mourn the death of Lazarus. When Martha heard that the Lord was nearing Bethany, she immediately went out to speak to him, but Mary remained in the house. We are not told why Mary remained in the house. It seems likely that she was aware of the Lord's approach, but for whatever reason she chose to remain with their many guests. She no doubt knew that the Lord would soon be entering their home, for He had often resided there previously. Martha told the Lord that if He had been there, her brother would still be alive, but she also recognized that though Lazarus was dead, the Lord could still do something about it.

Indeed, the Lord replied, *"I am the resurrection and the life."* Martha departed to secretly tell her sister that the Lord was asking for her. Mary immediately came to the Lord and fell at His feet weeping. She repeated the same confidence in Him that Martha had already declared. He was moved to tears by her brokenness and her request. The Lord went to the tomb, the stone was removed, and Lazarus was called forth; he soon walked out of the tomb bound in grave clothes. Being broken at the Savior's feet results in the Son being glorified!

March 23 – Worshiping at the Lord's Feet
John 12:3

Then Mary took a pound of very costly oil of spikenard, anointed the feet of Jesus, and wiped His feet with her hair. And the house was filled with the fragrance of the oil.

On behalf of the Lord, the prophet Isaiah declared to Israel: *"I am the Lord, that is My name; and My glory I will not give to another, nor My praise to carved images"* (Isa. 42:8). There is only one God and He will not share His glory with another. God alone is to be revered and worshiped, a truth that the Lord Jesus confirmed when He was tested by Satan (Matt. 4:10). It is then no surprise that we witness God's Son, the Lord Jesus Christ, repeatedly being worshiped as God in the New Testament. The Magi worshiped the Lord when He was a young child (Matt. 2:11). The healed blind man worshiped the Lord Jesus after understanding that He was the Son of God (John 9:38). All the hosts of heaven will worship the Lamb, the Lord Jesus Christ (Rev. 5:12-14).

Another beautiful expression of worshiping the Lord Jesus occurred in the home of a previous leper named Simon six days before Christ's death (Mark 14:1-11). Lazarus, who had been raised from the dead, was sitting with the Lord at a table, while Martha was serving. Their sister Mary then arrived and anointed the Lord with a pound of a very expensive ointment called spikenard. This is a beautiful scene of Christian fellowship, service, and worship all in the Lord's presence.

Judas, the betrayer, condemned Mary for her wastefulness, but the Lord said, *"Let her alone; she has kept this for the day of My burial."* Mary apparently possessed a deeper understanding of what was coming than that of the disciples and she wanted to show her utmost appreciation. She gave her best to the Lord and kept none of the oil for herself. It would be inappropriate to speak of personal cost or limiting gratitude for the One possessing all things who was yet willing to give His life for her to live. John notes that the house was filled with the sweet fragrance of Mary's worship. Genuine, selfless worship will refresh the hearts of all those who love the Lord Jesus. At the Lord's feet, Mary was taught, she prayed, and she worshiped – her example is a superb one to follow. Let us remember that *"Christ came, who is over all, the eternally blessed God"* (Rom. 9:5) and He deserves our best.

85

March 24 – Follow My Example
John 13:14-17

If I then, your Lord and Teacher, have washed your feet, you also ought to wash one another's feet. For I have given you an example, that you should do as I have done to you. Most assuredly, I say to you, a servant is not greater than his master; nor is he who is sent greater than he who sent him. If you know these things, blessed are you if you do them.

The disciples gathered in an upper room with the Lord to eat the Passover together. Before the feast began, the Lord girded Himself as a slave, poured water in a basin, picked up a towel, and began washing the dirty feet of His disciples. Normally, this was the task of a household servant to refresh visitors, but since the Lord was the host and the disciples were His guests, He humbled Himself to serve them. They had been arguing among themselves as to who would be the greatest in the kingdom, so the Lord provided them with an example of how one works his or her way up in His kingdom – by humble service.

Peter did not appreciate the Lord's act of kindness and refused to have his feet washed. The Lord told Peter that in a future day he would understand what He was doing and then replied, *"If I do not wash you, you have no part with Me."* This statement caused Peter to reverse his position and to ask the Lord to bathe him. The Lord answered: *"'He who is bathed needs only to wash his feet, but is completely clean; and you are clean, but not all of you.' For He knew who would betray Him; therefore He said, 'You are not all clean'"* (John 13:10-11). The Lord was also revealing doctrinal truth about spiritual regeneration (a one-time act of the Holy Spirit at conversion) and the need for believers to confess sins afterwards to remain in fellowship with Him (1 Jn. 1:9). As we daily walk through a defiled world, some of its influences dirty our hands and feet, which then need to be cleansed.

On the eve of His crucifixion, God incarnate washed twenty-four dirty feet (two of which belonged to the betrayer Judas) for a reason: *"I have given you an example, that you should do as I have done to you."* Instead of arguing about their kingdom status, the disciples should exhibit the humble character of the King by serving each other. True humility is a quiet heart that expects nothing, gives its best, and is not offended when others expect what is not deserved.

March 25 – A New Commandment
John 13:34-35

A new commandment I give to you, that you love one another; as I have loved you, that you also love one another. By this all will know that you are My disciples, if you have love for one another.

God's love is the binding agent that marks Christians as a peculiar people in the world. Through the power of the Holy Spirit, Christ's love draws those who previously had nothing in common into intimate communion with each other. This is why Paul exhorts believers to behave *"with all lowliness and gentleness, with longsuffering, bearing with one another in love, endeavoring to keep the unity of the Spirit in the bond of peace"* (Eph. 4:2-3). Of course, the unity that the Holy Spirit labors to maintain within the Body of Christ is not divorced from the Truth. The Lord Jesus referred to the Holy Spirit as the Spirit of Truth: *"The Spirit of truth, whom the world cannot receive, because it neither sees Him nor knows Him; but you know Him, for He dwells with you and will be in you"* (John 14:17). Therefore, the type of love and unity God desires to be displayed in the Church will always have His truth as a basis. Genuine love cannot benefit others unless it is centered in God's will as demonstrated by God-honoring conduct.

How is the world to see Christ? The Lord Jesus told His disciples: *"By this all will know that you are My disciples, if you have love for one another."* Christ would be known when the disciples exhibited the same love for each other that Christ had already demonstrated to them. Christian love is a powerful weapon against the enemy, for it practically conveys the gospel message to the lost. If we are not displaying the love of Christ in what we do, we are wasting our time:

And though I have the gift of prophecy, and understand all mysteries and all knowledge, and though I have all faith, so that I could remove mountains, but have not love, I am nothing (1 Cor. 13:2).

The love of the saints is a rich heritage; may we always value each other above temporal things. Lord, we give You thanks for the gracious benefits of a loving community of saints in our local church. Lord, if we cannot give You thanks for this, please use us so that we can.

March 26 – Ask the Father in My Name
John 14:12-14

Most assuredly, I say to you, he who believes in Me, the works that I do he will do also; and greater works than these he will do, because I go to My Father. And whatever you ask in My name, that I will do, that the Father may be glorified in the Son. If you ask anything in My name, I will do it.

John's Gospel presents a strong connection between prayer and knowing and doing the will of God. In fact, the Lord Jesus refers to His Father's "will" *seven* times, speaking only His Father's words *seven* times, and that His disciples should pray only in His name on *seven* different instances. Hence, perfect praying centers in the will and the Word of God; it is not selfish. When we petition the Father in prayer, we are asking Him to grant our requests to honor His Son's name.

The only way to ensure this occurs is for the Holy Spirit to lead us into prayer after we have properly discerned God's will from studying His Word. Then with confidence we can close our prayer with a hearty "amen" which literally means "so be it." *"Now this is the confidence that we have in Him, that if we ask anything according to His will, He hears us"* (1 Jn. 5:14). We must know God's Word to know how to pray in a way that would honor Christ's name.

Prayer is not a "name it and claim it" – "blab it and grab it" – formula for success. Righteous praying centers in God's will and is motivated by love for the Savior's name. Prayer shows faith and dependence in God to initiate, direct, and complete each matter of our lives according to His will. Prayer transforms our hearts by conforming our thinking to the mind of Christ. For those who love the name of Jesus Christ and His will, prayer is a great blessing which moves the hand of God!

Prayer is reaching out after the unseen; fasting is letting go of all that is seen and temporal. Fasting helps express, deepen, confirm the resolution that we are ready to sacrifice anything, even ourselves to attain what we seek for the kingdom of God. ... The great thing in prayer is to feel that we are putting our supplications into the bosom of omnipotent love.

— Andrew Murray

March 27 – If You Love Me, Obey My Commandments
John 14:21

He who has My commandments and keeps them, it is he who loves Me. And he who loves Me will be loved by My Father, and I will love him and manifest Myself to him.

Five times the night before the Lord was crucified (while still in the upper room), He told His disciples of the inseparable tie between their love for Him and practical obedience to His commands: *"If you love Me, keep My commandments"* (John 14:15). He was going to demonstrate this truth the next day: *"But that the world may know that I love the Father, and as the Father gave Me commandment, so I do"* (John 14:31). There was no question of the love of the Father for the Son, or of the Son for the Father, but the Son was going to show the world how much He loved the Father through obedience.

John 14:21 contains a promise for all those who will likewise demonstrate love for God by simply obeying His Word: The Lord said He would *"manifest Myself to him."* John was the beloved disciple and, apparently, the least inhibited in expressing his love for the Lord – it was to him, the disciple who loved much, that a fuller manifestation of Christ was granted. It was John, and only John, who was an eyewitness to the Apocalypse, *"The Revelation of Jesus Christ"* (Rev. 1:1). The divine disclosure of Christ's glory to John is a direct testimony of the immensity of John's love for the Lord Jesus. Those who have been forgiven much love Christ more, those who love much obey Christ more, and those who obey Christ much comprehend Him more.

Humility before God and reverence for His Word result in blessing and further understanding of God's will. Willful ignorance, rebellion, or compromise should be unheard of responses to Scripture, that is, for those who truly long to know and experience God. The irresistible love of God can only be experienced by answering His invitation to know Him. Our understanding of God's plan and our commitment to live it out will be directly proportionate to the extent that we have known and experienced Him. Continued submission to divine truth is the pathway to intimately experiencing and knowing God in deepening degrees. It is this consistent contact with God's nature that results in our comprehension of His wondrous design for our lives.

March 28 – Abide in Me
John 15:1-6

I am the true vine, and My Father is the vinedresser. Every branch in Me that does not bear fruit He takes away; and every branch that bears fruit He prunes, that it may bear more fruit. You are already clean because of the word which I have spoken to you. Abide in Me, and I in you. As the branch cannot bear fruit of itself, unless it abides in the vine, neither can you, unless you abide in Me. I am the vine, you are the branches. He who abides in Me, and I in him, bears much fruit; for without Me you can do nothing. If anyone does not abide in Me, he is cast out as a branch and is withered; and they gather them and throw them into the fire, and they are burned.

Some have made this passage say what it does not – the analogy does not teach that true believers can lose their salvation. The subject of this passage is not salvation, but fruit bearing. Having just departed the upper room, the Lord is speaking only to His disciples (i.e., true believers, as Judas has already departed the group). The fact that Christ refers to "a man" and not "them" in verse 6 affirms that Christ knew the eleven were branches (true believers) in the Vine (in Him).

The key words in this text are: "love" (ten occurrences), "abide" (nine times mentioned), and fruit (found eight times). The Lord desires believers to be washed by the Word (v. 3), to be lifted up out of the muck of the world (the verb *airo* is better translated "lift up" than "take away" in v. 2), and to abide in Him. Why does the Lord want this for all believers? So that they can experience the love and joy of God, and bear "fruit" (v. 2), "more fruit" (v. 2), and "much fruit" (vv. 5, 8). Those who do not choose to abide in the goodness of Christ will be incapable of bearing spiritual fruit (v. 4).

Some may say that they are true branches, but their mimicked fruit-bearing will be proven to be counterfeit in time. True faith has a lasting reality (Jas. 2:17). You can fake it for a while, but not without zapping yourself dry; only Christ's resources can prompt fruit-bearing in believers: *"I am the vine, you are the branches. He who abides in Me, and I in him, bears much fruit; for without Me you can do nothing."* Without Christ I can do nothing to please God, but by abiding in Him, *"I can do all things through Christ who strengthens me"* (Phil. 4:13).

90

March 29 – The Benefits of Abiding in Christ
John 15:7-13

If you abide in Me, and My words abide in you, you will ask what you desire, and it shall be done for you. By this My Father is glorified, that you bear much fruit; so you will be My disciples. As the Father loved Me, I also have loved you; abide in My love. If you keep My commandments, you will abide in My love, just as I have kept My Father's commandments and abide in His love. These things I have spoken to you, that My joy may remain in you, and that your joy may be full. This is My commandment, that you love one another as I have loved you. Greater love has no one than this, than to lay down one's life for his friends.

The Lord Jesus has implored His eleven true branches to choose to abide in Him, their spiritual Vine. He has told them that without Him they can do nothing; branches must draw their life from the vine in order to bear fruit. Fruit bearing is one of five benefits that the Lord identifies for those branches abiding in Him (v. 8). Fruit bearing speaks of all that the Holy Spirit desires to do through us to honor Christ and bestow glory to God (e.g., giving to and serving others, using our spiritual gifts and resources to encourage others, praising God, etc.).

The second benefit of abiding in Christ is that we get to enjoy a powerful prayer-life (v. 7). If we are praying in the will of God, the Lord wants us to ask Him for anything and He will do it. This gives every believer the opportunity to see the good hand of God in his or her life and witness what could be the grace of God.

The third benefit of abiding in Christ is that we get to experience the love of God (v. 9). In Christ, the Father lavishes us with the same love He conveys to His Son. Catesby Paget puts the matter this way:

So near, so very near to God, I cannot nearer be;
For in the person of His Son, I am as near as He.
So dear, so very dear to God, more dear I cannot be;
The love wherewith He loves the Son: such is His love to me!

The fourth benefit of abiding in the Vine is to experience real, tangible joy that can only be sourced from God. Nehemiah tells us that *"the joy of the Lord is our strength"* in all of life's challenges.

The fifth benefit of abiding in Christ is the ability to love others as only God can. *"We love ... because He first loved us"* (1 Jn. 4:19).

March 30 – The World Hates You
John 15:14-15

If the world hates you, you know that it hated Me before it hated you. If you were of the world, the world would love its own. Yet because you are not of the world, but I chose you out of the world, therefore the world hates you.

The Lord had just told His disciples that He was leaving, but would come again for them. In His absence, they were to abide in Him and be fruitful. Yet, those who abide in Him must expect trouble. This chapter has the highest concentration of the word *hate* in the Bible (seven occurrences). The hate of the *world* (found six times) is contrasted with God's *love* (spoken of ten times). The synopsis is that God's love trumps the hate of the world. Believers living for Christ cannot escape the world's hate, but they can experience the goodness of God now, in ways not possible in heaven. Worldliness is any sphere in which Christ is excluded. Worldliness is the love of passing things, and things have no eternal value, except in how they are used to please God.

The Lord wanted His disciples to understand that because the world hated Him, it would also hate them for associating with Him (John 15:18-19). Furthermore, because the world persecuted Him, they should expect the same hostile treatment (John 15:20). Later, Paul stated that suffering persecution in the world was unavoidable if one chooses to *live godly in Christ Jesus* (2 Tim. 3:12). Clearly, the world does not love followers of Christ, so let us not invest into something that offers us nothing of tangible value and is under God's judgment.

Additionally, those of this world hate their sin being exposed (John 15:22-25). In contrast, citizens of heaven want their sin exposed and dealt with. Whether sins of omission, sins of wrong thinking, or sins of behavior we desire to be brought under the conviction of God's Word through the illumination of the Holy Spirit. In the next chapter, the Lord told His disciples that after His departure the Holy Spirit would come to actively convict the world of their sin, their need of a righteous standing before God, and to judge all those not receiving salvation in Christ (John 16:7-10). What was the purpose of all this information? That in Christ, the disciples would experience peace and joy despite suffering tribulations in the world, for He has *"overcome the world."*

March 31 – The Comforter Is Coming to Guide You
John 16:12-14

I still have many things to say to you, but you cannot bear them now.
However, when He, the Spirit of truth, has come, He will guide you
into all truth; for He will not speak on His own authority, but whatever
He hears He will speak; and He will tell you things to come. He will
glorify Me, for He will take of what is Mine and declare it to you.

Just before and then again after His death and resurrection the Lord
Jesus instructed His disciples to be expecting the coming of the Holy
Spirit. He, the Comforter, would infuse them with divine power to
enable their ministry. Knowledge of their divine calling and their
understanding of Scripture would be of no avail without God's
facilitating power.

The English word "advocate" is only translated once from the
Greek word *parakletos* in the New Testament. This word is usually
translated "comforter," as in the four references to the Holy Spirit in
John's Gospel. The role of an "advocate" or "comforter" is to legally
plead one's case or to speak on the behalf of another in a court of law –
a legal intercessor. Although in different aspects, both the Lord Jesus
and the Holy Spirit take up this role on behalf of believers.

Thayer's Greek Dictionary describes the application of *parakletos*
as pertaining to the Lord: "Christ's pleading for pardon of our sins
before the Father." But when does Christ plead our case? When we
acknowledge and confess our sins? First John 2:1 states that Christ *is*
our advocate when we sin, not when we confess our sins, though we
should (1 Jn. 1:9). This ensures that each time the devil accuses us of
wrongdoing before God's throne in heaven, Christ is able to point to
His wounds sustained at Calvary and declare that though our sin is
offensive, it has already been righteously judged. This upholds God's
righteous displeasure over our sin, but also that it has been dealt with.

While on earth the Holy Spirit is our "Comforter." He was sent by
the Lord Jesus to literally be "the One called alongside" to speak of
Christ and accompany the Church along the perilous journey
homeward. He is the Comforter, the Helper, the Teacher, the Convicter,
and the One who guides us into deeper truth and enables us to share it
effectively and accurately with others.

93

April 1 – That They May Be One
John 17:20-23

I do not pray for these alone, but also for those who will believe in Me through their word; that they all may be one, as You, Father, are in Me, and I in You; that they also may be one in Us, that the world may believe that You sent Me. And the glory which You gave Me I have given them, that they may be one just as We are one: I in them, and You in Me; that they may be made perfect in one, and that the world may know that You have sent Me, and have loved them as You have loved Me.

On the eve of His suffering, the Lord repeatedly acknowledged in His prayer recorded in John 17 the inseparable link between unity and the display of the glory of God. When the Church is unified, the glory of a triune God, who is always in unity, is displayed for all to witness. Peaceful unity and loving-kindness among men is not a naturally occurring phenomenon, so when it does transpire the world takes notice (John 13:35). The lost are prompted to consider what they see and by the grace of God some will be won to Christ! It is absolutely necessary for a local assembly to be of one accord before they can properly exhibit Christ to their neighborhoods.

If there is disunity in the local church, the work of the Holy Spirit is concentrated within the house of God in order to remove the rubble of pride, hypocrisy, willful sin, and doctrinal error. When the flesh-controlled operations are removed from the local assembly, then Spirit-controlled saints will rise up together and be more than conquerors for the glory of God. Let us all remember that *"it is honorable for a man to stop striving, since any fool can start a quarrel* (Prov. 20:3).

James ties strife and division with the work of the devil: *"For where envying and strife is, there is confusion and every evil work"* (Jas. 3:16; KJV). On the other hand, the unity of God's people is precious to Him: *"Behold, how good and how pleasant it is for brethren to dwell together in unity!"* (Ps. 133:1). In fact, unity within the Church is something that the Holy Spirit is constantly working to achieve; unfortunately our proud behavior opposes His efforts (Eph. 4:3). The inescapable consequence of grieving Him is powerless ministry and spiritual dryness. May we all strive for unity to show God's character and glory instead of striving with each other.

April 2 – Peace Be With You
John 20:19-20

Then, the same day at evening, being the first day of the week, when the doors were shut where the disciples were assembled, for fear of the Jews, Jesus came and stood in the midst, and said to them, "Peace be with you." When He had said this, He showed them His hands and His side. Then the disciples were glad when they saw the Lord.

It is difficult to serve the Lord fully and faithfully if we are anxious over present situations or are harboring guilt over past mistakes. The word *worry* means "to strangle something," while the word *anxiety* conveys the thought of "being pulled in different directions at the same time." Worry and anxiety rob us of our peace and in doing so prevent us from being a good testimony of Christ to the world. An individual must know the peace of God to effectively share it with others.

The Lord not only made *peace with God* on our behalf at Calvary (Rom. 5:1), but now offers us the *peace of God*: *"Be anxious for nothing, but in everything by prayer and supplication, with thanksgiving, let your requests be made known to God; and the peace of God, which surpasses all understanding, will guard your hearts and minds through Christ Jesus"* (Phil. 4:6-7). He not only offers salvation of the soul, but of the mind also. As before mentioned, the Greek word for "peace" in John 20 is *eirene*. It is derived from a verb meaning "to bond together," or "to be made at one again." The applied meaning of *eirene* in Romans 5:1 is that an individual is made "one again" with God in relationship after trusting the gospel; this is the saving of the soul. Yet, Philippians 4:7 refers to the saving of the mind – this is achieved when we are "one again" with Christ in thinking and attitudes.

The Lord Jesus understood the significance of being one with Him in salvation and in thinking. In fact, His first words to His disciples on the day of His resurrection conveyed this: *"Peace be with you."* From their vantage point, their Master had died, murdered by the same Jewish leaders that were now looking to do the same to them. Therefore, they were gathered together behind locked doors. But after hearing Christ's words and verifying that He was truly alive, their joy returned. It is the same for us: knowing the Lord's presence and meditating on His words will bring peace and joy to our hearts.

April 3 – Peace to You
John 20:21-22

So Jesus said to them again, "Peace to you! As the Father has sent Me, I also send you." And when He had said this, He breathed on them, and said to them, "Receive the Holy Spirit."

The disciples were together behind locked doors when the Lord Jesus suddenly stood before them. No doubt, at first, they were startled by His abrupt appearance; after all, they witnessed His death and burial. However, the Lord said to them, *"Peace be with you."* After the Lord showed them the wounds in His hands and side (the wounds in his feet would have been visible already), the disciples were filled with joy – truly their Master had risen from the tomb, just as He had previously told them He would. Through His finished work at Calvary, the disciples could enjoy oneness with God – have peace with God.

But the Lord did not end the conversation with this realization. He again said to them, *"peace to you."* Why did the Lord tell His disciples *"peace be to you"* twice? What followed the Lord's second declaration answers this question. Just as the Father had sent Him into the world to provide an opportunity for lost souls, enemies of God, to be reconciled with Him, He was sending them out into the world with the same message of peace. However, enjoying relational oneness with God through grace is not sufficient to convey this message to the world. His disciples would need a continuing work of grace in their hearts and minds to have God's peace while they conveyed His message of peace. The Lord knew that His apostles needed to have peace within before they could outwardly convey a message of peace.

It is impossible to convey peace to others unless the believer has laid hold of the peace of God. Whenever a believer is not at peace, he or she should ponder the question: "In what area of my life am I not one with Christ?" Being one again with Christ brings peace to the soul.

The Lord then breathed on them and they received the Holy Spirit. This particular ministry of the Holy Spirit seems to have equipped the disciples with understanding of their apostolic ministry: they now had the authority to tell those who received their message of peace by faith that their sins were forgiven. Their spiritual regeneration, baptism, sealing, etc. clearly occurred at Pentecost a few weeks later.

April 4 – Feed My Sheep
John 21:15-17

So when they had eaten breakfast, Jesus said to Simon Peter, "Simon, son of Jonah, do you love Me more than these?" He said to Him, "Yes, Lord; You know that I love You." He said to him, "Feed My lambs." He said to him again a second time, "Simon, son of Jonah, do you love Me?" He said to Him, "Yes, Lord; You know that I love You." He said to him, "Tend My sheep." He said to him the third time, "Simon, son of Jonah, do you love Me?" Peter was grieved because He said to him the third time, "Do you love Me?" And he said to Him, "Lord, You know all things; You know that I love You." Jesus said to him, "Feed My sheep."

Earlier, John presented Christ as the "Good Shepherd" who lays His life down for the sheep (John 10:7-18). His sacrificial love for the sheep stands in sharp contrast to the hireling shepherds of Israel, who led God's sheep astray, neglected their care, and then deserted them in times of danger; these would be judged accordingly (see Ezek. 34).

Those who have been charged with the care of God's sheep must attend to His flock. Peter is now called to be one of many shepherds (elders) of God's sheep (1 Pet. 5:1-2), and although he could only be martyred once for the Lord, he would die a hundred times in caring for God's sheep. Three times, in one fashion or another, the Lord Jesus asked Peter, *"Do you love Me?"* Peter affirmed a friendship kind of love for the Lord each time the Lord questioned him. However, the Lord had asked on the first two occasions if Peter had the deepest kind of love, sacrificial love, for Him. Peter did not affirm that kind of love for Christ, so on the third question the Lord asked Peter if he had a friendship type of regard for Him. After affirming this kind of affection for the Lord, the Lord implied that Peter should prove his love by feeding the Lord's lambs, tending His sheep, and feeding His sheep. Likewise, let all those who have a portion of the Lord's flock to care for prove their love to the Lord Jesus by tending His sheep (1 Pet. 5:3).

Sheep stink, they wander, they kick, they bite, and they glare, but they are still the Lord's sheep. He loves His sheep and we should love all those that Christ has redeemed by His blood. It is quite problematic to care for the Lord's sheep unless you are in love with the Good Shepherd. Only love for Christ can make this arduous task bearable.

April 5 – The Times and the Seasons
Acts 1:6-7

Therefore, when they had come together, they asked Him, saying, "Lord, will You at this time restore the kingdom to Israel?" And He said to them, "It is not for you to know times or seasons which the Father has put in His own authority."

If the Church had replaced Israel and was to be Christ's kingdom on earth, as *Replacement Theology* teaches, then this would have been a perfect opportunity for the Lord to correct His disciples' wrong thinking. But He did not tell them that they were the "new Israel." He simply told them it was not for them to know the time which the Father has predetermined for Israel to be blessed by Messiah's kingdom.

If God was finished with ethnic Israel, why would Paul ask: *"Has God cast away His people?"* and then respond so emphatically, "God forbid!" (Rom. 11:1). Paul's second rhetorical question concerning the Jewish nation had the same conclusion: *"Have they stumbled that they should fall?"* and his response was again, "God forbid!" (Rom. 11:11). He then asserted that the *"blindness in part has happened to Israel, until the fullness of the Gentiles comes"* (Rom. 11:25). Once the Church Age is complete, God would again work to refine His covenant people. At the conclusion of the Tribulation Period, *"all Israel shall be saved"* (Rom. 11:26). God is not finished with the Jewish Nation.

About six weeks earlier, the disciples had asked the Lord, *"What will be the sign of Your coming, and of the end of the age?"* (Matt. 24:3). The Lord responded to their question by describing several escalating signs of the coming Tribulation Period and chronological events that would occur during that seven-year period. He also told them, *"But of that day and hour no one knows, not even the angels of heaven, but My Father only"* (Matt. 24:37). This follows the Jewish custom of the father deciding when his son, the bridegroom, had properly prepared lodging for his bride and could bring her there. Christ will return for His Church when the Father says all is ready in heaven to receive her. Afterwards, the Lord will return to the earth to judge the wicked and to rule the nations. Every eye shall see Him and every man will reckon with Him (Matt. 24:30), but only the nation of Israel and those not bowing to the Antichrist will receive His mercy!

April 6 – Be My Witnesses
Acts 1:8

*But you shall receive power when the Holy Spirit has come upon you;
and you shall be witnesses to Me in Jerusalem, and in all Judea and
Samaria, and to the end of the earth.*

Acts 1 records the final post-resurrection meeting of the Lord with
His disciples before ascending back into heaven. This farewell occurred
on the Mount of Olives just east of Jerusalem. The Lord Jesus reminded
them that the Holy Spirit was coming to spiritually baptize them and
that they were to wait in Jerusalem until He arrived in a few days (Acts
1:4-5). We find out from the remainder of Acts 1 that a large group of
disciples (including Mary, the mother of Christ, and His half-brothers
now converted) obeyed the Lord's instructions and returned to
Jerusalem and were of one accord in prayer until the Holy Spirit
baptized and filled them ten days later at the Feast of Pentecost.

During the Lord's final address, He instructed them to be witnesses
for Him beginning at Jerusalem, then Judea, then Samaria, and then
they were to carry the gospel message to the ends of the earth. The
only way the latter command could be fulfilled is if following
generations of disciples completed the task. This would be how the
Lord would build His Church.

Accordingly, we understand that all believers are to be witnesses
for Christ in the world. Evangelists are special gifts of Christ to His
Church to encourage and equip all those believers who are not
evangelists to evangelize the lost (Eph. 4:12). The Great Commission
demonstrates God's great love for the lost and that He desires as many
as possible to be redeemed by the blood of His Son (2 Pet. 3:9).

The disciples were to follow the example that the Lord Jesus had
shown them in three plus years of ministry. They had moved about
Galilee, Samaria, and Judea seeking the lost sheep of Israel. Our Savior
did not expect wayward sheep to visit His family's carpentry business
in Nazareth to learn about the Good Shepherd; rather, He went out
seeking what was lost to Him. This was His evangelistic example, what
He taught, and then commanded His disciples to do after His departure
(also see Matt. 28:19-20).

April 7 – Unified and Increasing
Acts 2:1

When the Day of Pentecost had fully come, they were all with one accord in one place.

The first five chapters of Acts indicate that the early Church was successful in evangelism when there was unity and Christ-mindedness among the disciples:

So continuing daily with one accord in the temple, and breaking bread from house to house, they ate their food with gladness and simplicity of heart, praising God and having favor with all the people. And the Lord added to the church daily those who were being saved (Acts 2:46-47).

And through the hands of the apostles many signs and wonders were done among the people. And they were all with one accord in Solomon's Porch. Yet none of the rest dared join them, but the people esteemed them highly. And believers were increasingly added to the Lord, multitudes of both men and women (Acts 5:12-14).

When there were division and factions within the Church, their testimony was marred, the Spirit was quenched, and fruitfulness ceased (Acts 6:1-6). Yet, as soon as unity among the brethren was again achieved we read: *"Then the word of God spread, and the number of the disciples multiplied greatly in Jerusalem, and a great many of the priests were obedient to the faith"* (Acts 6:7). What is the lesson to be learned? Believers must lay hold of the mind of Christ to remain in unity. The Holy Spirit works to achieve unity among believers, but believers must labor to keep it (Eph. 4:3). This is achieved by humbling ourselves and putting the interest of others ahead of our own. A busybody inserts his or her interests into the affairs of others, but a Christ-minded believer puts the welfare of others above his or her own interests – this type of attitude ends strife. Having the mind of Christ ensures unity among His people.

Division has done more to hide Christ from the view of men than all the infidelity that has ever been spoken.

— George MacDonald

100

April 8 – They Continued Steadfastly (Part 1)
Acts 2:41-42

Then those who gladly received his word were baptized; and that day about three thousand souls were added to them. And they continued steadfastly in the apostles' doctrine and fellowship, in the breaking of bread, and in prayers.

The New Testament Christians continued in activities such as teaching, prayer, fellowship, and the Lord's Supper. In the Greek text, there is a definite article before the word "fellowship" in this verse, meaning that there was one particular fellowship that the Church enjoyed – Christ's fellowship. The Church is a living body composed of many members who enjoy divine fellowship with each other. Such body life will be manifested chiefly within the local assembly, but it is not restricted to it. The Lord's Table, mentioned in 1 Corinthians 10, is a place where all believers enjoy communion with each other and Christ, and receive from Him what is needed to serve Him. Local churches were commanded to receive other believers who desired to take part in the privileges and responsibilities of church fellowship (Rom. 15:7) and those received into the local church fellowship were instructed not to neglect it (Heb. 10:25). Each local church fellowship is a display of Christ's fellowship with the Church as a whole.

Believers, including new converts, relocating Christians, and traveling workers, who desired to be an active part of a local church were added to the fellowship in various ways. For example, we read that Barnabas provided a word of testimony to the saints in Jerusalem on Paul's behalf so that he would be received by them (Acts 9:27). New converts, after being water baptized, were received into church fellowship. As believers moved from one location to another, they carried with them letters of introduction from their home church meeting in order to be received into this fellowship with another assembly (Acts 18:26-27; Rom. 16:1; Col. 4:7-8). Letters not only introduced believers to other meetings, but affirmed their faithfulness to their profession of faith and their moral integrity. Such believers could be welcomed into the family life of the assembly without reservation. This biblical practice safeguards the assembly against wolves who want to secretly enter into the meeting and provides a huge blessing to those who desire Christian fellowship.

April 9 – They Continued Steadfastly (Part 2)
Acts 2:41-42

Then those who gladly received his word were baptized; and that day about three thousand souls were added to them. And they continued steadfastly in the apostles' doctrine and fellowship, in the breaking of bread, and in prayers.

Unfortunately, many church meetings today do not practice biblical reception and others have instituted the doctrine of church membership. Not only does this weaken the family atmosphere of the meeting, but both practices tend to allow a mixture of saved and lost individuals to comprise a local church. While church reception stresses privileges and responsibilities, local church membership conveys personal rights and spiritual status (e.g., one must be going to heaven if a member of a particular church). Whenever man allows what God does not, there will be problems; as children of God, we can only have fellowship with those who have fellowship with God. Only those who have experienced rebirth are members of the universal body of Christ (1 Cor. 12:13). Conferring to a lost person church membership only hinders him or her from coming to Christ and also works to weaken the body life of the local church – a child of the devil in league with God's people will never result in improving genuine devotion or godliness of the group.

Membership in a local church is never taught in Scripture. Rather, those who had a consistent profession of faith (Acts 2:41-42), were morally sound in life (2 Thess. 3:10-11; 1 Cor. 5:11), who were sound in doctrine (2 Thess. 3:6, 14; Titus 3:9-10), and who agreed to submit to the church elders as unto the Lord (1 Thess. 5:12; Heb. 13:17) were received into local church fellowships. Church membership stresses individual rights rather than the good of the body as a whole. The New Testament pattern of reception puts the emphasis on personal acceptance of the privileges and responsibilities which accompany family life in an assembly of believers. Those who engage in sin are dealt with in love through various stages of church discipline with the goal of repentance and restoration (1 Cor. 5:5; 2 Cor. 2:6-11). The Church is God's instrument to teach all those who witness its behavior that God is Holy, and that He desires and extends joyful and empowering fellowship to all those who seek to be holy too (1 Pet. 1:16).

April 10 – They Had Been With Jesus
Acts 4:13

Now when they saw the boldness of Peter and John, and perceived that they were uneducated and untrained men, they marveled. And they realized that they had been with Jesus.

The Lord Jesus understood that effective discipleship would require Him to be with His disciples: *"Then He appointed twelve, that they might be with Him and that He might send them out to preach"* (Mark 3:14). The impact of Christ's investment into His disciples was even noticed by the Jewish priests who had rejected Christ and His message, *"They realized that they had been with Jesus."* Because the disciples had been with Christ, they had learned of Him and had become like Him. Even the unregenerate recognized the surprising transformation of uneducated men to powerful witnesses. How was it possible for the disciples to perform supernatural miracles, to exhibit holy character, and to declare divine wisdom? The disciples had been with the Lord!

Paul's shepherding ministry among the Christians at Ephesus also serves as an excellent example of the commitment needed to see young believers mature in Christ. During his third missionary journey, Paul stayed at Ephesus for nearly three years (Acts 20:31). He remained among the Ephesians in order to teach and to show them what was necessary to experience victorious Christian living. In his farewell address to the elders at Ephesus, Paul acknowledged that he had remained with them to teach them God's Word (Acts 20:25, 35). Paul said to them, *"For three years I did not cease to warn everyone night and day with tears"* (Acts 20:31). Paul had both shared the gospel with the lost and taught those who believed wherever the people had been, whether in the synagogue (Acts 19:8), in the school of Tyrannus (Acts 19:9), in public (Acts 20:20), or in their homes (Acts 20:20).

Both the Lord's training of His disciples and Paul's apostolic ministry with those responding to Christ's message demonstrate the necessity of being with and investing time into the next generation of disciples. Unfortunately, the modern Church is so encumbered with busyness that its members have no time to invest in the mentoring of others. May we follow the Lord's and Paul's examples of selfless sacrifice in order to equip this generation to be able to equip the next.

April 11 – We Must Testify
Acts 4:18-20

So they called them and commanded them not to speak at all nor teach in the name of Jesus. But Peter and John answered and said to them, "Whether it is right in the sight of God to listen to you more than to God, you judge. For we cannot but speak the things which we have seen and heard."

The Jewish judicial body, the Sanhedrin, arrested and questioned the apostles concerning the religious propaganda they were spreading throughout Jerusalem. The Sanhedrin then prohibited the apostles from publicly preaching in the name of Jesus. But since the Lord Jesus had commanded them to preach the gospel message in Jerusalem and Judea before ascending into heaven, the apostles rejected this decree because they knew it was right to obey God, rather than the edicts of men.

From Scripture we understand that all authority (power to rule) comes from God alone (John 19:11). Christ told the apostles that He had obtained all authority (Matt. 28:18). The Lord taught that the greatest benefit of authority was not in rule, but in service, which He demonstrated by selflessly serving others (Matt. 20:25-26). He showed that we must remain under God's authority to have His power to do good and honor Him (Luke 7:1-10). The benefits of remaining under God's authority are: power to bless is received, confusion is ended, wickedness is restrained, and personal fruitfulness is enjoyed.

God-ordained authority on earth, though imperfect, is His means to teach us submission and to funnel down blessings to us (Prov. 29:2). There are only two authorities working in the world: God-ordained authority and satanic authority; Satan is the prince of this world (John 12:31). Therefore those rebelling against God-ordained authority do not escape authority, but rather put themselves under satanic authority. When a believer makes this choice, the result will be: a lack of God's blessing, a disordered life, and disdain on God's name (1 Cor. 14:33). The only time God-ordained authority is not to be obeyed is when it is in *clear* rebellion against God's authority, as in the scene before us (also Acts 5:29). At such times saints may disobey corrupt authority, but we should also be ready to willingly suffer the consequences of honoring the Lord by that decision (Acts 5:40; 1 Pet. 2:18-21).

April 12 – With One Accord
Acts 4:24

So when they heard that, they raised their voice to God with one accord and said: "Lord, You are God, who made heaven and earth and the sea, and all that is in them."

The Lord Jesus told the repentant thief on the cross, *"Today you will be with Me in paradise"* (Luke 23:43). After the repentant thief died, he would be with the Lord. Paradise is wherever the Lord is, meaning that the closest experience of heaven itself on this side of glory is to be gathered together with other believers in the presence of the Lord Jesus. Such was the case in Acts 4 when the saints were gathered in one place and were with one voice praising God and requesting boldness from Him to share the gospel message.

The gathering of the local assembly is a lampstand, a testimony to the world, and it should be loved, for it is a visible reminder to the world that Christ has a record of Himself here. Thus, it would be better for us to be in fellowship with ten believers who love the Lord, His Word, and His people than to be a part of a large congregation playing church. This was the conviction of Michael Faraday, one of the leading scientists of the 19th century. He trusted Christ at an early age and was part of a small fellowship of believers who gathered according to New Testament principles his entire life. He served as an elder in this church for several years. His devotion to the Lord and His people was revealed publicly on one occasion during the height of his scientific career.

Faraday was at the Royal Institute in London lecturing to a large audience. He spoke on the properties of the magnet, revealed one of his new discoveries, and concluded his lecture with a triumphant experiment that greatly excited the enthusiasm of his audience. After the applause had subsided, the Prince of Wales arose and made a motion of congratulation to Faraday. Normally, someone receiving such a motion would rise to the platform and verbally acknowledge the accolade with a short speech. But a hush soon came over the crowd after learning that the hero of the evening had hastily left the room just after concluding his speech. His intimate friends knew that the weekly prayer-meeting hour had arrived and he was holding fellowship with God and a group of Christians numbering less than ten.[14]

April 13 – Counted Worthy to Suffer Shame
Acts 5:40-42

And they agreed with him, and when they had called for the apostles and beaten them, they commanded that they should not speak in the name of Jesus, and let them go. So they departed from the presence of the council, rejoicing that they were counted worthy to suffer shame for His name. And daily in the temple, and in every house, they did not cease teaching and preaching Jesus as the Christ.

In Acts 4 the apostles were arrested, questioned, and warned not to preach in the name of Jesus Christ again. After departing the Jewish court, the apostles gathered with other believers to report the matter and to pray for boldness; they knew they should obey God rather than men. In response to their corporate prayer, the Holy Spirit infused them with power to preach Christ. The outcome of this enablement was that many people were healed of their ailments and disabilities, and many souls were added to the Church. Those from surrounding cities were now coming to Jerusalem to be healed by the apostles.

This was an alarming situation to the Sanhedrin, who again had the apostles arrested. But an angel visited the apostles that night and led them out of prison through open doors. Once freed, the angel told them to go to the temple and to speak words of life to the people (Acts 5:20). They obeyed and the apostles began teaching Christ at the temple early the next morning. At about the same time, the Jewish counsel met to decide the fate of the imprisoned apostles. They soon learned that the apostles were no longer in their prison (though the doors were secure).

Shortly after this they received a report that the apostles were again teaching at the temple. The Sanhedrin ordered them to be arrested again. The apostles were brought before the counsel without violence and questioned as to why they had not obeyed their previous warning. Peter answered them: *"We ought to obey God rather than men"* (Acts 5:29). After listening to the wise counsel of Gamaliel, the court decided to have the apostles beaten and to threaten them not to preach in the name of Jesus. Afterwards they were let go. Despite the counsel's warning, the apostles continued preaching Christ, and the Church multiplied. Instead of being depressed or bitter about their stripes, the disciples chose to rejoice in their Savior and trust in His sovereignty.

April 14 – Scattered Everywhere Preaching the Word
Acts 8:1-4

Now Saul was consenting to his death. At that time a great persecution arose against the church which was at Jerusalem; and they were all scattered throughout the regions of Judea and Samaria, except the apostles. And devout men carried Stephen to his burial, and made great lamentation over him. As for Saul, he made havoc of the church, entering every house, and dragging off men and women, committing them to prison. Therefore those who were scattered went everywhere preaching the word.

Saul had consented to the death of Stephen in Acts 7. Now the young Pharisee was zealously trying to stamp out Christianity, for its message opposed what he had learned about the Law of Moses and how Jews were to please God. In the next chapter, he will learn that Christ actually fulfilled the Law and also paid the penalty that the Law demanded for sin, but not for Himself, but for Saul's sins.

But presently Saul is busy arresting and imprisoning Christians wherever they can be found, including dragging them out of their homes. However, the result of this persecution did not stifle the Jesus Movement, but rather expanded it. As believers fled Saul's wrath, they took the precious seed of the gospel with them wherever they went. We do well to remember that even when things seem dark and threatening, the Lord is still accomplishing His work in ways that we usually do not appreciate at the time. Indeed, the Church was scattered abroad in Acts 8:1, but in Acts 9:31 we read, *"Then the churches throughout all Judea, Galilee, and Samaria had peace and were edified."* Both activities were under Christ's control and both outcomes blessed the Church in different ways. Christ knows how to build His Church!

When the Lord seems to be silent, we must wait for His marching orders, and when He clearly says "go," we must rise up and move forward with Him. He put His people in proper order to be a testimony of Himself to onlookers. This also required that He put them under orders that He might accomplish all His purposes for them. It is a great privilege to go on with the Lord and to face the unknowns and the challenges of the next day with confidence. The believer's union with Christ means that He meets every trial His redeemed encounter.

April 15 – Saul, Saul, Why Are You Persecuting Me?
Acts 9:3-5

As he journeyed he came near Damascus, and suddenly a light shone around him from heaven. Then he fell to the ground, and heard a voice saying to him, "Saul, Saul, why are you persecuting Me?" And he said, "Who are You, Lord?" Then the Lord said, "I am Jesus, whom you are persecuting. It is hard for you to kick against the goads."

Saul was on his way to Damascus to continue his crusade against Christianity. A bright light shone down on Saul from heaven which caused Saul to fall to the ground. The Lord Jesus asked Saul why he was persecuting Him. Saul did not know who was speaking to him, but he did realize that it was the Lord God. The Lord identified Himself as the One Saul was vehemently opposing – Jesus!

The Lord keenly felt Saul's attack on His Church (His people being imprisoned) and was intervening to end Saul's assault and turn him into an apostle to the Gentiles; he would later go by the name Paul. This reminds us, that in Christ, we have resources to overcome whatever challenge we encounter: *"For as the sufferings of Christ abound in us, so our consolation also abounds through Christ"* (2 Cor. 1:5).

Ananias visited Saul in Damascus as commanded. Saul had been blind and had been fasting since his encounter with the Lord Jesus three days earlier. Ananias healed Saul's blindness and through the laying on of hands, Saul received the Holy Spirit in the name of Jesus Christ. What did Saul do immediately after receiving the Holy Spirit? He ate some food to be strengthened, fellowshipped with other believers, was baptized, and then *"immediately he preached the Christ in the synagogues, that He is the Son of God"* (Acts 9:20). Interestingly, this is the only reference to Christ being the "Son of God" in Acts. Incredibly, the declaration comes from a zealous Pharisee, who could do backflips through the Old Testament, but now he knew of whom Scripture spoke of. He was willing to declare this truth no matter the cost, which as he soon learned included the possibility of death. Paul was a chosen vessel to bear Christ's *"name before the Gentiles, and kings, and the children of Israel"* (Acts 9:15). The highest occupation of the believer is to honor the name of Jesus Christ above all else, no matter what the personal cost might be – let us live out this vital truth.

April 16 – Is This Not He Who Destroyed?
Acts 9:21-24

Then all who heard were amazed, and said, "Is this not he who destroyed those who called on this name in Jerusalem, and has come here for that purpose, so that he might bring them bound to the chief priests?" But Saul increased all the more in strength, and confounded the Jews who dwelt in Damascus, proving that this Jesus is the Christ. Now after many days were past, the Jews plotted to kill him. But their plot became known to Saul. And they watched the gates day and night, to kill him. Then the disciples took him by night and let him down through the wall in a large basket.

The conversion of Saul is perhaps the most radical example of a changed life recorded in Scripture. Years later, he would tell the believers at Philippi that if anyone could impress God with their religious credentials or their good works done in the flesh, it was him:

Circumcised the eighth day, of the stock of Israel, of the tribe of Benjamin, a Hebrew of the Hebrews; concerning the law, a Pharisee; concerning zeal, persecuting the church; concerning the righteousness which is in the law, blameless. But what things were gain to me, these I have counted loss for Christ (Phil. 3:5-7).

After coming to Christ, he knew everything he had worked so hard for in the flesh meant nothing – God was completely unimpressed. However, after understanding the truth and being converted, nothing else mattered in his life but Christ. Besides to please the Lord, he was also compelled to fulfill his calling to try to offset his previous brutal treatment of Christians before his conversion (1 Tim. 1:15). He had learned on the Damascus road that when he hurt Christians, he was hurting the Lord. We all would do well to remember this truth.

Saul was the ideal choice to be an apostle to the Gentiles. He was fluent in both Greek and Hebrew languages (Acts 17:22-31, 21:40) and he spent much of his life learning Old Testament Scripture and the rabbinical writings (Acts 22:3). Because he was a Roman citizen, he knew the culture of the empire (Acts 16:37) and he also was aware of the Greek and Jewish customs of his day (Gal. 1:14). How the Lord Jesus radically changes lives and then uses them to accomplish His sovereign purposes is amazing evidence of who He is – the Son of God.

April 17 – What Is Clean and Unclean?

Acts 10:9-16

The next day, as they went on their journey and drew near the city, Peter went up on the housetop to pray, about the sixth hour. Then he became very hungry and wanted to eat; but while they made ready, he fell into a trance and saw heaven opened and an object like a great sheet bound at the four corners, descending to him and let down to the earth. In it were all kinds of four-footed animals of the earth, wild beasts, creeping things, and birds of the air. And a voice came to him, "Rise, Peter; kill and eat." But Peter said, "Not so, Lord! For I have never eaten anything common or unclean." And a voice spoke to him again the second time, "What God has cleansed you must not call common." This was done three times. And the object was taken up into heaven again.

Peter was abiding in the house of Simon, a tanner living in Joppa. At noon Peter ascended to the housetop to pray. While in the spirit of prayer, Peter received a vision. He saw a great sheet bound by its four corners coming down from heaven; it contained an assortment of unclean creatures. The Lord commanded, *"Rise, Peter; kill and eat."* Peter refused because the edicts of Leviticus 11 forbade it. The Lord responded: *"What God has cleansed you must not call common."*

Peter learned through this thrice-repeated vision that what God calls clean is clean, and that all men, not just Jews, could now be cleansed by the blood of Christ. Peter later explained what he had learned from the vision to Cornelius, a Gentile who feared and honored the Lord: *"You know how unlawful it is for a Jewish man to keep company with or go to one of another nation. But God has shown me that I should not call any man common or unclean"* (Acts 10:28). The Law prohibited the Jews from having any contact with Gentiles lest a Jew become defiled, but in the Church Age, the gospel is for Jew and Gentile (Rom. 1:16).

The Law was glorious because it pointed Israel to what would replace it, which was more glorious – salvation in Christ (2 Cor. 3:6-13). Peter already understood that much of the Law was no longer in effect. This is evident in that Peter had been staying with a new believer named Simon, who tanned animal skins for a living and would have been unclean by Levitical standards (Acts 9:43). The Jews were no longer to think of anyone as "clean" or "unclean"; the important distinction in the Church Age is whether a person is "saved" or "lost."

April 18 – Healing the Oppressed Through His Name
Acts 10:38-43

How God anointed Jesus of Nazareth with the Holy Spirit and with power, who went about doing good and healing all who were oppressed by the devil, for God was with Him. And we are witnesses of all things which He did both in the land of the Jews and in Jerusalem, whom they killed by hanging on a tree. Him God raised up on the third day, and showed Him openly, not to all the people, but to witnesses chosen before by God, even to us who ate and drank with Him after He arose from the dead. ... To Him all the prophets witness that, through His name, whoever believes in Him will receive remission of sins.

Peter shares the gospel message to the household of Cornelius and explains that the remission of sins is only through Jesus Christ. Thankfully, all who heard this message believed it, received the Holy Spirit, and were then baptized. Luke speaks of another benefit of Christ's ministry: He came to free those being oppressed by the devil.

Scripture speaks of three main means in which Satan directly afflicts humans in opposition to God's rule: possession, oppression, and obsession. Possession happens when an unbeliever is indwelt by a demon(s) and they assume control of that person's mind and body.

Oppression speaks of mainly external hardships that Satan brings to bear on humanity; these try the patience of the faithful and are permitted and limited by the Lord. Satan's attack on Job's livelihood, posterity, and health would be an example of oppression or when Paul was buffeted or hindered by Satan (2 Cor. 12:7; 1 Thess. 2:18). Yet, the Lord used these experiences to teach Paul of His abounding grace.

Obsession is a satanic attack on the believer's mind. When believers allow strongholds to be erected in our minds, these can be easy stimulated by the devil to cause anxiety, distress and depression. Ananias is an example (Acts 5:3). If there are no strongholds (i.e., bitterness, anger, envy, greed, etc.), then Satan's efforts of injecting thoughts into our thinking would be ineffective and he would soon leave us. However, where a stronghold does existence, he can stimulate it through suggestion to keep a beachhead in our minds. Mental strongholds are removed by taking every thought captive to the obedience of Christ, and then in His grace resisting the solicitation.

April 19 – Wanting Others to See the Grace of God
Acts 11:22-25

Then news of these things came to the ears of the church in Jerusalem, and they sent out Barnabas to go as far as Antioch. When he came and had seen the grace of God, he was glad, and encouraged them all that with purpose of heart they should continue with the Lord. For he was a good man, full of the Holy Spirit and of faith. And a great many people were added to the Lord. Then Barnabas departed for Tarsus to seek Saul. And when he had found him, he brought him to Antioch.

The book of Acts supplies several good examples of mentoring; one of the most prominent is the relationship of Barnabas to Paul. A young, enthusiastic believer named Saul was introduced to the Christians in Jerusalem. Initially, they did not want to associate with him because he had persecuted the Church as a zealous Pharisee previously. Yet, Barnabas vouched for Saul (Paul) and persuaded them of the legitimacy of his conversion. Saul was then warmly received into fellowship.

However, Saul was greatly burdened for his own people, so he frequented synagogues and the temple in an effort to persuade the Jews of the necessity of trusting in Christ alone for salvation. His knowledge of Old Testament Scripture and his past religious education provided him with the necessary credentials to debate even with the elite religious leaders of his day. As a result, Jerusalem was in an uproar. Though Saul was sharing the truth, he did not possess the love and grace in his preaching at this time to achieve the best outcome. As a result, the wider efforts of other believers in Jerusalem to evangelize were being hindered by unnecessary hostility. It was necessary for Saul to leave Jerusalem; he returned to his hometown of Tarsus.

Not long after Saul departed from Jerusalem, the apostles heard that Gentiles were being saved in Antioch. Barnabas was sent to investigate the matter and found the rumors to be true. Barnabas must have thought Antioch would be a great place to mentor Saul and for him to see the grace of God at work, so he traveled north to Tarsus to retrieve him and to bring Saul to Antioch. There, both men assembled with the church at Antioch and labored side by side in a teaching ministry for one year. Let us remember the example of Barnabas and take young people to where the action is, so that they too may see the grace of God at work.

April 20 – First Called Christians in Antioch
Acts 11:26

So it was that for a whole year they assembled with the church and taught a great many people. And the disciples were first called Christians in Antioch.

Paul exhorts the Christians at Colosse to consider every aspect of their conduct and speech as an approval or disapproval of the name of Jesus Christ. *"And whatever you do in word or deed, do all in the name of the Lord Jesus, giving thanks to God the Father through Him"* (Col. 3:17). Each believer functions as an ambassador of Christ on earth (2 Cor. 5:20); we are to represent the Lord and conduct His affairs on earth in a manner which would honor Him. We are Christians, or *Christ-ones*. Warren Wiersbe summarizes what it means to bear up the name of the Lord Jesus as a Christian.

As Christians, we bear the name of Christ. The word *Christian* is found only three times in the entire New Testament (Acts 11:26; 26:28; 1 Peter 4:16). The name was given originally as a term of contempt, but gradually it became a name of honor. The name of Christ, then, means *identification:* we belong to Jesus Christ. But His name also means *authority*. A man's name signed to a check authorizes the withdrawal of money from the bank. The President's name signed to a bill makes it a law. In the same way, it is in the name of Jesus Christ that we have the authority to pray (John 14:13-14; 16:23-26). Because Jesus Christ is God, and He has died for us, we have authority in His name. All that we say and do should be associated with the name of Jesus Christ. By our words and our works, we should glorify His name. If we permit anything into our lives that cannot be associated with the name of Jesus, then we are sinning. We must do and say everything on the authority of His name and for the honor of His name. Bearing the name of Jesus is a great privilege, but it is also a tremendous responsibility.[15]

It is a great honor to be intimately associated with the name of Jesus Christ, but as Paul declares, it also entails responsibility: *"that the name of our Lord Jesus Christ may be glorified in you"* (2 Thess. 1:12). Those who show His glory now will be glorified with Him soon.

April 21 – Separate to Me, Barnabas and Saul
Acts 13:1-3

Now in the church that was at Antioch there were certain prophets and teachers: Barnabas, Simeon who was called Niger, Lucius of Cyrene, Manaen who had been brought up with Herod the tetrarch, and Saul. As they ministered to the Lord and fasted, the Holy Spirit said, "Now separate to Me Barnabas and Saul for the work to which I have called them." Then, having fasted and prayed, and laid hands on them, they sent them away.

The Holy Spirit called Barnabas and Paul from their fruitful ministry in Antioch to serve as foreign missionaries. The Holy Spirit is not the force of God or the invisible influence of God, but rather He is one of three persons of the Trinity. Thus, He has a will and directs the affairs of believers (Acts 16:6-7; 1 Cor. 12:11), but not in a way that is out of sync with the will of the Son or the Father (John 16:13-15).

This was a deep cut for the church at Antioch; forty percent of their teachers were being summoned by God for ministry outside of the assembly. They committed the matter to the Lord in prayer and fasting and agreed to send (literally "to release") Barnabas and Paul to the grace of God (Acts 14:26). The verb rendered "sent" in verse 3 is in the active voice, which means the Antioch leaders made the decision themselves; they were not forced to send Barnabas and Paul into the mission field. This is what prayer accomplishes for us – it aligns our thinking with God's thinking and settles our minds with His peace. The church at Antioch hence commended them to the work to which they had been called and Paul and Barnabas departed from Antioch as peers.

Acts 13 provides a good pattern to follow in sending out workers to reach lost people groups today. Such workers were sent out, supported, and supervised by local churches, not Christian organizations. The missionaries in Acts did not raise funds in order to be sent; rather, they *were* sent and the Lord provided for them as they went (Acts 14:26, 15:40). They lived by faith and, when necessary, worked with their own hands (Acts 18:3). They were accountable to their commending assembly (Paul gave a report to the church in Antioch after each of his missionary journeys). Reports of the Lord's work were supplied to other assemblies for encouragement also (Acts 15:4).

April 22 – Paul and Barnabas
Acts 13:43

Now when the congregation had broken up, many of the Jews and devout proselytes followed Paul and Barnabas, who, speaking to them, persuaded them to continue in the grace of God.

In the early chapters of Acts, whenever Barnabas and Paul are spoken of together, the mentor's name is always mentioned first; however, after Acts 13:46, Paul is generally mentioned first. The only two exceptions to this developed pattern is the reference to both men in Acts 14:14, and during the Jerusalem counsel in Acts 15 (as Barnabas was more familiar to the saints at Jerusalem). So why does Scripture switch the order of Paul's and Barnabas' names? Paul, who had been mentored by Barnabas at Antioch, and who had then served with him as a colleague, had now surpassed his mentor in speaking ability.

The first missionary journey had provided Paul opportunities to develop his speaking gift and he became a powerful preacher and the lead spokesman of the missionary team. This would be the last time the two men would labor together; each would depart on their next separate missionary journeys with a new apprentice to be mentored through "on-the-job" training. Barnabas' ministry to Paul serves as a great example to us – may each of us train people for Christ who will train others and who, by God's grace, will all go beyond our own accomplishments!

A mentor must be available, be willing, be accountable, and be a good example to follow. To provide the specialized care a new convert needs will require one's time and resources. Good mentoring is a costly ministry and one which cannot be accomplished without a significant amount of personal interaction. Paul and Barnabas exhibited the above characteristics in their mentoring ministries and are considered good examples to follow. Barnabas invested in Paul, who later poured himself into Silas, the Ephesians, and many others. In the case of the Christians at Ephesus, he spent three years teaching and training them without regard for his own needs. These testimonies agree with the four key aspects of what Peter says it takes to be a good shepherd of God's people: availability, willingness, accountability, and an exemplary lifestyle (1 Pet. 5:2-3). Of course, the ultimate example of a selfless mentor is found in the Good Shepherd Himself.

April 23 – Filled With the Holy Spirit (Part 1)
Acts 13:49-52

And the word of the Lord was being spread throughout all the region. But the Jews stirred up the devout and prominent women and the chief men of the city, raised up persecution against Paul and Barnabas, and expelled them from their region. But they shook off the dust from their feet against them, and came to Iconium. And the disciples were filled with joy and with the Holy Spirit.

Though not directly prayed for by believers in Scripture, the believer is commanded to be Spirit-filled: *"And be not drunk with wine, wherein is excess; but be filled with the Spirit"* (Eph. 5:18). The Greek verb *pleroo* is rendered "filled" in this verse. It means to "cram," "make full," or "to fill to completeness." It is used to describe a sponge filled with vinegar (Matt. 27:48) or pots filled to the brim (John 2:7) or a house filled with the odor of spikenard (John 12:3). *Pleroo* means to "be saturated with or completely full" of something. The verb in Ephesians 5:18 is in the present tense, passive voice, and imperative mood. This means we have an ongoing responsibility to be filled by the Holy Spirit. Our charge is obedience to God's revealed will; God responds to our submission by enabling us to do His will. We are to do what we are supposed to do and God does what only He can.

Spirit filling does not mean we get more of the Holy Spirit but He gets more of us and then we are further enabled to bring glory to God. We are either saved and have the Holy Spirit, or we are dead in trespasses and sins without Him; He is not given in measure (John 3:34; Rom. 8:9).

Spirit filling should not be confused with spiritual baptism which places us in the Body of Christ. Spirit filling is repeatable. For example, the apostles were filled by the Holy Spirit and baptized into Christ at the Feast of Pentecost (Acts 2:4). Yet, after a corporate prayer meeting, they were again Spirit-filled which enabled them to preach the gospel message boldly (Acts 4:31). This enabling power of the Holy Spirit became a telltale sign of those called for particular ministries according to the sovereign will of God. For example, deacons were selected for serving based on the evidence of Spirit filling (Acts 6:3). Barnabas was Spirit-filled to strengthen the new work of God at Antioch (Acts 11:23). Saul was filled with the Holy Spirit to rebuke a sorcerer (Acts 13:9). In summary, Spirit filling is an active and repeatable work of the Holy Spirit that enables believers to perform God's bidding.

April 24 – Filled With the Holy Spirit (Part 2)
Acts 13:49-52

And the word of the Lord was being spread throughout all the region. But the Jews stirred up the devout and prominent women and the chief men of the city, raised up persecution against Paul and Barnabas, and expelled them from their region. But they shook off the dust from their feet against them, and came to Iconium. And the disciples were filled with joy and with the Holy Spirit.

Spirit filling was a common, repeatable, and desirable experience for the believers in Acts. Here are some of the recorded occurrences:

- Acts 2:4: Believers waiting in Jerusalem for the Holy Spirit were filled, which enabled them to share the gospel message in various distinct languages to those foreigners visiting Jerusalem for the feast. Peter powerfully preached Christ to the Jews and 3,000 souls were saved.
- Acts 4:29: The Church was praying in one accord for boldness to preach the gospel to the lost (note, they were not praying for Spirit filling); they were filled and "spoke the Word of God with boldness" (Acts 4:31).
- Acts 7:54-60: Stephen was full of the Spirit, which enabled him to preach Christ to the Sanhedrin and for him to willingly give his life for Christ.
- Acts 9:17-20: Paul was regenerated and filled with the Holy Spirit; he then immediately began preaching Christ in Damascus.

The New Testament highlights other enabling benefits of Spirit filling for believers: to gain a Christlike character (Gal. 5:22-23), to properly worship and praise God (Eph. 5:18-20), to have a submissive heart and to exhibit self-control (Eph. 5:21), and to enjoy an effective prayer life (Eph. 6:18). There is no example in the New Testament of a saved person praying for or commanding the filling of the Holy Spirit. It is a sovereign act of God in the life of an obedient believer to bring about His purposes in time.

There is also no example in the New Testament of the Holy Spirit filling believers to enable them to speak gibberish (i.e., in a non-distinct language). When the Holy Spirit fills someone, He has a Christ-exalting purpose in mind; He does not prompt chaos or disorder. Obedience to God's revealed Word makes believers available for Spirit-filling and to be used in God's mysterious work to honor the name of Jesus Christ!

117

April 25 – Reporting What God Had Done
Acts 14:26-28

From there they sailed to Antioch, where they had been commended to the grace of God for the work which they had completed. Now when they had come and gathered the church together, they reported all that God had done with them, and that He had opened the door of faith to the Gentiles. So they stayed there a long time with the disciples.

Being commended from the church in Antioch, Paul and Barnabas first visited Cyprus, then Pamphylia and southern Galatia on their first missionary journey. Sadly, Barnabas' young nephew John Mark abandoned the apostles at Perga and returned to Jerusalem (13:13). (Through Barnabas' masterful encouragement, John Mark is later restored to fruitfulness.) Thankfully, many believed the gospel message and churches were established before Paul and Barnabas returned to Antioch to tell of the great things they had witnessed.

After being commended to the grace of God by the church at Antioch again, Paul launched out with Silas on his second missionary journey. They visited the areas in southern Asia that had been previously evangelized with a goal of building up the new disciples in doctrine. A young believer named Timothy from Lystra joined them, as did Luke at Troas. Then, having been summoned by the Holy Spirit into Europe, the missionary team visited major cities in Macedonia and Achaia before sailing back to Caesarea and returning home to Antioch.

Paul's third missionary journey again began at Antioch. Luke summarized the next phase of their trip: *"he [Paul] went over the region of Galatia and Phrygia in order, strengthening all the disciples"* (Acts 18:23). Paul went on to Ephesus and there joined with Aquila and Priscilla, who were fellow tentmakers and zealous believers for the Lord. Paul never requested funds for his own ministry, but trusted the Lord to provide for his needs (which meant working with his own hands at times). After the riot in Ephesus, Paul departed to revisit churches that had been formed in Macedonia and Achaia previously. He then returned to Asia through Macedonia and sailed back to Caesarea and made his way to Jerusalem where he was received by the brethren (21:15-17). May we follow Paul's humble example of wherever we are or go, report *"all that God had done with"* us.

April 26 – The Churches Were Strengthened in Faith
Acts 16:4-5

And as they went through the cities, they delivered to them the decrees to keep, which were determined by the apostles and elders at Jerusalem. So the churches were strengthened in the faith, and increased in number daily.

Christ is the Head of His Church (Eph. 1:22-23). The Church is to worship God, and to adore and honor Christ's authority and position over her. Distortion of this reality occurs when elected church officials and headquarters undermine Christ's headship. Believers are to gather in autonomous groups according to the order commanded in Scripture. Local churches are to be interdependent on each other, but no group of believers has the authority to control any other local church.

This is demonstrated by the outcome of the Jerusalem Council in Acts 15. The apostles and elders convened this meeting to discuss whether or not Gentile believers should be circumcised. Though a doctrinal decision was affirmed at this meeting, counsel, not a mandate, was provided for the consideration of the various churches established elsewhere. The apostles and elders described how the Gentiles should behave among Jewish believers, but no attempt was made to enforce the ruling. Letters were sent out to various churches and Gentile believers considered the ruling and decided to follow its implications. As a result the churches, which now possessed more godly wisdom and truth, were built up in the Lord and continued growing.

Regrettably, much of the Church today has compartmentalized into denominational organizations which govern a collective of churches. As A. P. Gibbs explains, Scripture does not endorse this practice:

In early Christianity there were congregations of believers but no Congregationalists; baptized believers but no Baptists; there were elders or presbyters in the assembly but no Presbyterians; there were methods in their meetings but no Methodists; there were bishops (elders) in the church but no Episcopalians; they trembled at the Word but there were no Quakers; they all shared in the blessing of Pentecost but there were no Pentecostals; they were all united in Christ but there were no United Brethren; they all had charisma (gift of grace) but there were no Charismatics. ... The early believers simply met in the Name of the Lord Jesus Christ and so were labeled by the world as Christians.[16]

April 27 – The Spirit Did Not Permit Them
Acts 16:6-7

Now when they had gone through Phrygia and the region of Galatia, ***they were*** *forbidden by the Holy Spirit to preach the word in Asia.* ***After they*** *had come to Mysia,* ***they tried*** *to go into Bithynia, but the Spirit did not permit* ***them***. *So passing by Mysia,* ***they came*** *down to Troas. And a vision appeared* ***to Paul*** *in the night. A man of Macedonia stood and pleaded with him, saying, "Come over to Macedonia and help us." Now* ***after he*** *had seen the vision,* ***immediately we*** *sought to go to Macedonia, concluding* ***that the Lord had called us*** *to preach the gospel to them* (Acts 16:6-10; several pronouns and verbs are identified by bold text for emphasis).

There were times that the Holy Spirit constrained the missionary team from venturing into a particular area and other times that He directed the team where God wanted them to go. Paul and the missionary team were being led by the Holy Spirit. It is evident from this text that God often uses older servants of His to confirm the calling of younger believers into His work. Paul was used of God in Timothy's calling and then assisted him in fulfilling it (2 Tim. 1:6).

Shortly after Timothy departed from Lystra to join the missionary team, we read the above narrative. Though the team labored together to proclaim the gospel, it was the veteran worker that received direction from the Lord. Paul's call became the call of all those with him. So initially, Paul mentored and guided Timothy in ministry, but later, they co-labored as peers. This working relationship lasted some twenty years and is a wonderful testimony of the grace of God in their lives.

Timothy was called to a ministry and not a location. The record of Acts shows that the Lord's servants rarely remained in one location for long. Aquila and Priscilla were used first in Corinth, then in Ephesus, then at Rome, and then again in Ephesus to disciple Christians and start local church gatherings. According to Scripture, Paul's two-and-a-half-year stay in Ephesus was the longest period of time he spent serving in one location. As a principle, this example is contrary to the *resident worker* pattern which prevails in Christianity today. The pattern of older, spirit-led saints mentoring and equipping younger ones for service is a biblical example and forms the foundation of discipleship.

April 28 – Praying and Singing Hymns While Suffering
Acts 16:23-25

And when they had laid many stripes on them, they threw them into prison, commanding the jailer to keep them securely. Having received such a charge, he put them into the inner prison and fastened their feet in the stocks. But at midnight Paul and Silas were praying and singing hymns to God, and the prisoners were listening to them.

Pagans at Philippi accused Paul and Silas of wrongdoing. They were not extended their civil right to a fair trial, but instead were beaten, chained, and put into prison. In the inner prison, the air circulation was poor. The stench of open wounds, feces, and body odor that accompanied the smoke from torches would make breathing difficult. How did these two servants of the Lord respond to this cruel situation? *"But at midnight Paul and Silas were praying and singing hymns to God, and the prisoners were listening to them"* (Acts 16:25).

They prayed (the right tactic for gospel expansion), and they rejoiced in their God through singing, which declared their confidence in God to everyone listening to them. How did the Lord respond to their praying and rejoicing? He brought an earthquake, which released them from their captivity and then provided an opportunity for the jailer and his whole family to hear and believe the gospel of Jesus Christ.

Instead of choosing to be depressed or bitter about their stripes, Paul and Silas chose to rejoice in their Savior. It may be that our rejoicing does not specifically or immediately bring relief or conclusion to our difficulty, but God has promised to work a greater good and glorify Himself through every situation (Rom. 8:28). Rejoicing in the Lord demonstrates a trusting faith in God's sovereign control over every matter of life. Consequently, suffering followed by willful rejoicing is what led to the beginnings of the Church in Philippi, for the Philippian jailer and his household came to Christ through the powerful testimony of Paul and Silas.

Writing to the Corinthians, Paul relates some of the incredible difficulties he faced in his ministry, but then concludes by declaring, *"As sorrowful, yet always rejoicing"* (2 Cor. 6:10). Paul had a choice to complain about their lack of support towards him or to rejoice in his laboring which in time brought the Corinthians to maturity.

April 29 – Searching the Scriptures Daily
Acts 17:10-11

Then the brethren immediately sent Paul and Silas away by night to Berea. When they arrived, they went into the synagogue of the Jews. These were more fair-minded than those in Thessalonica, in that they received the word with all readiness, and searched the Scriptures daily to find out whether these things were so.

One of the challenges of life is discerning between holy truth which does not change or contradict itself from evil deception which does. Luke endorsed the behavior of the Bereans as a good example to follow because they were *"more fair-minded than those in Thessalonica, in that they received the word with all readiness, and searched the Scriptures daily to find out whether these things were so."* They were confronted with the gospel message and sought to verify or disprove it by investigating Old Testament Scripture. Moreover, because they wanted to know the truth, they were willing to search the Scriptures daily until they could either prove or disprove the message that the apostles had conveyed to them. Similarly, every child of God should be like the Bereans, proving matters out to determine what is true and false. We should be discerning! Paul exhorted Timothy:

Be diligent to present yourself approved to God, a worker who does not need to be ashamed, rightly dividing the word of truth. But shun profane and idle babblings, for they will increase to more ungodliness (2 Tim. 2:15-16).

John instructed believers, *"Believe not every spirit* [teacher]*, but test the spirits whether they are of God"* (1 Jn. 4:1-4). He also informed them of an anointing that they had received at spiritual rebirth which would give them spiritual discernment (1 Jn. 2:26-27). There is no need to pray for this anointing; every believer already has it. It is always spoken of in the past tense and has the purpose of giving spiritual discernment concerning what is truth and what is false. God's Word must be used to validate what is from Him (truth) and to identify what is deception from the devil. Truth will not contradict itself. Let us all be good Bereans, for slothfulness leads to embracing deception.

April 30 – The Word of the Lord Grew Mightily
Acts 19:19-20

Also, many of those who had practiced magic brought their books together and burned them in the sight of all. And they counted up the value of them, and it totaled fifty thousand pieces of silver. So the word of the Lord grew mightily and prevailed.

Paul spent more time at Ephesus than any other location during his years of itinerant ministry. As previously mentioned, during his third missionary journey, Paul stayed at Ephesus for nearly three years (Acts 20:31). He taught the Ephesian believers what was necessary to experience victorious Christian living. Paul shared the gospel with the lost and taught those who believed wherever they were – whether in the synagogues, in the school of Tyrannus, in public, or in the homes of those who would receive him.

At Ephesus, God enabled Paul to do many unusual miracles (Acts 19:11-12). He healed the sick and drove the demons out of the oppressed in the name of Jesus Christ. Several Jewish exorcists gathered in a house to try to mimic Paul's ministry. They were going to perform an exorcism by calling on *"the Jesus, whom Paul preaches."* The evil spirit told these men that he knew who Jesus and Paul were, but did not recognize them, meaning they had no authority over him. The attempt ended badly with all the men being wounded and running out of the house for their lives. However, this situation became widely known in Ephesus, which caused great fear to fall among the general populous and also the magnification of the Lord Jesus.

Many people engaging in pagan and occult practices repented and turned to Christ for salvation. They now knew that all their past spirituality was against the one true God and His Savior for humanity. To show that they had a change of heart and did not value the things in their former lives, they brought all their magic books to a public place and burned them. It was an enormous fire, as all the books were valued at 50,000 pieces of silver, but to the new believers it would be sin not only to keep the books, but to sell them also. Why propagate a message contrary to the truth? Oh, that all of the Lord's people would purge everything from their homes that distracts from the truth and then ensure no one else would ever be stumbled by the deceptive clutter.

May 1 – Breaking Bread Weekly on Sunday
Acts 20:6-7

But we sailed away from Philippi after the Days of Unleavened Bread, and in five days joined them at Troas, where we stayed seven days. Now on the first day of the week, when the disciples came together to break bread, Paul, ready to depart the next day, spoke to them and continued his message until midnight.

Prior to the Church Age, the Sabbath day ordinance provided a simple test as to what the Jews valued – their own private affairs or what the Lord deemed important. The Lord is honored when His people remember and honor Him as requested, instead of doing what they are inclined to do for themselves on the day set aside for God. Today, the Church is not under the Law (Rom. 7:4) and the Jews are no longer under the Law either (2 Cor. 3:6-18), but the Ten Commandments still reflect God's moral standard to be lived out in His people (Rom. 3:20).

Christians are not commanded to keep the Sabbath, but there is a principle throughout Scripture of setting aside one day in seven to honor God, and the early Church set a precedent for gathering on Sunday for this purpose. To draw a distinction between Christianity and the Law (and, more importantly, the humanized religion from it), the early Church met on Sunday, rather than on Saturday. Christians continued to gather corporately on one day out of seven to worship the Lord, but they did so on the first day of the week, the day of Christ's resurrection (1 Cor. 16:2). For example, Paul remained an entire week at Troas in order to be with the saints when they gathered on Sunday to remember the Lord through the breaking of the bread (Acts 20:7). He also taught them doctrine into the wee hours of the morning.

Sunday is referred to as "the Lord's Day" by the apostle John (Rev. 1:10). Let us seek to make the Lord's Day a special day for the Lord. Saints should put aside their own personal ambitions and should gather to hear the preaching of the Word, to break bread, to pray, to encourage each other, and to engage in ministry which would draw people to Christ. The Lord's Day should be a special day for all spiritually-minded Christians – a day set aside to remember and honor the Lord with other believers. We are not under law in this matter, but we are bound by love to show our appreciation for the Lord.

May 2 – Finish My Race With Joy
Acts 20:22-24

*And see, now I go bound in the spirit to Jerusalem, not knowing the
things that will happen to me there, except that the Holy Spirit testifies
in every city, saying that chains and tribulations await me. But none of
these things move me; nor do I count my life dear to myself, so that I
may finish my race with joy, and the ministry which I received from the
Lord Jesus, to testify to the gospel of the grace of God.*

Although Paul had encountered opposition to the gospel message
previously, Acts 16 records the first brutal act of persecution again him.
He and Silas were beaten, chained, and placed in prison based solely on
an accusation; they were permitted no civil trial. This would have
occurred in the autumn of 50 A.D. Through the experience of suffering,
Paul had learned the power of rejoicing in Christ regardless of one's
circumstances. As mentioned previously, the outcome of their suffering
and rejoicing was that a local church was established in Philippi.

The events recorded in Luke's narrative above occurred about six
and a half years later, in the spring of 57 A.D. Paul had suffered several
whippings and beatings, and had endured at least one stoning by this
time (2 Cor. 11:23-26). His body was heavily scarred from the abuse.
Paul experientially knew that suffering for Christ was inescapable (2
Tim. 3:12), but also that rejoicing in Christ was the secret to displaying
the grace of God in every arduous situation. In Acts 16, he had merely
experienced joy in suffering, now he expected joy to accompany him
all the way to the finish line of his earthly ministry.

Then, about four years later, when Paul was a prisoner in Rome, he
wrote a letter to the church at Philippi and exhorted them to choose to
rejoice in Christ in every hardship. Christ is in heaven and all that
matters is to magnify Him (i.e., bring Him into every situation) so that
others can see Him. This was to be done whether in death or in life for
the furtherance of the gospel of Christ. Paul had *experienced* the power
of rejoicing through repeated trials to the point that he now *expected* to
have a lifelong ministry marked by joy, and as a result, could teach
others how to rejoice in their circumstances. So he *exhorts* them to
follow his example – rejoicing is a choice and results in seeing God's
handiwork in ways not possible if overwhelmed by sorrows.

May 3 – Elders Appointed by the Holy Spirit
Acts 20:28

Therefore take heed to yourselves and to all the flock, among which the Holy Spirit has made you overseers, to shepherd the church of God which He purchased with His own blood.

There is a three-stage process for recognizing church elders: A divine call, the internal call, and recognized by all. The Holy Spirit calls (appoints) them (Acts 20:28), the internal call is shown by active, selfless shepherding (1 Tim. 3:1), and eventually the serving brother will be morally and spiritually scrutinized according to the requirements of Titus 1 and 1 Timothy 3 and publicly recognized as an elder. If a brother with a blameless testimony just cannot keep from doing shepherding work in the assembly, and is marked by faithfulness despite the personal cost to himself, he is likely God's man. The man who cries "Pick me" is most assuredly not God's choice. Rather, God's man respects the office and is often leery of the responsibility because he can already identify with the work and the cost of doing it.

Those who are elders and those who may be recognized as elders are not perfect men, but they should be blameless brothers of high moral standards and character. A prospective elder who is drawn to shepherding work and exhibits the qualities of 1 Timothy 3:1-7 is most likely the man that God has raised up *from among His sheep* (Acts 20:28) to be *shepherds among His sheep* (1 Pet. 5:1). Recognizing in haste a man whom God has not called will be one of the most painful mistakes an assembly can make. However, engaging in prayer and careful observation, while waiting on the Lord to make it obvious to everyone will be the safe approach in appointing those He has called to lead. A brother, who is called by God to shepherd, will be shepherding God's people long before he is actually recognized as an elder.

We understand from Acts 20:28 that the Holy Spirit appoints elders in the local church from among that gathering; elders do not come in from outside the local church in question. (How else will you really know their character?) Hence, Peter exhorts church elders to willingly remain among those God has entrusted into their care and to maintain an exemplary life fostered in humility before them (1 Pet. 5:2-3). Pastoral care of God's people cannot be accomplished from a distance.

May 4 – Not Ashamed of the Gospel of Christ
Romans 1:16

For I am not ashamed of the gospel of Christ, for it is the power of God to salvation for everyone who believes, for the Jew first and also for the Greek.

Paul declares his unwavering allegiance to share God's gospel message to a lost world. He faithfully warned others of God's judgment for disobedience and their need to repent and receive the Lord Jesus Christ for the forgiveness of their sins. He had the joy of seeing many turn to Christ and experience the power of God to salvation, but he also suffered in that gospel ministry. As noted before, Paul was repeatedly scourged and beaten with rods, and was once stoned and left for dead.

Salvation itself is a three-part reality consisting of a process of God sandwiched between two acts of God. Salvation begins when an individual believes the Gospel of Jesus Christ and is, consequently, regenerated (born again) by the Holy Spirit (John 1:12-13; Titus 3:5). The soul is saved at this time and eternal life with God is assured. After this act of God, the long process of sanctification begins – this process is to morally make us like Christ (Rom. 8:29). Salvation concludes with glorification, an act of God which transforms the believer's lowly body and makes it holy and fit for heaven (1 Cor. 15:51-52).

Through sanctification, the believer is separated and carved out of the world to be like the Lord Jesus, to be used by Him, and to glorify God. The Holy Spirit, thus, saves the believer from being ruled by his or her inherent depraved nature and from the clutches of the corrupt world system. God uses His Word and various trials, tests, persecutions, sufferings, etc. to conform the believer to the likeness of His Son. The Holy Spirit provides encouragement, enablement, conviction, chastening, etc. to accompany each experience we enter during the refining process. From start to finish, our salvation in Christ is a stunning work of God that we should want everyone to experience.

Despite the hostility that sometimes accompanies sharing the gospel, may we follow Paul's example of declaring God's message of love and truth to those who urgently need to hear it. Sadly, many Christians today want to be raptured from responsibility. God will not hold us guiltless if we withhold His words of life (Ezek. 33:6-7)!

May 5 – The Just Shall Live by Faith
Romans 1:17

For in it the righteousness of God is revealed from faith to faith; as it is written, "The just shall live by faith."

"The just shall live by faith" is a quotation from Habakkuk 2:4. At first the prophet Habakkuk did not understand why God was not punishing His corrupt and idolatrous people. After he learned that God did have plans to punish and refine His covenant people, the prophet was perplexed how God could use a wicked nation like Babylon to accomplish His agenda. The Lord informed His servant that wicked Babylon would be judged also. God's exhortation to Habakkuk is that "the just shall live by faith." Man cannot understand all that God is achieving or is destined to accomplish, therefore, it is best just to trust Him and believe that He will do what is best. This brought great joy to the prophet's soul and ours also if we put the verse into practice.

Habakkuk 2:4 is quoted three times in the New Testament to explain enjoying spiritual life in Christ through faith (Rom. 1:17; Gal. 3:11; Heb. 10:38). Romans emphasizes that those justified in Christ should be characterized by "just" behavior. The Galatian reference focuses on pleasing God by "living" in the resurrection power of Christ's life. The writer of Hebrews reminds us of the necessity of genuine "faith" to progress in the Lord's work and that the believer's faith and hope are tied together. Both aspects have their culmination in Christ's coming for His Church: *"For yet a little while, and He who is coming will come and will not tarry. Now the just shall live by faith."* Though Scripture repeatedly emphasizes hope in the Christian experience, many believers today unfortunately do not know what their hope is and hence dread the future. But the just shall live by faith!

The message to Habakkuk (and to us too) is that trusting God and obeying His Word result in life (communion with Him), while pride and rebellion lead to death (separation from Him; Rom. 6:23). Habakkuk was not to trust his feelings or emotions, but rather to have faith in God and His choices: God would chasten Judah, judge Babylon, and in the process exalt His great name in all the earth. The greatest good is accomplished when we live by faith and trust God with our fate. Even if all is lost, we still have the great God of our salvation.

128

May 6 – Creation Demands a Creator
Romans 1:18-21

For the wrath of God is revealed from heaven against all ungodliness and unrighteousness of men, who suppress the truth in unrighteousness, because what may be known of God is manifest in them, for God has shown it to them. For since the creation of the world His invisible attributes are clearly seen, being understood by the things that are made, even His eternal power and Godhead, so that they are without excuse.

Creation provides an adequate testimony of a Creator! The Bible declares that God is the Creator, which then provides a test for all of us: Will we grip the evidence by faith or reject it? *"By faith we understand that the worlds were framed by the word of God, so that the things which are seen were not made of things which are visible"* (Heb. 11:3). In the first chapter of Romans, Paul explains that suppressing creation's evidence for a Creator will result in four inescapable realities:

1. Rejecting the Creator leads to the worship of creation (including one's self; Rom. 1:22-23).

2. Worshiping creation results in immoral and vile sin (rebellion against God's creation order results in homosexual behavior; Rom. 1:24-27).

3. Those who do such things inherently know that they deserve God's judgment (Rom. 1:32).

4. Rejection of the Creator, as evidenced by immoral living and idolatry, leads to divine judgment (Rom. 1:18-21).

The first three of these realities may be observed presently in our Western culture – the fourth reality is coming soon. The post-modern society of our day, in general, has departed from creation's witness of God; consequently, immorality is rampant: More and more couples are shunning the commitment of marriage and opting for a lifestyle of fornication (sex outside of marriage). Many of those engaging in immorality admit that deep down they know it is not right, yet they enjoy gratifying their own lusts too much to think too deeply about it. It is as if sex has become a narcotic to numb their conscience from the harsh reality of their conduct and the gravity of their future judgment.

May 7 – Is Your Conscience Offended? (Part 1)
Romans 2:12-13

For as many as have sinned without law will also perish without law, and as many as have sinned in the law will be judged by the law (for not the hearers of the law are just in the sight of God, but the doers of the law will be justified).

Why do we feel guilt after engaging in certain behaviors which no written law forbids? We have a moral law implanted within us which forces its way into the reasoning mechanics of the brain. David writes: *"The fool has said in his heart, 'There is no God.' They are corrupt; they have done abominable works; there is none who does good"* (Ps. 14:1). Though the atheist may be a socially moral person, one significant motivation for atheism is that man is enabled to do as he pleases when he pleases; if he chooses to pursue a life of sin, there is no divine consequence, only the *possibility* of social retribution. An individual who denies God's existence, regardless of intellectual rationale, ultimately does so to obtain liberation from divine authority.

Man apart from God cannot *perfectly* do good deeds to please God (Rom. 3:10-12). God declares that the *sum total* of man's self-working is putrid in His sight (Isa. 64:6). So, whether atheist, agnostic, insubordinate theist, etc., the reality of not being good is fostered in rejection of divine truth. From a natural perspective, all mankind, no matter what the religious bias or social backdrop, suffers the same moral ill; we cannot continue in well-doing even when we try our best, a fact to which our conscience bears witness.

So why do world cultures, even isolated societies, generally agree that it is morally wrong to kill, to steal, to commit adultery, to lie, to be disrespectful to parents, etc. Why is there a uniform code of ethics that spans the globe and is observed to be independent of time and culture? The answer is that the One who designed us has integrated a moral code of ethics within our being to beckon each person to look inward for evidence of a Creator. The Creator is commanding each of us to behave in one perfect way. Unfortunately, none of us behaves perfectly – that is, as God does. *"For all have sinned and fall short of the glory of God"* (Rom. 3:23). We cannot continue in well-doing. If you have ever felt guilt after doing something, then you know this to be true.

May 8 – Is Your Conscience Offended? (Part 2)
Romans 2:14-16

(For when Gentiles, who do not have the law, by nature do the things in the law, these, although not having the law, are a law to themselves, who show the work of the law written in their hearts, their conscience also bearing witness, and between themselves their thoughts accusing or else excusing them) in the day when God will judge the secrets of men by Jesus Christ, according to my gospel.

It is our conscience deep within our essence that produces feelings of guilt when we transgress the moral law God placed within us. *"Therefore, to him who knows to do good and does not do it, to him it is sin"* (Jas. 4:17). Natural man cannot identify the source of these intense feelings of guilt. What can be done to quiet the deafening apprehension of a wounded conscience? Pondering his loathsome situation, man rationalizes, "If doing something I know to be wrong induces mental anguish, then doing what I know to be right should ease my guilty pangs." As a result, except for Christianity, the religions of the world are founded on the "need of doing" to obtain a supernatural blessing. Works-based religion is a natural product of a depraved human conscience trying to ease its own grieving. The fact that we feel guilt is evidence to us that we did not continue in well-doing; we did not obey what we instinctively knew was right behavior (Rom. 2:15). Thus, we prove to ourselves that we are sinners, that we fall below the perfect standard of righteousness needed to enter heaven (Rom. 3:23).

If we are honest about the matter, each of us has a natural propensity to engage in sinful thoughts and deeds – we gravitate to that which we know is wrong. For God to save us, we must acknowledge that we are spiritually dead and in sin, repent from all we thought would earn us a right standing before God and receive Jesus Christ as our Savior.

Christianity declares that you cannot "do" something to earn your way to heaven – you could never do enough, and what is necessary to gain entrance has already been "done" at Calvary. The world's religion cries "do," while Christianity declares "done." Hence, we must realize that every aspect of our being has been affected adversely by sin, and only through Christ and the power of the Holy Spirit can the matter be resolved. My conscience bears witness to me that I need a Savior!

May 9 – Living the Circumcised Life
Romans 2:25-29

For circumcision is indeed profitable if you keep the law; but if you are a breaker of the law, your circumcision has become uncircumcision. Therefore, if an uncircumcised man keeps the righteous requirements of the law, will not his uncircumcision be counted as circumcision? And will not the physically uncircumcised, if he fulfills the law, judge you who, even with your written code and circumcision, are a transgressor of the law? For he is not a Jew who is one outwardly, nor is circumcision that which is outward in the flesh; but he is a Jew who is one inwardly; and circumcision is that of the heart, in the Spirit, not in the letter; whose praise is not from men but from God.

Circumcision was a "token" of Abraham's righteous standing gained by faith in God's promise (Gen. 15:6), not by the act of circumcision itself. Abraham was justified by faith before he was circumcised at the age of 99 (Rom. 4:11). However, as a perpetual sign of His covenant with Abraham, the Lord required Abraham's male descendants to also be circumcised (Gen. 17:1-14). This command was later reiterated and incorporated into the Mosaic Law (Lev. 12:3).

Over time, the Jews wore male circumcision like a badge that identified them as God's chosen people destined for blessing because of God's covenant with Abraham and later with them. In other words, the sign of the covenant became more vital than living out the moral law linked with the sign. It would be similar to a married man boasting of his beautiful gold wedding ring, but then commits blatant adultery – by breaking his wedding vows he mocks the symbol of his vow.

By stripping away the foreskin from the organ that best identified an individual as a male, God was symbolizing the stripping away of an old identity and the need to rely on God for a new way of life. Male circumcision would be a constant reminder to have no confidence in the flesh. It is the same for believers today; in Christ we become a new creation with a new identity in Him (2 Cor. 5:17). Yet, our new identity in Christ demands that we live the "circumcised life," which is the "cutting off" or "putting to death" of the desires and the will of our flesh. Paul summarizes in Romans 2:29 that it is the circumcision of the heart God wants in a believer's life, not just an outward show.

May 10 – Justified Freely by His Grace
Romans 3:23-24

For all have sinned and fall short of the glory of God, being justified freely by His grace through the redemption that is in Christ Jesus.

The New Testament epistles provide further details about how justification is accomplished. Paul informs us that a believer is justified by God's grace (Rom. 3:24), by Christ's blood (Rom. 5:9), and by faith (Rom. 5:1). James declares another astounding fact pertaining to justification: *"You see then that a man is justified by works, and not by faith only"* (Jas. 2:24). Humanly speaking, this may seem confusing. How can justification be so complicated if God simply accredited Abraham a righteous standing based on his faith (Jas. 2:23)?

Using your God-given imagination for a moment, in your mind's eye envision a huge reservoir in the upper elevations of a mountain range. Water from melting snow from mountain grandeur gently streams down into bubbling brooks, which, in turn, fill this reservoir to full capacity. An enormous dam holds back the vast resource except for what water is rushing out from its base into a deep channel. This channel conveys the water a great distance to a collection pool in the flat plains below. As individual headgates about this collection pool are opened, the vital blessing of the reservoir is applied to parched fields already sown with seed. Thus, the immense reservoir so far above in the mountains is responsible and necessary for an abundant harvest to follow below. Justification is, from a biblical sense, depicted in this imaginary scene. The reservoir pictures God's vast grace waiting to be bestowed from heavenly realms above. The channel represents the means in which God's grace is conveyed to mankind – through the blood of Jesus Christ. The act of opening the headgates symbolizes an individual trusting in the gospel message and, thus, receiving God's manifold grace through the blood of Christ. The harvest of good works that follows is the practical demonstration of a justified soul (Jas. 2:17).

Thus, a believer is justified by grace, through Christ's blood, by personal faith, and is evidenced by good works. True faith produces good deeds, including obedience. A soul that has been declared righteous by God should seek to live righteously. Those who have been justified in Christ should live to show Christ to others in their actions.

May 11 – Put Off the "Old Man" – He Is Dead
Romans 6:5-7

For if we have been united together in the likeness of His death, certainly we also shall be in the likeness of His resurrection, knowing this, that our old man was crucified with Him, that the body of sin might be done away with, that we should no longer be slaves of sin. For he who has died has been freed from sin.

Positionally speaking, co-crucifixion took place at the cross and became effectual for a believer at his or her conversion. At the cross, the old man, the man in Adam, the man that we once were before salvation, the man who was dominated and controlled by the flesh – that man died with Christ. Paul conveys the practical aspects of this positional truth to the believers at Galatia: *"Those who are Christ's have crucified the flesh with its passions and desires"* (Gal. 5:24). The believer has been positionally crucified with Christ so that his or her flesh nature will lose its controlling influence as he or she matures in Christ. It is not that the flesh nature diminishes in strength, but rather that the Holy Spirit within the believer overpowers it. What originated in the world cannot compete with that which is supernatural; thus, a yielded, dependent life cannot be overcome by the flesh nature.

Practical sanctification occurs in the believer as his or her flesh nature loses its influence (its control dies out) and the likeness of Christ becomes apparent; this process will be complete at glorification. Hence, Paul commands believers to "mortify" (or put to death) the deeds of the flesh (Col. 3:5) and in Romans 13:14 to starve the lusts of the flesh. The goal of these activities is that Christ and not the *nature* of the Old Man is seen in the believer's life. All believers were crucified with, died with, buried with, made alive with, and raised up with Christ in order to declare the power of His resurrection in daily life.

When a believer thinks upon what is corrupt, it must lead to a legitimate harvest of corruption (Gal. 6:7-8). It will be realized long after the initial seeds were sown and the repercussions will be far more devastating than what could have ever been imagined. Believers must desire to be controlled by the Holy Spirit and not their lusting flesh – only then are the deeds of the flesh mortified and fellowship with God maintained. This is what God considers living for Him (Rom. 8:13).

May 12 – Put On the "New Man" – He Is Alive
Romans 6:8-11

Now if we died with Christ, we believe that we shall also live with Him, knowing that Christ, having been raised from the dead, dies no more. Death no longer has dominion over Him. For the death that He died, He died to sin once for all; but the life that He lives, He lives to God. Likewise you also, reckon yourselves to be dead indeed to sin, but alive to God in Christ Jesus our Lord.

Paul tells us that "the Old Man" (i.e., what we were in Adam by nature) was crucified and died when Christ died, so that we are no longer slaves to sin (Rom. 6:6, 20-23). Because Christ rose from the grave, those trusting in Him receive eternal life in Him and the ability to overcome sin through the power of the Holy Spirit (John 3:16; Rom. 8:13). From a practical standpoint, all of us were born spiritually dead in Adam (Rom. 5:12). Although many will never admit that they are dying because of sin, those who do realize their hopeless condition can escape eternal condemnation and experience the full love of God by trusting in Christ for healing. God has much more for us than just escaping death; He wants us to experience His love and newness of life – and live as a "New Man."

Paul told the believers at Ephesus that because they had heard and learned Christ (i.e., believed), they had the ability to put off the former conduct of the *Old Man* and live as a *New Man* in Christ: *"that you put off, concerning your former conduct, the old man which grows corrupt according to the deceitful lusts, and be renewed in the spirit of your mind, and that you put on the new man which was created according to God, in true righteousness and holiness"* (Eph. 4:22-24). Positionally speaking, the Old Man is what we were in Adam and the New Man what we are in Christ; may we live Christ and not like a dead man.

From Colossians 3:5-14, the works of the flesh (the behavior of the Old Man) to be put off include: fornication, uncleanness, covetousness, unrighteous anger, wrath, malice, blasphemy, lying, and filthy speech. Activities that the New Man should put on include: being renewed in the knowledge of Christ, practically putting off the deeds of the Old Man, and being holy, merciful, kind, humble, meek, longsuffering, forbearing and forgiving.

May 13 – Do Not Let Sin Reign
Romans 6:12-13

Therefore do not let sin reign in your mortal body, that you should obey it in its lusts. And do not present your members as instruments of unrighteousness to sin, but present yourselves to God as being alive from the dead, and your members as instruments of righteousness to God.

Believers today must desire to be controlled by the Holy Spirit, and not by their lusting flesh – only then are the deeds of the flesh mortified and fellowship with God maintained: *"If by the Spirit you put to death the deeds of the body, you will live"* (Rom. 8:13). Positionally speaking, co-crucifixion took place at the cross and became effectual for a believer at his or her conversion (Rom. 6:6). The Greek verb translated "put to death" or "mortify" is in the present tense and active voice, meaning that believers are to be on active duty to mortify the deeds of the flesh. If your flesh nature raises its ugly head – you are to inflict a mortal blow against it. The only way to deal with lusting flesh is to put it to death; no pity, no mercy, and no procrastination.

Death and dying are not pleasant topics of conversation. There is a certain finality associated with death that our flesh loathes, because it ceases to function. But from God's standpoint, as Paul reminds the Galatians, Christians have already died positionally with Christ, and should therefore live out this truth: *"Those who are Christ's have crucified the flesh with its passions and desires"* (Gal. 5:24). The purpose of crucifixion was to end a life, though death would occur sometime after the victim was crucified. Accordingly, the cross ensures that as time moves on, there will be less of the believer's flesh and more of Christ apparent in his life.

Ultimately, complete freedom from the pull of sin within will be achieved at glorification. Until then, consistent mortification which gives the flesh no provision to fulfill its lusts is to be an ongoing exercise of all believers (Rom. 13:14). Gratification and mortification are the only two things the flesh understands. The danger is that if we choose to gratify the flesh, even a little, it will want more the next day because the flesh is never satisfied (Eccl. 1:8). The only spiritual recourse to deal with our lusting flesh is to deal it a deadly blow and to keep on mortifying it day after day – this is God's will for all of us!

May 14 – The Flesh Is Never Satisfied
Romans 7:5

For when we were in the flesh, the sinful passions which were aroused by the law were at work in our members to bear fruit to death.

Though the phrase "the flesh" sometimes refers to the human body, it is normally applied in the New Testament Epistles to refer to the fallen, independent nature which allows sin its opportunity within us. Paul states that through the fall of Adam, sin and spiritual death entered the world (Rom. 5:12). Every individual coming from Adam's line is born with Adam's inherited fallen nature (Ps. 51:5, 58:3); that is, we are born sinners and separated from God. This is why John states that those who reject Christ's offer for salvation are already condemned (John 3:17); we are all conceived and born into this lost spiritual condition. John further explains that the *"lusts of the flesh"* within us are not found in God, but are of the world – a system apart from God and under Satan's delegated control (1 Jn. 2:16).

In Romans 7, Paul describes his personal struggles to obey God's Law apart from divine power. Paul reminds us that our flesh wants to do what our conscience knows is wrong to do. The flesh, governed by the fallen nature, is never satisfied; it wants more than what is reasonable or lawful. Solomon put it this way: *"The eye is not satisfied with seeing, nor the ear filled with hearing"* (Eccl. 1:8). Instead of drinking *"a little wine for [one's] stomach's sake"* (1 Tim. 5:23), the flesh longs to be drunk with wine (Eph. 5:18). This is because when a person is drunk, the restraining influence of reason is lost and it becomes easier for the flesh to rule the moment.

Consequently, everything God says about the flesh is negative. In the flesh there is *"no good thing"* (Rom. 7:18). The flesh profits *"nothing"* (John 6:63). A Christian is to put *"no confidence"* in the flesh (Phil. 3:3). He is to make *"no provision"* for the flesh (Rom. 13:14). A person who lives for the flesh is living a negative life. Living for what belongs to the condemned life (what we inherited from Adam) will only bring the believer shame and suffering because the flesh always wants more than what has God's approval.

May 15 – No Good Thing
Romans 7:18-20

For I know that in me (that is, in my flesh) nothing good dwells; for to will is present with me, but how to perform what is good I do not find. For the good that I will to do, I do not do; but the evil I will not to do, that I practice. Now if I do what I will not to do, it is no longer I who do it, but sin that dwells in me (Rom. 7:18-20).

Paul understood that there was nothing in his flesh nature that would naturally want to honor the Lord. Instead of eating what is necessary to maintain a fit body, the flesh engages in gluttony (Prov. 23:21, 28:7). Scripture exhorts us to dress modestly to avert flaunting our bodies before others (1 Tim. 2:9; 1 Pet. 3:3), and not to seek to be the center of attention (Luke 14:8), but the flesh wants to be noticed and admired by others. The marriage covenant protects the sexual relationship between a husband and a wife, but unchecked cravings lead to fornication, which is a great offense against God (1 Thess. 4:3; Eph. 5:5-6) and against one's own body (1 Cor. 6:18).

Paul spoke of a law within his members (Rom. 7:23) which continued to oppose the law of God in his mind (i.e., his understanding of what God demanded of him). He referred to this nature as the law of sin (Rom. 7:25) and he knew it was an abiding evil presence within himself. There is no need to put a pre-conversion or post-conversion label to the latter portion of Romans 7; an unregenerate person or a believer not walking in the Spirit will both struggle as Paul describes.

However, after conversion Christians should be governed, not by the law of sin within them, but rather by the Spirit of God (Rom. 8:13). Moderation and self-control are a testimony to others that God is the One controlling a believer's actions (Phil. 4:5). Apparently, many in the church at Corinth did not have such a testimony because they were being controlled by their lusting flesh. In the opening verses of 1 Corinthians 3 Paul tells them three times that they are "*carnal*." The normal Greek word translated "flesh" in the New Testament is *sarx*, and Paul uses this word as a modifier (*sarkikos*) to describe their carnal behavior; they were "fleshly." Their flesh was governing their behavior within the assembly, and, as a result, the testimony of the church was suffering because their communion with Christ was being hindered.

May 16 – A Losing Battle
Romans 7:21-23

I find then a law, that evil is present with me, the one who wills to do good. For I delight in the law of God according to the inward man, but I see another law in my members, warring against the law of my mind, and bringing me into captivity to the law of sin which is in my members.

Though Paul's inner man (i.e., his spirit) desired to obey God, he found no natural wherewithal to do so. Yet, as a believer, it is this spiritual part of our essence which must govern our thinking and our actions (2 Cor. 4:16). Before we can understand how this is possible, we need a better understanding of how God created us.

God, who is triune, created man in His image. Man is not God, nor triune, but is tripartite. God is three distinct persons (Father, Son, and Spirit), while man is one person with three parts (spirit, soul, and body). The Holy Spirit acknowledges that each of us possesses a spirit, a soul, and a body (1 Thess. 5:23). These human components are interrelated, but are exclusive in their properties. The body is "world-conscious," the soul is "self-conscious," and the spirit of man is "God-conscious." The spirit is the noblest part of man and refers to the innermost area of our being – the "inner man." The body is the lowest portion of our existence and forms the outermost being. Between these two components dwells the soul. The soul comprises our intellect, our emotions, our personality, and our will. The soul links with the physical realm through the five senses, and through the spirit the soul connects with God. The soul is a bridge between the body and the spirit. When a believer is in fellowship with God, the Holy Spirit has the freedom to commune with man's spirit, which transmits godly thoughts to the soul. This in turn exercises the body to conform to the Spirit's control.

Before the fall of man, Adam's soul was completely under the control of his spirit. But the spirit cannot act directly on the body; it cannot bypass the soul (the mind). Thus, man has the will to choose to ignore his spirit and follow the desires of the flesh. God created the soul of man to stand between the body and the spirit in order to exercise power over the whole of man. It has the ability to consider spiritual things and render decisions other than what natural reason would endorse.

May 17 – Who Will Deliver Me From This Body of Death?
Romans 7:24-25

O wretched man that I am! Who will deliver me from this body of death? I thank God – through Jesus Christ our Lord! So then, with the mind I myself serve the law of God, but with the flesh the law of sin.

After stating that all men, including himself, were incapable of continued moral correctness through natural efforts, Paul ponders this hopeless condition: *"O wretched man that I am! Who will deliver me from this body of death?"* Paul then proclaims the answer, *"I thank God – through Jesus Christ our Lord! ... There is, therefore, now no condemnation to them which are in Christ Jesus"* (Rom. 8:1). Though man does not have the natural wherewithal to obey what he understands of God's law to be true, there is a solution – the Lord Jesus Christ! Instead of being condemned in Adam, our position in the crucified and risen Christ is that we are dead to sin and alive unto God without condemnation (Rom. 5:16, 18). Thus, while we know that we still have the law of sin in our members and nothing good in our flesh, we can rest in the assurance that God does not view us in the flesh (Rom. 8:9).

Though we still have a nature within us that opposes God, we are not condemned for having it once we are in Christ. Wrong attitudes and thoughts will still be present in us, but our responsibility in Christ is neither to pursue nor fulfill them, and to yield to His work of sanctification (Gal. 5:16). The work of sanctification begins in the believer's life immediately after he or she answers the call of salvation. God begins to fashion the new believer into a holy vessel and each believer is exhorted to cooperate in the working out of what God is working into his or her life (1 Thess. 5:23). Ultimately, God will conform all believers to the moral image of Christ (Rom. 8:29). We are not to resist God's working in our lives, but instead to yield to it by surrendering to Him. God promises to chasten those who choose not to submit to Him in order that they may become broken in disposition before Him and experience sanctification (Heb. 12:6). Accordingly, sanctification in a practical sense is occurring in all believers, but some are more serious about it than others and, therefore, will reap the greater blessing of being further refined now. The limiting factor in this process is how much we allow our flesh to stand in the way.

May 18 – No Condemnation and Power Over Sin
Romans 8:1-4

There is therefore now no condemnation to those who are in Christ Jesus, who do not walk according to the flesh, but according to the Spirit. For the law of the Spirit of life in Christ Jesus has made me free from the law of sin and death. For what the law could not do in that it was weak through the flesh, God did by sending His own Son in the likeness of sinful flesh, on account of sin: He condemned sin in the flesh, that the righteous requirement of the law might be fulfilled in us who do not walk according to the flesh but according to the Spirit.

Paul now answers the question he posed at the end of Romans 7: How can believers escape the problem of indwelling sin? He identifies three things that the Holy Spirit does for the believer. First, through regeneration and becoming one with Christ, the believer is no longer condemned, despite still possessing a nature that wants its own way.

Second, Paul explains that the believer has received a new nature and that through the power of the Holy Spirit, this nature can control the believer so that his or her flesh nature (the big bully within) no longer rules his or her life: *"For the law of the Spirit of life in Christ Jesus has made me free from the law of sin and death"* (Rom. 8:2). This results in a new war within each believer, a war between the old and new natures. *"Let us cleanse ourselves from all filthiness of the flesh and spirit, perfecting holiness in the fear of God"* (2 Cor. 7:1). Thankfully, this is a battle in which the believer can be victorious, for the power of the Holy Spirit is now *available* to overcome his or her inherent depravity. Some have taught that the flesh nature is eradicated at conversion, but clearly Paul stated that there would be an ongoing war between these two natures within the believer; the flesh and the new nature are completely opposed to each other and both compete for control of an individual's mind (Gal. 5:16-17).

Third, the Spirit of God speaking through man's spirit is in direct opposition to the lusts of the body and mind. The Holy Spirit speaks, convicts, draws, and chastens us, but He does not force the believer to do what is right. The decision is left to us – who will we listen to and obey? If we listen to the Spirit (walk in the Spirit), then we enjoy a condition of spiritual fruitfulness that could never occur in the flesh.

141

May 19 – New Life and a New Nature
Roman 8:5-6

For those who live according to the flesh set their minds on the things of the flesh, but those who live according to the Spirit, the things of the Spirit. For to be carnally minded is death, but to be spiritually minded is life and peace.

Prior to trusting Christ as Lord and Savior, people do not have the ability to please God; in fact, their old nature directly opposes God in thought and in deed (Rom. 5:10, 8:7). In these verses, Paul minces no words on this important point: The believer needs a new nature that longs to please God and will perform His will; there is nothing in the old nature that will want to do this (Rom. 7:18).

This new nature is received from God at conversion through an act of *"regeneration and renewing of the Holy Spirit"* (Tit. 3:5). The Holy Spirit washes us by bringing us to see the wrong in our sinful attitudes and desires. He makes us feel their uncleanness, and leads us to repent of and repudiate them. Peter refers to the new nature received as a divine nature: *"By which have been given to us exceedingly great and precious promises, that through these you may be partakers of the divine nature, having escaped the corruption that is in the world through lust"* (2 Pet. 1:4). Regeneration is the implantation of a new life and a new order of living. This is why a regenerated person is referred to as a "new man" in Colossians 3:10; he or she received a new disposition which is to govern his or her thinking and behavior. This new disposition is God's own nature, which cannot sin (1 Jn. 3:9), though the believer may still sin by ignoring its moral reckoning (1 Jn. 1:9-2:1).

Before the one-time act of regeneration, the believer was spiritually dead, but through rebirth he or she is made spiritually alive! Imagine for a moment a peach seed placed within a coffin containing a rotting corpse. The seed contains life, while the coffin contains nothing but death. In time, the seed will sprout and grow into a fruit-bearing tree. Through the power of the Holy Spirit, God implants life within a repentant sinner; that which was once dead now lives to bear fruit to God (John 15:1-5). The implanted seed cannot die, nor can it be corrupted as it comes from God; it gives us the capacity to really live.

May 20 – Those In the Flesh Cannot Please God
Romans 8:7-8

Because the carnal mind is enmity against God; for it is not subject to the law of God, nor indeed can be. So then, those who are in the flesh cannot please God.

John refers to the new nature as a righteous seed implanted within a new believer. This seed cannot invoke sin or lead the believer away from what pleases God: *"No one who is born of God practices sin, because His seed abides in him; and he cannot sin, because he is born of God"* (1 Jn. 3:9; NASB). "Born of God" and "born again" are equivalent terms with the washing of regeneration (Tit. 3:5).

The Lord Jesus said that no one would enter heaven without being born again (John 3:3). The only way to be born again is by trusting Jesus Christ alone for salvation: *"But as many as received Him, to them He gave the right to become children of God, to those who believe in His name: who were born, not of blood, nor of the will of the flesh, nor of the will of man, but of God"* (John 1:12-13). Without being born again, a human soul will remain spiritually dead and without the capacity to please God. In this state, every individual will act as a child of the devil and be controlled by the lusts and desires of his or her flesh (Eph. 2:1-3). Consequently, if we are going to live for God, we must be born again and yield to that new and holy nature received from Him.

It is only by the conviction of the Holy Spirit and the power of God's Word resounding in our minds that we are enabled to repent, choose Christ, and receive eternal life in Him. Until then we are simply dead corpses marching in cadence with Satan, performing his rebel agenda, and coming ever nearer to his final destination – hell (Eph. 2:1-3). Once we trust Christ, we become a New Man in Him, and receive His nature through the Holy Spirit; what we positionally were in Adam (the Old Man) is gone, but we still have his old nature within us.

By being new creatures in Christ and thereby partakers of God's nature, believers have the means of constantly escaping *"the corruption that is in the world through lust"* (2 Pet. 1:4). May we long to think, speak, and act as God would…He makes it possible to do so! May the children of light never march again in Satan's zombie band.

May 21 – The Carnal Mind Is Death
Romans 8:9-11

But you are not in the flesh but in the Spirit, if indeed the Spirit of God dwells in you. Now if anyone does not have the Spirit of Christ, he is not His. And if Christ is in you, the body is dead because of sin, but the Spirit is life because of righteousness. But if the Spirit of Him who raised Jesus from the dead dwells in you, He who raised Christ from the dead will also give life to your mortal bodies through His Spirit who dwells in you.

There are many things for which our flesh can lust: social status, fame, food, vices, sexual pleasures, money, beauty, etc. It is impossible to allow our flesh to lust for what it wants and not to expect our behavior to adversely affect our spiritual vitality. Peter acknowledges that a believer cannot simultaneously live according to the flesh and be in the will of God (1 Pet. 4:2).

Clearly, when the believer is in the flesh, he or she cannot please God; this is a practical truth. God's solution for us in overcoming the flesh's impulses begins by understanding a positional truth. Positionally speaking, co-crucifixion took place at the cross and became effectual for a believer at his or her conversion (Rom. 6:6). In Adam, we were *"made subject to vanity"* (Rom. 8:20). At the cross, the Old Man, the man in Adam, the man that we once were, the man who was dominated and controlled by the flesh, died with Christ. Paul conveys the practical aspects of this positional truth to the Galatian believers: *"Those who are Christ's have crucified the flesh with its passions and desires"* (Gal. 5:24). The purpose of crucifixion was to end the life of someone, though death itself would occur sometime later. From God's perspective, believers have been crucified with Christ so that their craving flesh will eventually die (i.e., there should be a diminishing influence of the old nature in believers as they mature in Christ).

When a believer thinks on what is corrupt, it must lead to a legitimate harvest of corruption (Gal. 6:7-8). Consequently, believers must desire to be controlled by the Holy Spirit instead of their lusting flesh – only then are the deeds of the flesh mortified and fellowship with God maintained.

May 22 – Live After the Spirit and Live
Romans 8:12-13

Therefore, brethren, we are debtors – not to the flesh, to live according to the flesh. For if you live according to the flesh you will die; but if by the Spirit you put to death the deeds of the body, you will live.

Believers are to be on high alert and be willing to instantly mortify any fleshly thoughts or impulses whenever observed. Furthermore, Paul told the believers at Colosse not to feed (strengthen) the nature of the Old Man by doing deeds of the flesh (Col. 3:5).

The ungodly longings of the flesh (some of which are listed in Col. 3:5) should not be strengthened through sinful behavior or by wrong thinking, but rather these should be starved so that they lose their influence and can be "put off" from the believer's conduct completely. If not fed, these ungodly longings lose their hold on the believer's life and die out more quickly – although ultimate freedom will not be achieved until glorification. Paul conveys this same fundamental truth to the believers at Rome: *"Likewise you also, reckon yourselves to be dead indeed to sin, but alive to God in Christ Jesus our Lord. Therefore do not let sin reign in your mortal body, that you should obey it in its lusts"* (Rom. 6:11-12).

Mortification or gratification are the only two things the flesh understands, but if we choose to gratify the flesh, even a little, it will want more the next day because the flesh is never satisfied. The only spiritual recourse in dealing with the lusting of the flesh is to deal it a deadly blow and to keep on mortifying it day after day – this is God's will for every believer. Consistent mortification of the flesh ends the sway of the carnal mind to cause death (separation) – for the believer this is the loss of spiritual fellowship with the Savior.

Scripture presents the solution to sin and death: *"For the wages of sin is death, but the gift of God is eternal life in Christ Jesus our Lord"* (Rom. 6:23). We choose our sin, but it is God who chooses the consequences of our sin and offers consoling grace for those who regret and repent of their sin (1 Jn. 1:9). God's infinite grace and forgiving heart ensure that failures are never final unless we choose to wallow in self-pity rather than finding a joyful refuge in His grace.

May 23 – Help in Our Weaknesses
Romans 8:26-27

Likewise the Spirit also helps in our weaknesses. For we do not know what we should pray for as we ought, but the Spirit Himself makes intercession for us with groanings which cannot be uttered. Now He who searches the hearts knows what the mind of the Spirit is, because He makes intercession for the saints according to the will of God.

Paul tells us that the Holy Spirit helps us in our weaknesses. The Greek word translated "weaknesses" is *astheneia* and may speak of any kind of physical, emotional, or spiritual disability. But it is not just assistance in our weaknesses that is promised; the Holy Spirit also offers intercession on our behalf before the throne of grace when we do not even know what to pray for or how to adequately express ourselves in prayer. During times of deep distress or tragic grief it may be hard to formulate words while praying; it is at these times that the Holy Spirit perfectly expresses our needs to our High Priest in heaven without any audible sound. When we groan, the Holy Spirit also groans with spiritual ministry. This is not the speaking in tongues as some teach, because the ministry the Holy Spirit engages in is literally "without sound."

The English expression of action, "makes intercession" is derived from a Greek verb with a present tense, meaning that the Holy Spirit *keeps on interceding* on our behalf. We never need to worry about the Holy Spirit being unaware of our troubles and sorrows, or that He gets tired of groaning when we groan, or that some matter is not worthy of His attention. He is within us and before the throne in heaven to help us in all our weaknesses, which He understands better than we do. He continues to make ongoing intercession for us anytime we are in need.

With that said, Paul also instructed the Christians at Ephesus to be *"praying always with all prayer and supplication in the Spirit"* (Eph. 6:18). If we pray in the Spirit, we can be assured that we have the supplications of the Holy Spirit according to the will of God at God's throne (1 Jn. 5:14). So whether our prayers are audibly expressed or spoken to God in our spirit, we pray to God through the enablement of the Holy Spirit, knowing that He will perfect or supply whatever is necessary to provide complete intercession on our behalf. In this way, we can always be assured that He will help us in all of our weaknesses.

May 24 – Present Your Bodies as a Living Sacrifice
Romans 12:1-2

I beseech you therefore, brethren, by the mercies of God, that you present your bodies a living sacrifice, holy, acceptable to God, which is your reasonable service. And do not be conformed to this world, but be transformed by the renewing of your mind, that you may prove what is that good and acceptable and perfect will of God.

Each Christian is a believer-priest and is called on to be a continual, living sacrifice to God. Through the power of the Holy Spirit, this may be accomplished in various ways: rejecting the desires of the flesh that are beyond God's will (Rom. 8:13), offering up praise to God (Heb. 13:15), supporting the Lord's work through gifts (1 Cor. 16:2), and by frequently remembering the Lord Jesus by observing the Lord's Supper (1 Cor. 11:22-33). The Greek word rendered "present" in verse 1 is translated in the same way in Romans 6:12. Both verses speak of believer's ability to be a living sacrifice. To do what God wants us to do means that we had to say "no" to what we wanted; in other words, it costs us something to give to God what pleases Him – this is what it means to be an acceptable sacrifice to God and is our priestly duty.

Additionally, Paul suggests that one of the ways that believers worship the Lord is to reject the world's philosophies and attractions by renewing our minds on what is true and spiritual. This is accomplished by yielding to God's Word to avoid conformity to the world. Worldliness is a system of values which excludes Christ's authority and ignores God's standards of wholesomeness.

Scripture speaks of two complementary means that call the believer's heart out of the world. The first is to set one's mind on things above: *"If then you were raised with Christ, seek those things which are above, where Christ is, sitting at the right hand of God. Set your mind on things above, not on things on the earth"* (Col. 3:1-2). The second is to come to realize that the things below are temporary and shakable. As the writer of Hebrews reminds us, in a coming day, all that does not honor the Lord will be removed (Heb. 12:27-29). The world is evil and temporal, but heaven is wonderful and eternal. This is why we should devote not just ourselves to the Lord, but all our resources also. What is not for Him will ultimately burn up anyway.

May 25 – Think Soberly, as God Has Given in Measure
Romans 12:3

For I say, through the grace given to me, to everyone who is among you, not to think of himself more highly than he ought to think, but to think soberly, as God has dealt to each one a measure of faith.

Speaking through the grace that was given to him as an apostle, Paul reminds his audience that there is nothing in the gospel message that makes them superior to anyone else. Christ is the Head of the Body and all believers have equal status within the Body, though not the same calling, gift or giftedness. Having this understanding should cause believers to behave appropriately in desiring to serve Christ by using their spiritual gift(s).

First, no believer is to have an exaggerated idea concerning their importance in the Body or the application of their spiritual gift in the Body of Christ. In fact, a spirit of humility is necessary for the Holy Spirit to effectively enable believers to use their abilities and spiritual gifts in a way that will benefit the Church. Each believer is a unique trophy of God's grace and each believer has a unique function in the Body of Christ to perform. Everyone is needed for the work of ministry of building up the Body (Eph. 4:12).

Second, there is no room for being envious of other saint's spiritual gifts or giftedness. God chooses the calling of each believer in the Body and then equips him or her to fulfill their assigned ministry (1 Cor. 12:11). For example, if your heart, because of boredom, decided to be a foot for a day, you would be in deep trouble. Likewise, believers who ignore their place in the Body of Christ and pursue ministry that they are not equipped for will do more damage than good – it is only what God energizes that will benefit the Church.

Third, believers are to use spiritual discernment in the application of their gift(s). If you receive joy in a particular ministry and others are clearly blessed by it, then continue doing what God is blessing. However, if what you are doing is drudgery and there appears to be no benefit to anyone, then seek the Lord on the matter. Obtain godly counsel, pray for wisdom, and wait until the Lord reveals a different type of ministry to explore. We must rely on God's wisdom and grace, and then by faith draw upon the full measure of strength He supplies.

May 26 – Gifts Differing According to Grace (Part 1)
Romans 12:4-6

For as we have many members in one body, but all the members do not have the same function, so we, being many, are one body in Christ, and individually members of one another. Having then gifts differing according to the grace that is given to us, let us use them: if prophecy, let us prophesy in proportion to our faith.

The human body has many unique *members* (i.e., organs and functional parts) that depend on each other for the welfare of the entire body. Similarly, the Body of Christ also has many unique members with important roles to be performed if the Church is to function as Christ desires it to. Only when all believers are in fellowship with the Lord and enabled by the Holy Spirit to use their spiritual gifts in full measure that God gives will the Church adequately represent Christ in the world. We need each other and each other's abilities in the Body.

Prophesying (*propheteuo*) has several meanings: to speak forth with divine inspiration, which may include the foretelling of future events, or simply to utter forth divine truth that has already been revealed through God's written Word. In the apostolic age, prior to the canonization of Scripture, God spoke directly through the apostles and prophets to convey truth to His people. Today we understand that a modern day "prophet" would be *forthtelling* truth and not *foretelling* the future (1 Cor. 13:8-10). God's prophets were rarely tactful or soft-spoken mouthpieces for God; rather they were forthright and no-nonsense. Prophets keenly felt God's anger when His character had been affronted by His wayward people and that tenor was reflected in their ministry. Today, the gift of prophecy might be evident when an individual, having properly discerned the spiritual disparity between the Church's behavior and God's Word, bluntly sets the matter straight.

Any man approaching God, to either speak to Him in prayer or to speak for God to others (prophecy or teaching), should visibly salute God by having their heads uncovered (1 Cor. 11:4). Their uncovered head represents God's glory and authority in the assembly. Any woman present when this occurs should be silent and have her head covered to conceal glories that compete with God's glory (i.e., her head represents man's glory and her hair her own glory; 1 Cor. 11:5-7; 14:34).

May 27 – Gifts Differing According to Grace (Part 2)
Romans 12:7

Or ministry, let us use it in our ministering; he who teaches, in teaching.

Paul speaks of two more spiritual gifts bestowed in grace to believers in verse 7: ministry (or serving) and teaching. Those with the gift of ministry were to focus on what God had called them to do; likewise those given a teaching gift were to be diligent in using it.

God bestows to some believers a servant's heart. Observation would indicate that there are two broad variations of this gift, *helps* and *service*. Believers with the gift of *helps* will be people-oriented; they enjoy rubbing shoulders with others as they serve. Not only do these saints get things done for others in need, but they also provide an emotional component that is therapeutic for the soul also. Other believers are more focused on getting things done, that need to be done, without the human interaction. They are happy to clean the church building or paint someone's house, even when no one else is nearby. Both these aspects of ministry in the Body of Christ are much needed.

It should be understood that the title "minister" is not biblically applied to those in church leadership; in fact, the term is applied in a variety of ways in the New Testament: it is spoken of as a spiritual gift (Rom. 12:7), and is applied to those in civil authority (Rom. 13:1-4), to different believers as they serve Christ in various capacities (1 Cor. 3:5, 4:1; 2 Cor. 6:4, 11:15) and to Christ, who is a minister of the truth to the Jews (Rom. 15:8). It is never used as a title before a proper name anywhere in Scripture. In summary, every believer is a minister and should function in the Body of Christ according to the ministry he or she has been called by the Lord to do.

A teacher is able to rightly discern the meaning of Scripture and then is able to effectively explain and apply it for the benefit of his or her audience. The priest Ezra was a scribe, an instructor of the Law. His passion as a teacher is recorded in Ezra 7:10: *"Ezra had prepared his heart to seek the Law of the Lord, and to do it, and to teach statutes and ordinances in Israel."* Ezra spent time in God's Word to understand it, he obeyed what he knew to be true, and he desired others to know God's Word also. Effective teachers do what they teach others to do.

May 28 – Gifts Differing According to Grace (Part 3)
Romans 12:8

He who exhorts, in exhortation; he who gives, with liberality; he who leads, with diligence; he who shows mercy, with cheerfulness.

God knows that we need both encouragers (like Barnabas) and exhorters in our lives. The Greek verb *protrepomai* is rendered "encouraged" in Acts 18:27 (RV): *"The brethren encouraged him [Apollos]."* The first portion of this word, *protrepo,* literally implies "to urge forward." When God's people do well, especially in areas in which they tend to struggle, believers should add energy to the right behavior with praise and encouragement in order to reinforce it.

Encouragement is not the same thing as *exhortation*, the gift Paul identifies in this verse. Believers need constant exhortation to serve the Lord properly: *"Exhort one another daily"* (Heb. 3:13). "To exhort" is translated from the Greek word *parakaleo*, which means "to call near and invoke." If a believer has lost his or her direction, those with maturity are to draw near in love and redirect his or her path. We are to literally "come along side and turn." Exhortation is for small course changes, whereas admonishing and rebuke are for correcting more serious matters of foolishness and sin, respectively. Exhortation is most effective when the receiver knows that the exhorter loves them!

The spiritual gift of *giving* provides astute perception of those in need, how to best supply those needs and a compassionate burden to do so. People with this gift joyfully offer what they have liberally, often beyond their means to alleviate someone's lack or to support a ministry.

The spiritual gift of *administration* enables individuals to organize people and activities in such a way that an efficient, orderly, and effective outcome is realized. These leaders have a special knack for getting things done and getting the most out of the time they have.

Those with the spiritual gift of mercy have a God-given ability to aid and comfort those in distress. While this may include meeting a distressed person's necessities, mercy supplies a cheerful component that settles one's anxiety and infuses hope for the future: "All is not lost...you will get through this...I will do whatever I can to help you get through this."

God distributes differing spiritual gifts according to His will and then gives us whatever strength and ability is needed to use what He has given.

151

May 29 – Gifts Differing According to Grace (Part 4)
Romans 12:6

Having then gifts differing according to the grace that is given to us!

The Holy Spirit distributes spiritual gifts to believers *"as He wills"* (1 Cor. 12:11). The number of gifts per believer will vary (1 Cor. 12:4), but every believer receives at least one spiritual gift (1 Cor. 12:7). Also, the manner in which these gifts will be used will differ (1 Cor. 12:5), as will the beneficiaries of the gifts (1 Cor. 12:6).

One way of identifying spiritual gifts is to observe how believers react in difficult situations. Their first impulse will often indicate how God has provisioned them to serve the Church. For example, picture the following scene in your mind. A church is gathered to remember the Lord on Sunday morning by keeping the Lord's Supper. While one man named Tony passes the communion tray across the aisle to another man, Frank, it is dropped on the floor – the cups and their contents spill out on the floor. Obviously, this is a stressful situation which provides an opportunity for different believers to use their spiritual gifts. A sister with the gift of helps quickly rises from her seat and ventures to the kitchen to retrieve a damp rag and some towels to clean up the mess. Another sister with the gift of mercy pats Tony on the shoulder and says, "Don't worry about it; I drop things all the time." "Frank, you did not receive a cup, I was considering not partaking anyway, so please take mine" says a brother with the gift of giving. The teacher says, "If you would have held the tray with two hands while passing it, you would not have dropped it." A brother with the gift of administration stands up, and asks a believer to retrieve the tray and refill the cups while the sister with the gift of helps is cleaning up the mess; he then informs everyone that the Lord's Supper will continue as soon as the tray is refilled. This situation probably does not occur often in your assembly, but it does illustrate how the Lord equips different believers to serve others.

All the spiritual gifts in your local church are important and all need to be identified, exercised, and developed. There is no need to ascribe names to what people do, but rather believers should be cheered to keep doing ministry that brings them joy and blesses the Church. If you are weary of serving or are harming the Body – stop what you are doing!

May 30 – Let Love Be Without Hypocrisy
Romans 12:9-13

Let love be without hypocrisy. Abhor what is evil. Cling to what is good. Be kindly affectionate to one another with brotherly love, in honor giving preference to one another; not lagging in diligence, fervent in spirit, serving the Lord; rejoicing in hope, patient in tribulation, continuing steadfastly in prayer; distributing to the needs of the saints, given to hospitality.

Perhaps one of the most neglected ministries within the Church and among the lost is hospitality. Some believers decline to use their homes in ministry because they do not believe they have the ability to do so. Others set their expectation so high they feel inadequate. Yet, there is nothing in Scripture that suggests that hospitality is a specific spiritual gift per se, or that there is some standard to which we must comply. Hence, Peter exhorts his audience *"to use hospitality one to another without grudging"* (1 Pet. 4:9). Every believer should be given to hospitality. The home is a lovely setting to console the grieving, refresh the weary, exhort the erring, and reach the lost with the gospel.

Our English word "hospitality" is translated from the Greek noun *philoxenos* or verb *philonexia*, which together only occur five times in the New Testament. Hospitality literally means to be "fond of strangers (guests)." Paul, John, and Peter urge their audiences to engage in hospitality and also identify hospitality as an act of genuine love towards others.

To the Romans, Paul writes: *"Love without hypocrisy...given to hospitality."* We are not to be respecters of persons, but attempt to have profitable relationships with those believers with whom we are associated. Thankfully, God's love towards us is not hypocritical; He has intimates, but no favorites (Acts 10:34). Consequently, James warns *"if you show partiality, you commit sin"* (Jas. 2:9). Hospitality is a means for enhancing Christian fellowship, especially with those with whom you may feel uncomfortable or with whom you are not prone to interact. Perhaps there are believers in your home assembly or in your local community that you do not know well; why not invite them over for a meal? If it is awkward to meet with them alone, invite others to join you as well.

153

May 31 – Minister to Your Brethren
Romans 12:15-16

Rejoice with those who rejoice, and weep with those who weep. Be of the same mind toward one another. Do not set your mind on high things, but associate with the humble. Do not be wise in your own opinion.

In these verses, Paul exhorts believers as to how they should consider and treat each other. Having the same mind does not mean that all believers are to think alike, but that we should have the mind of Christ (Phil. 2:1-5). This type of thinking is not high-minded of one's opinions and accomplishments, but rather elevates the interests of others above our own and sees the good of the Body as a higher objective than personal gain. Our nature from Adam craves the pampered life, recognition and fame, but Paul says to associate with the humble and not to seek high status. This is how Christ lived while on the earth and expects us to live in Him during our sojourn also.

A few hours before the Lord's arrest on the Mount of Olives, He was speaking to His disciples about future things. He told them that in a coming day He would separate the sheep from the goats and only the sheep would enter His kingdom (i.e., the Judgment of Nations after the Tribulation Period). The King would honor those who do not side with the Antichrist, but rather choose to care for Him (speaking of the good deeds done to His suffering brethren the Jews). The Sheep (the righteous) did not understand the King's accolade, so He clarified the matter: *"And the King will answer and say to them, 'Assuredly, I say to you, inasmuch as you did it to one of the least of these My brethren, you did it to Me'"* (Matt. 25:40). In application, the way we treat the lowliest believer in the Body of Christ shows our esteem for Christ.

Our tendency is to rub shoulders with those of status and that are well-to-do and snub those of humble estate. We tend to avoid identifying and associating with those who are burdened, persecuted, and suffering. But all believers are one in Christ; we all are members of His Body, of His Church, and compose His Bride. When one member of the Body suffers – all of its members suffer. This spiritual reality must compel us to have the same care for one another that Christ would have for us (1 Cor. 12:25-26). Indeed, weep with those who weep!

June 1 – Overcome Evil With Good
Romans 12:17-21

Repay no one evil for evil. Have regard for good things in the sight of all men. If it is possible, as much as depends on you, live peaceably with all men. Beloved, do not avenge yourselves, but rather give place to wrath; for it is written, "Vengeance is Mine, I will repay," says the Lord. Therefore, "If your enemy is hungry, feed him; if he is thirsty, give him a drink; for in so doing you will heap coals of fire on his head." Do not be overcome by evil, but overcome evil with good.

Moses reminded the Israelites, before they entered the Promised Land, that vengeance and recompense for wrongdoing was the Lord's business (Deut. 32:35). Paul quotes Moses' command here, but then adds further instructions for believers in the Church Age. Christians have the indwelling Holy Spirit and are commanded to fulfill the greater intention of the Law – to love selflessly, for example, by giving to others in lieu of merely not stealing from them (Rom. 13:8-10). Recognizing God's righteous standard is the focus of keeping the Law, but demonstrating His irresistible love in righteousness is paramount in fulfilling the Law – and this we must do to win the lost to Christ!

Christians, therefore, should desire to pluck lost souls out of hellfire much more than they desire to get even for wrong done to them. Paul exhorts us to show the love of God to those who oppress us, even giving our enemies food and drink if they are hungry and thirsty. In so doing we heap coals of fire on their heads, so to speak. William MacDonald explains Paul's idiom: "If the live coal treatment seems cruel, it is because this idiomatic expression is not properly understood. To heap live coals on a person's head means to make him ashamed of his hostility by surprising him with unconventional kindness."[17]

The "heap coals of fire" expression may refer to the ancient Egyptian custom of carrying coals of fire in a vessel on one's head as an expression of kindness to a neighbor that one desired to be reconciled with. Starting household fires for cooking and heat was problematic in those days, so gifting burning coals was a gesture of goodwill. In a coming day, the Lord will set right all that has been wrong. Until then, may we endeavor to show love when wronged that the lost might recognize that there is something beyond just being right.

June 2 – There Is No Authority Except From God
Romans 13:1

Let every soul be subject to the governing authorities. For there is no authority except from God, and the authorities that exist are appointed by God.

God instituted human government to teach us submission to His authority, so when those who are representing Him become corrupt, His retribution is severe because His character has been blasphemed (Gen. 9:6; Rom. 13:1-5). Whether it is civil authority, home authority, or church authority, no instituted form of government is perfect on this side of Christ's rule in the Kingdom Age. Regardless, the Lord is teaching us to yield ourselves in willful submission to those that He has put in place to rule over us. Sometimes, this authority becomes corrupt, but as much as possible we are "to salute the uniform" so to speak and not the person or establishment wearing the uniform dishonorably.

The righteous will rejoice when the honorable Judge over all the earth vindicates His name by judging those who misused His authority. At that time, God will avenge the oppressed. In Psalm 58:10-11, David tells us that it is better to be mistreated and happy in the Lord than to be numbered with those who taint God's name by corrupt authority.

Isaiah notes several telltale signs of a nation in declension (Isa. 3:1-11): First, there is an absence of wise and just judges and governors for which a society's general welfare depends. Second, immature and impulsive leaders take their place. Third, the absence of godly leaders upholding an ethical compass to guide the people results in a divided society. This dynamic often causes an age-gap rift where the younger generation rebels against their elders. Fourth, an air of despair permeates the nation as moral values are compromised by those trying to transform the society. Sadly, emotional or carnal enticements are employed to win the hearts of the undiscerning populace.

Since our civil officials are placed in office by the Lord, we must realize that, at times, God may be reproving us rather than seeking our prosperity. One can hardly deny that the same social features that Isaiah spoke of long ago are already evident in many Western countries which once held to a Christian heritage, but now are provoking the Lord to anger. Hence, hardship, not divine blessing, should be expected.

June 3 – Do Not Resist God by Resisting Authority
Romans 13:2

Therefore whoever resists the authority resists the ordinance of God, and those who resist will bring judgment on themselves.

After our first parents disobeyed God in Eden, their initial response was to hide from Him. Ever since that loathsome event, humanity has been denying God's authority and trying to hide from the associated responsibility. For example, Scripture clearly lays out God's order for authority in the home, in the Church, and in civil affairs, but we often ignore it. Men are instructed not to squander their earnings on frivolous toys and entertainment, but rather they are to provide for their households (1 Tim. 5:8) and those in need (Rom. 12:13; Eph. 4:28). They are to be the spiritual leaders of their homes, not passive spectators (1 Cor. 14:35). Women are not to supplant the authority of their husbands (Eph. 5:22-23; 1 Tim. 2:11-14), and they are to be keepers of the home (Tit. 2:4) and helpers to their husbands (Gen. 2:18). Children are to obey their parents as unto the Lord (Eph. 6:1-2); they are not to rebel against their authority. Believers are not to forsake the accountability of the local assembly (Heb. 10:25), but rather they are to obey the leadership that God has put over them (Acts 20:28; Heb. 13:17). Citizens are to obey their governmental leaders for the fear of the Lord (Rom. 13:1-2), and to pay taxes (Rom. 13:7), and they are not to speak evil of those in authority (2 Pet. 2:10).

There are only two authority structures in the world: God's and Satan's. After Lucifer rebelled against God (Isa. 14:12-15), he injected his own proud and selfish spirit into the world (1 Jn. 2:16). This independent thinking and rebel spirit then caused humanity to fall. Consequently, there are now two authority structures in the world, and they stand completely opposed to one another. God's authority is supreme, while Satan's authority is tolerated within boundaries, until God's purposes have been served. God allows Satan to test man's moral resolve. Believers are to serve God in all things and it is understood that the various authority structures He has placed over us are for the purpose of teaching us to submit to Him. Thus, we honor God by obeying those He has placed in authority over us; compliance is rendered to win not the esteem of men, but the approval of God.

June 4 – Obey God's Minister
Romans 13:3-5

> *For rulers are not a terror to good works, but to evil. Do you want to be unafraid of the authority? Do what is good, and you will have praise from the same. For he is God's minister to you for good. But if you do evil, be afraid; for he does not bear the sword in vain; for he is God's minister, an avenger to execute wrath on him who practices evil. Therefore you must be subject, not only because of wrath but also for conscience' sake.*

Paul suggests two reasons for obeying the authority that God has placed over us. First, those who resist God-established authority resist the One who originated it (Rom. 13:2). No authority exists unless God allows it; therefore, disobedience to home, civil, and church authority is rebellion against God's rule (unless such authority is acting contrary to God's authority). The fear of God's judgment is a sobering deterrent against defying those who represent Him and are being used by Him to teach us submission and to bless us.

Second, our conscience tells us that we should obey God's authority over us (1 Tim. 1:5). Just as children instinctively know that it is proper to submit to the authority of their parents (in the Lord), we all know that it is appropriate to submit to the church elders and civil officials that He has placed over us. Those in positions of authority are God's ministers for accomplishing good and justice ideally. Sadly, this privileged position of representing the Lord to others is often abused by corruption.

Is there any time that we should not obey the authorities God has placed over us? If those in authority are clearly in contradiction to specific commands recorded in God's Word, the believer should submit to the higher authority and suffer the temporary consequences of the lower authority patiently (Acts 4:19-20, 5:29). At times we are called to endure as Christ did; He suffered undeservingly in righteousness to leave us an example to follow. This has nothing to do with suffering justly for wrongdoing, for Christ was sinless, but rather yielding ourselves to God and patiently suffering for the misconducts of others while we wait for Him to set all things right (1 Pet. 2:18-20). To please God, rather than to be chastened by Him, and to have a clear conscience before God are good reasons for respecting and yielding to His authority.

June 5 – Fulfill the Law
Romans 13:8-10

Owe no one anything except to love one another, for he who loves another has fulfilled the law. For the commandments, "You shall not commit adultery," "You shall not murder," "You shall not steal," "You shall not bear false witness," "You shall not covet," and if there is any other commandment, are all summed up in this saying, namely, "You shall love your neighbor as yourself." Love does no harm to a neighbor; therefore love is the fulfillment of the law.

Paul instructed the Christians in Rome to *"Owe no one anything except to love one another, for he who loves another has fulfilled the law."* Previously, Paul informed his audience that the purpose of the Mosaic Law was to show that man was sinful and needed a Savior – Christ (Rom. 3:20-25). If someone stole something, it proved that they could not "keep" the law and were sinful. The law declares God's holiness and man's depraved state. But once the Holy Spirit indwells a believer, he or she becomes able to "fulfill" the law. When one chooses not to steal, that is keeping the law; but fulfilling the law is not just *not stealing* from another – it is *giving to* that person. Giving expresses love. God's holiness is reflected in keeping the law, but His gracious character is represented in fulfilling the law. Through the power of the Holy Spirit, the believer conveys the love of God to others in a supernatural way. It is not natural to love our enemies, to do good to those who persecute us, to bless those who curse us, or to withhold vengeance when it is just. Only by the power of the Holy Spirit in our lives are we able to demonstrate the love of God in such ways.

The believer should never be satisfied with his outward projection of God's love. Can a husband love his wife too much? No, he will never love his wife as Christ loves the Church (Eph. 5:25). Thus, there will always be room to abound more and more. The church at Thessalonica was thriving in the midst of Jewish persecution, yet Paul exhorts, *"And the Lord make you to increase and abound in love one toward another, and toward all men, even as we do toward you"* (1 Thess. 3:12). The Lord would receive the most glory, they would receive the most joy, and the Holy Spirit would accomplish the most blessing when they chose to invoke love to resolve "people problems."

June 6 – Handling Debatable Things
Romans 14:1-3

Receive one who is weak in the faith, but not to disputes over doubtful things. For one believes he may eat all things, but he who is weak eats only vegetables. Let not him who eats despise him who does not eat, and let not him who does not eat judge him who eats; for God has received him.

In contrast to the Mosaic Law, the Church has been given few commandments to obey. Through the new covenant established by Christ's blood we live in the Age of Grace. God bestows us much freedom in working out the questionable things of our salvation (Phil. 2:12). God knows that love is a better motive to inspire service to Him than the fear of judgment alone (1 Jn. 4:18). Interestingly, the Lord Jesus taught more often about wise and foolish behavior than about what was blatantly right and wrong. It is obviously wise to do what God requires us to do and to abstain from what He forbids us to do; doing otherwise would be foolish. Christian liberty, however, pertains to the realm of debatable things and personal preferences, not to issues of evil or sin. Accordingly, Paul exhorts us to not judge one another in matters of liberty, but *"let every man be fully persuaded in his own mind"* (Rom. 14:5), *"for whatever is not of faith is sin"* (Rom. 14:23).

In the above verses Paul provides three principles that should guide our attitudes concerning judging the liberty of others. First, we are to accept those weaker in the faith. This means that we will not burden them with uneventful quarreling about areas of Christian liberty. It is not profitable to persuade those young in the faith into a particularly way of thinking about questionable matters before they have the maturity and time to work through the matter before the Lord, themselves.

Second, we are to have mutual forbearance with each other in the realm of Christian liberty. We realize that godly believers will not think the same way on questionable matters and we are willing to accept these non-doctrinal differences with patience and tolerance to ensure that Body life is not needlessly negatively impacted.

Third, Paul reminds us that only a master judges his own servants. Servants have no authority to judge each other. Our Master is quite capable of judging the motives and convictions of all that are His!

June 7 – Servants Do Not Judge Fellow Servants
Romans 14:4-8

Who are you to judge another's servant? To his own master he stands or falls. Indeed, he will be made to stand, for God is able to make him stand. One person esteems one day above another; another esteems every day alike. Let each be fully convinced in his own mind. He who observes the day, observes it to the Lord; and he who does not observe the day, to the Lord he does not observe it. He who eats, eats to the Lord, for he gives God thanks; and he who does not eat, to the Lord he does not eat, and gives God thanks. For none of us lives to himself, and no one dies to himself. For if we live, we live to the Lord; and if we die, we die to the Lord. Therefore, whether we live or die, we are the Lord's.

Paul forbade Christians from legislating special days, feast days, or Sabbaths and from forcing their personal convictions on others (Col. 2:16). Rather Paul says, *"Let every man be fully persuaded in his own mind"* about such things. Let us remember that Scripture only endorses one special day for the Church to regard; everything else originated in human vanity. The early Church dedicated the first day of the week for corporate worship and service (Acts 20:7). Moreover, it is wise to rest the body one day out of seven, which follows the pattern exemplified by God in the first workweek (Gen. 2:1-3).

Combining both features, we believe that it is honorable to God to rest our bodies and to worship Him together on Sunday. In this way, believers observe the Lord's Supper at least once a week and should continue doing so until entering into God's final rest in heaven. In the Church Age, there are no biblical holidays to observe. In fact, most of the traditional holidays that believers are absorbed with today distract from honoring the Lord Jesus as He has requested in Scripture.

Christians are to judge the behavior and doctrine of other professing Christians, but we are not to judge fellow believers in the areas of personal liberty, their motivation for or profitability of ministry, or whether they are actually saved; only the Lord knows the genuine quality of their faith. Jesus Christ bought us with a great price, His own blood. Hence, believers are dead to self; they are not to be driven by human traditions or selfish desires, or to issue egocentric judgments of others, but rather to behave in such a way that pleases their Savior, Jesus Christ.

June 8 – Christ Alone Will Judge His Servants (Part 1)
Romans 14:10-12

But why do you judge your brother? Or why do you show contempt for your brother? For we shall all stand before the judgment seat of Christ. For it is written: "As I live, says the Lord, every knee shall bow to Me, and every tongue shall confess to God." So then each of us shall give account of himself to God.

The Lord pays a fair wage to the unregenerate – the wages of sin is death (Rom. 6:23); this will ultimately occur at the Great White Throne judgment (Rev. 20). The Lord also rewards those believers who serve Him faithfully according to revealed truth (Rom. 10:2-3; 2 Cor. 5:10). Paul affirms that every believer will stand before the Lord to give an account of how he or she lived for Him. *The Judgment Seat of Christ* is not a judgment of salvation, but one of works. Good works will be amply rewarded and everything else will be burned up (1 Cor. 3:11-15). What was done by Christ through us (1 Cor. 3:11), done willingly (1 Cor. 9:17), done for the Lord with right motives (Col. 3:23-25), while not seeking the praise of others (Matt. 6:1-5) will be rewarded.

The *Judgment Seat of Christ* occurs immediately after the Church is raptured into heaven (1 Thess. 4:17). The Lord will have His reward with Him when He returns to the air for His Church (Rev. 22:12). In John's vision of things to come, we find the twenty-four elders (representing the redeemed from the earth; possibly including Old Testament saints) on thrones and wearing crowns before God's throne in heaven (Rev. 4:4). Afterwards, the Lord Jesus receives His title deed to all things from the hand of His Father; the Tribulation Period begins after He opens the first of seven seals (Rev. 6:1). After the Tribulation Period concludes seven years later, the Church returns to the earth with the Lord, who will establish His earthly kingdom (Rev. 19:7-16). Martyred Tribulation saints will experience glorification at that time and be rewarded for their faithfulness (Rev. 14:13, 20:4). A refined remnant of Israel will be restored to God at Christ's Second Advent (Zech. 12:10; Rom. 11:25). The Abrahamic covenant will be fulfilled.

Those in Christ have eternal life and a great inheritance reserved in Him. May we live each and every day by anticipating His sudden appearing to take us home to be with Him forever (1 Cor. 15:51-52).

Daily Devotions

June 9 – Christ Alone Will Judge His Servants (Part 2)
Romans 14:11-12

For we shall all stand before the judgment seat of Christ. For it is written: "As I live, says the Lord, every knee shall bow to Me, And every tongue shall confess to God." So then each of us shall give account of himself to God.

The *Judgment Seat of Christ* is also referred to as *the Day of Christ*, or *the Day of the Lord Jesus* which believers are to long for (1 Cor. 1:8, 5:5; Phil 1:6, 10, 2:16). *The Day of Christ* is not to be confused with *the Day of the Lord*, an Old Testament term to speak of divine judgment on earth and used in the New Testament to speak of the Tribulation Period through the millennial reign of Christ, the destruction of the earth, and the Great White Throne Judgment (1 Thess. 5:1-11; 2 Pet. 3:10). Paul clarifies both terms in 2 Thessalonians 2:1-10. Peter also spoke of a third day, *The Day of God*, which is the eternal state (2 Pet. 3:12).

The *Judgment Seat of Christ* is where the believer's works will be judged for reward or burned up (1 Cor. 3:11-15). Eternal glory has a weight to it (2 Cor. 4:17) that gives a believer an appreciation of heaven and a reflective glory of Christ. Our clothing in heaven reveals our rewarded righteous acts (Rev. 19:8): some saints will shine brighter than others (1 Cor. 15:41-42) and some may be ashamed (1 Jn. 2:28).

What types of rewards are given at the Judgment Seat of Christ? There are likely many, but five are specifically mentioned in Scripture:

1. The *Crown of Life*: given for patiently enduring trials (Jas. 1:12).
2. The *Crown of Rejoicing*: given for soul-winning (Phil. 4:1; 1 Thess. 2:19). *"He who wins souls is wise."*
3. The *Crown of Righteousness*: given to those who love Christ's appearing (2 Tim. 4:8).
4. The *Crown of Glory*: given to church elders who shepherd God's flock well (1 Pet. 5:4).
5. The *Incorruptible Crown*: given to those controlling the lusts of the flesh (1 Cor. 9:25).

These rewards enable saints to worship God in heaven. Revelation 4:11 speaks of saints casting their crowns before God's throne, yet the Greek word rendered "cast" is also translated "pour" (Rev. 12:15-16): Believers will have the opportunity to *pour out* worship to God forever.

June 10 – Make for Peace and Edify Each Other
Romans 14:19

Therefore let us pursue the things which make for peace and the things by which one may edify another.

Paul exhorts Christians not to pursue debatable activities which will promote disunity, contention and the like. Endeavor to maintain peace with others as much as possible (Rom. 12:18). It may be technically permissible for me to walk across the kitchen floor with muddy boots on, but it certainly will not make for peace with my wife. It would be best to sacrifice an extra minute of my time to remove my boots than to suffer potential wrath for my foolish liberty!

Paul exhorts the believers at Ephesus to endeavor *"to keep the unity of the Spirit in the bond of peace"* (Eph. 4:3). Only the Holy Spirit can create peace in a Christian home or in a gathering of God's people. Paul exhorts these Christians to work hard to keep intact what the Holy Spirit has labored to achieve. Sarcasm, teasing, name-calling, rude jesting, pointed jokes, and the like will only provoke the flesh and rob your home or local assembly of peace. Through the laying hold of the mind of Christ and maintaining His thinking, the Holy Spirit maintains peace among those who know Christ as Savior.

Scripture declares to us the mind of Christ and accordingly, how we should think about and serve others. If we behave like Christ would, then we would not unnecessarily rile believers to act in the flesh and stir up strife. Believers must be determined to bring Christ's thinking into every situation in lieu of the world's wisdom and methods. The carnal man wants to exalt himself, tear others down, and get even when wronged. If that is the philosophy applied in our homes and local churches, we will be a most miserable and fruitless people. May we heed Paul's warning to the saints in Galatia:

For you, brethren, have been called to liberty; only do not use liberty as an opportunity for the flesh, but through love serve one another. For all the law is fulfilled in one word, even in this: "You shall love your neighbor as yourself." But if you bite and devour one another, beware lest you be consumed by one another! (Gal. 5:13-15).

June 11 – Be Convinced Before You Act
Romans 14:22-23

Do you have faith? Have it to yourself before God. Happy is he who does not condemn himself in what he approves. But he who doubts is condemned if he eats, because he does not eat from faith; for whatever is not from faith is sin.

As believers, it is often difficult to work out the *gray* areas of our liberty. This may be a permissible activity, but is it wise for me to engage in it? The tenor of the Testaments is quite different on this subject matter. The Old Testament contained hundreds of laws that could never be fully obeyed (Gal. 3:10-12). The purpose of the Law was to show sin and to point the Jews to the solution – their Messiah Jesus Christ (Rom. 3:20; Gal. 3:24). In the New Testament, grace reigns on behalf of the believer; consequently, very few "dos and don'ts" are levied. God desires that love and not fear be the motive for service (1 Jn. 4:18). Obviously, what God says to do, we should do, and what God says that we should not do, we should not do. But, what about all those facets of living in which Scripture is silent? The Lord desires us to work out our salvation (i.e., sanctified living) with fear and trembling before Him (Phil. 2:12). He desires us to be holy priests.

The task then is to reduce the gray area of our liberty into appropriate personal conduct that neither offends one's conscience or the edicts of Scripture. The believer does not function in a fog of unclear notions, but becomes fully persuaded in his or her mind what is right and what is wrong behavior. This behavior glorifies God and does what is spiritually edifying for self and others; it does not stumble the lost or a weaker brother or make provision for the flesh to be master.

If we lack wisdom in a particular matter, James tells us to ask God for what we need and it will be supplied: *"If any of you lacks wisdom, let him ask of God, who gives to all liberally and without reproach, and it will be given to him"* (Jas. 1:5). God is patient and wants us to understand and be confirmed in our mind as to what is right and appropriate before we act. Satan is the high-pressure salesman that desires to catch us off guard and to cause us to act before we have had the opportunity to fully investigate Scripture, to pray for guidance, to obtain godly counsel, and to become settled in faith!

June 12 – If You Are Strong, Bear With the Weak
Romans 15:1-3

We then who are strong ought to bear with the scruples of the weak, and not to please ourselves. Let each of us please his neighbor for his good, leading to edification. For even Christ did not please Himself; but as it is written, "The reproaches of those who reproached You fell on Me."

Throughout much of Israel's history (as recorded in the Old Testament), we find only brief periods in which the entire nation was benefiting from God's presence among them. The conquest of Canaan, under Joshua's leadership, and the reigns of King David and King Solomon are a few of these special times of blessing and prosperity. However, most of Israel's history is marred by spiritual complacency, or idolatry and carnality, such that God's presence was not with His people. But God loved His covenant people too much to allow them to go their own way, so He chastened them, to make them realize that they would never be happier or more prosperous than remaining in communion with Him. These eras of discipline caused much misery, and even resulted in the dispersion and death of many Jews.

But even during these dismal times, God's energizing power was evident in faithful individuals, such that there was no need for the weakness of the vessels to be known. This reality was quite evident in whom God chose as leaders in the era of the Judges. When God's people depart from Him, He responds not by withholding a deliverer, but by supplying one in keeping with the spiritual condition requiring one. Such was the outshining of God's goodness through the apostles in the infancy of the Church Age. God chose common, uneducated men to marvelously confront the spiritual deadness of their day (Acts 4:13).

At that time the ecclesiastical testimony was clear, bright, and powerful and hordes of lost souls were added to the Church. Sadly, that is not the testimony of the Church today. Generally speaking, the modern church is settled into Laodicean complacency and materialism. It should then be no surprise that God may use those marred by imperfections or of less than admirable character, but yet have faith to accomplish feats of sovereign grace during this present day of ruined testimony. If God can use you as a testimony of His grace during this era of declension, be strong and strengthen what remains (Rev. 3:2)!

June 13 – Receive One Another
Romans 15:7

Therefore receive one another, just as Christ also received us, to the glory of God.

Believers, including new converts, relocating Christians, and traveling workers, who desired to be a part of a local church were added to the fellowship in various ways. For example, we read that Barnabas provided a word of testimony to the saints in Jerusalem on Paul's behalf so that he would be received by them (Acts 9:27). New converts, after being water baptized, were received into church fellowship (Acts 2:41-42). As believers moved from one location to another, they carried with them letters of introduction from their home church meeting in order to be received into this fellowship with another assembly (Acts 18:26-27; Rom. 16:1; Col. 4:7-8). Yet, a believer who was widely known to have a good testimony, such as Paul, would not need a letter of introduction to be received, as he would already be known by the church (2 Cor. 3:1-2).

Letters not only introduced believers to other meetings, but affirmed their faithfulness and their moral integrity. For example, Paul tells the believers in Rome to receive sister Phoebe from the church in Cenchrea and also notes that she was a helper of many, including Paul (Rom. 16:1-2). The believers at Ephesus wrote a letter of reception on behalf of Apollos to the saints at Corinth (Acts 18:27). Once he arrived at Corinth, he was received into the fellowship and *"greatly helped those who had believed."* Such believers with letters of introduction could be welcomed into the family life of the assembly without reservation. This biblical practice safeguards the assembly against wolves who want to secretly enter into the meeting and also provides information as to how incoming believers have been used previously to bless God's people.

The Greek word translated "receive" in Romans 15:7 is a present tense, middle voice, imperative mood verb. Believers are commanded to actively receive those who desire to be added to the local fellowship unless there is a good reason not to (e.g., he or she does not have a sound profession of Christ, or is not sound in doctrine or in life). The middle voice tells us that it is good for us to receive other believers into the body-life of the local church. We should desire everyone to be plugged into the privileges and responsibilities of church family life.

June 14 – It Is Your Duty!
Romans 15:25-27

But now I am going to Jerusalem to minister to the saints. For it pleased those from Macedonia and Achaia to make a certain contribution for the poor among the saints who are in Jerusalem. It pleased them indeed, and they are their debtors. For if the Gentiles have been partakers of their spiritual things, their duty is also to minister to them in material things.

Moses stressed the fair and kind treatment of beasts of burden: *"You shall not muzzle an ox while it treads out the grain"* (Deut. 25:4). An ox that was serving its master by trampling stalks of grain on the threshing floor in preparation for winnowing should be permitted to eat some of the stalks. Paul then refers to this verse to show that those laboring for the Lord were likewise worthy of financial support from those who had benefited from their preaching (1 Cor. 9:9).

The New Testament indicates that Church workers were employed by the Lord, not by local churches. Serving the Lord is not a career to be chosen, but a heavenly calling to be fulfilled! God enables the worker's ministry and is responsible for supporting them financially (Phil. 4:10-19; Col. 4:17). As He most often accomplishes this through His people, Paul emphasizes that those who had been spiritually blessed by ministry had a "duty" to support those who blessed them (Rom. 15:27). Examples of not muzzling the laboring ox in principle would include the support of:

- The evangelist (1 Cor. 9:14).
- A teaching elder (1 Tim. 5:17-18).
- A teacher in general (Gal. 6:6).
- A commended worker (1 Cor. 9:4).

At times workers may need to engage in secular employment for financial reasons (Acts 18:3), but nowhere in Scripture do we see them making public appeals for their own financial support. Commended workers serve the Lord (Acts 14:26), and thus the Lord wants His people to freely and amply provide for them in His name. This arrangement permits His workers to do His bidding and for the Lord to endorse their efforts by attending to their daily needs.

June 15 – Priscilla and Aquila
Romans 16:3-5

Greet Priscilla and Aquila, my fellow workers in Christ Jesus, who risked their own necks for my life, to whom not only I give thanks, but also all the churches of the Gentiles. Likewise greet the church that is in their house.

If you had Priscilla and Aquila's names in your address book, you would have many blotted out entries for them – they were on the move in the Lord's work. Many Jews settled in Greece after being expelled from Rome by the decree of Claudius in 49 A.D. Jewish immigrants from Rome such as Aquila, born in Pontus, and his wife Priscilla settled in Corinth (Acts 18:2-3). Paul first arrived at Corinth in the spring of 51 A.D. during his second missionary journey. He apparently lived with Priscilla and Aquila much of the time he was in Corinth, as they were fellow tent-makers by trade. After one and a half years, Paul set sail for Syria and took Priscilla and Aquila with him as far as Ephesus. They remained behind while Paul went back to his commending assembly at Antioch to give a report (Acts 18:18-22).

Paul returned to Ephesus in the spring of 53 A.D. (his third missionary journey). While in Ephesus, he wrote the believers at Corinth and passed on greetings from Priscilla and Aquila, who were still in Ephesus and had a church meeting in their home (1 Cor. 16:19). While in Ephesus, Aquila and Priscilla met a zealous open-air preacher, a Jew, named Apollos. The couple strengthened Apollos by teaching *"him the way of God more accurately."* In Acts 18, Luke breaks his practice of mentioning Priscilla's name first, probably to indicate Aquila's leadership role in discipling Apollos. Afterwards, the brethren from Ephesus sent Apollos to the assembly at Corinth (Acts 18:27-19:1). Claudius died about this time, so Priscilla and Aquila returned to Corinth to serve the Lord, possibly accompanying Apollos.

In about 57 A.D., Paul addresses Priscilla and Aquila, his *"fellow workers,"* who were then in Rome. Paul praises their faithfulness to him: *"who risked their own necks for my life, to whom not only I give thanks, but also all the churches of the Gentiles"* (Rom. 16:4). Early Church workers were not sedentary; the Lord's servants were mobile, versatile, and available to serve in whatever ministry they were led into.

June 16 – Note Those Who Cause Divisions
Romans 16:17

Now I urge you, brethren, note those who cause divisions and offenses, contrary to the doctrine which you learned, and avoid them.

There is much confusion concerning the meaning of the word "discipline," as we normally associate it with the administration of "pain." The concept that "pain" and "discipline" are synonymous falls miserably short of the biblical meaning of discipline. Biblical discipline includes a number of tools which can be used in order to affirm good behavior or to correct wrong or undesired behavior.

There is *instruction* which conveys truth in an understandable way so that God's people are not ignorant of God's will. There is *encouragement* to reward and reinforce right behavior when it occurs, especially in areas where the recipient tends to struggle. There is *exhortation*, which means "to come alongside and turn" – all believers need course corrections by those who love them. When someone becomes insubordinate or troublesome, they must be admonished by God's Word. *Admonition* literally means "to put in mind" and calls attention to a subject matter by giving a mild rebuke or warning.

Not every behavior will require stern reproof. *Correction*, a milder form of calling attention to foolish or lacking behavior, will be used much more often. The Greek word translated "correction" in 2 Timothy literally means to "straighten up again." A believer that is unruly is to be warned to submit to the church elders (1 Thess. 5:14). When a believer has transgressed either known boundaries or obvious ones, there should be a *rebuke*. Rebuke has the thought of "putting honor upon something" and is used often in the Gospels to describe the Lord's sharp reproof of a wrong attitude, often in a stressful situation.

The disorderly (2 Thess. 3:11, 14, 15) and those that are divisive (Rom. 16:17) or factious (Titus 3:10-11) are to be *avoided* completely (Acts 20:28-31). The purpose of shunning is to help another person see that he or she is out of fellowship with God, and therefore out of fellowship with His people. A believer engaging in gross sin and who has rejected Biblical reproof should be dealt with by *excommunication* (1 Cor. 5:11-13). This has the effect of delivering the rebellious to Satan for buffeting, possibly ending in that person's death (1 Tim. 1:20; 1 Cor. 5:5).

June 17 – Crushed Under Your Feet
Romans 16:19-20

For your obedience has become known to all. Therefore I am glad on your behalf; but I want you to be wise in what is good, and simple concerning evil. And the God of peace will crush Satan under your feet shortly. The grace of our Lord Jesus Christ be with you. Amen.

Paul invokes unusual imagery borrowed from a story in the book of Joshua to encourage believers to stand strong in the Lord against evil and false teachers. Joshua is a strong type of Jesus Christ. Even the meaning of both their names is the same – "Jehovah's salvation." After a spectacular military victory over the five armies of southern Canaan, it was time for their leaders to be judged. Joshua commanded that the five kings be brought out of their cave prison; then He addressed his captains: *"'Come near, put your feet on the necks of these kings.' And they drew near and put their feet on their necks. Then Joshua said to them, 'Do not be afraid, nor be dismayed; be strong and of good courage, for thus the Lord will do to all your enemies against whom you fight'"* (Josh. 10:24-25). After Joshua's captains stepped on the necks of the kings, Joshua slew all five kings with a sword and had their bodies hung on five trees as a public testimony of their defeat. The pressing of one's foot on the neck of an enemy was an Eastern custom to demonstrate complete victory. Spiritually speaking, Christ allows His followers to share in the victory that is only possible through Him. Likewise, it was Joshua, not the captains, who actually slew the enemy!

The overall picture before us has its prophetic origin in Genesis 3:15, which foretold that Christ would bruise the serpent's head. The Lord Jesus fulfilled this prophecy at Calvary (John 12:31-33). In Eden, God had said to the serpent (Satan), *"And I will put enmity between you and the woman, and between your seed and her Seed* [Christ]*; He shall bruise your head, and you shall bruise His heel"* (Gen. 3:15). At Calvary, Satan was defeated by the seed of the woman.

Paul may be referring to Christ's future victory over Satan and the wicked at His second advent to the earth (Rev. 19:17-20:3) or he may be speaking of the victory that a believer can have over evil today in Christ. As a believer relies on God's grace to accomplish holy living, the victory is won through Christ, and the devices of Satan are spoiled.

June 18 – He Who Glories, Glory in the Lord
1 Corinthians 1:27-31

But God has chosen the foolish things of the world to put to shame the wise, and God has chosen the weak things of the world to put to shame the things which are mighty; and the base things of the world and the things which are despised God has chosen, and the things which are not, to bring to nothing the things that are, that no flesh should glory in His presence. But of Him you are in Christ Jesus, who became for us wisdom from God – and righteousness and sanctification and redemption – that, as it is written, "He who glories, let him glory in the Lord."

The believers at Corinth were glorying in all sorts of things besides Christ, which was causing disunity and division in the assembly. By glorying in their favorite preachers or newfound liberty, they were actually robbing Christ of honor. Paul reminds them that every part of their salvation, including their sanctification, was in Him, *"you are in Christ Jesus."* Thus, all their bragging and glorying should be in Him.

Through the prophet Isaiah, the Lord had foretold how, when, and why He would cause Babylon's fall after using that nation to chasten His covenant people (Isa. 40-48). He did this that His people especially would realize that no idol could foreknow or accomplish such things and that He alone was the true God: *"For My own sake, for My own sake, I will do it; for how should My name be profaned? And **I will not give My glory to another"** (Isa. 48:11). God's past dealings with Israel and His desire to honor His own name should prompt believers today to consider what we do and say – let us not rob God of the glory due His name either. He is still the One in control and is accomplishing His purposes in us for His own honor and glory.

God continues to prompt our admiration and worship by using weak and foolish things (including people) to confound what is powerful and wise by secular standards. Understanding that without Christ we can do nothing (John 15:5), but in Christ we can do all things (Phil. 4:13) should keep believers from glorying in themselves. Any and all praise must be the Lord's. When we glory in ourselves, we follow Lucifer's example and act like his children, which God is determined to bring to nothing.

June 19 – You Are Carnal
1 Corinthians 3:3-4

For you are still carnal. For where there are envy, strife, and divisions among you, are you not carnal and behaving like mere men? For when one says, "I am of Paul," and another, "I am of Apollos," are you not carnal?

The Church at Corinth was plagued by petty divisions and hero worship. Some believers had their favorite preachers and were apparently arguing over the matter (1 Cor. 1:12). Paul exhorts them:

I plead with you, brethren, by the name of our Lord Jesus Christ, that you all speak the same thing, and that there be no divisions among you, but that you be perfectly joined together in the same mind and in the same judgment (1 Cor. 1:10).

The divisions among them had resulted because believers had become earthly focused instead of being heavenly minded. Paul calls them "carnal." This church had a number of doctrinal and church order problems, but Paul begins his corrective ministry by affirming the headship of Christ in the Church. In fact, he refers to the Lordship of Christ some six times in the first ten verses of 1 Corinthians.

Much of the division within the Church would be resolved if believers kept focused on Christ's manifold perfections and not on the imperfections of others. He is Lord alone, and all other believers have an equal standing as "brethren," a term which includes the "sisteren" (Matt. 23:8; Gal. 3:28). Accordingly, let us not exalt men to a higher rank than what Scripture permits.

Our religious pride, condescending attitudes, and fleshly tactics merely ensure that God is opposing our endeavors, no matter how lofty we think our intentions are. How can God empower us to serve Him, when we engage in the very behavior He hates – pride and sowing discord among the brethren (Prov. 6:16, 19)? We do well to remember that *"God resists the proud, but gives grace to the humble"* (Jas. 4:6).

However sweet the word may sound, any sectarian boasting is but the babbling of a babe. The divisions in the Church are due to no other cause than to lack of love and walking after the flesh.

— Watchman Nee

173

June 20 – Laboring With God
1 Corinthians 3:7-9

So then neither he who plants is anything, nor he who waters, but God who gives the increase. Now he who plants and he who waters are one, and each one will receive his own reward according to his own labor. For we are God's fellow workers; you are God's field, you are God's building.

The believers at Corinth were carnally touting their favorite preachers in a divisive way; they had forgotten the bigger picture of ministry altogether. It is not the particular laborer that matters in the work of the Lord, but rather that the Lord is laboring with His people. To confront this dangerous sectarianism, Paul reminds the Corinthians that all believers are important and are especially equipped to serve God. Believers are tools in God's hands. Saints labor for the Lord, but it is He who blesses their efforts to further His purposes.

The Jews had discovered many times throughout their history that without the Lord they were helpless, but with the Lord, even giants could not stand against them. Paul uses a horticulture illustration to recognize this same condition of service in the Church Age. While God uses some to till, others to plant, others to water, and others to reap, it is He who gives the harvest; the laborers alone cannot produce anything.

It is natural for us to boast of our temporal accomplishments, but this is not profitable for eternity. May we remember that if the Lord is not in the work – we are wasting our time and resources! Conversely, when we are in the will and strength of God, *"we are more than conquerors through Him who loved us"* (Rom. 8:37). Also, let us remember that *isms* tend to create *schisms* in the Body of Christ, so let us not be followers of men, lest the work of God suffer through needless disunity.

The Lord reminded His disciples at His ascension that though He was departing from them, He would still continue laboring with them (Mark 16:19-20). We do not labor for the kingdom alone or in vain, for it is Christ's work, and He labors with us to achieve it. We are His eyes to discern the needs of others and His hands to serve them; *"we are God's fellow workers."* Being yoked with Christ ensures that all God wants us to accomplish for the honor of His Son's name is doable!

June 21 – Stewards Must Be Found Faithful
1 Corinthians 4:1-2

Let a man so consider us, as servants of Christ and stewards of the mysteries of God. Moreover it is required in stewards that one be found faithful.

In a coming day, each of us will have to give a stewardship account to the Lord. How did we use our time, resources, and spiritual gifts to further His kingdom? Here are some ideas to improve our stewardship:

1. Sacrifice the *Fluff of Life* – purge what is robbing your time (e.g., sports amusements, gaming, etc.). The permissible must not replace the best.

2. Prioritize and Cut – stick to your calling, learn to say "no," and put boundaries on new activities in order to stay effective in ministry.

3. Minimize Travel Time – accomplish as much communication as possible through email, phone calls, texting, video calls, etc. rather than traveling, which expends much time and resources.

4. Do Not Waste Time Entertaining Goats – Christ's teachings are to be committed to faithful believers who will in turn teach others (2 Tim. 2:2). New converts require special care but there should be fruitfulness in time. If Satan can keep us busy with his people – he will.

5. Improve Organization – develop an efficient filing system of storing past emails, messages, letters, studies, spreadsheets, receipts, etc. This will reduce time in tax preparations, to responding to questions already answered previously, or in future ministry and study development.

6. Develop Teaching Materials – if you are a teacher, completely develop electronic copies of both questions and answers for your students so that repeat studies in the future will require minimal preparation.

7. Minimize Social Media and Unnecessary Phone Calls and Messaging – These means of communication can waste a lot of time when a brief email or text message could have sufficed. We really do not need to know what our friends ate for lunch – stick to what is pertinent info.

8. Limit Distractions – set aside study time without distractions (the early morning hours are a great time of the day to spend time with the Lord).

June 22 – You Have Only What You Received
1 Corinthians 4:6-7

Now these things, brethren, I have figuratively transferred to myself and Apollos for your sakes, that you may learn in us not to think beyond what is written, that none of you may be puffed up on behalf of one against the other. For who makes you differ from another? And what do you have that you did not receive? Now if you did indeed receive it, why do you boast as if you had not received it?

The Corinthian believers had a tendency to hero-ize certain teachers within the assembly and also itinerant preachers (1 Cor. 1:10-13). This practice of favoring certain ministers and being critical of others was fostered in pride, so the result was division in the church. What is of the flesh will always work to undermine God's best for His people!

Paul transferred the issue to a simplified illustration involving him and Apollos to ensure the Corinthians understood his point. He then reminded them that he and Apollos, and indeed every minister of Christ, received their ability and calling from God. Both were given a specific ministry to fulfill and the divine enablement to perform it. Since different teachers were given various abilities and ministries according to God's will, why should we compare God's servants, especially to their detriment? If all we have comes from God, who are we to question what He gives or why He gives it?

Our carnal flesh yearns to compare what we have to what others have in order to justify dissatisfaction in what God has given. We even compare the abilities, the assets, and the ministries of other people to suggest that God did a better job expressing His wisdom with one person than another person. We are to compare what we do to Scripture in order to align our lives with God's will, but comparing believers' giftedness or the ministries they have been chosen to do is demeaning to God. We should be thankful for what He does give!

Without Christ, the believer is nothing, has nothing, and can do nothing for God. But in Him we inherit all things (Rom. 8:17), rule over all things (2 Tim. 2:12), and can do all things that God endorses (Phil. 4:13). Let us maintain this big-picture reality and not squabble about distinctions that have no bearing on furthering the cause of Christ. *"He who glories, let him glory in the Lord"* (1 Cor. 1:31).

June 23 – Fools for Christ
1 Corinthians 4:8-13

You are already full! You are already rich! You have reigned as kings without us – and indeed I could wish you did reign, that we also might reign with you! For I think that God has displayed us, the apostles, last, as men condemned to death; for we have been made a spectacle to the world, both to angels and to men. We are fools for Christ's sake, but you are wise in Christ! We are weak, but you are strong! You are distinguished, but we are dishonored! To the present hour we both hunger and thirst, and we are poorly clothed, and beaten, and homeless. And we labor, working with our own hands. Being reviled, we bless; being persecuted, we endure; being defamed, we entreat. We have been made as the filth of the world, the offscouring of all things until now.

Because the apostles were abiding by Christ's callings for their lives, they often suffered: hunger, thirst, inadequate clothing, homelessness, ridicule, and various persecutions including beatings. Hence, worldlings considered them to be the filth and scum of the earth. In contrast, many of the Corinthians believers were rich, full, and prospered as kings because they were not submitting to Christ's calling for their lives. There would be a future day when all believers would enjoy ruling and reigning with Christ in His kingdom, but now was not the time for such things. They were to be Christ's representatives in the world, not to enjoy the world's pleasantries by neglecting their calling.

The Greek word for Church is *ekklesia*, which means "called out ones." The Church is a company of believers who are *kaleo* (called) – *ek* (out of or from) something. But what are God's people called out from? Randy Amos explains, and may we live accordingly:

- They are called *out of* the world's thinking and system (John 15:19)
- They are called *out of* the perishing nations (Acts 15:14)
- They are delivered *from* this present age (Gal. 1:4)
- They are delivered *from* the power of Satan's darkness (Col. 1:13)
- They will be physically delivered *out of* this world into heaven (2 Cor. 5:8; Rev. 3:10)
- They are commanded to come *out of* the wicked Babylonian system (Rev. 18:4)[18]

June 24 – When You Are Gathered Together
1 Corinthians 5:4

In the name of our Lord Jesus Christ, when you are gathered together, along with my spirit, with the power of our Lord Jesus Christ.

Although the local church gathers together for various reasons (Acts 2:42), all of its meetings possess a central theme – we are to gather in the name of the Lord Jesus and, hence, in the authority of that Name. How did Paul assist the church at Corinth to overcome their divisions and cliques? In his first epistle to them, he affirmed the Lordship of Christ six times in the first ten verses and then repeatedly referred to Christ's authority in the Church: *"In the name of our Lord Jesus Christ, when ye are gathered together"* (1 Cor. 5:4). Whether it is a simple feast of bread and wine to remember Him and to publicly proclaim the value of His death, or around His Word to learn His mind, or before His mercy seat to tell Him of our needs and request grace to fulfill our high-calling in Christ – we meet with Him and in His name. The Lord and His presence alone draw us to all the church meetings. I want to be at every meeting because the Lord will be at every meeting. When a believer justifies careless absenteeism, in effect he or she is casting a vote to close down the assembly and remove Christ's name from the community! On the subject of gathering in Christ's name, C. H. Mackintosh writes:

> Of the many favors conferred upon us by our ever-gracious Lord, one of the very highest is the privilege of being present in the assembly of His beloved people, where He has recorded His name. We may assert with all possible confidence that every true lover of Christ will delight to be found where He has promised to be. We may rest assured that anyone who willfully neglects the assembly is in a cold, dead, dangerous state of soul. To neglect the assembling of ourselves is to take the first step on the inclined plane that leads down to the total abandonment of Christ and His precious interests.[19]

The Lord extended this promise to His disciples: *"For where two or three are gathered together in My name, I am there in the midst of them"* (Matt. 18:20). Wherever the Lord is at is where His people should long to be also.

June 25 – Leaven Must Be Purged
1 Corinthians 5:6-8

Your glorying is not good. Do you not know that a little leaven leavens the whole lump? Therefore purge out the old leaven, that you may be a new lump, since you truly are unleavened. For indeed Christ, our Passover, was sacrificed for us. Therefore let us keep the feast, not with old leaven, nor with the leaven of malice and wickedness, but with the unleavened bread of sincerity and truth.

Leaven, in Scripture, speaks of sin, corruption, or evil doctrine (Matt. 13:33; 1 Cor. 5:8). Interestingly, the first mention of leaven in the Bible describes the simple meal Lot's wife prepared for the two visiting angels (Gen. 19:3). The unleavened bread stood in sharp contrast to Lot's "leavened" life (speaking of his failure to separate from worldliness). The next reference to leaven in the Bible relates to the unleavened bread which was to be a part of the Passover Feast (Ex. 12).

Only unleavened bread was eaten on the night of the Passover, but a further restriction was observed during the following seven days of the feast of Unleavened Bread; there was not to be any leaven in any of the Jewish homes (Ex. 12:15, 19). Though the Israelites were immersed in a pagan culture, its filth and corruption should not be in their homes. Though they were in the world, they were not to be of the world. Those Jews eating the Passover Lamb to escape God's wrath in Egypt must maintain an unleavened life. Those partaking of Christ for salvation in the Church Age are also to live a consecrated life to Him.

The Corinthian believers were boasting of a brother in their assembly who was engaging in sexual sin with his step-mother. They thought such things were now permissible in grace, but Paul tells them that they were erroneously "puffed up" over the matter. This is what leaven within us does – it "puffs up" (causes us to glory in what offends God). Paul warns the Corinthians to not fellowship with someone identifying with Christ, but was not in fellowship with the Lord because of stubborn sin. A little leaven leavens the whole lump of dough, so false doctrine or ongoing sinful behavior has a cascading effect that can spread throughout the assembly if unchecked. If sin in the Church is not dealt a deadly blow by God's people, it will thoroughly corrupt all who do not esteem holiness as necessary for maintaining fellowship with Christ.

June 26 – No Fellowship With Believers in Ongoing Sin
1 Corinthians 5:9-11

I wrote to you in my epistle not to keep company with sexually immoral people. Yet I certainly did not mean with the sexually immoral people of this world, or with the covetous, or extortioners, or idolaters, since then you would need to go out of the world. But now I have written to you not to keep company with anyone named a brother, who is sexually immoral, or covetous, or an idolater, or a reviler, or a drunkard, or an extortioner – not even to eat with such a person.

Paul's edict to the assembly at Corinth reflects God's passion for holy living. Believers are commanded to abstain from fornication, which is any sexual relationship outside the bounds of marriage: *"For this is the will of God, even your sanctification, that ye should abstain from fornication"* (1 Thess. 4:3, KJV). If married, a man is to have only his wife and the wife only her husband; there is to be no sexual lusting after, or "touching," of another person for sensual reasons (1 Cor. 7:1). God's judgment falls not only on fornicators, but also upon those who *"approve of those who practice"* fornication (Rom. 1:32). Believers are not to even look on those committing fornication with any sense of approval. It is this *looking* upon sexual perversions to achieve pleasure that has become a scourge to our society.

Pornography and *porneia* rendered "fornication" are closely associated in meaning. *Porneia* speaks of all forms of sexual impurity and wanton behavior. The word initially meant "to act the harlot" but later evolved to mean "to indulge in unlawful lust." *Porneia* describes various types of sins: premarital sex (1 Cor. 7:1-2), physical adultery (Matt. 19:9), any form of unchaste conduct (1 Cor. 6:13, 18), harlotry or prostitution (Rev. 2:20-21), homosexuality (Jude 7), and spiritual adultery (Rev. 14:8, 17:4). When sins are listed in the New Testament, fornication normally tops the list (Col. 3:5). Besides hurting others, fornication is a grievous sin that afflicts one's own body (1 Cor. 6:18).

All sin grieves God, but the devastating nature of sexual immorality is why the fornicating man at Corinth was to be excommunicated. Moreover, believers are not to have any casual contact with any professing Christian who is in unrepentant sin. This clause did not apply to the lost, as contact with them is needed to share the gospel.

June 27 – The Church Should Judge Itself
1 Corinthians 6:1-4

Dare any of you, having a matter against another, go to law before the unrighteous, and not before the saints? Do you not know that the saints will judge the world? And if the world will be judged by you, are you unworthy to judge the smallest matters? Do you not know that we shall judge angels? How much more, things that pertain to this life? If then you have judgments concerning things pertaining to this life, do you appoint those who are least esteemed by the church to judge?

Under the Law, any Jew having a controversy or an offense to be judged would have never thought about bringing it before a Gentile tribunal. Rather, it was to be heard by the priests and appointed judges of Israel (Deut. 16:18-22). Jehovah was in the midst of His people, thus it would have been insulting to Him for His people to ask Gentile pagans, who did not know Him or His Law, to judge their grievances.

Paul affirms a similar protocol for believers in the Church Age. Christians were not to take each other into Gentile courts to resolve their differences; rather, they were to submit to the judgment of the wise among them and to the elders of the church (1 Cor. 6:1-9). Paul reminded the Corinthians that it was much better to be willing to be defrauded by another believer (to part with temporal things) than to disdain the name of the Lord Jesus Christ in secular courts of law.

To enhance his point, the apostle reminds his brethren at Corinth that in a coming day they will "judge the world" and "judge the angels." Why then would they want to take each other to a secular court for judgments – such mundane matters were minuscule in comparison to the eternal matters they would be judging under Christ's authority in His Kingdom. At the Great White Throne judgment, all of the wicked, including the angels, will be judged by Christ and cast in the Lake of Fire. Believers will take part in that judgment process. The believer has a bright future in Christ! Besides the opportunity to praise and worship the Lord with unhindered affections and unfailing strength, the believer also rules and reigns with Christ, judges the wicked with Christ, and inherits all things with Christ (Rev. 21:7). Being with Christ ensures that heaven will be a wonderful place to spend eternity. Being heavenly minded now supplies the proper perspective for living as we should.

June 28 – Such Were Some of You
1 Corinthians 6:9-11

Do you not know that the unrighteous will not inherit the kingdom of God? Do not be deceived. Neither fornicators, nor idolaters, nor adulterers, nor homosexuals, nor sodomites, nor thieves, nor covetous, nor drunkards, nor revilers, nor extortioners will inherit the kingdom of God. And such were some of you. But you were washed, but you were sanctified, but you were justified in the name of the Lord Jesus and by the Spirit of our God.

Any sexual relation other than between a husband and wife is referred to as fornication in the Bible. This is why Paul says *"to avoid fornication, let every man have his own wife"* (1 Cor. 7:2). Fornication then includes adultery, pre-marital relationships, homosexuality (e.g., sodomy), bestiality, etc. Under the Law, any Jew engaging in these sexual sins was to be put to death (Lev. 20:10-13), except for those engaging in pre-marital sex who were to marry (Deut. 22:29).

When it comes to God's standard of purity, nothing has changed in the New Testament; the only difference is that expedient punishment for sexual sins is not demanded by God. Such sins are still offensive to God and will be punished, but not by immediate death. To say that the New Testament does not condemn fornication is absurd (1 Cor. 6:13, 18; 1 Thess. 4:5). Paul and John both confirm that those engaging in such sin will not go to heaven, but will be cast in the Lake of Fire (Eph. 5:3-5; Rev. 21:8). God is offended when people exchange divinely revealed truth for a lie; He responds by turning them over to their own reprobate thinking; homosexuality was a primary behavior that resulted when God removed His convicting influence (Rom. 1:21-28).

Some at Corinth had been saved out of all kinds of sinful behaviors including gross immorality. Being new creations in Christ meant that they could not continue in sin (1 Jn. 3:9), thus Paul says, *"such were some of you."* The Greek verb translated *"were washed"* is in the middle voice meaning that the Corinthians freely chose to trust in the gospel message and be washed clean by the blood of Christ. The verbs rendered "sanctified" and "justified" are in the passive voice, meaning that God responded to their faith by doing only what He can do – justifying them in Christ and using them for His glory. Praise the Lord!

June 29 – Can I Be Mastered by It?
1 Corinthians 6:12

All things are lawful for me, but all things are not helpful. All things are lawful for me, but I will not be brought under the power of any.

The Mosaic Law could never be fully obeyed no matter how hard one tried to be compliant (Gal. 3:10-12). This was by design. God wanted His covenant people to understand that they could not approach Him, their holy God, by merely doing good works. No amount of good deeds could ever compensate for one sin and no one can continue in well-doing; hence, all of us stand before God condemned. The purpose of the Law was to show sin and point the guilty to God's only solution for salvation, the Lord Jesus (Rom. 3:20; Gal. 3:24).

Through Christ, grace is extended to believers to work out the questionable areas of life with fear and trembling before the Lord (Phil. 2:12). Scripture refers to this privilege and responsibility as Christian "liberty." Believers are to heed the guidelines and warnings of Scripture, glean from the good examples of godly saints in Scripture, and also learn to avoid the mistakes and failures of those who missed the mark. Obviously biblical commands are nonnegotiable; we must do what God commands and avoid doing what He prohibits.

Paul reminds the believers at Corinth that though there were many permissible activities, not all would be profitable for them to engage in. In fact, some could enslave them. It would be far better never to start what you cannot stop later. Many begin various forms of drug use to feel good, but after they become addicted, they take drugs not to feel bad. Sometimes addiction is referred to as "substance abuse," but such debilitating circumstances abuse the person, not the substance. Many believers today are mastered by activities which are not inherently evil, but have become enslaved by them nonetheless: gaming, social media, amusements, sports, education – the list is endless. Sadly, our time, resources, and affections are wasted on what has no value for eternity.

The Christian's only goal in life is to give our Savior honor and glory through complete submission to His will. To achieve this goal, the believer must be liberated from all controlling hindrances. In this way, our God has a visible means to express His lovingkindness from heavenly realms into an evil and cursed world, which needs to see Him.

June 30 – Do Not Live for What Is Temporary
1 Corinthians 6:13

Foods for the stomach and the stomach for foods, but God will destroy both it and them. Now the body is not for sexual immorality but for the Lord, and the Lord for the body.

In this section, Paul implores the believers at Corinth to sanctify their temples (their individual bodies) unto the Lord. He has just told them to be careful not to be mastered by permissible activities that rob from them, instead of edifying them in the Lord. Now he warns them about focusing their interests on temporal things rather than living for what counts for eternity. He uses the illustration of food and the stomach to make his point.

God has wonderfully designed our stomachs to digest food in order to supply needed nutrients and fuel to keep our bodies healthy. Likewise, the Lord has created foods for us to eat that our stomachs can digest. But food is a temporary thing and only has a brief benefit. Yet, eating proper foods and maintaining a well-balanced diet enables us to keep our bodies fit for God's use. In this manner what was temporary in nature provides the opportunity to accomplish something eternal in nature, something that God values. Paul's point is that we need food to live, but if we live for food, we will be a poor testimony for Christ. The self-disciplined life is a beautiful testimony of the Savior who lived such a life during His own earthly sojourn.

Generally speaking, it has been my observation through the years that what and how one eats is a litmus test of how well that person keeps the carnal impulses of his or her flesh in check. If a person shows no discernment about what they eat (either an out-of-balance diet or one that favors things like grease and sugar), or gluttony is observed, that is usually an indication of a weak character. Yearning for temporal thrills is rarely limited to one aspect of indulgence. I have watched men in past years gorge themselves with food, only to learn later that they were also engaging in secret sins which eventually destroyed their marriages, families, and even assemblies. Overeating and not properly exercising one's body may seem like trivial things, but really these give evidence of a deeper disposition which devalues eternal things. Let us not live for fleeting thrills, but for what has lasting value to God.

July 1 – Do Not Defile God's Temple
1 Corinthians 6:18-20

Flee sexual immorality. Every sin that a man does is outside the body, but he who commits sexual immorality sins against his own body. Or do you not know that your body is the temple of the Holy Spirit who is in you, whom you have from God, and you are not your own? For you were bought at a price; therefore glorify God in your body and in your spirit, which are God's.

The New Testament speaks of several types of temples that were important to God. Besides Jehovah's temple in Jerusalem, built under Zerubbabel's leadership in the sixth century B.C., the Lord also spoke of His own body as a temple: *"Destroy this temple, and in three days I will raise it up"* (John 2:19). In Himself He had the authority and power to lay down His life and raise it up again (John 10:17-18).

At Pentecost, the Church was formed when all believers were baptized into Christ by the Holy Spirit to create a spiritual Body called the Church. Because God lives within believers, Scripture refers to this mysterious spiritual Body as God's living temple on earth (1 Tim. 3:15; 1 Pet. 2:5). Accordingly, all believer-priests compose the temple of God and may lift up worship and living sacrifices to God wherever and whenever they desire (Rom. 12:1; Rev. 1:6).

Sometimes the temple of the Lord relates to the testimony of believers gathered at one location – the local church (1 Cor. 3:16-17), which is to be a lampstand of God to a lost world (Rev. 2:5). However, in the above verses, Paul exhorts individual believers to understand that their bodies are temples of the Holy Spirit and that they should render their whole self in consecrated service for the glory of God.

The Lord Jesus cleansed the temple in Jerusalem twice during His public ministry, once at the beginning (John 2:14-17) and once at the end of His ministry (Matt. 21:12). Man had turned God's house of prayer into a place of commerce and corruption and the Lord keenly felt the offense. In John's account we read, *"When He had made a whip of cords, He drove them all out of the temple, with the sheep and the oxen, and poured out the changers' money and overturned the tables."* Remembering that the Lord Jesus is in you, dear believer (Rom. 8:9-10), what might He desire to drive out of His temple today?

July 2 – Knowledge Puffs Up, but Love Edifies
1 Corinthians 8:1-3

Now concerning things offered to idols: We know that we all have knowledge. Knowledge puffs up, but love edifies. And if anyone thinks that he knows anything, he knows nothing yet as he ought to know. But if anyone loves God, this one is known by Him. Therefore concerning the eating of things offered to idols, we know that an idol is nothing in the world, and that there is no other God but one.

Paul now introduces a new subject concerning the sacrifice of personal liberty (choosing wise behavior in permissible things) for the good of another believer. He begins by saying we (believers) know that an idol is nothing; it is merely a figment of man's fallen imagination, for there is only one God. This was a fact they all knew to be true. The specific situation he is addressing relates to marketplace practices in a city with a pagan temple. Idols do not eat much, so the good quality meat offered to idols was sold in the market at a reduced price. So believers understanding that there is only one God could buy this good low-cost meat with a good conscience, but they should not serve it to those who might be offended by it or boast about it. This action, for example, might stumble new believers who may have just been saved out of idolatry and did not fully understand their liberty in Christ.

Paul's point is that truth alone is not sufficient to guide our behavior; we need to show each other the love of Christ while still holding to the truth. Love without truth is hypocrisy and the truth without love is brutality; both virtues must guide what we do. In chapter 5, the Corinthians had love without the truth; they showed tolerance to a brother in gross sin and were "puffed up" about it. Paul now warns them that just having the truth and not love will cause them to be "puffed up" in pride also. This is what leaven does, it puffs up, and acting in truth without love (i.e., doing what we know will not benefit others) carries with it the stench of pride (i.e., self-promotion).

If someone has a spot of skin cancer on his or her arm, a surgeon could remove the patient's entire arm or the surgeon could skillfully remove only the malignant part. Both actions remove the dangerous threat, but the repercussions of the former action leaves the patient disabled for life. Executing truth at any cost is disguised cruelty!

July 3 – A Brother Is More Important Than Food
1 Corinthians 8:9-13

But beware lest somehow this liberty of yours become a stumbling block to those who are weak. For if anyone sees you who have knowledge eating in an idol's temple, will not the conscience of him who is weak be emboldened to eat those things offered to idols? And because of your knowledge shall the weak brother perish, for whom Christ died? But when you thus sin against the brethren, and wound their weak conscience, you sin against Christ. Therefore, if food makes my brother stumble, I will never again eat meat, lest I make my brother stumble.

In Paul's day, the consciences of some Christians were offended when other believers ate meat that had been offered to idols. This was usually high-quality, secondhand meat available at a reasonable price in the marketplace. Paul writes: *"I know and am convinced by the Lord Jesus that there is nothing unclean of itself; but to him who considers anything to be unclean, to him it is unclean"* (Rom. 14:14). This indicates it would not be a sin to eat meat that had been offered to idols if one had a clear conscience in the matter (Rom. 14:23). However, whatever the believer's persuasion might be on the matter of proper healthy diet, or economical purchases, it should be understood to be an area of liberty. Such liberties are to be forfeited, if need be, to avoid offending others unnecessarily who do not understand such things.

This means we do not cause division by promoting our alimentary convictions among those who see things differently (Rom. 14:1-3), and that we gladly yield our rights if there is the potential for stumbling another believer by our eating and drinking. Our meal times should be marked by thanksgiving and joyful fellowship, not unprofitable opinions and meddling pride. The dietary laws issued to the Jews were specific to them; these were to accentuate their need for holiness in all areas of life, for holy Jehovah resided with them. Thus, at that juncture of time, non-compliance with these specific "dos and don'ts" would be a sin. However, in the Church Age, the matter of what a believer eats is not a moral issue, but rather one of wisdom. The believer would be wise to eat what is good for the body and likewise foolish to ingest or drink what is harmful to the body. A believer would also be wise not to eat or drink what might offend others who are of a different conviction.

187

July 4 – Deserving of Financial Support
1 Corinthians 9:3-7

My defense to those who examine me is this: Do we have no right to eat and drink? Do we have no right to take along a believing wife, as do also the other apostles, the brothers of the Lord, and Cephas? Or is it only Barnabas and I who have no right to refrain from working? Who ever goes to war at his own expense? Who plants a vineyard and does not eat of its fruit? Or who tends a flock and does not drink of the milk of the flock?

Some at Corinth did not believe Paul was a true apostle of Christ, or at least he was an inferior one to the apostles that were Christ's original disciples. This view was further bolstered by the observation that Paul and Barnabas (itinerant apostles) behaved quite differently than the apostles at Jerusalem. These men were apparently married and were well supported financially. The lives of Paul and Barnabas, on the other hand, could not be characterized by these features.

Although Paul did receive gifts from various individuals and churches, he was a tentmaker by trade, and at times, had to withdraw from ministry to labor with his own hands to supply his needs. Some of the Corinthian believers believed that this reality proved that Paul was not really an apostle; otherwise, the Lord would support his ministry, such that he would not need to suspend it.

However, Paul corrects their conclusion by saying that he and Barnabas had the right to receive support, to marry, to have a family, but had chosen not to exercise such privileges, lest their ministry suffer from doing so. They were itinerant preachers that often suffered rejection, harsh living conditions, various persecutions, and were under the constant threat of death for preaching Christ. Would that be a good living situation for a wife and children? To ensure that their motives for ministry were not questioned, lest the gospel message be hindered, they chose not to demand any compensation from those they were serving. They deserved recompense for their labors, just as a soldier who wars, a man who plants a vineyard, and a shepherd caring for sheep deserved wages, fruit, and milk, respectively. If it is appropriate for these earthly occupations to receive support, how much more so for the Lord's servants who engaged in heavenly and eternal service for God.

188

July 5 – Determined Not to Hinder the Gospel
1 Corinthians 9:11-12

If we have sown spiritual things for you, is it a great thing if we reap your material things? If others are partakers of this right over you, are we not even more? Nevertheless we have not used this right, but endure all things lest we hinder the gospel of Christ.

As laboring apostles of Christ, Paul and Barnabas deserved financial support from the church at Corinth, but to ensure that their motives for preaching would not be questioned, they did not demand compensation for their ministry. It was more important to the apostles that the gospel message be shared blamelessly in Corinth, than knowing where their next meal was coming from. They worked for the Lord and He was responsible to provide for their needs. If the Corinthian believers were not moved to supply their necessities, the Lord would move others to do so in order for the work to continue.

As shown from the apostles' example, there will be occasions that require us to sacrifice our liberty in Christ in order to remain blameless, lest the unregenerate are hindered from hearing the gospel message (1 Cor. 10:33). We also do not want to engage in any behavior that would cause the lost to blaspheme the Lord's name. Here are a few ways that this could occur: First, if we claim to be a child of God, but then do not keep His commandments, we cause children of the devil to blaspheme God (Rom. 2:23-24). Second, if we engage in personal conduct that even God's enemies regard as immoral, God's name is dragged through the dirt (2 Sam. 12:13-14). Third, if Christian husbands and fathers do not provide for their families' needs, they are considered worse than pagans by those observing (1 Tim. 5:8). Fourth, if wives and mothers do not love their husbands and children, and keep their homes in order, the word of God is blasphemed (1 Tim. 5:14; Tit. 2:4-5). Fifth, if Christians express disrespect for those in authority over them, this causes God's name to be blasphemed (1 Tim. 6:1).

Whether the matter is sacrificing our Christian liberty or living in a way that defies the Lordship of Christ, the unregenerate are watching. We should not do anything that would stumble the lost from hearing the good news message, or even worse, cause them to blaspheme the One who entrusted us with sharing it with them.

July 6 – Fulfill Your Calling Willingly
1 Corinthians 9:16-18

For if I preach the gospel, I have nothing to boast of, for necessity is laid upon me; yes, woe is me if I do not preach the gospel! For if I do this willingly, I have a reward; but if against my will, I have been entrusted with a stewardship. What is my reward then? That when I preach the gospel, I may present the gospel of Christ without charge, that I may not abuse my authority in the gospel.

Christ had assigned Paul a task to do, preach the gospel message to the Gentiles, and he was going to do it to the best of his ability in the grace that God provided. If for the love of Christ, Paul obeyed his calling and did what he was required to do, then he would receive a heavenly reward, but if he neglected his calling, he knew that he would be chastened by God for doing so: *"Woe is me if I do not preach the gospel."* Because of this great accountability in ministry, Paul was determined not to charge for his service, but to rely on the Lord to supply all His needs. He knew the best way to fulfill his calling and not suffer loss at the Judgment Seat of Christ was to remain blameless.

God likewise equips believers today with the resources needed to worship and serve Him. First of all, the Christian is indwelt by the Holy Spirit (1 Cor. 6:19), Who leads and guides us. Second, in Christ we possess all spiritual blessings in heavenly places (Eph. 1:3), which enable us to manifest the character of Christ to the world. A believer can, by faith, lay hold of all the love, grace, and peace he or she desires to exhibit in his or her life. Third, God supplies physical resources to those who desire to willingly serve Him.

Yet, as Paul's resolve demonstrates, it is not the lack of time or financial backing that hinders our ability to serve God, but rather, our commitment to serve the Lord instead of ourselves. Paul had placed all of his time and resources at the Lord's disposal. He felt that his ministry was so critical to saving lost souls from hellfire that he did not reserve his time or his resources: *"And I will very gladly spend and be spent for your souls; though the more abundantly I love you, the less I am loved"* (2 Cor. 12:15). We may be ready to pray, but not to labor, or labor and not pray, but Paul teaches us that we really cannot serve as we should until all that we have is at the Lord's disposal.

July 7 – Becoming All Things to All Men
1 Corinthians 9:16-18

For though I am free from all men, I have made myself a servant to all, that I might win the more; and to the Jews I became as a Jew, that I might win Jews; to those who are under the law, as under the law, that I might win those who are under the law; to those who are without law, as without law (not being without law toward God, but under law toward Christ), that I might win those who are without law; to the weak I became as weak, that I might win the weak. I have become all things to all men, that I might by all means save some. Now this I do for the gospel's sake, that I may be partaker of it with you.

Paul was versatile in his preaching ministry. He was keenly aware that though the gospel message could not be altered, the method of presenting it to different audiences should vary. His goal: *"I have made myself a servant to all, that I might win the more."* Paul had a passion for winning souls to Christ and knew it was wise to do so (Prov. 11:30).

Paul notes three ways that he had *become all things to all men.* First, to the Jew, he became a Jew. Although Paul was a Jew by birth, and was highly trained in the Law, in Christ, he was no longer bound to the ceremonies or traditions of Judaism. Yet, we see Paul observing certain Jewish rituals, honoring the Patriarchs, speaking in Hebrew, and quoting the Old Testament to gain an audience with his brethren.

Second, to those without the Law (the Gentiles), he became a Gentile. Paul approached them differently; he dressed like them, ate with them, and went to where they gathered – the Law did not permit a Jew to act this way. At the Areopagus in Athens, he spoke to a group of Greek intellectuals about the shrine they had erected "TO THE UNKNOWN GOD" (Acts 17:23). Paul informed them of His name, revealed His divine attributes, and the message that their Creator wanted them to know concerning salvation in Christ.

Third, to the weak, he became weak, likely a reference to slavery. Although Paul was a free man who had privileges as a Roman citizen, he willing put aside his civil rights to reach slaves for Christ. About half of the Roman Empire was enslaved at this time, meaning there were many people to reach who had nothing and no reason to live. Quartus (meaning *four*) was likely a believing slave (Rom. 16:23).

July 8 – Running for the Prize
1 Corinthians 9:24-25

Do you not know that those who run in a race all run, but one receives the prize? Run in such a way that you may obtain it. And everyone who competes for the prize is temperate in all things. Now they do it to obtain a perishable crown, but we for an imperishable crown.

Paul illustrates consecration by using athletic imagery. The Corinthians would have been familiar with both the Greek Olympic Games and their own Isthmian Games. As Warren Wiersbe explains, Paul likens a competitor in a foot race to the Christian experience:

An athlete must be disciplined if he is to win the prize. Discipline means giving up the good and the better for the best. The athlete must watch his diet as well as his hours. He must smile and say "No, thank you" when people offer him fattening desserts or invite him to late-night parties. There is nothing wrong with food or fun, but if they interfere with your highest goals, then they are hindrances and not helps. The Christian does not run the race in order to get to heaven. He is in the race because he has been saved through faith in Jesus Christ. Only Greek citizens were allowed to participate in the games, and they had to obey the rules both in their training and in their performing. Any contestant found breaking the training rules was automatically disqualified.

In order to give up his rights and have the joy of winning lost souls, Paul had to discipline himself. That is the emphasis of this entire chapter: Authority (rights) must be balanced by discipline. If we want to serve the Lord and win His reward and approval, we must pay the price. The word *castaway* (1 Cor. 9:27) is a technical word familiar to those who knew the Greek games. It means "disapproved, disqualified." At the Greek games, there was a herald who announced the rules of the contest, the names of the contestants, and the names and cities of the winners. He would also announce the names of any contestants who were disqualified. Only one runner could win the olive-wreath crown in the Greek games, but *every* believer can win an incorruptible crown when he stands before the Judgment Seat of Christ. This crown is given to those who discipline themselves for the sake of serving Christ and winning lost souls. They keep their bodies under control and keep their eyes on the goal.[20]

July 9 – Running for the Prize
1 Corinthians 9:24-26

Do you not know that those who run in a race all run, but one receives the prize? Run in such a way that you may obtain it. And everyone who competes for the prize is temperate in all things. Now they do it to obtain a perishable crown, but we for an imperishable crown. Therefore I run thus: not with uncertainty. Thus I fight: not as one who beats the air.

By God's grace, Paul was determined to keep his flesh from ruling his behavior, lest he lose his testimony and become unprofitable in ministry. Paul didn't shadow-box his own flesh; he landed the blows. He knew drastic measures were required to keep his bully under wraps. Paul was in a long, grueling race, but he was not competing against other Christians – he was competing against himself. His goal was to keep one stride ahead of his flesh nature in order to finish well.

Paul was determined that his inner man, and not his flesh, would govern his actions. He knew that if he achieved this objective, he would receive an incorruptible crown at the Judgment Seat of Christ, as would all believers who competed with the same spiritual tenacity. All runners have the same motive: whatever we do during this race must ultimately be for the glory of God (1 Cor. 10:31).

Believers do not compete against each other; for God has given each believer a specific calling to fulfill and that will not be finished until the race is over. We do not race against each other, the competition is within ourselves. Like Paul, you and I have the daily challenge of staying a stride ahead of our own nasty flesh.

Besides personal discipline, Paul had another running strategy that he shared with the Christians at Philippi: *"forgetting those things which are behind and reaching forward to those things which are ahead"* (Phil. 3:13). It is wise to learn from our mistakes, but past failures (or victories, for that matter) should not hinder Christians from pressing onward in their heavenly calling. Falling is a normal part of learning to walk properly; it is not falling that makes us a failure, but rather, it is remaining down after the fall and wallowing in self-pity: *"For a righteous man may fall seven times and rise again, but the wicked shall fall by calamity"* (Prov. 24:16).

July 10 – I Will Not Be Disqualified
1 Corinthians 9:27

But I discipline my body and bring it into subjection, lest, when I have preached to others, I myself should become disqualified.

None of us was born with discipline. Discipline in the Christian life is learned through trials, various experiences, and accomplishments which God uses to shape us into Christ-likeness. As we place ourselves in subjection to Christ and the authority of His Word, we learn tenacity, temperance, and self-control. Discipline is aligning our wants with what God wants most for us and then going on with Him to obtain it.

In the Christian race we don't want to burn out, or rust out; we want to last out for Christ. The goal is to maintain a consistent, God-honoring life to maximize our capacity to serve Him and to finish the race well. Paul knew what his flesh nature was capable of doing and that he had to maintain a disciplined life to finish well, else he would be sidelined because of sin. Anytime that we allow the flesh to rule our behavior, we become disqualified to run for Christ: *"So then, those who are in the flesh cannot please God"* (Rom. 8:8). We are either moving forward with the Lord or we are backsliding away from Him.

The writer of Hebrews tells us that as long as backsliding believers choose to fall away, they actively put Christ to shame and cannot be brought to repentance or fruitfulness. One cannot turn back to the Lord (i.e., repent) if he or she is actively backsliding away from Him. Those living in a falling away spiritual condition are "near to cursing," but are not cursed (Heb. 6:8). Backsliding believers are not fruitful, nor can they be; yet, fruit *should* accompany salvation (Heb. 6:9). A believer in this condition has a burned up testimony which ruins their ministries and disgraces Christ (Heb. 6:8; John 15:4-6). Those who are actively falling away from the truth are said to be "rejected" according to Hebrews 6:8. The same word is translated "castaway" (KJV) or "disqualified" (NKJV) in 1 Corinthians 9:27. Paul was surely not speaking of losing his own salvation; rather, the term refers to the loss of one's testimony and one's opportunity for profitable ministry that occurs as a result of giving in to carnal lusting. The bottom line: Any child of God who willfully forsakes going on with the Lord will be miserable, fruitless, and cause the name of Christ to be disdained.

July 11 – The Lord's Supper (Part 1)
1 Corinthians 11:23-26

For I received from the Lord that which I also delivered to you: that the Lord Jesus on the same night in which He was betrayed took bread; and when He had given thanks, He broke it and said, "Take, eat; this is My body which is broken for you; do this in remembrance of Me." In the same manner He also took the cup after supper, saying, "This cup is the new covenant in My blood. This do, as often as you drink it, in remembrance of Me."

We read of four times that the Lord Jesus personally met with Paul to convey vital doctrine; one such event was to ensure that the Lord's Supper was not changed into something that He did not institute.

While it is true that the Lord Jesus invites all believers to participate in the Lord's Supper, a local assembly of God's people should not welcome just anyone into their midst to break bread. It is not that the Lord's Supper needs to be protected per se, but rather that we do not want to grieve the Holy Spirit by allowing the unregenerate, those in sin, or those who are embracing false doctrines to participate as if they were sanctified believer-priests fit for worship (1 Pet. 2:5, 9).

Who should participate in the Lord's Supper? First, only those who have a sound profession of Christ should participate; the Lord's Supper was given by the Lord to His disciples as a memorial feast (Luke 22:19). Second, those who partake must be doctrinally sound (2 Thess. 2:6, 3:14; 2 Jn. 9-10) and, third, morally sound (1 Cor. 5:1-5, 11, 13). If these aspects are not met, those individuals are welcome to observe, but they should not partake of the bread and wine, nor participate audibly.

Letters were used to validate these priestly qualities in believers journeying from one church to another (Acts 18:26-27; Rom. 16:1; Col. 4:7-8). These letters enabled visiting believers to be received into another local church fellowship with joy and all the privileges and responsibilities of a believer-priest (Rom. 15:7). To preclude the Lord's discipline, only believer-priests who exhibit His life should partake of the wine and the bread. This is why all believers are commanded to examine themselves before partaking of the emblems (1 Cor. 11:27). Believer-priests who come together to remember the Lord in the beauty of His holiness with hearts full of adoration should always be welcome.

July 12 – The Lord's Supper (Part 2)
1 Corinthians 11:27-31

Therefore whoever eats this bread or drinks this cup of the Lord in an unworthy manner will be guilty of the body and blood of the Lord. But let a man examine himself, and so let him eat of the bread and drink of the cup. For he who eats and drinks in an unworthy manner eats and drinks judgment to himself, not discerning the Lord's body. For this reason many are weak and sick among you, and many sleep. For if we would judge ourselves, we would not be judged.

A narrative in Numbers 9 highlights the significance God ascribes for us in keeping His memorial feasts. The Passover was to be kept on the fourteenth day of the first month in the Hebrew calendar. However, there was a man who had become ceremonially unclean by attending to a dead body at the time of the Passover. This created a dilemma; the unclean man could not eat the Passover, but was commanded to do so by the Law. Moses consulted the Lord and He added a provision for those unclean at the time of the Passover to hold it a month later. This provision affirms the significance that God puts on His people memorializing the Passover annually as required.

With this observation in mind, C. H. Mackintosh notes the importance of believers continually keeping the Lord's Supper today:

The Christian reader should understand the immense importance and deep interest of the ordinance [the Lord's Supper in view of the Passover ordinance] as viewed on the double ground of subjection to the authority of Scripture, and responsive love to Christ Himself. Furthermore, we are anxious to impress the seriousness of neglecting to eat the Lord's Supper ... it is dangerous ground for any to attempt to set aside this positive institution of our Lord and Master. It argues a wrong condition of soul altogether. It proves that the conscience is not subject to the authority of the word, and that the heart is not in true sympathy with the affections of Christ. Let us therefore see to it that we are honestly endeavoring to discharge our holy responsibilities to the table of the Lord – that we forbear not to keep the feast – that we celebrate it according to the order laid down by God the Holy Spirit.[21]

Indeed, any professing Christian who can carelessly ignore the Lord's dying request to remember Him suffers from coldness of heart!

196

July 13 – Diversities of Spiritual Gifts
1 Corinthians 12:4-7

There are diversities of gifts, but the same Spirit. There are differences of ministries, but the same Lord. And there are diversities of activities, but it is the same God who works all in all. But the manifestation of the Spirit is given to each one for the profit of all.

Each believer in the Body of Christ is both equipped and called to serve Christ. At their conversion, the Holy Spirit distributes spiritual gifts to believers *"as He wills"* (1 Cor. 12:11). The number of these spiritual gifts per believer will vary, but each will receive at least one spiritual gift. The manner in which these gifts will be used will differ. The degree of the gift given will vary, as will the beneficiaries (those who receive the spiritual ministry). For example, let us consider the spiritual gift of teaching. There are many flavors of teaching: counseling, instructive, exhortative, expositional, illustrative, encouraging, prophetic, academic, etc. Some will receive a five-star teaching gift and others a one-star enablement, yet each believer is to be faithful to whatever ability God has bestowed to them.

The intended beneficiaries of the spiritual gift of teaching will also widely vary. Some will provide marriage and family counseling to those in need. Some will speak from pulpits, others in classrooms, others at the kitchen table leading Bible studies, and still others will engage in itinerant ministries. There are women who shepherd other women, while other sisters long to teach children. Each spiritual gift is multi-dimensional in nature and purpose, which makes ascribing one particular name to a received gift from the Holy Spirit problematic.

Using one's gift(s) in wisdom as enabled by the Holy Spirit is what is important, not having a name for the spiritual gift. Pursuing ministry which has not been enabled by the Holy Spirit will cause more damage than good to the Body of Christ. This is why it is important to understand what your spiritual gift is and how the Lord wants you to serve others. If what you are doing is genuinely blessing others and you are not burdened by the ministry, but rather enjoy doing it – then keep on doing it and see if the Lord opens the door to further opportunities to serve. The Lord fully equips us for the service that He has called us to perform in His Body. A heart loves being a heart, and a foot – a foot!

July 14 – Enjoying Good Body Life
1 Corinthians 12:15-26

If the foot should say, "Because I am not a hand, I am not of the body," is it therefore not of the body? And if the ear should say, "Because I am not an eye, I am not of the body," is it therefore not of the body? If the whole body were an eye, where would be the hearing? If the whole were hearing, where would be the smelling? But now God has set the members, each one of them, in the body just as He pleased. And if they were all one member, where would the body be? But now indeed there are many members, yet one body. And the eye cannot say to the hand, "I have no need of you"; nor again the head to the feet, "I have no need of you." No, much rather, those members of the body which seem to be weaker are necessary. And those members of the body which we think to be less honorable, on these we bestow greater honor; and our unpresentable parts have greater modesty, but our presentable parts have no need. But God composed the body, having given greater honor to that part which lacks it, that there should be no schism in the body, but that the members should have the same care for one another. And if one member suffers, all the members suffer with it; or if one member is honored, all the members rejoice with it.

Paul tells us what good body life in the Church should look like: First, no believer should disdain another's spiritual gift, as all gifts are important to body life. Second, God has placed each member in the Body to accomplish a divine purpose. Third, the Body is composed of many members, but some members are weaker than others, but still important to the body. An arm is stronger than the liver, but the liver is vital to the body. A foot is tougher than an eye, but without the eye the foot would be injured. Fourth, some members are not attractive or elegant, but still deserve respect. These members of our body are covered with clothing or skin so that they become less noticeable. Thus, the functional performance of each member is understood to be far more important to the entire body than the outward appearance of any particular member. Fifth, all members are different, but are needed to allow the body to function. Sixth, each member should care for others. There should be no division. When one member hurts, the whole body hurts, and when one member does well, the whole body rejoices.

July 15 – Many Members and All Are Important
1 Corinthians 12:24-27

For as the body is one and has many members, but all the members of that one body, being many, are one body, so also is Christ. For by one Spirit we were all baptized into one body – whether Jews or Greeks, whether slaves or free – and have all been made to drink into one Spirit. For in fact the body is not one member but many.

Paul affirms that all believers, whether Jew or Greek, male or female, free or slave, have become one in Christ (Gal. 3:28). Indeed there are many members of that Body, all of which have a designated role in the Body, and therefore all believers are important to the proper functioning of the Body. This means every believer is to strive to exercise and develop his or her spiritual gift without striving with each other. The Church can only represent Christ to the unregenerate when the Body is behaving as its Head desires.

When there are divisions and factions within the Church, her testimony is marred, the Spirit is quenched, and fruitfulness ceases. Only by laying hold of the mind of Christ through the Holy Spirit can unity be maintained in the Church to reveal the glory of God. On the eve of Calvary, the Lord repeatedly affirmed in His prayer in John 17 the inseparable link between unity and displaying God's glory:

I do not pray for these alone, but also for those who will believe in Me through their word; that they all may be one, as You, Father, are in Me, and I in You; that they also may be one in Us, that the world may believe that You sent Me. And the glory which You gave Me I have given them, that they may be one just as We are one: I in them, and You in Me; that they may be made perfect in one, and that the world may know that You have sent Me, and have loved them as You have loved Me (John 17:20-23).

When the Church is unified, the glory of God is displayed in it for all to see. Peaceful, cooperative unity among men is not a naturally occurring phenomenon, so when it does transpire, the world takes notice. The lost are prompted to consider what they see and by the grace of God some will be won to Christ! Hence, a local assembly must be in one accord before they can exhibit Christ to their neighborhoods.

July 16 – What Does Genuine Love Look Like?
1 Corinthians 13:4-7

Love suffers long and is kind; love does not envy; love does not parade itself, is not puffed up; does not behave rudely, does not seek its own, is not provoked, thinks no evil; does not rejoice in iniquity, but rejoices in the truth; bears all things, believes all things, hopes all things, endures all things.

The subjects of 1 Corinthians chapters 12 and 14, respectively, are Church body life and Church order. Paul sandwiches the subject of Church love in between these two topics for a specific purpose: Biblical love should govern the use of spiritual gifts and ministry in the assembly. The Corinthian believers were being selfish and self-focused in the use of their spiritual gifts. In the first three verses of this chapter Paul categorically states that what we do for the Lord, even martyrdom, means nothing, if not motivated by genuine love.

Paul begins by describing what selfless love looks like, then moves to what love is not, before concluding with what genuine love is.

What love is:	What love is not:
Suffers long – it is patient	Does not envy – rejoices when others are honored
Kind – tender and compassionate	Does not boast of self – quiet with own accomplishments
Centers in the truth – rejoices in it	Not proud – all abilities come from God
Bears all things – commitment based	Keeps no list of wrongs
Believes the positive possibility first	Does not seek self-interest above others
Hopes – rejoices in God's promises	Not easily provoked to anger
Endures – longsuffering of offenses	Does not rejoice in sin or failures of others
God's love is inexhaustible/eternal	Does not think evil – thinks positively or gives the benefit of the doubt

Because the source of true love is God, all that His love motivates will reflect the fruit of the Holy Spirit. Biblical love is sacrificial by nature: *"For God so loved the world that He gave His only begotten Son"* (John 3:16). The only way that we can love others as God loves is to experience His selfless, sacrificial love: *"We love because He first loved us"* (1 Jn. 4:19).

July 17 – That Which Is Perfect Has Come (Part 1)
1 Corinthians 13:8-10

Love never fails. But whether there are prophecies, they will fail; whether there are tongues, they will cease; whether there is knowledge, it will vanish away. For we know in part and we prophesy in part. But when that which is perfect has come, then that which is in part will be done away.

"That which is perfect" may refer to our complete understanding of the *Faith* in heaven, or more likely to the completed canon of Scripture given during the Apostolic Age which reveals all that God desires man to know presently. In a sense, both understandings are true. The canon of Scripture (the good news of God revealed to man) is complete (Jude 3; Hebrews 2:3-4); however, our unity in the faith (complete understanding of what is revealed) will not occur until after the Church is in Heaven (Eph. 4:12-13). In this respect, believers are mere children beholding something not fully understood. So looking into the mirror may describe our sojourn on earth with the Bible as our only source of written revelation, and seeing face to face may speak of our complete understanding of truth in heaven. Or Paul may have been alluding to the Apostolic Age, where the Church patiently waited for God to reveal what He wanted her to know – Scripture. Church history gives the latter view more credence, as prophecy (foretelling), speaking in tongues, and revelations generally concluded towards the end of the Apostolic Age. The evidence within Scripture indicates that the sign gifts generally concluded by approximately 60 A.D. The majority of the New Testament was written after this date with no recorded occurrences of such gifts. After this date, these gifts are referred to in the past tense (1 Tim. 1:18, 4:14; Heb. 2:3-4; 2 Pet. 2:19-21) and were not available to heal Timothy in 64 A.D. (1 Tim. 5:23) or Epaphroditus in 60 A.D. (Phil. 2).

Notice that while prophecies and the gift of knowledge (revelation from God to the Church) and tongues (representing sign gifts) will cease, love will endure forever. This is why love is greater than faith and hope (Rom. 13:13); once we are in heaven, the latter two virtues will have served their purpose, but believers will bask in the love of God forever. If divine visions and dreams occur today, it will be of local or individual benefit, not new revelation for the Church to heed.

July 18 – That Which Is Perfect Has Come (Part 2)
1 Corinthians 13:8-10

Love never fails. But whether there are prophecies, they will fail; whether there are tongues, they will cease; whether there is knowledge, it will vanish away. For we know in part and we prophesy in part. But when that which is perfect has come, then that which is in part will be done away.

The Old Testament contains many examples of individuals receiving a direct commission from God. God personally spoke to Abraham, Moses, Gideon, Samuel, Isaiah, Jeremiah, and Ezekiel to convey their calling. Saul, David, and Elisha received God's message for their lives from prophets. The means by which their callings were given are quite unique also: Abraham saw *the God of glory*, Samuel heard a still, quiet voice, Isaiah and Ezekiel witnessed the majestic throne of God, and Moses bowed before a burning bush.

The New Testament also records the direct and specific calls of the disciples to ministry. So, should Christians today expect to receive a personal visit from God to call them into service? Should we expect a voice from heaven, a vision, or a prophetic utterance to confirm God's calling for us? During the early days of the Church Age, prophets were given to the Church as a check against false teachers – they confirmed the oral transmission of the Word of God before it was written down. Since believers have a divine anointing to understand truth (1 Jn. 2:20, 27) and the Word of God is now complete (Jude 3; 1 Cor. 13:9-10), modern Christians should not expect a prophetic confirmation of their ministry, at least in the normative sense. God may reveal Himself directly, but it should not be expected of Him to do so.

The apostles that the Lord commissioned died long ago and there are no biblical references to sign gifts being used after 60 A.D. The book of Acts reveals a clear historical transition from "apostles" to "apostles and elders" to just "elders" (local church leaders). Hence, we should not expect a sign or utterance to confirm God's ministry calling for us. Practically speaking, how would you know a supernatural sign or a prophetic utterance was from God anyway? It might be from the devil to lead you astray. Moreover, we tend to read into situations what we want them to be, which makes us vulnerable to being deceived.

July 19 – A Silence That Honors God (Part 1)
1 Corinthians 14:33-35

For God is not the author of confusion but of peace, as in all the churches of the saints. Let your women keep silent in the churches, for they are not permitted to speak; but they are to be submissive, as the law also says. And if they want to learn something, let them ask their own husbands at home; for it is shameful for women to speak in church.

We live in days in which the devil is relentlessly trying to undermine the rudiments of God's creation order in Genesis 1: What is life? What is the origin of life? What is gender? What is marriage? What is work? Unfortunately, many have fallen prey to humanized thinking which seeks to erode God's purposes. While discussing *Creation Order*, Paul explains that what is created by or from another becomes the glory of the originator: God created man from the dust of the ground; thus man represents God's glory. God created the woman (the gender) from the side of the first man; thus the woman symbolizes man's glory. The woman's long hair originates from her and is hence her glory (1 Cor. 11:3-15). But what originates from another should not rule over the originator (1 Tim. 2:13-14). Paul states that this order of authority is to carry over into the audible ministry also.

The meanings of two Greek words connected with silence must be understood. First, the verb *sigao* means "to keep secret" or literally to speak within oneself or under one's breath without impeding another person's speech (e.g., Luke 18:39). For example, anyone speaking in tongues was to yield to (be silent) if someone had received a prophetic word. Paul then applies *sigao* to preclude women from speaking publicly in the church meetings in the same way (1 Cor. 14:28-32). In church meetings, women are to *sigao* (i.e., have no singular leading voice). However, *sigao* does not mean total silence because everyone should participate in singing and congregational *amens* (1 Cor. 14:16).

The second Greek word of importance is **hesuchia**, a noun rendered "silence" twice in 1 Timothy 2:11-12. *Hesuchia* conveys the idea of submissive quietness or to "settle down" (as in Acts 22:2; 2 Thess. 3:12). When both genders gathered for spiritual exercise (e.g., a Bible study), the women were to receive instruction from male leaders with quiet subjection, but they were not forbidden from audibly contributing.

July 20 – A Silence That Honors God (Part 2)
1 Corinthians 14:33-35

For God is not the author of confusion but of peace, as in all the churches of the saints. Let your women keep silent in the churches, for they are not permitted to speak; but they are to be submissive, as the law also says. And if they want to learn something, let them ask their own husbands at home; for it is shameful for women to speak in church.

Paul first instructs men (not women) *"to pray everywhere while lifting up holy hands"* (1 Tim. 2:8). The lifting of hands while leading God's people in prayer followed the practice of priests and kings (Lev. 9:22; 1 Kgs. 8:22). Paul then instructs the women to wear discreet attire and to express godliness in doing good works (1 Tim. 2:9-10). Clearly, women are to dress modestly and engage in godly conduct beyond the church meetings, just as men were encouraged to lead in prayer "everywhere." Clearly then, Paul's instruction had a wider application than just meetings of the church. William MacDonald explains:

> Wherever a mixed group of Christians is gathered together for prayer, it is the men and not the women who should lead in this exercise. … Neither is a woman to have authority over a man. That means that she must not have dominion over a man, but is to be in silence or quietness. Perhaps we should add that the latter part of this verse is by no means limited to the local assembly.[22]

Paul is addressing situations in which Christians might gather (for prayer, for Bible studies, for ministry events, etc.). For informal gatherings (when the local church is not gathered in one place), men should lead in teaching and in prayer, but in such settings women could read Scripture, contribute thoughts to the study, and ask questions. At such times, women are to be "settled down" or in "quietness" (the meaning of *hesuchia* rendered "in silence" in 1 Tim. 2:11-12), but audibly non-leading participation is permitted. However, when the local church is gathered in one place, women are not to have a distinct voice but to "keep silent" (the meaning of *sigao* ensures that she is not to disrupt the male speaker in any fashion; 1 Cor. 14:33). It is noted that *Home Order* poses no limitations on wives, mothers, or daughters in praying or sharing scriptural thoughts with other family members.

July 21 – Christ's Resurrection Central to the Gospel
1 Corinthians 15:1-4

Moreover, brethren, I declare to you the gospel which I preached to you, which also you received and in which you stand, by which also you are saved, if you hold fast that word which I preached to you – unless you believed in vain. For I delivered to you first of all that which I also received: that Christ died for our sins according to the Scriptures, and that He was buried, and that He rose again the third day according to the Scriptures.

Paul understood that the resurrection of the dead was more than just an "I hope so" crutch to get the believer through tough times; it was an essential part of the believer's salvation. He stated that if there was no resurrection of the dead, *"then also those who have fallen asleep in Christ have perished. If in this life only we have hope in Christ, we are of all men the most pitiable"* (1 Cor. 15:18-19). Without resurrection there is no salvation! *"For if the dead do not rise, then Christ is not risen. And if Christ is not risen, your faith is futile; you are still in your sins!"* (1 Cor. 15:16-17). Paul stated that if the resurrection of Christ did not occur, then we would still be spiritually dead even though we had trusted in Christ. We would just be forgiven dead people!

The Lord Jesus was judicially punished for all of our sin at Calvary, and because He was raised from the dead, believers can not only be forgiven of their sins, but they in Him receive His life. The Lord Jesus gave up His life that we might live out His life now. This is why the Lord could say, *"I give them eternal life, and they shall never perish; neither shall anyone snatch them out of My hand"* (John 10:28). In Christ there is life; outside Christ there is only death!

Paul adamantly states that those in Christ have salvation and will never experience divine wrath: *"Much more then, having now been justified by His* [Christ's] *blood, we shall be saved from wrath through Him"* (Rom. 5:9). Why could Paul be so sure that believers would never suffer God's wrath? Because God would be unjust to punish believers for crimes He had already punished His Son for on their behalf. To do so would mean that Christ did not satisfy God's judicial wrath for sin. But Christ's resurrection proves that God was satisfied, meaning that we can have God's forgiveness and His life.

July 22 – Evil Company Corrupts Good Habits
1 Corinthians 15:33-34

Do not be deceived: "Evil company corrupts good habits." Awake to righteousness, and do not sin; for some do not have the knowledge of God. I speak this to your shame.

It has often been stated that you become like those you spend time with. The book of Proverbs certainly upholds this point of view:

He who walks with wise men will be wise, but the companion of fools will be destroyed (Prov. 13:20).

Make no friendship with an angry man, and with a furious man do not go, lest you learn his ways and set a snare for your soul (Prov. 22:24-25).

Fools mock at sin, but among the upright there is favor (Prov. 14:9).

Likewise, Paul warns the believers at Corinth that bad companions will corrupt good character. If we closely associate with an angry person – we will become angry also. Spending time with foolish people does not increase our wisdom, but rather prompts more folly.

The marks of a disciple of Christ are to learn the Master (Matt. 11:29) and to become like Him (Matt. 10:25). This means that if we have close fellowship with the Savior, we will be more like Him. Time in Christ's presence as we meditate on Him through His Word enables us to learn His mind and gain His moral likeness (Phil. 2:1-5).

Even the Sanhedrin, the Jewish judicial body, had nothing kind to say about the Lord Jesus or His disciples, but after arresting the disciples for preaching Christ, they inadvertently gave them a compliment: *"they realized that they had been with Jesus"* (Acts 4:13).

How did the Jewish leaders come to this conclusion? After hearing Peter's speech and observing the bold but gracious, Christlike behavior of the disciples, the Jewish elders knew who the disciples had been with – Jesus! Because they had spent much time with the Lord, the character of their words and behavior reminded others of Christ. This same spiritual testimony is possible today; may others know today that we have been with the Lord Jesus Christ also.

July 23 – The Incorruptible Body (Part 1)
1 Corinthians 15:50-54

Now this I say, brethren, that flesh and blood cannot inherit the kingdom of God; nor does corruption inherit incorruption. Behold, I tell you a mystery: We shall not all sleep, but we shall all be changed – in a moment, in the twinkling of an eye, at the last trumpet. For the trumpet will sound, and the dead will be raised incorruptible, and we shall be changed. For this corruptible must put on incorruption, and this mortal must put on immortality. So when this corruptible has put on incorruption, and this mortal has put on immortality, then shall be brought to pass the saying that is written: "Death is swallowed up in victory."

Presently, you and I do not have a physical body fit for heaven. However, in a coming day, the Lord Jesus will come to the air for His Church and in a twinkling of an eye all believers in Christ will either be raised up from their graves with a glorified body, or, if living, will instantly experience glorification (1 Thess. 4:13-18).

Have you ever wondered what kind of body believers will have in heaven? Some in Paul's day were pondering this question, but others were challenging the teaching of resurrection because they could not understand how a physical body could exist in heaven. Paul uses a horticultural example to explain this difficulty. Just as a seed must fall into the ground and die in order to bring forth life, we must die to experience resurrection. Our future resurrected bodies will draw characteristics from our earthly bodies, in the same way a corn plant acquires its characteristics from the kernel of corn that was sown (1 Cor. 15:36-38). The plant is not the seed per se, but what it is was drawn from the seed. Accordingly, individuality of our human soul will be maintained in heaven, though our visible form will be different.

Paul says that our present bodies are perishable, weak, and natural; however, our glorified bodies will never perish, will be powerful, and spiritual (1 Cor. 15:51-53). The former body often dishonors the Lord, while that would be impossible with the latter body – there is no flesh nature within it to cause the glorified body to rebel against the Lord. John states that believers will have a body like the Lord Jesus' body, which obviously cannot commit sin (1 Jn. 3:2). Praise the Lord!

July 24 – The Incorruptible Body (Part 2)
1 Corinthians 15:50-54

Now this I say, brethren, that flesh and blood cannot inherit the kingdom of God; nor does corruption inherit incorruption. Behold, I tell you a mystery: We shall not all sleep, but we shall all be changed – in a moment, in the twinkling of an eye, at the last trumpet. For the trumpet will sound, and the dead will be raised incorruptible, and we shall be changed. For this corruptible must put on incorruption, and this mortal must put on immortality. So when this corruptible has put on incorruption, and this mortal has put on immortality, then shall be brought to pass the saying that is written: "Death is swallowed up in victory."

Not only John, but Paul also explains that at glorification (at the rapture of the Church) saints will receive Christ-like bodies that will be fit for heaven:

For our citizenship is in heaven, from which we also eagerly wait for the Savior, the Lord Jesus Christ, who will transform our lowly body that it may be conformed to His glorious body, according to the working by which He is able even to subdue all things to Himself (Phil. 3:20-21).

Having a Christlike body in heaven means that believers will morally act like God forever and they will possess perfect bodies that will never diminish in vitality. There will be no ill thoughts about other people, no crippling bents, no temptations, nor will there be any addictions with which to grapple. God is a holy God, and to dwell in His presence, we will have to be holy too.

Paul states that the appearing of the Lord Jesus is the blessed hope of the Church (Tit. 2:13) and that those who love the Lord's appearing will be rewarded with a special crown (2 Tim. 4:8). John says that those who live expectant of Christ's return will live purely, because the Lord is pure and because a believer would not want to be ashamed when He does suddenly come for His people (1 Jn. 2:28, 3:3). So although we have not received our resurrection bodies yet, we are to live as though we have! We are to enjoy the resurrection power of Christ's life now and in the future we will be blessed with a Christ-like eternal body!

July 25 – Regularly Giving to the Lord
1 Corinthians 16:2

On the first day of the week let each one of you lay something aside, storing up as he may prosper, that there be no collections when I come.

The early Church settled on a pattern of gathering together weekly on the day of Christ's resurrection, Sunday (also see Acts 20:7). Paul exhorts the church at Corinth about regularly giving to the Lord each Lord's day. There is a fourfold exhortation about giving in this verse: First, all believers are to regularly give to the work of the Lord and giving weekly is implied. Under the Law there were rigid tithes and gifts that were demanded of the Jews, but during the Church Age, believers are not told how much to return to the Lord. So a tithe (a tenth), as required by the Law, may be a good initial guide for our giving, but love for the Lord and not compulsion is to motivate giving in the Church Age.

Second, *"Let each one of you"* means that our giving is a personal matter and should not be publicized (Matt. 6:3). To boast about what we give to the Lord or to others means that we are looking for the praise of men and not the honor of God. Regrettably, the eternal value of such gifts is diminished or altogether lost.

Third, "storing up" means that there must be prayerful preparation in deciding how much should be given to the Lord. Our giving to the Lord is a private matter. We should not give what we do not have; otherwise we are in reality giving what someone else possesses and there is no sacrifice in that.

Fourth, our giving should be proportionate to how God has prospered us. Generally speaking, the Lord does not expect us to give back to Him what is beyond our means. He does expect us to support His work to the degree He has equipped us to do so. The Lord was delighted more with the two mites given by a poor widow than with the more lucrative gift of a self-righteous Pharisee. Our giving to the Lord is a good indication as to what we truly value in life.

Clearly, from Paul's instructions to the believers at Corinth, the Lord does not expect us to contribute the same amounts, but He does expect us to give to the work of the Lord willingly and regularly.

July 26 – Comfort Others as You Have Been Comforted
2 Corinthians 1:3-5

Blessed be the God and Father of our Lord Jesus Christ, the Father of mercies and God of all comfort, who comforts us in all our tribulation, that we may be able to comfort those who are in any trouble, with the comfort with which we ourselves are comforted by God. For as the sufferings of Christ abound in us, so our consolation also abounds through Christ.

Paul and his ministry companions had suffered many adversities, poverties, and persecutions in fulfilling their God-given callings. Yet, through their difficulties they had become more acquainted with the God of all comfort. By continuing to walk in faith, they had enjoyed a higher experience with God than they would have without the hardships. Paul wanted the Corinthian believers to know God in this way also. He wanted them to be comforted in their trials and sorrows by the same means that he had come to appreciate and expect.

Being one with Christ means that everything that comes into our lives also comes into His life. The Lord abandoned the supreme glory of Heaven to be the incarnate man born of a virgin, to live in a sin-cursed world, to endure the contradiction of sinners for thirty-three-plus years, to endlessly serve those in need to the point of exhaustion, to be rejected and betrayed, to lay down His life and to be cursed of God to save others from Hell that they might enjoy the abundant life of God.

The Lord keenly feels our sorrows and our harsh circumstances, and He not only sympathizes with us, but He also provides the only kind of comfort that quiets worry and anxiety. We are then able to pass along our testimonies of comfort to assist those who are going through similar circumstances. We comfort with the comfort we have received; this is often how ministries begin. H. A. Ironside explains:

Many a saint is permitted to go through deep waters, to pass through severe trial both of body and mind, not only for his own profit, but that he may be the better fitted to be a channel of blessing to his brethren when cast down and in distress. Happy is the saint who is thus subject to the will of God and enabled to be His agent in consoling his discouraged fellows and restoring them, through a ministry received in times of sorrow.[23]

210

July 27 – The Fragrance of Christ
2 Corinthians 2:14-16

Now thanks be to God who always leads us in triumph in Christ, and through us diffuses the fragrance of His knowledge in every place. For we are to God the fragrance of Christ among those who are being saved and among those who are perishing. To the one we are the aroma of death leading to death, and to the other the aroma of life leading to life. And who is sufficient for these things?

The Levitical priests were anointed with holy oil containing fragrant spices. Thus, at all times, and at all places in the tabernacle, the fragrance of the holy oil would be enjoyed. In the same spiritual sense, believers in the Church Age are to carry the sweet fragrance of Christ everywhere they go as they perform their priestly duties (1 Pet. 2:5, 9). Believers today compose the Church, the House of God (1 Tim. 3:15).

The olive oil within in the anointing oil represents the work of the Holy Spirit (Zech. 4:2-6), which means believer-priests today can only express the sweet moral excellencies of Christ in what they do by the power of the Holy Spirit. As each believer is controlled by the Holy Spirit, the sweet fragrance of Christ will be powerfully disseminated to all, but as Paul notes, not everyone will appreciate the fragrance of Christ. The lost are able to witness the Lord Jesus through the selfless acts and godly character of believers. As the lost observe divine love, joy, peace, faith, self-control, and humility, they are prompted to take note, breathe in, and ponder the sweetness of the Lord Jesus. Some will be repulsed by what they sense, but others will be prompted to breathe again, and some will never again desire to inhale anything but Christ.

God had previously told Moses that the priests were to be anointed with olive oil when they were purified by blood and consecrated to the Lord (Ex. 29:7). This undoubtedly symbolizes the initial work of the Holy Spirit at conversion to bring a vile sinner under the power of Christ's blood. However, the priests were to be anointed a second time with the fragrant oil before serving in the Holy Place. Again, the work of the Holy Spirit is emphasized, but this time it is in the believer's life and service. It is only what God controls within us that has the potential for propagating the sweet fragrance of Christ to the world that so desperately needs to be awakened to His sweetness.

July 28 – Being Changed From Glory to Glory
2 Corinthians 3:18

But we all, with unveiled face, beholding as in a mirror the glory of the Lord, are being transformed into the same image from glory to glory, just as by the Spirit of the Lord.

Paul informed the Corinthians as to why Moses had covered his face after returning from Mount Sinai the final time; he did not want Israel to see the fading brilliance of his face (2 Cor. 3:13-16). The Law that he had just given Israel was glorious, but it would be replaced by a better covenant that was sealed by Christ's own blood, making it more glorious. The New Covenant did not have a fading glory.

Moses was extended a great privilege, but in this present dispensation, the humblest Christian is brought nearer to beholding the glory of God by viewing Christ through Scripture than Moses was when he was in the cleft of the rock. Paul says that as we peer into the Holy Page, the Spirit of God shows us the glory of Christ in God and to the extent that we desire to behold His glory, we are changed into the same image. Every believer should long to see Christ's glorious appearing, but while waiting for that day, may each of us earnestly beseech the Lord, as Moses did, *"Please, show me Your glory."* God longs for His children to be like Himself in thought and deed (Rom. 8:29). *"Be you holy; for I am holy"* (1 Pet. 1:16).

How is it possible to morally behave as God does? Paul states that it is as we keep our faces unveiled before God by confessing and forsaking sin. We gain a greater understanding of righteousness as we behold the mirror, the Word of God (Jas. 1:23-25), and see ourselves in contrast to God's holiness. By yielding to divine truth, the believer is transformed into deeper shades of Christ-likeness. Occupation with the splendor and glory of Christ and submission to the control of the Holy Spirit will truly usher holiness into our lives. H.A. Ironside explains this concept in his book, *Holiness – The False and the True*:

> I have been learning all along my pilgrim journey that the more my heart is taken up with Christ, the more do I enjoy practical deliverance from sin's power, and the more do I realize what it is to have the love of God shed abroad in that heart by the Holy Spirit given to me, as the earnest of the glory to come.[24]

July 29 – The Outward Man Is Perishing
2 Corinthians 4:16

Therefore we do not lose heart. Even though our outward man is perishing, yet the inward man is being renewed day by day.

Solomon exhorts man's natural dependency: *"Remember now your Creator in the days of your youth, before the difficult days come"* (Eccl. 12:1). Throughout one's life, a person should revere God, obey His commandments, and render faithful service to the Creator. The coming difficult days in this verse refer to the body's degradation that accompanies old age. To ensure his younger audience would be able to relate to his warning, Solomon colorfully describes the condition of those trudging on through their autumn years:

In the day when the keepers of the house shall tremble, and the strong men shall bow themselves, and the grinders cease because they are few, and those that look out of the windows be darkened and when the doors are shut in the streets, and the sound of grinding is low; when one rises up at the sound of a bird, and all the daughters of music are brought low (Eccl. 12:3-4).

It is natural for older women to fall, for men to slump over with age, and for the elderly to lose their teeth and eyesight. Additionally, they may lose their hearing and often suffer from insomnia, weakened vocal cords, fearfulness, and diminished natural desires (e.g., taste for food, sexual vigor, etc.). Paul puts the matter this way: the *"outward man is perishing"* (2 Cor. 4:16). Solomon remarks this unavoidable degenerative process is nature's way of preparing us for our long-lasting abode: death, man's eventual end under the sun. It would be wise, then, for us to honor God in our brief existence, for as Solomon notes, a dead and decaying body has no opportunity to do so.

Paul explains that though our physical bodies diminish in ability with time, our inner man (i.e., our spirit) is strengthened through the power of the Holy Spirit. In contrast to a waning, aging body, our union with Christ ensures an endless resource of resurrection power. So while we may have decreasing ability to demonstrate love in our earthly relationships, our union with Christ ensures an increasing capacity to appreciate and demonstrate our devotion to Him regardless.

July 30 – The Reward of Our Light Affliction
2 Corinthians 4:17-18

For our light affliction, which is but for a moment, is working for us a far more exceeding and eternal weight of glory, while we do not look at the things which are seen, but at the things which are not seen. For the things which are seen are temporary, but the things which are not seen are eternal.

It is quite amazing that Paul could refer to his jail-time, his beatings, and being stoned and left for dead as "light affliction," but in the grand scheme of things he understood all that he had endured patiently had earned him an eternal weight in glory. He realized that God had used these hardships to better him, to declare the gospel more powerfully, to encourage weaker brethren to do the same, and would give him a greater opportunity to worship the Lord throughout eternity.

Dear believer, the Lord remembers your selfless and arduous service and will reward you for it. The Lord is watching. He knows. He cares. He remembers. He will reward appropriately and abundantly:

For I consider that the sufferings of this present time are not worthy to be compared with the glory which shall be revealed in us (Rom. 8:18).

For God is not unjust to forget your work and labor of love which you have shown toward His name, in that you have ministered to the saints, and do minister. And we desire that each one of you show the same diligence to the full assurance of hope until the end, that you do not become sluggish, but imitate those who through faith and patience inherit the promises (Heb. 6:10-12).

We do not know when Christ will return for us and remove us to His abode, but He has provided everything that we need until that time. We can be assured that He will not rest until all believers are brought into His full inheritance and eternal rest! Then, we all will be shocked to learn how little we practically appreciated the reality of *"all spiritual blessings in heavenly places in Christ."* Paul had learned to rely on God's grace to accomplish what could be and a reward that would be. May we appropriate, in full measure, the grace of God afforded to us now in Christ – an exceeding and eternal weight of glory is worth it!

July 31 – Absent From the Body, Present With the Lord
2 Corinthians 5:6-8

So we are always confident, knowing that while we are at home in the body we are absent from the Lord. For we walk by faith, not by sight. We are confident, yes, well pleased rather to be absent from the body and to be present with the Lord.

When the Lord saves a repentant sinner, He completely redeems that person's spirit, soul, and body. The soul and the spirit are immediately delivered from the penalty of sin when one confesses his sinfulness before God and accepts Christ's free gift of salvation (John 5:24). The body practically realizes salvation when it is raptured from the presence of sin, after a complete overhaul called glorification. This transformation will occur for all living believers (simultaneously) at the coming of the Lord Jesus for His Church (1 Thess. 4:13-17). In a twinkling of an eye, what was corruptible will be incorruptible, and what was mortal will be immortal (1 Cor. 15:51-52). The believer's body will be instantly transformed: sin and pain will cease to exist in it.

The believer's glorified body will be enabled to worship and to please God without any hindrances of the flesh or ills of its previously fallen state. In summary, an individual's soul and spirit are eternally saved when he or she trusts the gospel message, while salvation of the body is to be greatly anticipated in a coming day. This was Paul's blessed hope and his earnest expectation. *"Now is our salvation nearer than when we believed"* (Rom. 13:11).

God's offer for salvation is a complete salvation of the whole of man through Jesus Christ! The spirit is saved (Acts 7:59; 1 Cor. 6:20; 1 Cor. 5:5), the soul is saved (Jam. 5:20; Matt. 10:28), and the body will be saved (Phil. 3:21). It is through Christ that all man's deepest needs are satisfied.

In Christ we are significant, for we are one with Him; we are both needed and wanted. In Christ we find security, for we are eternally safe and all our needs are provided for as He sees fit. We have God's assurance that if we die before the saving of our bodies (i.e., at the rapture of the Church), our spiritual essence will be in His presence (Rev. 6:9). *"We are confident, I say, and willing rather to be absent from the body, and to be present with the Lord"* (2 Cor. 5:8).

August 1 – The Love of Christ Compels Us
2 Corinthians 5:14-16

For the love of Christ compels us, because we judge thus: that if one died for all, then all died; and He died for all, that those who live should live no longer for themselves, but for Him who died for them and rose again. Therefore, from now on, we regard no one according to the flesh. Even though we have known Christ according to the flesh, yet now we know Him thus no longer.

As shown with God's dealings with His covenant people in the Old Testament, He will not tolerate a divided heart in His people. Their religious formalities and idolatry were severely punished. It is impossible to live a holy life for God's glory unless single-hearted devotion guides the way. From Israel's inception, the Lord desired communion with a holy nation, not a double-minded, mostly-pagan people (Lev. 11:44). Regrettably, much of Israel's history shows that they had forgotten from where they came, a pit of hopeless slavery, and why God had delivered them from Egypt, to rescue them from Egypt's corruption to be His special redeemed possession.

Believers in the Church can also forget from where they came. As children of the devil, we were dead in trespasses and sin and enslaved to sin. Similarly, the Lord Jesus wants a spotlessly pure bride for Himself (Eph. 5:27), one that does *"abstain from the appearance of evil"* (1 Thess. 5:22). This means fully consecrating one's spirit, soul and body for God's purposes by abhorring evil in thought and deed. This means recalling that what the believer was positionally in Adam is dead and gone (Eph. 4:22; Rom. 6:6). All that we were before Christ is no more – we died with Christ at Calvary. Because believers have been legally declared dead, they receive a new life – Christ's life through rebirth. Now the love of Christ compels us to live daily as He would, which means we cannot pursue our own ambitions or lusts.

James reminds us that *"a double-minded man* [is] *unstable in all his ways"* (Jas. 1:8) and *"that friendship with the world is enmity with God,"* in fact God considers it spiritual adultery (Jas. 4:4). When God's people venture away from the Lord, it always results in an unstable life and in failure of those things which matter for eternity. When we spurn the love of Christ for carnal and secular thrills, God is greatly offended.

August 2 – Let There Be Equality
2 Corinthians 8:13-15

For I do not mean that others should be eased and you burdened; but by an equality, that now at this time your abundance may supply their lack, that their abundance also may supply your lack – that there may be equality. As it is written, "He who gathered much had nothing left over, and he who gathered little had no lack."

Paul is teaching about giving to the Lord in 2 Corinthians chapters 8 and 9. He commences by revealing the motive for being generous in giving to the Lord: *"For you know the grace of our Lord Jesus Christ, that though He was rich, yet for your sakes He became poor, that you through His poverty might become rich"* (2 Cor. 8:9). Contemplating all that the Son of God had to set aside in glory to become God's Lamb for sacrifice (for our sin) should prompt us to want to give back to Him what we can. If we gave Christ everything we have, we still could never repay the debt that He paid on our behalf.

Interestingly, the first mention of "riches" is in Genesis 13:2: Abraham returned to Canaan from Egypt with great wealth. This posed a new difficulty though; Abraham and Lot could no longer dwell together because of the abundance of their stuff (Gen. 13:6). What effect do too many possessions have on God's people? The result is strife among the brethren (Gen. 13:7). When brethren strive together, they cease to be a testimony for God.

How are brethren to consider their possessions? The early Church held the proper view of "equality" and thus maintained and enjoyed unity: *"And the multitude of those that believed were of one heart and of one soul; neither said any of them that any of the things which he possessed was his own; but they had all things common"* (Acts 4:32).

In the above verses, Paul taught the Corinthians that there should be equality among the brethren. If a brother is in need and another brother is able to meet that need, he should readily do so. Equality is not communism. Holding all things in equality is not the same as everyone having equal portions. When God's people properly value God, the things of God, and His people, they will enjoy unity; if their focus is shifted to temporal things, they will experience envy, dissatisfaction, and coveting. It is better to be united, rather than to be divided by stuff!

217

August 3 – God Loves a Cheerful Giver
2 Corinthians 9:6-8

But this I say: He who sows sparingly will also reap sparingly, and he who sows bountifully will also reap bountifully. So let each one give as he purposes in his heart, not grudgingly or of necessity; for God loves a cheerful giver. And God is able to make all grace abound toward you, that you, always having all sufficiency in all things, may have an abundance for every good work.

The Jewish tithing statutes of the Law were abolished in the New Testament. In the Church Age each believer is required to regularly and proportionately give back to the Lord as God has prospered him or her (1 Cor. 16:2). God makes no demands as to the specific amount we are to give back to Him; rather, we are permitted to evaluate our situation, and to freely express our love and appreciation to Him through giving. Our giving back to the Lord is a means of expressing: *"Thanks be to God for His indescribable gift!"* (2 Cor. 9:15).

The Greek word rendered "cheerful" is *hilaros*. The English word "hilarious" is derived from *hilaros*. Interestingly, *hilaros* only occurs twice in the New Testament and both incidences relate to giving (Rom. 12:8 is the other). God loves a *hilaros* giver because it is how He gives.

God has wonderfully shown us that true giving commences with selfless sacrifice: *"For God so loved the world that He gave His only begotten Son"* (John 3:16). The Lord Jesus affirmed *"to whom little is forgiven, the same loves little"* (Luke 7:47)! In summary, the portion that we return of what we have received from the Lord directly reflects how much we believe we have been forgiven and how much we love Him. Those who have been forgiven much give much, because they love much!

Many of the present financial practices of the Church are not found in Scripture. In New Testament days, there was no collection agency, no forced giving, no personal solicitations, no fund-raising campaigns, only voluntary giving as each person was exercised by the Lord. Paul reminds us of two important truths: First, a joyful and thankful heart should guide our giving to the Lord, for He loves a cheerful giver. Second, *"he who sows sparingly will also reap sparingly, and he who sows bountifully will also reap bountifully."*

August 4 – Pulling Down Strongholds
2 Corinthians 10:3-5

For though we walk in the flesh, we do not war according to the flesh. For the weapons of our warfare are not carnal but mighty in God for pulling down strongholds, casting down arguments and every high thing that exalts itself against the knowledge of God, bringing every thought into captivity to the obedience of Christ.

We learn from a number of Old Testament examples that God's ways are not man's ways in overcoming the enemy. Whether it is Samson slaying a thousand Philistines with the jawbone of an ass, or causing the walls of Jericho to fall with a shout, or fighting using an ox goad to fight men armed with shields, spears, and swords, God gives His people spectacular victories with what the world deems as feeble and indeed laughable means. This was repeatedly done to teach His covenant people not to rely on their physical strength to conquer their enemies, but rather His. The Lord chooses to work this way so that our flesh has no opportunity to glory in His presence (1 Cor. 1:30).

Like Israel, believers in the Church Age must also realize that all our engagements with the enemy are the Lord's battles and that every victory is the Lord's victory. We have no strength against the devil, other than what the Lord provides. Thus, we need a supernatural work of God's grace in our lives to pull down the strongholds in our minds and overcome the enemy's evil tactics and power against us.

Though Paul is speaking to the Corinthians about the threat of being mastered by false teachers, the provision of deliverance he mentions has much broader ramifications. John highlights this wonderful principle in his first epistle: *"For whatever is born of God overcomes the world. And this is the victory that has overcome the world – our faith. Who is he who overcomes the world, but he who believes that Jesus is the Son of God?"* (1 Jn. 5:4-5). Though there will be satanic opposition to hinder the work of God that we are engaged in, the solution is before us. In faith, the Israelites daily marched around Jericho until God miraculously delivered the city into their hands. In faith, Shamgar charged six hundred Philistines with an ox goad. These victories and more were not accomplished through carnal weapons of war, but in divine response by faith and obedience to God's Word.

August 5 – Transforming Themselves Into Apostles
2 Corinthians 11:13-15

For such are false apostles, deceitful workers, transforming themselves into apostles of Christ. And no wonder! For Satan himself transforms himself into an angel of light. Therefore it is no great thing if his ministers also transform themselves into ministers of righteousness, whose end will be according to their works.

Many people these days are seeing visions and hearing voices. Paul warns that Satan mimics God's means of declaring revelation in order to deceive those desiring something beyond what God has already revealed in Scripture (2 Cor. 11:14). During the Apostolic Age, prophecy, visions, dreams, and audible commands were prevalent to express divine revelation. Yet, we must realize that the Lord Jesus is the Father's ultimate revelation to the world (Jn. 1:1-2, 1:14). Christ has not left us in the dark concerning truth; He has declared to us the divine revelation needed for salvation, godly living, and bringing Him glory. This revelation was brought by the apostles for us to follow (Heb. 2:3) and is complete in declaration (Jude 3). With this said, God is God, and He can do anything He pleases. It is suggested that if the reader does witness some supernatural manifestation, the following checklist should be reviewed to determine the source of the event:

1. All that flows from God will agree with His nature and what He has previously declared as truth in Scripture.

2. Based on the pattern of New Testament Scripture, revelation was conferred only to individuals who had consecrated themselves to holy living (e.g., Joseph, Mary, Simeon, Anna, Stephen, Paul, etc.).

3. Visions from the Holy Spirit will occur when the believer's mind is fully active and not hindered by medications, drugs, fatigue, etc. The opposite is true with evil spirits, as drug abuse is common in satanic rituals.

4. God conveys revelation when our minds are clear and active and when we are in spiritual communion with him. This means that there will be no strongholds within our minds which Satan can use to hinder God's voice.

5. Is the revelation confusing or coercing you to an immediate action? God does not force truth on us in such a way that we are reduced to mindless puppets. God is patient and wants us to affirm the truth before acting.

August 6 – A Thorn in the Flesh
2 Corinthians 12:7-9

And lest I should be exalted above measure by the abundance of the revelations, a thorn in the flesh was given to me, a messenger of Satan to buffet me, lest I be exalted above measure. Concerning this thing I pleaded with the Lord three times that it might depart from me. And He said to me, "My grace is sufficient for you, for My strength is made perfect in weakness." Therefore most gladly I will rather boast in my infirmities, that the power of Christ may rest upon me.

Paul had an ongoing infirmity that he asked the Lord to remove on three different occasions. The Lord was determined not to take away Paul's "thorn in the flesh," but rather that he would learn to rely on His grace each and every day despite the limitation. We are not told what this thorn was, but it is speculated by his statement to the Galatians that he suffered from poor eyesight (Gal. 4:15, 6:11).

Although Paul was disappointed in the Lord's decision, he knew that the Lord knew what was best to keep him humble and dependent on God's grace. Consequently, Paul accepted his situation and praised the Lord for His grace – he could actually take pleasure in his infirmities because he would be a witness of God's grace in action.

Paul would gladly remain weak so that the power of Christ would be more obvious in him. In this sense, the day of small things is but the beginning of greater things where God is concerned. When little men think of themselves as small, an infinite God goes big!

The Lord Jesus conveyed this idea in His *Sermon on the Mount*: *"Blessed are the poor in spirit, for theirs is the kingdom of heaven. Blessed are those who mourn, for they shall be comforted. Blessed are the meek, for they shall inherit the earth"* (Matt. 5:3-5). The Lord does not need our wealth or religious feats; He simply wants our hearts soft, pliable, and beating for Him. Once Paul understood why he must continue suffering with his infirmity, he was pleased to do so. The Lord delights to demonstrate His power through the weakness of His people, and it liberates our minds to realize that this is always best for us because it honors Him. If you do not think you have much to offer the Lord because of your infirmities or weaknesses, you are just the kind of person He is looking for to honor Himself.

August 7 – No Ethnic Barriers in the Body
Galatians 2:11-13

Now when Peter had come to Antioch, I withstood him to his face, because he was to be blamed; for before certain men came from James, he would eat with the Gentiles; but when they came, he withdrew and separated himself, fearing those who were of the circumcision. And the rest of the Jews also played the hypocrite with him, so that even Barnabas was carried away with their hypocrisy.

Paul refers to a time when he, Barnabas, and Titus (a Greek believer) visited the apostles in Jerusalem to privately discuss an issue that they were constantly encountering in ministry. Certain Jews were teaching that though Gentiles were saved by the gospel of Christ, they must continue in the Law to maintain their salvation. Titus, a Greek believer, who labored with Paul, was presented as a test case to the apostles. This meeting appears to be the precursor to the Council of Jerusalem (Acts 15), a full-blown convention to resolve the matter once and for all. The apostles concluded that there was no reason for Titus to be circumcised. As a Gentile, he was never under the Law, so why should he, who had been liberated by grace, be placed into bondage of a system that only condemned and gave no help for victorious living?

During this trip the apostles in Jerusalem also affirmed that Paul was preaching the same gospel that they were to the Jews, but Paul had been commissioned by the Lord to preach it to the Gentiles.

Later, Peter came to Antioch and had open fellowship with Paul, Barnabas, and Gentile believers. Peter even ate with the Gentiles, which was forbidden by the Law. However, when some hardline Judaizers arrived from Jerusalem, Peter, and even Barnabas, separated from the Greeks. Paul saw their actions as an affront to the gospel message which made Jew and Gentile one in Christ. Paul would not permit a false peace to undermine God's working of grace among the Gentiles. Any mingling of the Law with grace in Christianity would void the worth of Christ's sacrifice. Paul, the apostle to the Gentiles, publicly rebuked Peter, an apostle to the Jews, for his hypocrisy. Paul's action shows that the apostles were mere men and were not above other believers in the Body intrinsically; though each had a unique apostolic ministry, they were still accountable to each other and to the Lord.

August 8 – Walk in the Spirit
Galatians 5:16-17

I say then: Walk in the Spirit, and you shall not fulfill the lust of the flesh. For the flesh lusts against the Spirit, and the Spirit against the flesh; and these are contrary to one another, so that you do not do the things that you wish.

What does it mean to walk in the Spirit? First, notice that it is the opposite of living in the flesh. The Holy Spirit and our carnal flesh (as controlled by our fallen nature inherited from Adam) have nothing in common. Each wants to control our behavior (what we walk after), the former for God, and the latter for whatever we crave after.

Listen to Paul's medley of exhortations concerning the walk of the believer: do not walk as fools (Eph. 5:15), the way you formerly did (Eph. 5:8), or the way the Gentiles walk in the vanity of their minds (Eph. 4:17); walk as children of light (Eph. 5:8). In other words, don't be foolish; walk according to the truth, not in the darkness as before. The Lord Jesus promised that if we obey His commandments, He will manifest Himself to us in deeper fellowship (John 14:21). In order to walk with the Lord, we must be in agreement with Him on the matter of sin, for *"can two walk together except they be agreed?"* (Amos 3:3). Surely, light has no communion with darkness; thus, may each of us walk with God according to divine truth and in moral integrity.

The Lord Jesus said of Himself: *"I am the light of the world. He who follows Me shall not walk in darkness, but have the light of life"* (John 8:12). The ultimate test of whether someone has truly trusted Christ for salvation is whether they continue in sin (i.e., the practicing of whatever displeases the Lord). A true child of God does not persist in sin (1 Jn. 3:9); a child of light does not blatantly walk in darkness. Why? Because a true believer longs for God's abiding presence and fellowship. Not only are there deep longings to be with God, but a profound remorse under the conviction of the Holy Spirit should lead a true child of God to repentance and restoration.

To walk in the illumination, the enablement, the guidance, the instruction, and the fruit of the Spirit is to enjoy unhindered fellowship with God. To walk after the flesh is to break fellowship with God, for nothing done in the flesh can please God (Rom. 8:8).

August 9 – The Fruit of the Spirit
Galatians 5:22-23

But the fruit of the Spirit is love, joy, peace, longsuffering, kindness, goodness, faithfulness, gentleness, self-control. Against such there is no law.

On several occasions the Lord Jesus told His disciples that only good trees bear good fruit, and, likewise, that bad trees produce according to their nature (Matt. 7:17). His point was that a true believer is known by his or her fruit in the same way that *"a tree is known by its fruit"* (Matt. 12:33). Apple trees do not produce pears; they bear only apples. This means that true Christians will be characterized by the fruit of the Spirit, not by works of the flesh.

Paul refers to "the fruit of the Spirit," not "the fruits of the Spirit." The fruit of the Spirit is homogenous in expressing the character of God in the believer's behavior, thus "fruit" and not "fruits." The qualities of this fruit relate to three categories of associations: Love, joy, and peace pertain to our union with Christ. Longsuffering, gentleness, and goodness relate to our interaction with others. Faithfulness, meekness, and self-control are in relationship to self.

The Holy Spirit longs for us to experience the love, joy, and peace of Christ in our lives; these eternal qualities are only found in God. The Holy Spirit also enables us to be patient, kind, gentle, longsuffering, forgiving in our interactions with others; we want to show others the goodness of God that we ourselves are experiencing. The Holy Spirit also wants us to be full of faith, and to keep our carnal nature in check. All that we do and say should be guided by meekness and self-control.

While it is true that not every Christian matures as he or she ought, every genuine child of God will grow and bear fruit to some extent; this is evidence of salvation (Jas. 2:17). Various reasons for a lack of maturity are possible. The sluggish believer may not be spending time in the Word of God as he or she ought, due to a preoccupation with temporal things and activities. They may not be serious about keeping short accounts with God by expediently confessing sin. All these carnal behaviors grieve and quench the Holy Spirit (Eph. 4:30; 1 Thess. 5:19). As believers, we do not want the Holy Spirit to confront or to oppose us, but rather to fill and control all that we do.

224

August 10 – Are You Spiritual?
Galatians 6:1

Brethren, if a man is overtaken in any trespass, you who are spiritual restore such a one in a spirit of gentleness, considering yourself lest you also be tempted.

The civil war that occurred in Israel, as recorded in Judges 20, provides valuable insight into the type of attitude God's people should have in dealing with unrighteous brethren. Some in the tribe of Benjamin had and were committing lewd acts that were an abomination to the Lord. Rather than relinquishing the perpetrators for judgment, the tribe of Benjamin decided to protect them, which resulted in a civil war that nearly wiped out the tribe of Benjamin. The other eleven tribes were caught up in holy zeal to uphold justice and holiness in Israel, but without a spirit of brokenness, so the Lord was not with them.

It took the deaths of about 40,000 men to bring them to brokenness and utter dependence on the Lord; then the Lord permitted them to judge their brethren. H. L. Rossier summarizes why the final battle was successful in removing the evil done in Israel, and the practical lesson to be gleaned for the Church today:

> Benjamin was defeated by a humbled people who showed themselves weaker than he. It is the principle of all discipline in the assembly. Without love, without dependence on God and His word, without self-judgment, discipline will always be defective, and it is only under such conditions that an assembly can purge out the old leaven.[25]

Believers cannot properly deal with a sinning brother or sister unless they are first humbly before the Lord in innocence, have pure motives, and are dedicated to obeying His Word. Only through this type of attitude can the work of rebuke and restoration be effectively accomplished. Only those who are truly spiritual in this way can restore a fellow brother or sister who has been overtaken by sin.

Paul reminds us that we are all of like passions, and if it were not for the grace of God, each of us would be capable of doing the most vile works of unrighteousness. Realizing that should keep us broken before the Lord. It should hurt us to have to deal with another's sin!

August 11 – Bear One Another's Burdens
Galatians 6:2

Bear one another's burdens, and so fulfill the law of Christ.

Deuteronomy 15:11 reads, *"For the poor will never cease from the land; therefore I command you, saying, 'You shall open your hand wide to your brother, to your poor and your needy, in your land.'"* Although this verse does not legally apply to Christians today, it does highlight what God deems appropriate conduct for His people throughout all ages, that is, to rally around and help each other during times of distress. Paul affirms that it is Christlike to *"bear one another's burdens."* The Greek word rendered "bear" means "to carry" and the word translated "burdens" implies a crushing load. There are times in life when we may be unexpectedly buried by a crushing load; it is at those times believers are to support each other.

For example, the early Church cared for their poor widows (Acts 6:1; 1 Tim. 5:3-5). These Christians did not value their possessions (of which they were merely God's stewards) more than each other (Acts 4:32). As a result of this loving, unselfish spirit, all of the Lord's people were wonderfully sustained: *"nor was there anyone among them who lacked"* (Acts 4:34). They experienced exactly what both Moses and Solomon promised and laid up treasures in heaven in the process (Matt. 19:21). God forbid that we, who have received so much goodness in Christ, should *"oppress one another"* by withholding our temporal possessions from our brethren in need (Lev. 25:14, 17).

Paul speaks of a different load a few verses later:

But let each one examine his own work, and then he will have rejoicing in himself alone, and not in another. For each one shall bear his own load (Gal. 6:4-5).

The *load* in verse 5 closely resembles that of a soldier's backpack. It is used here to speak of the daily burden that we are assigned and expected to bear for the Lord. This represents the daily tasks each soldier of the cross is to expected to perform for the Lord; no one is to take those assigned duties from us. So let us do what we know we should do and be ready to help those who did not know what was coming.

August 12 – Share With Those Who Share With You
Galatians 6:6

Let him who is taught the word share in all good things with him who teaches.

Paul twice refers to an edict from the Mosaic Law that stressed the fair and kind treatment of beasts of burden (1 Cor. 9:9; 1 Tim. 5:18): *"You shall not muzzle an ox while it treads out the grain"* (Deut. 25:4). An ox that was serving its master by trampling stalks of grain on the threshing floor in preparation for winnowing should be permitted to eat some of the stalks. Paul refers to this Old Testament command to show that those laboring for the kingdom of God were likewise worthy of financial support from those who had benefited from their preaching.

The New Testament indicates that Church workers were employed by the Lord, not by local churches. Serving the Lord is not a career to be chosen, but a heavenly calling to be fulfilled! God enables the worker's ministry and is responsible for supporting them financially (Phil. 4:10-19; Col. 4:17). As He most often accomplishes this through His people, Paul emphasizes that those who had been spiritually blessed by ministry had a "duty" to support those who blessed them (Rom. 15:27). Examples of not muzzling the laboring ox in principle would include the support of:

- The evangelist (1 Cor. 9:14).
- A teaching elder (1 Tim. 5:17-18).
- A teacher in general (Gal. 6:6).
- A commended worker (1 Cor. 9:4).

Gaius provides a good example to follow in the care of the Lord's servants. He extended hospitality to itinerant church workers and then did not send them away empty-handed (3 John 5-8). At times workers may need to engage in secular employment for financial reasons, but nowhere in Scripture do we see them making appeals for their own support. Commended workers serve the Lord (Acts 14:26), and thus the Lord wants His people to freely and amply provide for them in His name. This arrangement permits His workers to do His bidding and for the Lord to endorse their efforts by attending to their daily needs.

August 13 – Do Not Grow Weary in Well Doing
Galatians 6:9-10

And let us not grow weary while doing good, for in due season we shall reap if we do not lose heart. Therefore, as we have opportunity, let us do good to all, especially to those who are of the household of faith.

While it is certainly possible to grow weary in the Lord's work, we never want to adopt a mental disposition of being weary of the Lord's work or reach a point of physical exhaustion. The Lord's servants can only give out what they receive from the Lord themselves.

What God has assigned us to do is important to do regardless of how we feel about it or doing it. Paul encourages us to be especially motivated to serve those in the Body of Christ – *"let us do good to all."* Those who faithfully serve the Lord now, despite expenses, hardships and persecutions, will be amply rewarded in due season, speaking of the Judgment Seat of Christ. Then, all of our laboring and warring associated with our earthly sojourn will be over.

Paul applies the sowing and reaping principles of verse 7-8 to faithful service and rewards in verses 9-10. Those who sow to the flesh will reap corruption and those who sow to the Spirit will reap life:

Do not be deceived, God is not mocked; for whatever a man sows, that he will also reap. For he who sows to his flesh will of the flesh reap corruption, but he who sows to the Spirit will of the Spirit reap everlasting life (Gal. 6:7-8).

There are three inescapable laws of the harvest associated with carnality and spiritual life. First, we reap what we sow: if we sow to the flesh, we reap corruption, but if we sow to the Spirit of God we reap a spiritual harvest which God will reward. Second, we reap later than we sow: if we sow to the flesh, the corruption continues to come a long time afterwards, and if we sow to the Spirit, a harvest of spiritual benefits are obtained forever. Third, we reap more than what we sow: the results of sowing to the flesh are much more devastating than what we could have ever imagined; likewise our eternal reward for sowing to the Spirit will be far more than we can comprehend. May we keep laboring with the Lord and not lose heart – we will be glad we did later.

August 14 – The World Has Been Crucified to Me
Galatians 6:13-15

For not even those who are circumcised keep the law, but they desire to have you circumcised that they may boast in your flesh. But God forbid that I should boast except in the cross of our Lord Jesus Christ, by whom the world has been crucified to me, and I to the world. For in Christ Jesus neither circumcision nor uncircumcision avails anything, but a new creation.

Under the Law, the Jews were bound to circumcise their male infants eight days after birth. God had given Abraham and his posterity circumcision as a reminder of His covenant with Abraham and his descendants (Gen. 17). What was given to the Jewish nation at Sinai by Moses was only for them; it was not given to the Gentiles (Acts 15:10). This is why Paul exhorts the Gentile believers in Galatia not to give ear to the Judaizers. These legalists were teaching that salvation was by grace through Christ, but that a believer had to continue to keep the Law to maintain his or her salvation. As the Galatians had never been under the Law, it was irrational for the Judaizers to place them under its bondage now, especially since the Law only condemned as no one could keep it and it provided no assistance in living for Christ.

Hebrews contains the Jewish complement of this message: Israel was no longer under the Law; the entire system had been replaced by what it anticipated in Christ. The Law was not dead, for it still declares the righteousness of God, but the Jews were dead to it, in that they had been liberated by Christ from its condemning outcome (Rom. 7:4-6).

Accordingly, Paul uses the strongest language he can to say that once someone has trusted in the gospel of Jesus Christ and become a new creation, he or she can never embrace legalized religion or secular ideologies of the world. Paul says that *"the world has been crucified to me, and I to the world."* The Greek verb rendered "crucified" is in the imperative mood, passive voice, and perfect tense. In other words, how could Paul boast in anything but the cross of Christ, seeing that through it the power of God had carved him out of the world forever. Spiritually speaking, he could never be a part of an anti-God system that hates Christ ever again. Christ's cross is like a sharp knife that divides believers out of what was dead and makes them alive forever.

August 15 – Laying Hold of Our Spiritual Blessings
Ephesians 1:3

Blessed be the God and Father of our Lord Jesus Christ, who has blessed us with every spiritual blessing in the heavenly places in Christ.

In the Church Age, believers do not labor for a *place* of rest as Israel did and still does; our rest and inheritance are in a *Person* – Christ in heavenly places. This is why Paul could pray for fellow believers, *"The Lord of peace Himself give you peace in every way"* (2 Thess. 3:16) and also share his life's aspiration with them:

Not that I have already attained, or am already perfected; but I press on, that I may lay hold of that for which Christ Jesus has also laid hold of me. Brethren, I do not count myself to have apprehended; but one thing I do, forgetting those things which are behind and reaching forward to those things which are ahead, I press toward the goal for the prize of the upward call of God in Christ Jesus (Phil. 3:12-14).

Christ is the believer's inheritance and resting place. The practical blessings of our present, heavenly possessions in Christ will be experienced through faith and obedience as one engages in active conquest now through His resurrection power. In the Christian experience, the inheritance we each possess presently relates directly to how we have experienced the Lord's gracious and holy character.

The Lord does not bestow such things as power and authority lightly; these are received in measure and in accordance to our capacity to retain each gift of grace in faith, love, and humility. To apprehend that which cannot be managed in wisdom would surely result in a worse outcome than not having a possession at all. Believers have different spiritual gifts, callings of ministry, talents to serve, and developed maturity in Christ. This means that each of us has different and varying capacities to receive and retain resurrection power as a spiritual possession (Phil. 3:10-16).

Paul affirms His desire to know Christ more and further experience His resurrection power in his own life. Paul was not perfect. He had not apprehended all that was available to him, but was determined to press forward to obtain all that could be possessed.

August 16 – "To the Praise of His Glory"
Ephesians 1:11-12

In Him also we have obtained an inheritance, being predestined according to the purpose of Him who works all things according to the counsel of His will, that we who first trusted in Christ should be to the praise of His glory.

After Paul speaks of the wonderful blessings those who have been redeemed by Christ have in Him, the apostle highlights why Christ still has His Church in the world: that we *"should be to the praise of His glory."* Paul mentions this idea three times in this narrative (Eph. 1:6, 12, 14).Why is the Church not in heaven with Christ? The main reason we remain on the earth is to show the goodness of Christ to others – to make Him look good – to be the praise of His glory. When Christ determines that work is complete, then He will come to the air, receive His Bride, and return to heaven with His Church.

Through our spiritual sanctification the Lord gets more glory from us as we become more like Him (Rom. 8:29). Believers should sin less with spiritual maturity (Rom. 6:1), though sinless perfection will not be achieved until we experience glorification at His coming (1 Jn. 3:2-3). To be *the praise of His glory*, believers must be marked by righteous living. Believers do not practice sin (1 Jn. 3:8-9), but when we do sin, we are to quickly confess it, repent of it and ask Christ for His cleansing and forgiveness (1 Jn. 1:9).

Nearness to Christ enables us to experience Him and permits us to express His glory. God the Father greatly desires for us to honor the name of His dear Son. This should prompt us to consider what we do and say, and to stay near to the Lord Jesus.

Matthew Henry wisely remarks, "Idleness gives great advantage to the tempter. Standing waters gather filth. The bed of sloth often proves the bed of lust."[26] Straying from the Lord's will, His work, and His presence will always lead us into trouble! Dear believer, by staying near to God and keeping busy in His work we afford the devil fewer opportunities to recruit us into his business. The only reason that the Lord permitted us to rise from our slumber this morning is that we should be to the praise of His glory today. To the extent possible, let us live each and every day to make the Lord Jesus look good!

231

August 17 – A Prayer for Illumination
Ephesians 1:17-19

That the God of our Lord Jesus Christ, the Father of glory, may give to you the spirit of wisdom and revelation in the knowledge of Him, the eyes of your understanding being enlightened; that you may know what is the hope of His calling, what are the riches of the glory of His inheritance in the saints, and what is the exceeding greatness of His power toward us who believe, according to the working of His mighty power.

In verses 15-16, Paul revealed why he was motivated to pray for the Ephesians and also to praise God for their testimony. First, he was prompted to praise God for their good testimony, which was marked by faith in action and demonstrating God's love to others. Second, he acknowledged that as he gave thanks to God for them, he was also inspired to pray for them. Although he did not know their individual needs, he knew that they would be more fruitful and joyful if God granted them further illumination *in the knowledge of Christ.*

Paul asked the Lord to give the Ephesians the spirit of wisdom and a greater personal understanding of Christ. The apostle wanted them to have a deeper experiential and devotional knowledge of God. A loving heart does not depend on intelligence, but rather on knowing God.

Next, Paul wanted them to know what the hope of Christ's calling was in them. Ultimately, this is the same for all believers, which is to be morally like Him (Rom. 8:29) and to be fully son-placed and receive all the inheritance destined by God for those coming into full maturity. This will occur after the Church has been raptured and is with Christ.

Additionally, the apostle prayed that they would be aware of the riches of the glory of Christ's inheritance in the saints. Believers are Christ's own special people (1 Pet. 2:9; Tit. 2:14) and will inherit all things with Christ. The believer will rule and reign with Christ on the earth during the Millennial kingdom (2 Tim. 2:12).

Lastly, Paul wanted them to experientially experience the exceeding greatness of God's power. The same power God used to raise up Christ from the grave to the heights of heaven will also save and preserve the saints of God unto glorification. The Church would do well today to yearn for more understanding of these same aspects of eternal life.

August 18 – Three Enemies to Fight
Ephesians 2:1-3

And you He made alive, who were dead in trespasses and sins, in which you once walked according to the course of this world, according to the prince of the power of the air, the spirit who now works in the sons of disobedience, among whom also we all once conducted ourselves in the lusts of our flesh, fulfilling the desires of the flesh and of the mind, and were by nature children of wrath, just as the others.

Before regeneration, we were children of the devil, walking according to secular philosophies and the passions of our fallen nature. We were dead in trespasses and sins and enslaved by these three masters, but through Christ we have been liberated to serve Him now. Yet, this does not mean that we are not vulnerable to the evil influences of our old masters, the devil, the world, and the flesh. Although we are not enslaved to them anymore, they still seek to master us. Believers must learn that different defenses are needed to combat their efforts.

The first enemy, the devil, is not to be directly confronted, but resisted by submitting to God in faith (Jas. 4:7). There is no need for believers to fear or flee the devil; if they continue resisting him in truth, he will be the one to flee. Believers are to be knowledgeable of his tactics so that he does not gain an advantage over them (2 Cor. 2:11).

Those who have been born again overcome the world by faith as they submit to God's Word: *"For whatever is born of God overcomes the world. And this is the victory that has overcome the world – our faith"* (1 Jn. 5:4). By faith we hold to the truth and reject God-denying philosophies and traditions, rather than be ruined by them (Col. 2:8).

A different strategy is needed to overcome the flesh. Victory over the flesh is achieved by identifying with Christ in His death and in His life (Rom. 6:1-10), choosing not to strengthen the flesh nature by engaging in its deeds (Col. 3:5), but rather through the power of the Holy Spirit mortifying desires outside of God's will for us (Rom. 8:13). This strengthens our inner man to resist future temptation (Eph. 3:16).

May God give us grace to *slay* the deeds of the flesh, to *submit* by faith to the truth, lest we become ensnared by secular ideas, and to *stand* fast in the faith to resist evil!

August 19 – His Workmanship
Ephesians 2:10

For we are His workmanship, created in Christ Jesus for good works, which God prepared beforehand that we should walk in them.

In Psalm 139, David acknowledged that God not only knew everything that he would do before he did it, but he also knew his thoughts afar off. God is omniscient and omnipresent, which ensures that He knows all things within and outside of time. God knows what we will do, what we will say, and what we will think even before we were ever created. Foreknowing our choices and steps in time, God has predestined good works for us to do for His glory and for our reward.

Because time poses no limitations on God, He foreknows our failures and our obedience, which permits Him to preordain specific works for us to accomplish. This is why Peter exhorts Christians to *"make your election sure,"* and Paul instructs us to *"walk in the works that God has foreordained."* Only by the empowerment of the Holy Spirit can we have such a testimony for Christ! Accordingly, Paul says that each believer is God's workmanship (literally a "poem") of His grace and beauty. What God expresses through us pleases Him and results in blessing and joy for us, but what is of carnal motives and pride does not honor Him and results in our sorrow and suffering.

God's work will be accomplished by one means or another; if we are hesitant because of weak faith, He is faithful to enhance our faith, usually by involving those with faith in His purposes. Such individuals will then receive the reward that we might have earned for eternity; deficient faith has many consequences. May God help us when our faith is weak to do those good works in which He has graciously predetermined for us to walk in for His glory. In so doing, we too may echo the words Paul spoke just before his death, *"I have fought the good fight, I have finished the race, I have kept the faith"* (2 Tim. 4:7).

Christians who do not pursue their divinely appointed roles in the body of Christ will not benefit from the Holy Spirit's enabling power. This normally results in harm to the Body and the disdain of Christ's name! May we instead, for the Glory of God, bestow on Him our best years, our best resources, our best abilities, and our spiritual gifts under His control so that we can fulfill His best intentions for us.

August 20 – A Prayer of Apprehension
Ephesians 3:16-21

That He would grant you, according to the riches of His glory, to be strengthened with might through His Spirit in the inner man, that Christ may dwell in your hearts through faith; that you, being rooted and grounded in love, may be able to comprehend with all the saints what is the width and length and depth and height – to know the love of Christ which passes knowledge; that you may be filled with all the fullness of God. Now to Him who is able to do exceedingly abundantly above all that we ask or think, according to the power that works in us, to Him be glory in the church by Christ Jesus to all generations, forever and ever.

In chapter 1, Paul prayed that the Ephesians would receive further spiritual illumination in comprehending Christ. He now prays that this further understanding would prompt them to better apprehend Christ, so that they could further experience His resurrection power.

Before beginning his prayer, he requested that the Ephesians would "not lose heart" concerning his present tribulations, which had been for their benefit. Given what had been accomplished by his ministry, they should view his imprisonment as a glory (a triumph), not as disgrace.

Then, the apostle prayed that God would bless them with particular blessings. First, he asked that they would be strengthened in the inner man according to the riches of Christ's glory. A rich man might give to someone "out of his riches" a trifle amount to assist someone in need. Not so with the Lord; He gives "according to His riches." He lavishes us with what is proportional to His wealth! Second, Paul prayed that Christ would dwell in their hearts by faith. Christ takes up residence within a repentant sinner at his or her conversion and regeneration. Paul is not talking about the possibility of Christ leaving the believer, but rather how much Christ feels at home while residing in the believer.

Third, Paul requested that they might know the love of Christ and then be rooted and grounded in that love. Maintaining unrestricted access before the throne of grace permits the believer to be deeply rooted in love. Fourth, the apostle requested that they would be filled with all the fullness of God; this comes through fully knowing and adoring Christ. In closing, Paul tells them to remember that Christ was able to bring about much more than they can imagine or even ask for.

August 21 – Walk Worthy of Your Calling
Ephesians 4:1-3

I, therefore, the prisoner of the Lord, beseech you to walk worthy of the calling with which you were called, with all lowliness and gentleness, with longsuffering, bearing with one another in love, endeavoring to keep the unity of the Spirit in the bond of peace.

Believers in Christ get a new walk – a new lifestyle to be lived out (Eph. 4:17). We are to walk worthy of our calling in Christ, lest we disgrace His name. Such a lifestyle will exhibit Christ's love (Eph. 5:2), abide in the truth (Eph. 5:8), and display wisdom (Eph. 5:15). Such a walk of integrity is only possible by walking in the Spirit (Gal. 5:16). Paul then describes the behavior of a believer being controlled by the Holy Spirit:

- Lowliness: Genuine humility that is cognizant of our own nothingness and lifts the interests of others above our own.

- Meekness/gentleness: This is power in control and submits to God's working in our lives without a rebel attitude.

- Longsuffering: A spirit of patience even under long, difficult circumstances.

- Bearing with one another: Showing love to those who hurt, irritate, or disturb you.

- Keeping unity: The Spirit makes for unity in the Body, but it is up to us to keep it; we are to live in peace with each other.

When believers are in communion with the Lord through willing submission, they will be in fellowship with each other and be able to serve the Lord together better. Believers are to *"keep the unity of the Spirit in the bond of peace."* The Holy Spirit is the only One who can create unity in the Church, and believers are the only ones who through carnal behavior and impure thinking can destroy that unity. If we are not in fellowship with God, it will be impossible for us to be in fellowship with each other or to serve the Lord in a cooperative way. His peace and blessing will be missing in all we attempt to do.

August 22 – A Sevenfold Unity to Be Enjoyed
Ephesians 4:4-6

There is one body and one Spirit, just as you were called in one hope of your calling; one Lord, one faith, one baptism; one God and Father of all, who is above all, and through all, and in you all.

Paul had just exhorted the Ephesians to be *"endeavoring to keep the unity of the Spirit in the bond of peace."* The Holy Spirit draws together all believers in Christ, equips them to serve each other, and to lubricate the Body, so to speak, so all the serving members, or moving parts, do not generate too much friction! In local churches where believer-priests are sitting on the premises instead of standing on the promises, there is little friction because there are few moving parts.

Paul then reminds the Ephesians of seven unities that all believers enjoy together. We enjoy these same aspects of Body unity today. First, there is one Body. The Church is composed of all believers from all different ethnic backgrounds over the entire Church Age. This spiritual temple is still being constructed, and when the last believer is added to the Body, then Christ will return for His Church.

Second, there is one Spirit. The third person of the Trinity is fully God and thus omnipresent, omniscient, omnipotent, immutable, and eternal. He does what is needed and indwells all believers forever.

Third, there is one hope. For the Church, this blessed hope is the Lord's coming for His bride, which we often refer to as the rapture (or "the catching up") of the Church from the earth into glory.

Fourth, there is one Lord. The Lord Jesus Christ is the centerpiece of heaven and to be the object of our attention and affection. He is our Master and Savior and we are to serve Him faithfully.

Fifth, there is one faith. There is only one divinely given doctrine (by revelation to the apostles) that forms the basis of the Christian faith.

Sixth, there is one baptism. Since the spiritual bond of Jew and Greek in Christ is spoken in the "one body" (v. 4), baptism here likely speaks of the profession of Christ's Lordship by both Jew and Greek at water baptism. Else, the idea of spiritual baptism would be redundant.

Seventh, there is one divine Father. As God, the Father is above all, through all, and in all believers. Instead of magnifying all of our differences, may we ponder all that we have in common in Christ.

August 23 – Equipping of the Saints
Ephesians 4:11-12

And He Himself gave some to be apostles, some prophets, some evangelists, and some pastors and teachers for the equipping of the saints for the work of ministry, for the edifying of the body of Christ.

Christ gives various individuals to the Church *for the equipping of the saints for the work of ministry, for the edifying of the Body.* Every believer has a work of ministry, the benefit of which will bless the entire body. Apostles were "sent ones" that were commissioned personally by the Lord and were given special authority by Christ to do signs and wonders (Heb. 2:4). The apostles led the Church in its infancy, until church elders were in place for each local assembly. The last mention of the apostles having a leadership role in the affairs of the Church is recorded in Acts 16:4. This is in reference with them working with church elders at the Council of Jerusalem in Acts 15 to determine whether or not Gentile men should be circumcised after trusting in Christ for salvation. The apostles provided the Church the foundational doctrines of the Faith (Heb. 2:3). Once Scripture had been God breathed and canonized, the ministry of the founding apostles and teaching prophets was fulfilled (1 Cor. 13:9-10). The prophets spoke for God to the saints until Scripture was canonized; this would involve both private and public ministry (Acts 21:9; 1 Cor. 14:29-32).

Evangelists equip saints to evangelize, often through personal example. It is a misconception to think of evangelists primarily as soul-winners. While it is true that evangelists have a passion for souls and are bold in sharing the gospel message, their primary task is to stir up and equip the Body of Christ to fulfill the Great Commission. All believers are to be witnesses for Christ (Acts 1:8), and evangelists help those of us who are not evangelists to evangelize others. Pastors are those who would shepherd God's people. Most elders would certainly be included in this group, but it also would include men who are not elders and women who shepherd women and children. It is noted that there is no definite article in front of teachers, thus, rules of Greek would connect "pastors" and "teachers" to signify the same individual. Teachers are those who expound truth and exhort others to follow it, both in word and in deed (they live out what they teach).

August 24 – The *Poimen* Gift
Ephesians 4:11-12

And He Himself gave some to be apostles, some prophets, some evangelists, and some pastors and teachers for the equipping of the saints for the work of ministry, for the edifying of the body of Christ.

Two Greek words are used in the New Testament to identify those men who hold an office of leadership in their respective local churches: *presbuteros* (elder) and *episkopos* (overseer). These two words (including their verb forms) relate to a church position which was not given at spiritual rebirth, but gained as a result of spiritual maturity, divine calling, and public recognition. A man may serve as a *presbuteros* and *episkopos* in one assembly, but if he relocates he may not be in the leadership of another church. A third word, *poimen,* is normally used to speak of the shepherding work in which both elders and non-elders engage. It is one of five spiritual gifts that Christ bestows to individuals in the Church at their conversion (Eph. 4:11-12). Thus, the pastoral gift remains within the recipient throughout his or her entire lifetime, regardless of where he or she may take up residence.

The gift *poimen* is not gender-specific, nor can it be equated directly with the office of elder, though certainly many elders will have this spiritual gift. It is noted that the only instances in which *poimen* is used in the New Testament to describe a specific person is when it is applied to the Lord Jesus. He is the Good *Poimen* (John 10:11), the Chief *Poimen* (1 Pet. 5:4), and the Great *Poimen* (Heb. 13:20).

The Greek word *presbuteros* and the related word *presbuterion* are used seventeen times to speak of church elders. *Episkopos* (and its verb form) is used six times in the New Testament to address the "overseers" (again referring to church elders). It is noted that no spiritual gift criterion, such as *poimen,* is required for a church elder. In summary, elders (a plurality of godly men) are to govern each assembly; they are to pastor those whom God puts into their care, although some of them may not have received the pastoral spiritual gift. All the elders of a meeting have equal authority, but they do not necessarily have equal gifts or equal administrations of a gift – this is what brings strength and balance to a plurality of church leadership. Brothers serving in unity are a lovely representation of the triune nature of God at work!

August 25 – The Work of Ministry
Ephesians 4:11-12

And He Himself gave some to be apostles, some prophets, some evangelists, and some pastors and teachers for the equipping of the saints for the work of ministry, for the edifying of the body of Christ.

The Lord Jesus gave individuals, such as evangelists and teachers, as gifts to the Church *"for the equipping of the saints for the work of ministry."* Every believer in the body of Christ has a work of ministry to engage in, the benefit of which will bless the entire Body. As believers rightly use their spiritual gifts, they equip others in the Body to do ministry, which then passes the original blessing along to other believers in order to further edify the body.

Visualize for a moment several children standing perfectly still in a wading pool while another child jumps into the pool. The resultant wave glides across the surface of the water and eventually bounces off every child in the pool. Each time the wave comes in contact with a child, it is also reflected back across the pool, eventually making contact with every other child in the pool, and so on. This wave-motion phenomenon illustrates how the initial edification of one member in the Body equips other members to minister to the Body; the blessing then continues to spread throughout the Body.

The outcome of such body-life enables individuals to reach their full potential in Christ and fulfill God's sovereign purpose for their lives. For example, though the evangelist is skillful in reaching the lost for Christ, his or her main ministry to the Church is to equip and to stir up others within the Body to evangelize wherever God has placed them as a testimony. The result is that, in a collective sense, the Church is stimulated and enabled to obey the great commission (Matt. 28:19-20).

Beneficial Church body-life is enjoyed as each member learns and practices sound doctrine while also learning how to properly use his or her spiritual gifts. Scripture supplies a foundation of truth for each believer to live out and practical sanctification occurs when he or she yields to it. Inevitably, all believers will suffer failure; conviction, correction, and reproof are God's means for restoring the wayward to righteous living. The Holy Spirit and other believers will assist in this ministry. God-honoring service becomes more feasible with maturity.

August 26 – Do Not Be Tossed to and Fro
Ephesians 4:14

That we should no longer be children, tossed to and fro and carried about with every wind of doctrine, by the trickery of men, in the cunning craftiness of deceitful plotting.

The Lord Jesus commanded the Church to be occupied with three main ministries in His absence: the upward ministry of *exaltation*, the inward ministry of *edification*, and the outward ministry of *evangelism*. These three important ministries of the Church can be summarized by the short slogan: "Lift up, build up, and reach out." Some refer to these as the "Three E's" or "E³": the *Exaltation* of God, the *Edification* of believers, and the *Evangelism* of the lost.

If an assembly has great worship, but no evangelism, in time they will die out. If a church engages in evangelism, but neglects discipleship, the babes in Christ will tend to be blown to and fro with every wind of doctrine. Many will eventually leave the church to find one better suited to their comfort level. If a local church has tremendous teaching, but fails to stimulate new believers to love and honor the Lord, those being discipled will not have the right motive for service, nor will they be inclined to flee sin. Those who don't grow in their love and appreciation for Christ will not live for Him; even if they know the truth, they have no reason to make personal sacrifices for it.

The inward ministry centers in the *edification* of all believers. The Bible likens this ministry to that of a shepherd (John 21:15-17; Acts 20:28-31; 1 Pet. 5:1-3). The Lord commissioned His disciples to teach those responding to the gospel message all the things that they had been taught by Him (Matt. 28:20). Believers in the early Church readily taught new disciples what they knew to be true, by referring them to His Word (Acts 2:42, 4:2, 5:42, 11:26, 13:1, 20:35). The apostles also instructed believers to engage in this important ministry, and again, *"Preach the word! Be ready in season and out of season. Convince, rebuke, exhort, with all longsuffering and teaching"* (2 Tim. 4:2). Teaching, reproof, instruction, and correction through the use of God's Word is absolutely necessary to refine believers' characters in such a way as to make them profitable unto good works (2 Tim. 3:16-17). The need for discipleship ministries in the Church is paramount today.

August 27 – Cooperation in the Body
Ephesians 4:16

From whom the whole body, joined and knit together by what every joint supplies, according to the effective working by which every part does its share, causes growth of the body for the edifying of itself in love.

Paul informed the believers at Ephesus that all believers should engage in Spirit-led worship and service. All believers are equipped with spiritual gifts to serve and edify the body of Christ (1 Cor. 12:4-7). Only when all believers use their spiritual gifts with the full measure of faith that God gives will the Church be fully functional (Rom. 12:3; 1 Pet. 4:10). The New Testament reveals ministries and offices that individuals were associated with, but no believer was given a personal title as part of his or her fulfillment of these. For example, there were apostles, elders, deacons, evangelists, pastor-teachers, etc. in the early Church, but no disciple of Christ was referred to by a title before his or her name. However, for centuries it has been the practice of the Church to ascribe to men names and labels that they ought not to have.

In truth, all believers have been equipped to serve Christ. Accordingly, all believers have common designations in Christ and should not seek titles or use terminologies that elevate themselves to unbiblical roles in the Church or that displace Christ's supreme position over the Church or lessen the oneness that all believers enjoy together. For example the idea of clergy and laity is totally foreign to Scripture.

Although the Lord provides elders to shepherd local assemblies, these men are not referred to as the Pastors of that particular church. Those in local church leadership have a ministry to the Chief Shepherd, not an elevated position above fellow-believers. Whatever authority the elders have springs forth from lives of godliness and subjection to the Lord, and not from human ambitions, certificates, or titles.

No title of position can be found before the name of any disciple of Christ anywhere in Scripture; in fact, the Lord forbids such nomenclature (Matt. 23:9-11). Why? Because all titles of honor are reserved for Him. This helps ensure that we continue to regard Him as the only Lord of the Church, and ourselves as merely brethren. We must avoid thinking more highly of ourselves than we ought to think.

August 28 – Put Off and Put On
Ephesians 4:22-25

That you put off, concerning your former conduct, the old man which grows corrupt according to the deceitful lusts, and be renewed in the spirit of your mind, and that you put on the new man which was created according to God, in true righteousness and holiness. Therefore, putting away lying, "Let each one of you speak truth with his neighbor," for we are members of one another.

As previously mentioned, when a believer thinks upon what is corrupt, it must lead to a legitimate harvest of corruption (Gal. 6:7-8). It will be realized long after the initial seeds were sown and the repercussions will be far more devastating than what could have ever been imagined. Consequently, believers must desire to be controlled by the Holy Spirit and not their lusting flesh – only then are the deeds of the flesh mortified and fellowship with God maintained: *"If by the Spirit you put to death the deeds of the body, you will live"* (Rom. 8:13). By doing so, we put on the *new man* that we are in Christ! Practically speaking, the believer has been crucified with Christ (Rom. 6:6) so that his or her craving flesh will eventually die (i.e., the old nature loses control in the believer's life as he or she matures in Christ).

Moreover, Paul commanded the saints at Colosse to *"Put to death your members which are on the earth: fornication, uncleanness, passion, evil desire, and covetousness, which is idolatry"* (Col. 3:5). In addition to the believer's lusting flesh eventually dying and the need to mortify its deeds whenever observed, Paul told the believers at Colosse not to feed (strengthen) the nature of the old man, but rather to put him off (Col. 3:9). The ungodly longings of the flesh (some of which are listed in Col. 3:5) should not be strengthened through sinful behavior or by wrong thinking, but rather these should be starved so that they lose their strength and can be "put off" from the believer's conduct completely. If not fed, these ungodly longings lose their hold on the believer's life and die out more quickly – though ultimate freedom will not be achieved until glorification. Mortification or gratification are the only two things the flesh understands. The only spiritual recourse in dealing with the lusting of the flesh is to extend it a deadly blow and to keep on mortifying it every day – this is God's will for every believer.

August 29 – Do Not Steal, but Labor to Give to Others
Ephesians 4:28

Let him who stole steal no longer, but rather let him labor, working with his hands what is good, that he may have something to give him who has need.

Paul reminded the believers at Corinth not to be proud concerning their possessions: *"For who makes you differ from another? And what do you have that you did not receive? Now if you did indeed receive it, why do you boast as if you had not received it?"* (1 Cor. 4:7). Whatever we have comes from God; there is no room for pride. Paul exhorted the Ephesians that, rather than stealing from others as they may have done before they were saved, they instead ought to work hard to supply their own necessities and then to assist those in need. Let us not think so highly of ourselves and our possessions that we are not willing to assist others with what God has graciously placed in our stewardship.

We also should remember that God has ordered our laboring: Husbands labor (usually outside the home) to provide for their family's basic necessities, while wives labor within the home accomplishing domestic duties and caring for children (Gen. 3:19; 1 Tim. 5:14). When these priorities are met, we are not to labor more to indulge our flesh with frivolous luxuries and extravagances. These only tend to strangle the spiritual man and pull our hearts away from the Lord. If our necessities are satisfied, we are to labor for others in legitimate need.

Because our time is important, we want to labor efficiently. Our best proficiency in serving will occur as we apply the very skills that have already been developed in normal laboring. You would seek a plumber, not a painter, if you had a leaky pipe. The painter might be able to do the work, but it would take longer and perhaps be of lower quality. Hence, men should labor in their normal jobs to provide extra income for those in need, while women will assist the needy with their in-home abilities or perhaps with other specific proficiencies developed by years of experience. One of the biggest travesties of 21st century church-life is that women enter the workforce after their children depart from home, instead of assisting younger wives and mothers with the domestic knowledge they have accumulated. But this is a crucial ministry ordained by God and it should not be neglected (Tit. 2:3-5).

August 30 – Do Not Grieve the Holy Spirit
Ephesians 4:30

Do not grieve the Holy Spirit of God, by whom you were sealed for the day of redemption.

Paul had a specific prayer request for the Christians at Thessalonica: *"Now may the God of peace Himself sanctify you completely; and may your whole spirit, soul, and body be preserved blameless at the coming of our Lord Jesus Christ"* (1 Thess. 5:23). It is God's desire that we, in our entirety, be "set apart" for His purpose, including our minds. As the believer's mind is one of the primary focuses of satanic assault, it stands to reason that the mind should be strengthened defensively and ready to minister a proper spiritual response. This is achieved by learning and rightly applying Scripture to various situations, instead of letting secular reasoning, our emotions, or flesh nature control our actions. The more we know of God's Word, the more our minds will be open and pliable to the leading, conviction, and caution of the Holy Spirit in directing the affairs of life.

Wrong thinking and behavior grieves the Holy Spirit and quenches His full activities within the believer (1 Thess. 5:19). Submission and holy behavior result in Spirit filling (Eph. 5:17-18) which enables the believer to pour out the blessings of God to others. It is essential for believers to learn the mind of Christ and learn to think with the same compassion, humility, and wisdom that Christ would in various situations. This ensures that the Holy Spirit will not be hindered from operations, thus allowing the infusing power of God to pass through the believer as electricity passes through wire. William Kelly reminds us that what often begins as an unchecked thought can quickly blossom into sin – all that is not Christ-like grieves the Holy Spirit:

> How often through lack of prayer and watchfulness fleshly lusts spring from sincere esteem and pure affection unawares gliding into carnality! How readily little fond familiarities follow by degrees, in the intimacy of Christian love ripening into unhallowed freedom, if not the worst evil. These fleshly desires, many of which men praise as doing well to self, war against the soul and are an abomination in God's sight. How mischievous and debasing to the Christian! They grieve the Holy Spirit, dishonor Christ, and fight against the soul.[27]

August 31 – No Bitterness, Rage, or Resentment
Ephesians 4:31

Let all bitterness, wrath, anger, clamor, and evil speaking be put away from you, with all malice.

Anger is an emotion, not a behavior. Anger can serve God or serve the flesh (Eph. 4:26). Scripture identifies four main outlets in which our anger will manifest itself. Two of these behaviors are God-honoring, while the remaining two lead to sin. Two behaviors are Spirit-controlled and two are flesh-motivated. We will cover the latter first.

First, there is *rage* or "blowing up": In this verse it is called *wrath*, as derived from the Greek word *thumos*. Rage is violent, an expression of uncontrolled anger – a work of the flesh with visible harm. It is sometimes referred to as *Open Aggression* and is "a self-preserving stand for personal worth, needs, and convictions at someone else's expense." Rage doesn't think; it vents in order to satisfy selfish need.

Second, there is *resentment* or "clamming up": It is referred to as *anger* in this verse, translated from the Greek *orge*. Resentment represses feelings of anger, which then smolder and ultimately seek covert revenge. Often it is social etiquette that forces us to resolve expressions of rage and to choose resentment as a more acceptable form of expressing anger. Denying the existence of angry feelings and pushing them down inside creates resentment and eventually bitterness.

Third, there is *righteous indignation* or "lifting God up." Indignation sacrifices selfish interest in order to intensely and actively pattern God's own abhorrence of sin. The Lord was "displeased" with His disciples for forbidding children to come to Him (Mark 10:14).

Fourth, there is *release* or "giving anger up." The word *charizomai* is often rendered "forgiving," as in the next verse. *Release* determines not to take revenge for an offense, but is determined to suffer loss and simply entrust the Lord with the outcome. It waits patiently for the opportunity to extend forgiveness when the offending party confesses sin (Luke 17:3); until such time the matter remains in the background of one's thinking. The main word rendered "forgive" in the Gospels is *aphiemi* and means "let be." However, in the Epistles, we learn of how we have been fully forgiven by God through Christ, thus, we are to willfully release offenses to God, rather than just take no action.

September 1 – Forgiving One Another
Ephesians 4:32

And be kind to one another, tenderhearted, forgiving one another, even as God in Christ forgave you.

The Greek word *charizomai* is found twenty-four times in the New Testament. It is translated as various forms of "forgive" fourteen times. Interestingly, only two of these fourteen references are found in the Gospel accounts (both are contained in one parable in Luke 7); the remaining occurrences are contained in the Epistles. *Charizomai* means "to bestow a favor unconditionally or to freely give." It expresses the type of unconditional *releasing* attitude a Christian should maintain when offended by others. To freely release the matter means that one does not seek revenge, vengeance or become resentful.

The mechanics of forgiveness are mainly addressed in the Gospel accounts and are associated with a different Greek word *aphiemi*, which means "to send away" and by implication "let it be – take no action." For example, Matthew 18:15-18 informs us how to go about problem resolution with others, while Luke 17:3 instructs us not to *declare* personal forgiveness until the offending party has repented.

Why did the Holy Spirit mainly use *aphiemi* in the Gospel accounts and *charizomai* in the Epistles to speak of forgiveness? Apparently, because the Epistles better express the proper motive for forgiveness: *"Forgiving one another, if anyone has a complaint against another; even as Christ forgave you, so you also must do"* (Col. 3:13).

In view of the believer's immense debt of sin that has been forgiven because of Calvary, we must be ready to forgive those who offend us. This will free us from being in bondage to bitterness and enable us to pray for those who despitefully use us. The unresolved matter is, thus, immediately left in the Lord's hands. This liberating activity allows a believer to move the offense into the background of their thinking and not keep it in the foreground. The unresolved issue, though not forgotten, does not rule one's daily life, for it has been given to Christ.

When the offending individual does confess his or her wrongdoing, we have already been well prepared to personally declare the matter forgiven. In light of the huge debt we have been forgiven, we must be willing to forgive the petty offenses, in comparison, of others.

247

September 2 – No Fornication or Even Joking About It
Ephesians 5:3-5

But fornication and all uncleanness or covetousness, let it not even be named among you, as is fitting for saints; neither filthiness, nor foolish talking, nor coarse jesting, which are not fitting, but rather giving of thanks. For this you know, that no fornicator, unclean person, nor covetous man, who is an idolater, has any inheritance in the kingdom of Christ and God.

The Lord Jesus affirmed God's design for marriage – a covenant between one biological man and one biological woman until death separates them (Matt. 19:4-6). This is the pattern that the apostles, church elders, and deacons adhered to (1 Cor. 9:5; 1 Tim. 3:1-12); consequently, there are no examples of Christians engaging in polygamy, open-marriages, or homosexual relationships in the New Testament. There are, however, many warnings and prohibitions against fornication. Jude includes a history lesson in his warning: *"Even as Sodom and Gomorrah, and the cities about them in like manner, giving themselves over to fornication, and going after strange flesh, are set forth for an example, suffering the vengeance of eternal fire"* (Jude 7). Any sexual relation other than between a husband and a wife is referred to in Scripture as fornication. This is why Paul says *"to avoid fornication, let every man have his own wife"* (1 Cor. 7:2). Fornication then includes adultery, pre-marital unions, homosexuality (e.g., sodomy), bestiality, etc. Under the Law, any Jew engaging in these sexual sins was to be put to death (Lev. 20:10-13), except those engaging in pre-marital sex were to marry (Deut. 22:29).

God's standard for sexual behavior in the New Testament is unchanged (1 Cor. 6:9-11, 18; 1 Thess. 4:3; Rev. 21:8); the only difference is that expedient punishment for sexual sins is not demanded by God for the Church. Because such sins are offensive to God, Paul warns the believers to avoid: uncleanness, covetousness, and filthiness. Uncleanness would be looking at impure pictures or suggestive material. Covetousness would be lusting to satisfy one's sexual appetites outside marriage. Filthiness would be engaging in dirty jokes, foolish talk, coarse jesting, or puns with sexual overtones. Fornication is such a serious sin that believers are not to even joke about it.

September 3 – Exposing Works of Darkness
Ephesians 5:11-13

And have no fellowship with the unfruitful works of darkness, but rather expose them. For it is shameful even to speak of those things which are done by them in secret. But all things that are exposed are made manifest by the light, for whatever makes manifest is light.

Someone who truly knows the God of the Bible understands that God knows our thoughts and all that we do. Hence, there are no excuses which can fool Him, no place dark enough to hide from Him, and no possibility that He will forget what offends Him. The all-wise Creator will judge our motives for what we do for Him and our behavior that disappoints Him, including willful silence amid injustice.

Believers are instructed to *"have no fellowship with the unfruitful works of darkness, but rather expose them."* Jacob did nothing after hearing that his son Reuben had slept with Bilhah (Jacob's concubine; Gen. 35:22). Jacob did not reprove his son's sin, but rather waited to the end of his life (some forty years later) to announce the repercussions of Reuben's behavior (Gen. 49:4). But during that interim, his silence excused the sin. Suppose that you and your children are walking through a park and see teenagers breaking glass bottles on the sidewalk. This behavior is new to your children and they wait for your instruction concerning it. If you say nothing, you have approved the act in their minds. Wrong and sinful behavior must be reproved.

If the light of our testimony does not confront the darkness of sin, something is wrong; silence condones sin! William MacDonald explains why believers cannot be silent spectators of unrighteousness:

When innocent people are being led off to gas chambers, ovens, and other modes of execution – when unborn babies are destroyed in abortion clinics – it is inexcusable to stand by and not seek to rescue them. It is also useless to plead ignorance. As Dante said, "The hottest places in hell are reserved for those who in a time of great moral crisis maintain their neutrality."[28]

Our society is in great moral crisis! Those who would side with God cannot be silent against social depravity; we must seek and love good while shunning and confronting evil. Our light must shine!

September 4 – Redeeming the Time
Ephesians 5:15-16

See then that you walk circumspectly, not as fools but as wise, redeeming the time, because the days are evil.

Moses and Aaron faithfully delivered Jehovah's demand for Pharaoh to release the Israelites so that they could worship Him in the wilderness. However, Pharaoh surmised that his slaves apparently had too much time on their hands if they were thinking about an extended holiday in the desert. His remedy for this perceived inefficiency and idleness was to command the Jews to *"get to their burdens"* and he increased their workload *"the same day"* (Ex. 5). Not only would the Jews have to perform their existing duties, but they now also had to scavenge for their own straw to produce bricks. Pharaoh's solution to Moses and Aaron's request was to keep the Jews so busy they would have no time to think about getting alone with their God.

The same tactic is used today by Satan to divert the Lord's people from spending time alone with their Savior and from serving Him. The world system that Satan controls devalues the things of God and exaggerates the value of what is temporary and sensual. Consequently, undiscerning believers have been deceived into forsaking the best for that which may be permissible, but which steals their available time. Satan's strategy: those Christians can have their religion, but I will not let them have any time to enjoy fellowship with their Savior.

Many families have allowed the teen culture of our day and its associated busyness to rule the home. Much time is expended transporting children to "fluff of life" activities while dads are beguiled into working more hours to financially support the extra entertainment and amusements of their children. Consequently, not only do many families have no time to be families, they have no time to whole-heartedly pursue the Lord. The home thus loses its appeal as a safe haven and a place of significance and importance to the children. The lack of family devotions and family time together is devastating to the family unity and promotes the isolation of its members. The way in which we use our time speaks frankly of our love for the Lord. We cannot *buy back* time per se, but we can *buy up* opportunities to serve God. Let us have no regrets later for how we spent our lives now.

September 5 – Know What the Will of God Is
Ephesians 5:17

Therefore do not be unwise, but understand what the will of the Lord is.

Through sanctification, the believer is separated and carved out of the world to be like the Lord Jesus, to be used by Him, and to glorify God. In this manner the Holy Spirit saves the believer from being ruled by his or her inherent depraved nature and from the clutches of the corrupt world system. Although God uses a host of ways to conform the believer to the likeness of His Son, two general means are employed. First, an individual must invest time in God's Word to know Him and His will (John 15:3, 17:17). Second, God will orchestrate various trials, tests, sufferings, persecutions, and other circumstances in our lives in order to fashion holy character in us and to bring us closer to Him. Both of these activities enable the believer to better understand the will of God in our lives.

Normally, when Scripture speaks of the will of God, it explicitly states what it is. The will of God is not some abstract concept that is variable for different believers, but rather the Bible expresses God's will in terms of the proper conduct and holy living which is required of all Christians. There is no mystery about it; God has declared to us His general will for our lives; we are to understand the will of God and to submit to it (Eph. 5:17; 1 Thess. 4:3, 5:18; 1 Pet. 2:15). What we desperately need from the Lord is day-by-day guidance: *"Trust in the Lord with all your heart, and lean not on your own understanding; in all your ways acknowledge Him, and He shall direct your paths"* (Prov. 3:5-6). If you are toiling in the Word to know God's will and submitting to what you do understand, you need not be anxious about the daily specifics of your life; His faithful hand will guide you.

In summary, the pertinent question is not what the will of God is for my life, but will I obey the revealed will of God for my life? A lack of love for the Lord will be shown through an unyielding spirit and through disobedience (John 14:15). Dear believer, life is short, a fleeting vapor in time; don't waste it pursuing things that you know are outside of God's will for your life. What you do for eternity the world cannot destroy, nor can anyone steal (Matt. 6:19-20).

September 6 – Be Filled With the Spirit
Ephesians 5:18

And do not be drunk with wine, in which is dissipation; but be filled with the Spirit.

Drunkenness is consistently forbidden throughout Scripture. Paul exhorts believers not to be controlled by excess wine, but rather be controlled by the Holy Spirit. The Greek verb *pleroo* is rendered "be filled" and means "to have influence or control over." In moderation, the fruit of the vine may stir up joy, but if abused, it certainly will control our behavior. Both the Holy Spirit and wine can be permitted to have influence within us that affects our behavior. Paul is not suggesting that believers get more of the Holy Spirit through being filled by Him, but rather He gets more of us. Both alcohol and the Holy Spirit can cause us to behave abnormally; the former promotes folly, and the latter only what pleases God.

It would be impossible for a believer to be filled with wine (controlled by the effects of alcohol) and also be filled with the Holy Spirit. In actuality, there are a host of things that we can permit into our lives that influence our thinking negatively besides abusing alcohol. How can the Holy Spirit fill us up, if we have allowed our minds to be flooded with things that do not have God's approval? If we are pursuing selfish or carnal lusts, or have strongholds of envy, pride, or bitterness in our hearts, what room is there for the Holy Spirit to add His goodness? We cannot be filled by Him, if we are already full of ourselves. Under His conviction, we must first empty ourselves in order to yield to Him and experience His control. F. B. Hole writes:

> The contrast is between what is fleshly and what is spiritual. We are to decline what excites the flesh that we may know the power of the Spirit. ... When thus filled we can offer the sacrifice of praise.[29]

As the believer submits to the known will of God, the Holy Spirit responds by filling that individual and equipping him or her for service with divine power. The idea of "filling" is not that the Spirit just pours into the believer, but rather he or she is crammed full of His divine presence. Submission leads to Spirit-filling, which results in usefulness and fruitfulness; without Spirit-filling we can do nothing to please God.

September 7 – Psalms, Hymns, and Spiritual Songs
Ephesians 5:19

Speaking to one another in psalms and hymns and spiritual songs, singing and making melody in your heart to the Lord.

Paul wrote something similar to the church at Colosse: *"Let the word of Christ dwell in you richly in all wisdom, teaching and admonishing one another in psalms and hymns and spiritual songs, singing with grace in your hearts to the Lord"* (Col. 3:16). Clearly, the purpose of the Church's singing is to reaffirm Scriptural truth and to worship and praise God.

Many churches at present are singing the hymns of old along with more modern praise choruses. The vast majority of the hymns we sing today have been brought into doctrinal correctness through years of editing; very few of the older hymns are in their original form. J. N. Darby and G. V. Wigram heavily edited the *Little Flock Hymnbook.* Samuel Trevor Francis, a notable poet, refused to have his hymns included in the *Little Flock Hymnbook* because he objected to Wigram's meddling. Regrettably, many of the modern choruses have not undergone the same degree of scrutiny, and many of the lyrics associated with Christian music today have not been developed by theologians and Bible teachers, but by musicians who favor pleasant sounding poetry. Consequently, much of the fervent aspirations of Crosby, Watts, and Wesley are not heard in today's music.

Listen to the aspirations of David's heart beating aloud for God: *"I will behave myself wisely in a perfect way ... I will walk within my house with a perfect heart"* (Ps. 101:2). Though David had not yet attained, he sometimes spoke of his highest aspirations as realized facts. Christian poetry and music should compel us to reach *"forth unto those things which are before – toward the mark for the prize of the high calling of God in Christ Jesus"* (Phil. 3:13-14).

Regrettably, the Church accepts error more readily through music than through preaching, and Satan knows it! Understanding that music is a powerful medium in which to convey both our thoughts to God and messages to each other, let us be careful to ensure that what we are singing is doctrinally sound and that the composition does not stir up the flesh to carnal behavior or thinking.

September 8 – Giving Thanks Always (Part 1)
Ephesians 5:20

Giving thanks always for all things to God the Father in the name of our Lord Jesus Christ.

How is it possible to offer God thanks *for all things*, when much of what we suffer in our sin-cursed world is distasteful, harsh, unjust, and sometimes deadly? The idea here is not just to find something in a bad situation to thank God for, but to actually show appreciation for His sovereign care, even when it does not seem reasonable to. Here are five reasons to give God thanks even when we do not feel like it:

First, we are commanded to give thanks (1 Thess. 5:16-18; Eph. 5:20; Col. 3:15-17). From these three passages we learn that we are to be thankful: *"in everything," "for all things,"* and *"in whatever we do in word or deed."* Moses also reminds us that our complaining is insulting to God, who controls all the events of our lives (Ex. 16:8). We may not feel like being joyful or thankful after a particular hardship, but we must; later, we will be glad that we did (Phil. 3:15-16)! We cannot be strong, but we can choose to rejoice in Christ – strength will come. Daniel was in a life-threatening ordeal but chose to give thanks to God (Dan. 6:10). Afterwards he was promoted and his God was exalted throughout the Persian Empire. Choosing to give God thanks at arduous times provides an opportunity for God to exalt Himself.

Second, it demonstrates that we know God (Rom. 1:20-21; Ps. 26:7; Ps. 116:17). To thank the Lord when circumstances dictate otherwise shows that we understand His character and attributes, and count Him faithful. When things go wrong, do not go wrong with them; rather, rejoice in the Lord, who will right all wrongs. King Jehoshaphat provides an example of this disposition. The Moabites, Ammonites, and Edomites were set to invade Judah. King Jehoshaphat did not know what to do. He chose to turn his eyes to the Lord and caused the people to rejoice before Him. The congregation was led by singers towards the enemy, but this was God's fight alone and He delivered His people from harm and gave them the spoil of their enemies (2 Chron. 20). Jehoshaphat's response of rejoicing permitted an opportunity for God to show Himself strong and do the impossible.

September 9 – Giving Thanks Always (Part 2)
Ephesians 5:20

Giving thanks always for all things to God the Father in the name of our Lord Jesus Christ.

How is it possible to offer God thanks *for all things*, even when we are suffering from injustice or a tragedy? Five biblical reasons are offered to answer this question. The first two have already been discussed; it is commanded and it shows that we know our God.

Third, giving thanks invigorates our praying, which settles our minds (Col. 4:2; Phil. 4:4, 6-7). Those who have peace with God are also offered the peace of God. The Lord told His disciples twice: *"peace be with you"* after His resurrection (John 20:19-21). The Lord's presence put their minds at peace, but they would need additional peace to properly convey Christ's message of peace to others. Choosing to rejoice provides an opportunity for God's peace to rule our hearts (e.g., Mary's choice to praise God, despite future unknowns; Luke 1:46-47).

Fourth, giving thanks affirms that we want to know and be like Christ (Rom. 8:28-29; Col. 2:6-7). Rejoicing in God while in hardship permits us to be drawn deeper into the secret of His presence, which gives us an opportunity to experience God. Paul "rejoiced greatly" despite his trial; He had been initiated into the secret of God's goodness and hence was content (Phil 4:10-11). In prison Paul wrote: *"Rejoice in the Lord ... I also count all things loss for the excellence of the knowledge of Christ Jesus my Lord ... that I may gain Christ ... that I may know Him and the power of His resurrection, and the fellowship of His sufferings, being conformed to His death"* (Phil. 3:1-10).

Fifth, giving thanks reckons that suffering must precede glory (Rom. 8:18, 25; 2 Cor. 4:16-18). *"If indeed we suffer with Him, that we may also be glorified together"* (Rom. 8:17). Giving thanks provides an opportunity to obtain eternal glory. Suffering would be most miserable if there was no God; there would be no purpose in it. But suffering in Christ benefits us now and also in eternity. Thus, we can thank God for the opportunity! This is Christ's example: *"Ought not the Christ to have suffered these things and to enter into His glory"* (Luke 24:26)?

Beloved, even when you do not feel like it – give God thanks. Later you will be glad you did! You may have to fake it – till you make it!

September 10 – Wives, Submit to Your Own Husbands
Ephesians 5:22-24

Wives, submit to your own husbands, as to the Lord. For the husband is head of the wife, as also Christ is head of the church; and He is the Savior of the body. Therefore, just as the church is subject to Christ, so let the wives be to their own husbands in everything.

Submission to order includes dependency on the authority over us. God funnels blessings from heaven through proper channels of authority. All of us are under some authority. Since the days of Noah, this has been His tool for teaching human submission to Himself. The Church is dependent upon Christ for provision and blessing. The Lord Jesus, during His earthly ministry, was dependent on the Father. A wife is to be dependent upon her husband to provide for her needs and to protect her. The term "head" (e.g., 1 Cor. 11:3) refers to someone who has authority and, thus, the one to whom subjection is to be yielded. Biblical headship includes three main spheres of authority: church order, home order, and civil order. Each sphere must be in adherence to divine authority for the maximum blessing of God to be obtained.

In *Home Order*, wives are to be submissive helpers and to respect the authority of their husbands (Gen. 3:16; Col. 3:18; Tit. 2:5). The deepest need of the man is to be respected, whereas the deepest need of a woman is to know that she is significant and secure in her husband's love. Positionally, the wife is equal to her husband, yet God has given the husband authority over the wife in the marital relationship. It was God who designed and initiated the marriage relationship in Genesis 2:23-24; therefore, His rules apply. The Lord Jesus confirmed that God's order for marriage had not changed (Matt. 19:5-6). Warren Wiersbe summarizes God's plan to bless the home:

> God does all things "decently and in order" (1 Cor. 14:40). If He did not have a chain of command in society, we would have chaos. ... True spiritual submission is the secret of growth and fulfillment. When a Christian woman is submitted to the Lord and to her own husband, she experiences a release and fulfillment that she can have in no other way. This mutual love and submission creates an atmosphere of growth in the home that enables both the husband and the wife to become all that God wants them to be.[30]

September 11– Husbands, Love Your Wives
Ephesians 5:25-28

Husbands, love your wives, just as Christ also loved the church and gave Himself for her, that He might sanctify and cleanse her with the washing of water by the word, that He might present her to Himself a glorious church, not having spot or wrinkle or any such thing, but that she should be holy and without blemish. So husbands ought to love their own wives as their own bodies; he who loves his wife loves himself.

It has been said that "an ideal wife is any woman who has an ideal husband" and "a good husband makes a good wife." Just as woman was fashioned from and for man, biblical manhood advocates biblical womanhood. For a wife to enjoy full femininity, she must comprehend the divine purpose for which she was created, her husband must be satisfying her essential needs, and she must be sustained by God's grace for the strenuous responsibility. In God's design, woman was created to be a helper for man, and man was created to satisfy her needs, thus assisting her to fulfill her God-given role.

In the Ephesian 5 narrative, Paul defines what true love for one's wife includes: stable leadership (vv. 22-24), sacrificial service (v. 25), sanctifying ministry (vv. 26-27), satisfying needs (vv. 28-30), and security (v. 30). In God's design for the family, the husband is to lead, provide, protect, and shepherd his family and love his wife in these biblical ways. The requirement for a church elder is literally to be *a one-woman man* and is a good pattern for all married men to follow (i.e., one's relationship with his wife is above reproach and reflects God's best design for marriage). Such a man is to be morally blameless in his marriage. This means no sexual misconduct, no inappropriate touching of either genders or children, no meetings with females alone, and no pornography or lascivious behavior (Prov. 5:15-20; Eph. 5:3-4).

The marriage covenant sanctifies and protects the sexual union of a man and a woman, but it does not condone what is inappropriate, unnatural, harmful, or offends the conscience (Deut. 23:17; Rom. 14:23; Heb. 13:4). Scripture supplies many principles and commands to guide proper bedroom behavior such that both parties maintain a clear conscience and enjoy a mutually satisfying experience. In fact, biblical love is shown by a husband attending to his wife's needs first.

September 12 – Children, Obey Your Parents in the Lord
Ephesians 6:1-3

Children, obey your parents in the Lord, for this is right. "Honor your father and mother," which is the first commandment with promise: "that it may be well with you and you may live long on the earth."

It is interesting that while speaking to the newly liberated Israelites, Moses tied two warnings together in Leviticus 19:3. He affirmed that children are to honor and obey their parents and that the Sabbath day was to be kept holy. Ultimately, the reverence for both commandments will be taught and observed in the home. If parents do not teach their children to respect God-ordained authority, they will, as adults, have little regard for law and order. Those who do not respect authority go their own way in life and suffer the harsh reality of an insubordinate spirit. Paul refers to the fifth of the Ten Commandments in his epistle to the Ephesians and notes the promise associated with it.

A child not corrected would be socially miserable and a nuisance to society. His sinful ways and rebellious manner would probably lead him into an early grave. Samson, Absalom, and Eli's sons are examples of such. However, a child who practices obedience is much more likely to live a happy and prosperous life.

The Greek word translated "children" in Ephesians 6:1 is *teknon,* which means "that which is derived of another" (i.e., children are derived from their parents). Age is not implied, meaning that the application of the word is not limited to small children. A different Greek word, *paidion,* is used to speak of infants and small children. Therefore, children should always respect and honor their parents regardless of how old they are. Of course, when children marry and have children of their own, the new parents become accountable to do what is God-honoring and best for their own family. The stipulative phrase, *"in the Lord,"* implies children are to serve their parents as unto the Lord in matters of righteousness, but not in matters of sin.

In the case of Korah, some of his sons refused to follow their father into rebellion against Moses and Aaron, and most importantly the Lord, and thus escaped the divine judgment which completely wiped out the rebels (Num. 16). They disobeyed their father in order to follow God's expressed will, which had been clearly shown to them.

258

September 13 – Fathers, Do Not Provoke Your Children
Ephesians 6:4

And you, fathers, do not provoke your children to wrath, but bring them up in the training and admonition of the Lord.

While God has bestowed husbands and fathers the authority to lead and oversee the care of their homes, they must also realize that whenever God gives authority, there is also accountability (e.g., Heb. 13:17; 1 Pet. 3:7). In a coming day every man will give an account to God for any abuse or neglect of his wife and children. During a Bible study with a group of young men, I asked the group how fathers could provoke their children to wrath. These were a few of the ways that were suggested: Being physically, sexually, emotionally abusive. Being overbearing, not acknowledging achievements, fault-finding or having a critical spirit, showing favoritism, exhibiting hypocrisy, reminding children of past failures, not being sensitive to needs or feelings, failing to keep promises, controlling, and reliving his life through his children.

The word "training" or "nurture" (KJV) is derived from the Greek word *paideia*. The word "chastise" comes from the same Greek root word as *paideia, paideuo,* meaning "to train by disciplinary punishment." Pilate employs *paideuo,* meaning "to chastise," just prior to the Lord's crucifixion: *"I* (Pilate speaking) *will therefore chastise Him, and release Him"* (Luke 23:16). In summary, *nurture* or *training* includes a broad range of educational methods, which also includes the provision "to train by pain." It is the measured response of the parent towards a child that has ignored instruction – measured in that it applies justice according to the previously stated order; measured also in that it considers influences which may have adversely affected the child's judgment. Under-measured chastisement mocks justice and will effectively undermine the weight of parental instruction. If the punishment is too harsh or undeserving, it will depress the child or provoke him or her to wrath. Nurturing supports instruction – the disciplinary rod is never without reproof (Prov. 22:15)!

The Greek word *nouthesia* is rendered "admonish," which means "to put in mind" or "to call attention to a subject matter by giving a mild rebuke or warning." A caution or gentle reproof is given by parents as they witness their children meandering toward forbidden territory. If a child is young and learning boundaries, use admonition.

September 14 – Wickedness in High Places
Ephesians 6:11-12

Put on the whole armor of God, that you may be able to stand against the wiles of the devil. For we do not wrestle against flesh and blood, but against principalities, against powers, against the rulers of the darkness of this age, against spiritual hosts of wickedness in the heavenly places.

The Epistle reaches its thematic crescendo at verse 11. Paul has spoken of the believer's position in Christ and the blessings associated with that union (Eph. 1-3). He has taught that the believer's union with Christ demanded an appropriate walk (lifestyle) that would honor Christ (Eph. 4-5). In Ephesians 6, Paul identifies the spiritual battle that wages on for those in Christ; we war against spiritual wickedness in heavenly places. Paul wanted the believers to *stand* strong against this powerful enemy. But they needed to understand the *sit-walk-stand* particulars of what he had written them to do, and so do we.

The Believer's Position in Christ – believers "sit" with Christ in heavenly places (Eph. 2:6). We must rest in this identification truth. Sitting means there is no strain on our legs (no walking, no standing). Spiritually speaking, we must learn to rest by faith in Christ; this means that we do not expend fleshly energy, rather we rest. God typically waits until we are willing to rest in Him before He acts on our behalf (though sometimes we exhaust ourselves before we do).

The Believer's Life in the World – believers are to "walk" worthy of their calling in Christ (the word *walk* occurs six times in Eph. 4-5). Believers are to *walk* in divinely arranged good works (Eph. 2:10) and in an orderly way marked by wisdom, godliness, and a general lifestyle worthy of our union in Christ (Rom. 13:12).

The Believer's Attitude Towards the Enemy – believers are to "stand" (6:11, 13, 14) against satanic powers. But we cannot stand strong unless our walk is honoring to God and we are resting in Christ in heavenly places. Although gospel work is offensive in nature, Paul's focus here is how we can withstand the enemy's brutal attack and thus defend the ground already conquered at the cross. The only way to defeat spiritual wickedness in heavenly places is to rest in the Lord who is in the highest place. Let us *sit-walk-stand* in Christ.

September 15 – "Take Up" To Stand
Ephesians 6:13

Therefore take up the whole armor of God, that you may be able to withstand in the evil day, and having done all, to stand.

The Ephesians were to stand against demonic forces that oppose Christ in the world. Paul mentions "to stand" three times and "to withstand" or "to resist" once in verses 11-14. Christ defeated Satan at the cross, and believers are to continue the victory already achieved at Calvary by resisting the enemy. Watchman Nee explains:

> Christ's warfare was offensive; he gained the victory over the devil at the Cross. Our warfare is mostly defensive – we war against Satan only to maintain and consolidate the victory which Christ has already gained – we hold what Christ has gained against all challenges. If we fight with the concept of gaining a victory, then we lose the battle at the onset. The Christian walk and warfare draw their strength from sitting before God and resting in Him. Satan's objective is to move us from the perfect ground of triumph, thus our armor is essentially defensive.[31]

To withstand such a powerful enemy, spiritual wickedness in high places, the believer must get up into the heavenly places and be strengthened in Christ. Kenneth Wuest translates verse 10 this way: "Be constantly strengthened in the Lord and in the active efficacy of the might that is inherent in Him." All affairs of our lives are not dependent on trying, but trusting in Christ in heavenly places (i.e., depending on His strength, not ours). Again Watchman Nee writes:

> No Christian can hope to enter the warfare of the ages without learning first to rest in Christ and in what he has done, and then through the strength of the Holy Spirit within, to follow him in a practical, holy life on earth. If he is deficient in either of these he will find that all the talk about spiritual warfare remains only talk; he will never know its reality. Satan can afford to ignore him for he does not count for anything.[32]

So believers are to stand, that is, take up a resistive opposition on the triumphant ground of Christ. We must be energized through prayer, clad with spiritual armor to stand. Verse 13 does not speak of standing in victory every day, but our ability to stand in every conflict any day.

261

September 16 – Having Girded Your Waist With Truth
Ephesians 6:14

Stand therefore, having girded your waist with truth, having put on the breastplate of righteousness.

Being a prisoner in Rome, Paul would have been quite acquainted with how a Roman soldier was dressed and equipped (Acts 28:16). He then applies what is a familiar scene as an illustration to teach about spiritual armor provided for all believers. The Greek narrative on the subject (vv. 14-18) is composed of two separate statements as initiated by imperative verbs "stand" in verse 14 and "take" in verse 17.

It is observed that Satan's voice is recorded only three times in Scripture (Gen. 3; Job 1-2; Matt. 4). This would seem to indicate that he is more likely to use subtle approaches to work his evil agenda rather than employing a direct assault. If you know that your enemy is approaching you for battle, then you will want to "take" and put on every provision of armor that you can to protect yourself. At such times, the believer should have the whole armor of God on.

However, Satan's subtle devices are not always obvious; this is why the first three pieces of armor should be worn at all times. Notice that "having" is connected with the belt of truth, the breastplate of righteousness, and feet shod with the gospel. "Take" and "taking" is connected with the latter three pieces of spiritual armor. We should remember that God permits Satan to test us in order to prove or to refine us and to make us more dependent on Him, and accordingly more fruitful to Him (Jas. 1:12-13; Job 1:6-12). This is an ongoing process, meaning we should be spiritually equipped appropriately with the belt, the breastplate, and the proper footwear all the time.

Having girded your waist with truth: Roman soldiers wore a long square tunic which could be pulled up and tied as to not hinder their movement. This action speaks of the readiness that believers are to have with the truth at a moment's notice. The soldier's sword hung on his belt. In the same way truth undergirds all of the believer's spiritual armor. But we cannot be ambassadors of truth if we are entangled by worldly affairs (2 Tim. 2:4) or are corrupted by hypocrisy (Col. 2:4). This is more than just knowing doctrine; the belt of truth readies the inner man by controlling his thoughts and affections based in the truth.

September 17 – The Breastplate of Righteousness
Ephesians 6:14

Stand therefore, having girded your waist with truth, having put on the breastplate of righteousness.

The Roman breastplate was composed of a solid piece of metal that was formed in the shape of a man's chest with a second piece of fitted metal for his back. The front and back components were held together by leather straps. The breastplate protected the soldier's vital organs from blows from the sword or penetration by spears or by arrows. This piece of armor was to be worn at all times.

Spiritually speaking, the breastplate of righteousness covers a pure heart and speaks of maintaining holy conduct at all times. Believers must keep short accounts with the Lord concerning the confession of sin and then seek to maintain a pure walk before Him. Righteous living provides a blameless testimony which will limit attacks of accusations. Isaiah tells us that this would be Messiah's example, when He came:

Then the Lord saw it, and it displeased Him that there was no justice. He saw that there was no man, and wondered that there was no intercessor; therefore His own arm brought salvation for Him; and His own righteousness, it sustained Him. For He put on righteousness as a breastplate, and a helmet of salvation on His head; He put on the garments of vengeance for clothing, and was clad with zeal as a cloak (Isa. 59:15-16).

Paul instructed the believers at Rome, *"but I want you to be wise in what is good, and simple concerning evil"* (Rom. 16:19). As believers, by God's grace, choose to be oblivious to evil and worldliness, we approve what is wise and the devices of Satan are spoiled. Those dedicated to holy living will enjoy a strong defense against the accusatory blows of the enemy. Believers walking hand in hand with Christ are invincible and immortal until their work on earth is done. At that time, the helmet of salvation, the shield of faith, and the breastplate of righteousness will hit the floor with a clang, for the battle days will be over and eternal rest will begin. Many who were waiting for the Lord's return have already been called home to heaven by the doorway of death. Until then, let us all wear the breastplate of righteousness!

September 18 – Having Shod Your Feet With the Gospel
Ephesians 6:15

And having shod your feet with the preparation of the gospel of peace.

The Roman soldier wore sandals fitted with hobnails on the bottom to ensure sound footing. This provision was especially helpful when a legion put their shields into various formations to protect each other from a bombardment of arrows and darts or when the enemy attempted to push through their shield barrier. Just as the Roman sandals provided firm footing, believers are to stand firm in the peace of the gospel while in enemy territory (i.e., the world's unrest and wickedness). This means that believers need to be ready at a moment's notice to be faithful witnesses for Christ (Acts 1:8) and to patiently use Scripture in whatever way is necessary to convey the truth of the gospel:

> *But sanctify the Lord God in your hearts, and always be ready to give a defense to everyone who asks you a reason for the hope that is in you, with meekness and fear; having a good conscience, that when they defame you as evildoers, those who revile your good conduct in Christ may be ashamed* (1 Pet. 3:15-16).

> *Preach the word! Be ready in season and out of season. Convince, rebuke, exhort, with all longsuffering and teaching* (2 Tim. 4:2).

Nehemiah shows us an application of this mindset when he created family/clan work-groups to continue building the wall of Jerusalem in the face of opposition. Half of the people were to have shields, bows, spears and coats of mail, while the other half worked (Neh. 4:16-17). Even those working had swords girded at their sides or they carried a trowel in one hand and a sword in the other. Both, in a spiritual sense, speak of the Word of God: the Trowel is to be used for the edification of the brethren and the Sword, which was once delivered to the saints, should be used to contend earnestly for the faith. Though in prison, Paul still used Scripture *"for the defense and confirmation of the gospel"* (Phil. 1:7-8). He handled Scripture to both defend the gospel against nonbelievers and to build up understanding for those in Christ. We should follow this example – building and defending are important ministries for strengthening and preserving the vitality of the Church.

September 19 – Taking the Shield of Faith
Ephesians 6:16

Above all, taking the shield of faith with which you will be able to quench all the fiery darts of the wicked one.

While some Roman shields were made of metal, the more widely used shield *thureon* was a two and a half by four foot thick piece of wood that was covered with leather. The leather was treated to make it fire resistant. This type of Roman shield was heavy, weighing about twenty pounds. The shield was capable of stopping fiery darts, spears, and arrows. The Roman shields could be connected or overlapped together to form a wall or ceiling, or both, depending on the type of protection needed. This also ensured that retreat was not an option; the soldiers were safer staying and working together to create an impenetrable barrier. Soldiers had to stand together to face the enemy.

Paul states that the shield of faith is needed to extinguish the fiery darts of the wicked one. The darts speak of demonic suggestions and enticements. The enemy can discourage us by planting doubts in our minds, or stimulating mental strongholds such as greed or bitterness, or causing anxiety over what we cannot control, or by deceiving us concerning the truth (Acts 5:3; 2 Cor. 11:14-15; Col. 2:4).

As spiritual armor for the believer, the shield represents trusting in the Lord for protection against the adversary. Soldiers of the cross are to stand firm on biblical truth and not withdraw from it. There are times when we all suffer from weak faith; doubts and discouragement come in like a barrage of flaming darts. At such times, those who are strong in faith can rally around the fainthearted and protect them from further attack with their own shields of faith. Like a Roman legion, believers who engage the enemy together provide encouragement and protection for the whole group.

The Roman shield was too heavy to carry around every moment of the day, but as soon as a threat was observed, the shields were to be quickly taken up and readied for action. Spiritually speaking, believers must be watchful with immediate readiness to take up their shields of faith when there is an obvious attack looming. Believers gathered for prayer and resting in God's truth and promises pose an impenetrable fortress against the fiery darts of the enemy.

September 20 – Take the Helmet of Salvation
Ephesians 6:17

And take the helmet of salvation, and the sword of the Spirit, which is the word of God.

As mentioned previously, the verb "take" in this verse is in the imperative mood (it is not another participle), thus dividing the believer's armor into two groups of three pieces. The Roman soldier's helmet, shield, and sword were heavy equipment. It was not necessary to wear the helmet, hold up the shield, and have one's sword drawn every moment of the day. However, these were to be accessible to take up quickly if it was obvious that a battle was imminent. For all other times, the belt, breastplate, and shoes were adequate protection.

The Roman helmet protected against the heavy broadsword which was swung like a bat by horse-mounted cavalry. The broadsword was used with the intention of removing the head of an enemy soldier; likewise, the devil desires that Christians lose their heads when opposed by Him. Hope invigorates the soldier in adversity and believers have the assurance of ultimate victory and eternal safety in God's presence (Rom. 8:31). Because Christ has already defeated Satan at Calvary, we know that our destiny is secure in Him. Accordingly, we are to wear the helmet which is *"the hope of salvation"* (1 Thess. 5:8).

The matter of destiny is settled; the eternal Christ is in and with the believers no matter how difficult our circumstances are in this present life. In application, Caleb's confidence in battle was the Lord's Word and His abiding presence, not his own strength or sword:

Now therefore, give me this mountain of which the Lord spoke in that day; for you heard in that day how the Anakim were there, and that the cities were great and fortified. It may be that the Lord will be with me, and I shall be able to drive them out as the Lord said (Josh. 14:12).

Effective spiritual warfare requires: First, maturity and training; we are on active duty and we are in the Lord's school. Second, we must be committed to holy living to ensure that we remain in His fellowship. Third, we must maintain full reliance on the Lord Jesus Christ. All beneficial spiritual exercise begins when we rest in Him, who is seated in the heavenly places. The helmet speaks of our security in Christ.

266

September 21 – Take the Sword of the Spirit
Ephesians 6:17

And take the helmet of salvation, and the sword of the Spirit, which is the word of God.

"Spirit" is in the genitive case in relationship to "sword" in this verse, meaning that the sword originated with the Holy Spirit – it is His sword. The sword of the Spirit is the Word of God used in the power of the Spirit. The sword could be used for offensive or defensive warfare. However, the context of this text highlights its defensive use.

God's Word properly applied is able to cut to the heart, or, more specifically, the human conscience:

For the word of God is living and powerful, and sharper than any two-edged sword, piercing even to the division of soul and spirit, and of joints and marrow, and is a discerner of the thoughts and intents of the heart (Heb. 4:12).

"Let all the house of Israel know assuredly that God has made this Jesus, whom you crucified, both Lord and Christ." Now when they heard this, they were cut to the heart, and said to Peter and the rest of the apostles, "Men and brethren, what shall we do?" (Acts 2:36-37).

The sword in verse 18 is the *machaira,* which was a six- to eighteen-inch two-edged sword used in hand-to-hand combat. It was sheathed and attached to the soldier's belt. The Greek word rendered "word" is *rhema.* The word *logos* is more often translated "word" in Scripture and is used to speak of a general concept or the full ramification of something. However, *rhema* is used to convey the idea of a specific thought or application. Spiritually speaking then, Paul is instructing believers to rightly know Scripture and by the power of the Holy Spirit precisely apply it to a specific situation.

The Lord's example of countering every attack by Satan with a precise application of God's Word from Deuteronomy is an excellent example of what Paul is speaking of here (Matt. 4:1-11). Owning a Bible does not mean we have a spiritual sword. We must know Scripture and discern its proper meaning, and then permit the Holy Spirit to call to mind the right passage to wield against a situation.

September 22 – Praying Always in the Spirit
Ephesians 6:18

Praying always with all prayer and supplication in the Spirit, being watchful to this end with all perseverance and supplication for all the saints.

In the Church Age we are invited to lift up our needs, cares, and burdens to the Lord: *"Therefore humble yourselves under the mighty hand of God, that He may exalt you in due time, casting all your care upon Him, for He cares for you"* (1 Pet. 5:6-7). Sincerely casting onto the Lord by prayer those things pressing down on our hearts is initially a laborious task, but ultimately results in abiding peace.

Prayer is work and believers must leave strength and time for effectual praying. The objective of prayer is not to shift our loads so that we can better shoulder them (that would be an exhausting waste of time), but rather to release our burdens to the Lord to deal with as only He can. But we must remember that groaning in prayer is not the same as grumbling or complaining to God about our difficulties (Rom. 8:22-27). The latter behavior reveals something lurking within us that inhibits praying in the Spirit (Eph. 6:18). The hindrance may be a rebellious spirit, doubt, or some level of distrust, or perhaps dissatisfaction with the Lord. We can escape these snares by candidly and genuinely lifting up our burdens to our caring Savior.

Grammatically speaking, prayer and alertness are tied with the use of the helmet and the sword. God's armor is not given to make us independent of Him; it can only be rightly used in the spirit of dependence on its Giver; we must pray "in the Spirit." Nee writes:

> Prayer in Christ's name unleashes the power, the authority, of His name in three ways: Preaching of the gospel, our warfare, and in our asking. We must be careful to invoke Christ's name on what is confirmed to be divine in purpose, per the word, and completely dependent on Him.[33]

Our spiritual armor is only effective when the power of God is working on our behalf. The proper defense against Satan is not our money, fame, organizing, wit, or intellect, but using *all* the spiritual armor (resources) that God provides us with.

September 23 – Let Your Love Abound
Philippians 1:9

And this I pray, that your love may abound still more and more in knowledge and all discernment.

Paul has a similar exhortation to the church at Thessalonica: *"The Lord make you to increase and abound in love one toward another, and toward all men, even as we do toward you"* (1 Thess. 3:12) and then he repeated it again in 1 Thessalonians 3:9-10. But earlier he wrote:

We give thanks to God always for you all, making mention of you in our prayers, remembering without ceasing your work of faith, labor of love, and patience of hope in our Lord Jesus Christ (1 Thess. 1:2-3).

But now that Timothy has come to us from you, and brought us good news of your faith and love (1 Thess. 3:6).

If the Thessalonians, a church suffering persecution for their faith, were characterized by consistent labors of love, why would Paul exhort them, *"to increase and abound in love one toward another, and toward all men"* and to "put on" love (1 Thess. 5:8)? Two reasons are suggested to answer this question: First, a believer can never love too much. The believer should never be satisfied with his outward projection of God's love. Can a husband love his wife too much? No, he will never love his wife in the same way that Christ loves His Church, but he should never quit trying (Eph. 5:25). Hence, there will always be room for us to abound more and more in love.

Second, God is love, and the more we love others, the more we will demonstrate Him to a lost world. The Lord Jesus told His disciples that their love one for another would be a strong testimony to the world of His love in them (John 13:34-35). For this reason Paul further instructs them how to abound in God's love: *"See that no one renders evil for evil to anyone, but always pursue what is good both for yourselves and for all"* (1 Thess. 5:15). The Lord would receive the most glory, they would receive the most joy, and the Holy Spirit would accomplish the most blessing when the Thessalonian believers chose to invoke love to address "people problems." It is the same for us; God's love is irresistible and we all need to abound in His love more and more.

September 24 – The Furtherance of the Gospel
Philippians 1:12

But I want you to know, brethren, that the things which happened to me have actually turned out for the furtherance of the gospel.

Philippi was where Paul and Silas witnessed the first European converts to Christ, Lydia and her household. After casting a spirit of divination from a servant girl, Paul and Silas were arrested, severely beaten, and imprisoned without a trial as commanded by the magistrates. While securely bound in the inner prison, the two evangelists began to sing praises to God. Then, a timely earthquake freed Paul, Silas, and the other prisoners from their bonds and cells. The jail keeper, knowing that he would be put to death if any of his prisoners escaped, sought to take his own life. Paul cried out to him not to do so and the keeper responded by asking the two missionaries how he could be saved. In short order, he and his household heard and believed the gospel message and afterwards were baptized. The church at Philippi was a direct outcome of suffering saints rejoicing in the Lord Jesus Christ.

So it is not surprising that in his Epistle to the Philippians, Paul teaches us that even during the most dismal of situations there is always a mental escape from depression; believers are called to rejoice – *rejoicing is a choice*. Though a prisoner in Rome, the apostle focused his mind on what great things God had accomplished through his imprisonment: Some in Caesar's household had come to Christ, timid brethren had become bold in the preaching of Christ, and even though some were preaching against Paul, he could still say, *"Christ is preached; and in this I rejoice, yes, and will rejoice"* (Phil. 1:18).

If Paul had focused his thoughts on his difficulties, he would have been overcome with despair. Instead, he chose to concentrate on the positive outcomes of his suffering, *"the things which happened to me have actually turned out for the furtherance of the gospel."* This is the single-mindedness that Paul had; whatever situation he was placed into, he wanted to bring Christ into it in order to further the spread of the gospel. He did not see his difficulties as stumbling stones, but rather as stepping stones into greater gospel opportunities. The *single mind* of chapter 1 leads to the *servant mind* of chapter 2, then to the *spiritual mind* of chapter 3, so that we can enjoy the *secure mind* of chapter 4.

September 25 – Rejoicing Is a Choice!
Philippians 1:15-18

Some indeed preach Christ even from envy and strife, and some also from goodwill: The former preach Christ from selfish ambition, not sincerely, supposing to add affliction to my chains; but the latter out of love, knowing that I am appointed for the defense of the gospel. What then? Only that in every way, whether in pretense or in truth, Christ is preached; and in this I rejoice, yes, and will rejoice.

In the writings to the Corinthians previously, Paul related some of the incredible difficulties he faced in his ministry, but then concludes by declaring, *"As sorrowful, yet always rejoicing"* (2 Cor. 6:10). The Lord had miraculously delivered him from many life-threatening circumstances (2 Cor. 11:23-28). Paul also informed the Corinthians that though his labor among them had cost him personally, he had maintained a sense of gladness. Rather than complaining, Paul chose to rejoice while serving the Corinthians, knowing that in time they would be brought to maturity.

Now, during his first Roman imprisonment, Paul informs the believers at Philippi that he has chosen to set his mind on those things in which he could rejoice, and thus he was not defeated by his harsh situation, but triumphed over it through faith. Then, in the closing chapter, he exhorted them to follow his example: *"Rejoice in the Lord always. Again I will say, rejoice!"* (Phil. 4:4). Satisfaction, full joy, and contentment are found only in the Lord – knowing and experiencing Him makes life worth living.

Whether we are confronted by intense opposition, daily suffering, or the disappointing regression of the Church, we must learn to trust and rejoice in the Lord. In such times of distress, may we too recall to mind Nehemiah's charge to his distressed fellow countrymen: *"The joy of the Lord is your strength"* (Neh. 8:10). Rejoicing is a choice and it is a command (1 Thess. 5:16). Rejoicing in truth revives the heart of the redeemed and opens the way for God to perform the spectacular!

It is both a great privilege and our duty to rejoice in our blessed Savior. To rejoice in Christ when everything around us shrieks of despair shows Him that we really know who He is and that we trust in Him no matter what.

September 26 – To Live Is Christ, and to Die Is Gain
Philippians 1:20-24

*According to my earnest expectation and hope that in nothing I shall
be ashamed, but with all boldness, as always, so now also Christ will
be magnified in my body, whether by life or by death. For to me, to
live is Christ, and to die is gain. But if I live on in the flesh, this will
mean fruit from my labor; yet what I shall choose I cannot tell. For I
am hard-pressed between the two, having a desire to depart and be
with Christ, which is far better. Nevertheless to remain in the flesh is
more needful for you.*

Paul had the mindset that He was going to glorify Christ in every
situation, no matter if the circumstances were favorable or ominous.
Presently, Christ sits at the right hand of His Father in heaven. Paul
viewed his body as a telescope and He was determined to magnify
Christ, that is to bring Christ closer (to make Him visible) so others
might see and know Him through Paul's Spirit-filled testimony.

Every child of God must remember that, though we are saved by
grace through the blood of Christ, we cannot worship or serve the Lord
apart from the continual energizing power of the Holy Spirit (Phil. 3:3).
Reliance on human wisdom, on the strength of the flesh, or on vain
religiosity will be futile substitutes for that real spiritual power which
has the capacity to fill the world with the aroma of Christ. We rest in
Christ alone for salvation and all that matters during this life is that He
be magnified through His Church in all things.

Paul had one hope, one earnest expectation, *the blessed hope*:
*"Looking for the blessed hope and glorious appearing of our great
God and Savior Jesus Christ"* (Tit. 2:13). While this may include
aspects of Christ's future kingdom as well, it certainly includes Christ's
coming for His Church (the rapture). Paul lived each and every day in
the anticipation of being imminently brought into the presence of
Christ. But though he yearned to be with the Lord, as long as the Lord
had work for him to do he would remain on earth to perform it. He
understood that his ministry was needful for the Church; thus, he
pressed onward until the Lord would call him home, either through
death or through glorification at Christ's coming for the Church.
Beloved, this is the pattern that each believer is to follow.

September 27 – Proof of Your Salvation
Philippians 1:27-28

Only let your conduct be worthy of the gospel of Christ, so that whether I come and see you or am absent, I may hear of your affairs, that you stand fast in one spirit, with one mind striving together for the faith of the gospel, and not in any way terrified by your adversaries, which is to them a proof of perdition, but to you of salvation, and that from God.

Suffering patiently for the cause of Christ is a proof of perdition to the lost and a token of salvation to the believer (Phil. 1:28; 2 Thess. 1:5). As shown in the conversion of the repentant thief, suffering with patience while relying on God's grace is a supernatural testimony to the lost; it is nonetheless a consolation to the believer that he or she is truly a child of God. Praying for those who persecute you is a demonstration of God's control of your will and it will be a safeguard to your mind – a defense against bitterness and overwhelming sorrow.

History records the intense persecution of the Church by the Roman Empire, but what is not as well-documented is the impact that the patient suffering of the early Church had on specific leaders within the empire. When Pliny was governor of Bithynia (about A. D. 110), he wrote a letter to the Roman Emperor Trajan to ask why Christians were being exterminated, then added:

> I have been trying to get all the information I could regarding them. I have even hired spies to profess to be Christians and become baptized in order that they might get into the Christian services without suspicion. Contrary to what I had supposed, I find that the Christians meet at dead of night or at early morn, that they sing a hymn to Christ as God, that they read from their own sacred writings and partake of a very simple meal consisting of bread and wine and water (the water added to the wine to dilute it in order that there might be enough for all). This is all that I can find out, except that they exhort each other to be subject to the government and to pray for all men.[34]

Not only is patiently suffering for the cause of Christ a testimony of supernatural wherewithal to the lost, but Paul told the saints at both Philippi and Thessalonica that it was proof of their salvation.

September 28 – Having the Mind of Christ
Philippians 2:3-5

Let nothing be done through selfish ambition or conceit, but in lowliness of mind let each esteem others better than himself. Let each of you look out not only for his own interests, but also for the interests of others. Let this mind be in you which was also in Christ Jesus.

All the disunity and contention within the Church today is the result of our pride in one form or another. Nothing good can come from pride! This is why Paul admonished the believers at Philippi to follow Christ's example of selfless humility: *"Let nothing be done through strife or vainglory; but in lowliness of mind let each esteem others better than themselves"* (Phil. 2:3; KJV). As R. C. Chapman attests, this is the best defense against the pride that naturally consumes us:

In 1 Corinthians 15:28 we read: "Then shall the Son also Himself be subject," and in Revelation, "The throne of God and of the Lamb." Christ is forever the Shepherd and forever the Lamb, and it is the lowly or little Lamb, the diminutive being used. There is an infiniteness in the lowliness of the blessed Lamb, and He is now at the utmost of His lowliness. Satan took upon himself the form of a master, being created a servant; instead of serving in obedience he would be lord, and "the condemnation of the devil" is in his self-will; he chose to take to himself what belonged only to God. What a rebuke to the devil the exaltation of the Son of God will be to all eternity – a mirror in which to see his own folly! Acquaintance with the Cross of Christ brings me to nothing! Let any thought of self-exaltation be to me as a serpent; I have nothing to do but to kill it![35]

Strife is the devil's way to get one's way, but lowliness permits God to judge legitimate wrongs His way, which is always the best way. How do we know this is true? Vengeance (i.e., justified wrath for sin) is the Lord's alone (Rom. 12:19); only He can rightly dispense wrath to humble the proud heart (Job 40:11-12) and the wrath of man does not work the righteousness of God (Jas. 1:20). David understood these wrath realities and thus asked the Lord to vindicate him and judge his oppressors; he reckoned that God was much better able to judge his oppressors than he ever could through strife (Ps. 35:1, 23-24).

September 29 – Working Out Your Salvation (Part 1)
Philippians 2:12-13

Therefore, my beloved, as you have always obeyed, not as in my presence only, but now much more in my absence, work out your own salvation with fear and trembling; for it is God who works in you both to will and to do for His good pleasure.

Notice that Paul does not say "work for" your salvation. He is merely instructing Christians to "work out," not "work for" their salvation. We can do absolutely nothing to earn good merit with God; we must simply trust Christ's finished work at Calvary for salvation (Eph. 2:8-9; Tit. 3:5). Legalism teaches that one is saved by grace through faith, but then must continue in keeping the Law to maintain that salvation. God is holy and desires His children to live up to the family image (1 Pet. 1:16), which involves searching the Word of God for truth to build one's faith upon, then seeking direction from the Lord through prayer and, in some cases, godly counsel.

Teaching younger believers to work out their salvation is extremely important – it provides them with tools for life in the discerning of wise and godly behavior. We don't want our children to get pulled into either the *world's religion* of doing or the *world's pleasure* of indulging. Even in Paul's day the undertow of these spiritual ills was apparent. The churches of Galatia were being pulled towards legalism – "I must do to please God," while the Corinthian church's motto was, "Christ died for all our sins – let's party." The world's religion says "do," but biblical Christianity says "done." The world's pleasure bewails, "Live for the day and for the moment – enjoy life," but Christ says, *"whosoever will lose his life for My sake, the same shall save it"* (Luke 9:24); in this way a Christian maintains an abiding joy in life.

The Lord's desire for us is to be wise and to do good and to avoid foolish and wrong behavior. To accomplish this we must build our lives on the foundation of His teachings and not secular wisdom:

Therefore whoever hears these sayings of Mine, and does them, I will liken him to a wise man who built his house on the rock: and the rain descended, the floods came, and the winds blew and beat on that house; and it did not fall, for it was founded on the rock (Matt. 7:24-25).

September 30 – Working Out Your Salvation (Part 2)
Philippians 2:12-13

Therefore, my beloved, as you have always obeyed, not as in my presence only, but now much more in my absence, work out your own salvation with fear and trembling; for it is God who works in you both to will and to do for His good pleasure.

In every local church, you will have saints who will tend to gravitate to either the world's religion of doing (legalism) or the world's pleasure of indulging (license). The believer's "old man" (what we were in Adam, before Christ) died with Christ (Rom. 6:6). The Galatians were figuratively doing CPR on the old man to revive him, while the Corinthian church was living as if he had never died. The proper Christian life is not *legalism* or *license*, but one of *liberty* – we must walk between these two natural pitfalls and live out Christ's life:

I have been crucified with Christ; it is no longer I who live, but Christ lives in me; and the life which I now live in the flesh I live by faith in the Son of God, who loved me and gave Himself for me (Gal. 2:20).

It is impossible to earn a greater status with God by doing good works, and it also is impossible to draw near to God by indulging our flesh. Younger believers need to learn to serve the Lord out of love. They should be taught not to fear the loss of acceptance or that God is going to smash them the first time they fail.

The child of God is to discern between what is holy and what is evil, what is wise and what is foolish. What is holy and wise should be obeyed, and what is evil and foolish should be shunned. The matter of discerning between right and wrong behavior is dependent upon knowing the commandments of Scripture. Discerning between what is wise and what is foolish is dependent upon knowing God's commandments, warnings, principles, promises, and the "lessons learned" from personal narratives in Scripture. In fact, the Lord addressed the matter of being wise and not foolish much more often than the matter of what is right and what is wrong, though the latter would be included in what is wise and foolish. Gaining discernment of what is wise and what is foolish requires prayer, study, the godly counsel of others, and the leading of the Holy Spirit in our lives.

October 1 – Counting What Was Gain to Be Loss
Philippians 3:7-8

But what things were gain to me, these I have counted loss for Christ. Yet indeed I also count all things loss for the excellence of the knowledge of Christ Jesus my Lord, for whom I have suffered the loss of all things, and count them as rubbish, that I may gain Christ.

Our family enjoyed living on a small farm in Illinois for about ten years. We had one dog of mixed pedigree named Daisy. She was a great watchdog and maintained a protective eye over our children. Daisy had only one problem; she was always overweight. It didn't matter what type of low-fat food we provided for her; she was always a lovable fat dog! One day, I discovered the secret to Daisy's obesity. I saw her relentlessly devouring something in the pasture – it turned out to be a cow pie (a hardened pile of manure). Cattle being prepared for slaughter digest large amounts of corn (or cracked corn in this case), which means they deposit corn-enriched waste products all over. If you were not aware of this fact, corn is one of the main ingredients in dog food. Daisy had an entire pasture full of corn-laced treats! There was no way to limit this putrid source of nutrition, so Daisy suffered from a chronic weight problem. Hopefully, by this point you are not too disgusted to learn the spiritual lesson of this illustration.

Paul likened all that he thought was important in his life before knowing Christ to "dung" or "rubbish" (i.e., manure). Paul counted all his religious accomplishments and all that the world had to offer him as worthless in contrast to knowing and living for Christ. When we adopt this type of spiritual mindset, we realize that feeding on what the world offers for sustenance is like choking down putrid cow pies with a ludicrous smack of enjoyment. "Barf!" the spiritual man exclaims.

Bragging about our secular feats is like calling people's attention to piles of dung we have sculpted into award-winning figurines. Apart from Christ, what we do in this world is completely worthless; no matter how good it looks on the outside, it is still manure to God. What is done in Christ is for His glory, not ours (1 Cor. 1:31). It goes without saying that manure is neither the food nor the prize of the child of God. Believers are called to be nourished by God's Word, to be empowered by His Spirit, and to do His will; they are not to be controlled by sin.

October 2 – That I May Know Him
Philippians 3:10

That I may know Him and the power of His resurrection, and the fellowship of His sufferings, being conformed to His death.

In the Christian experience, the inheritance we each possess presently relates directly to how each believer has experienced the Lord's gracious and holy character. The Lord does not bestow such things as power and authority lightly; these are received in measure and in accordance to our capacity to retain each gift of grace in faith, love, and humility. To apprehend that which cannot be managed in wisdom would surely result in a worse outcome than not having a possession at all. Believers have different spiritual gifts, callings of ministry, talents to serve, and developed maturity in Christ. This means that each of us has different and varying capacities to receive and retain resurrection power as a spiritual possession.

Even Paul, an apostle said, *"Not that I have already attained, or am already perfected; but I press on, that I may lay hold of that for which Christ Jesus has also laid hold of me"* (Phil. 3:12). Paul affirms His desire to know Christ more and further experience His resurrection power in his own life. Paul was not perfect. He had not apprehended all that was available to him, but was determined to press forward to obtain all that could be possessed. He informs those lacking in maturity that they may not understand this principle presently, but just to press forward in faith and obedience in what they knew to be true – spiritual maturity and blessing would come.

The same is true for us: There is much more inheritance to possess, but God is wise to grant only that portion for which we can both receive and retain presently. We are to thank God for what has been received, while at the same time continuing in conquest and requesting from Him a greater portion of His riches in Christ. May believers bless others with their possessions already received while continuing to rest in the Lord and increasing their capacity to receive more inheritance.

This was Paul's passion and why he could gladly associate proclaiming Christ with suffering for Christ. He knew this mindset would permit him to further know Christ and experience Him in ways that He had not previously known. May this be our passion also.

October 3– Forgetting Those Things Which Are Behind
Philippians 3:12-14

Not that I have already attained, or am already perfected; but I press on, that I may lay hold of that for which Christ Jesus has also laid hold of me. Brethren, I do not count myself to have apprehended; but one thing I do, forgetting those things which are behind and reaching forward to those things which are ahead, I press toward the goal for the prize of the upward call of God in Christ Jesus.

The goal of the Christian race is to maintain a consistent, God-honoring life day after day to maximize our capacity to serve Him and to finish the race well. *Press on* or *towards* expresses our aspiration to please Christ. It is certainly possible for believers to grow weary *in* the work God has given them to do, but they should never grow weary *of* the work. Also, believers do not compete against each other, for God has given each believer a specific calling to fulfill – a race to finish. Rather, we race against ourselves – to keep a stride ahead of our flesh.

Besides developing this personal discipline to ensure we are not disqualified from living for the Lord, Paul shared another running strategy with Christians at Philippi: *"forgetting those things which are behind and reaching forward to those things which are ahead"* (Phil. 3:13-14). Paul speaks of *the goal* or *mark* of his race, which would be the finish line of his earthly sojourn (either death or the rapture of His body to be with Christ). He also describes why he is running for the Lord – *the prize of the upward calling*. This would describe the crowns or rewards received at the Judgment Seat of Christ and also being in Christ's presence forever. The entire race from start (his conversion) to finish (his death) is described as *the upward call of God in Christ*. This encompasses all that God would desire to accomplish in Paul's life – salvation, sanctification, good works, conformity to Christ, etc.

Paul also mentions another aspect of this strategy – forgetting those things behind. It is wise to learn from our mistakes, but past failures should not hinder Christians from pressing onward in their heavenly calling. Falling is a normal part of learning to walk properly; it is not falling that makes us a failure, but rather, it is remaining down after the fall and not getting up in grace and finishing the race. Moreover, let us not glory in our past triumphs, as these can be a snare to our feet.

October 4 – Run Regardless, Maturity Will Come
Philippians 3:15-16

Therefore let us, as many as are mature, have this mind; and if in anything you think otherwise, God will reveal even this to you. Nevertheless, to the degree that we have already attained, let us walk by the same rule, let us be of the same mind.

Although Paul exhorted the Church at Philippi to follow his example of pressing on *"toward the goal for the prize of the upward call of God in Christ Jesus"* (Phil. 3:14), he also realized that many younger saints would not understand what he was talking about, so he continues, *"Therefore let us, as many as are mature, have this mind; and if in anything you think otherwise, God will reveal even this to you. Nevertheless, to the degree that we have already attained, let us walk by the same rule, let us be of the same mind"* (Phil. 3:15-16).

It is quite possible that you do not understand where the Lord is leading you at this present moment, but keep pressing on for the upward calling of God in Christ Jesus. Be faithful to what you know to be true; maturity will come and the confirmation of your calling with it. In God's timing, when He believes it is best for you, He will provide you with more clarity. Remember, God grows ministries as He grows people. In the growing interim, be faithful to what you know God has asked you to do and long for what is yet to come. We tend to focus on what is visibly spectacular, but God is interested in your character and how faithful you are to the mundane obligations. Those who are faithful in the little things will receive greater opportunities from God.

When the Lord opens the doors of a ministry, no one can close them (Rev. 3:7). When the Lord closes doors of ministry, He usually opens others (unless sin or foolishness is involved). But in any case, we can be *"confident of this very thing, that He who has begun a good work in you will complete it until the day of Jesus Christ"* (Phil. 1:6-7). *"For we are His workmanship, created in Christ Jesus for good works, which God prepared beforehand that we should walk in them"* (Eph. 2:10). God is sovereign and will preserve believers in this world until their homecoming. Until that time, may we diligently co-labor with Him (1 Cor. 3:9) in those things He has prepared for us to do to honor Him. Spiritual maturity and greater opportunities to serve will follow.

October 5 – Exhorting Properly
Philippians 4:1-3

Therefore, my beloved and longed-for brethren, my joy and crown, so stand fast in the Lord, beloved. I implore Euodia and I implore Syntyche to be of the same mind in the Lord. And I urge you also, true companion, help these women who labored with me in the gospel, with Clement also, and the rest of my fellow workers, whose names are in the Book of Life.

How can we reprove others in such a way that it is received without offense or questioning our motives? When a behavior needs to be reproved, corrections should be done personally. Don't write someone or send an email: this restricts communication to a factual level, is often cowardly, and rarely accomplishes anything positive. Talk to the person face to face (if in person is not possible, then video call), or if that is not possible, phone him or her, so that the one receiving the reproof can hear your love and sincerity in the tone and inflections of your voice. John had to address difficult topics in both his second and third epistles, but on the more sensitive matters he refused to write; he preferred to address those matters in person (2 Jn. 12; 3 Jn. 13). Face to face is by far the best format for approaching difficult issues. Often the Lord will allow the very things you want to address to come up casually in the conversation. Wait on the Lord and pray for the right timing and the Lord will assist you to discuss what is needful.

Paul used a lovely three-step technique to exhort two women in the church at Philippi. Euodia and Syntyche were bickering and causing disunity within the church. First, Paul began with a positive address: *"my brethren, dearly beloved and longed for, my joy and crown."* Second, he identified the issue and the solution: *"I beseech Euodia, and beseech Syntyche, that they be of the same mind in the Lord."* He also enlisted another person, likely Epaphroditus, to help these ladies to resolve their differences and to establish accountability for monitoring their progress – *"help these women"* (Phil. 4:3). Third, he concluded his exhortation with another positive statement, mentioning that both of these sisters *"labored with me in the gospel ... whose names are in the book of life."* This technique of sandwiching reproof between positive affirmations is a good pattern to follow.

October 6 – Be Anxious for Nothing
Philippians 4:6-7

Be anxious for nothing, but in everything by prayer and supplication, with thanksgiving, let your requests be made known to God; and the peace of God, which surpasses all understanding, will guard your hearts and minds through Christ Jesus.

Rejoicing in God and giving Him thanks during hard trials exhibits our confidence in His character and promises. The meaning of "anxious" is to be pulled in different directions at the same time and the idea of "worry" is to be strangled. Anxiety and worry are the principle thieves of the believer's joy. Yet, we cannot be robbed of God's peace if we choose to rejoice in Him instead of seeking happiness in favorable circumstances. The prophet Isaiah tells us that this is how we can enjoy God's *"perfect peace"* of mind:

You will keep him in perfect peace, whose mind is stayed on You, because he trusts in You. Trust in the Lord forever, for in YAH, the Lord, is everlasting strength (Isa. 26:3-4).

Nearness to God is the greatest defense against depression and the best means of promoting a stable mind. True peace is found in God alone. William Kelly reminds us that "strength depends upon what passes between our own souls and God, who in His gracious and vigilant care watches over His saints individually."[36] Each saint must personally appreciate Him and rest in Him to do what is appropriate and right each day. May we then heed Paul's exhortation, *"Set your affection on things above, not on things on the earth"* (Col. 3:2).

If you are anxious about something, we have a commanded remedy – take it to the Lord in prayer. If the matter is not worthy of casting it on the Lord, then it certainly is not worth fretting over. We either must pray or forget about it, for it is a complete waste of time and energy to agonize over things we cannot change by doing so.

Why worry when you can pray? Trust Jesus; He'll be your stay.
Don't be a doubting Thomas; rest fully in His promise.
Why worry when you can pray?
— Unknown

October 7 – Think on These Things
Philippians 4:8-9

Finally, brethren, whatever things are true, whatever things are noble, whatever things are just, whatever things are pure, whatever things are lovely, whatever things are of good report, if there is any virtue and if there is anything praiseworthy – meditate on these things. The things which you learned and received and heard and saw in me, these do, and the God of peace will be with you.

The mind is to be strengthened in the same way that the muscles of our body are – through exercise and proper diet. Paul provides the Philippians, and us too, a wholesome dietary menu that is sure to enhance the vitality of the believer's thought life. If we are going to expose our minds to violence, pornography, filthy language, coarse jesting, and extravagant indulgences, the heart will readily be conformed into a stagnant cesspool of carnal ambitions. *"For as he thinks in his heart, so is he"* (Prov. 23:7). Physically you are what you eat, but spiritually you become what you think upon.

When a believer feeds on (thinks upon) what is corrupt, it must lead to a legitimate harvest of corruption. It will be realized long after the initial seeds were sown that the repercussions were far more devastating than what could have ever been imagined. The nude images that a young man or husband tucks away in his mind will be used by Satan to stir up dissatisfaction with his own wife later for many years to come. So why hurt yourself, your wife, your family, and, most importantly, your God? The harvest of pain is just not worth it.

Thankfully, we have peace with God through the work of Christ at Calvary, but to enjoy the peace of God, Paul says that we must train our minds to feed on a spiritual diet. Posed as questions, these virtues are: Is it true – genuine, real, and reliably transparent? Is it noble – worthy of respect and honorable? Is it just – righteous and faultless? Is it pure – unmixed wholesomeness and high moral character? Is it lovely – admirable and appreciated by others? Is it of good report – or of good repute? These six patterns of thought are virtuous (of moral excellence) and praiseworthy (deserving of commendation). All that goes through the eye and ear gates should first pass the Philippians 4:8 filter! It is the only way to enjoy the presence of the God of peace.

October 8 – Learning Contentment
Philippians 4:11-13

Not that I speak in regard to need, for I have learned in whatever state I am, to be content: I know how to be abased, and I know how to abound. Everywhere and in all things I have learned both to be full and to be hungry, both to abound and to suffer need. I can do all things through Christ who strengthens me.

Remembering that God is sovereign over all things will defeat feelings of jealousy and discontent. God is in control and everything is as He allows it. Nothing occurs in creation, including our trials, which does not first pass over His desk, so to speak. It was through this disposition that Paul learned contentment during periods of lack.

At this moment you have exactly as much money as God wants you to have. If He wanted you to have more, your bank account would show it. The reason He has not bestowed more monetary blessings in your direction is that you do not need it, or you would be a poor steward of it, or He is teaching you lessons concerning budgeting and giving. The Lord knows what He is doing, and His doings serve our best *interest*. So let us appreciate what we have, assess our present condition with a spiritual mindset, adjust where we lack, and accept everything as from the Lord. Let us learn contentment also.

Learning contentment will keep coveting and unrighteous jealousy in check. King Saul, even after understanding that the kingdom had been promised to David, was lifted up in pride and jealousy. Saul could not accept God's sovereign rule or the just punishment he received for his own blunders. If we understand that we and our neighbors have exactly what God desires us to possess, what room is there for envy and coveting in our thinking? Haggai told the nation of Israel that because they were dwelling in their nice paneled houses, while God's house remained unfinished, He had blown their assets away in order to cause them to lack. The point being that sometimes lack is God's way of getting our attention, especially if the matter is one of disobedience.

Let us remember God's past goodness and faithfulness and that at all times, He is good and does good (Ps. 119:68). If you have done all that you can and still have legitimate lack, humbly petition Him for help, but remember that your joy is not in things; it is in Christ.

October 9 – God Shall Supply All Your Need
Philippians 4:14-19

Nevertheless you have done well that you shared in my distress. Now you Philippians know also that in the beginning of the gospel, when I departed from Macedonia, no church shared with me concerning giving and receiving but you only. For even in Thessalonica you sent aid once and again for my necessities. Not that I seek the gift, but I seek the fruit that abounds to your account. Indeed I have all and abound. I am full, having received from Epaphroditus the things sent from you, a sweet-smelling aroma, an acceptable sacrifice, well pleasing to God. And my God shall supply all your need according to His riches in glory by Christ Jesus.

Paul informed the saints at Philippi that they were the only church to share with him in the early days of his ministry in Europe (i.e., during his second missionary journey). They had shared with him shortly after he departed from Macedonia (v. 15), two more times afterwards (v. 16), another gift from Philippi is referenced in Paul's letter to the Corinthians (2 Cor. 11:9), and then a gift was received from them again during Paul's first Roman imprisonment (v. 14).

Paul acknowledges that there had been a gap in their giving to him, but he contributed that to the lack of their opportunity to do so, perhaps because he was a prisoner in Rome. However, the tenor of Paul's letter to the church at Philippi, to affirm the receipt of their latest gift, is one of joy. Five different Greek words occur in the Epistle to express joy, rejoicing, and gladness some eighteen times. Paul not only loved the Philippians, but he also rejoiced in them, and in their eternal reward.

After recognizing the giving spirit of the saints at Philippi, Paul noted that not only would they receive a heavenly reward for their generosity, but God would replenish their resources on earth to satisfy all their needs: *"My God shall supply all your need according to His riches in glory by Christ Jesus"* (Phil. 4:19). Those who are united with Christ are greatly blessed because of that union and will not lack resources to worship and serve the Lord. However, we should remember that it is not the lack of resources that hinders our ability to honor the Lord, but rather, our devotion to serve the Lord instead of ourselves with what we receive from Him.

October 10 – Filled With the Knowledge of His Will
Colossians 1:9-11

For this reason we also, since the day we heard it, do not cease to pray for you, and to ask that you may be filled with the knowledge of His will in all wisdom and spiritual understanding; that you may walk worthy of the Lord, fully pleasing Him, being fruitful in every good work and increasing in the knowledge of God; strengthened with all might, according to His glorious power, for all patience and longsuffering with joy.

Paul's prayer for the believers at Colosse emphasizes this maturing process: *"that you may be filled with the knowledge of His will in all wisdom and spiritual understanding; that you may walk worthy of the Lord, fully pleasing Him, being fruitful in every good work and increasing in the knowledge of God."* Note the progression from the knowledge of God, to the wisdom of that knowledge, to the outworking of both in fruitfulness, which then led to further knowledge of God. Not only were the believers to know the truth of Scripture, but they were also to grow in wisdom (the practical outworking of understood truth).

This dynamic of practicing and experiencing the truth to learn wisdom was evident in the life of the Lord Jesus. Though He was full of truth (John 1:14), yet He increased in wisdom and favor with God (Luke 2:52) and learned obedience by doing God's will for His life (Heb. 5:8). Experiencing the truthfulness of God's Word is necessary in the believer's life also. Tribulations, for example, practically test our faith and work into our faith a quality of patience that could not be achieved otherwise (Rom. 5:3; Jas. 1:3).

To be thoroughly equipped unto every good work, a believer, then, will rely on God's Word, the guidance of the Holy Spirit, and the mentoring assistance of spiritually-minded believers as he or she matures in Christ. Believers will accomplish their ministry within the body as they continue to grow spiritually, and exercise and develop; their spiritual gifts. The world is not to be the believer's playground it's God's classroom. Believers are called to maturity and to service – the two cannot be separated. Scripture testifies to the fact that God grows ministries as He grows people and we cannot grow spiritually without increasing in our knowledge and appreciation of the Lord Jesus.

October 11 – Do Not Be Deceived
Colossians 2:4

Now this I say lest anyone should deceive you with persuasive words.

The first question in Scripture belongs to Satan. Speaking to the woman (later named Eve), Satan projected doubt on what God actually had said to Adam: *"Has God indeed said, 'You shall not eat of every tree of the garden?'"* (Gen. 3:1). It was a leading question, for its purpose was not to provoke rational thought but to instill doubt and invoke rebellion. The tactic worked on the woman, who quickly slid from the ground of faith into human reasoning. Satan's question to the woman has a flavor of unfairness: "Could God be good and limit you in such an unfair way?" "Surely a good God would not keep you from all that is good." "Are you sure that you recalled exactly what God said?"

Satan began by questioning God's Word and presenting a half-truth, and mankind acted on the wrong half. Satan is never more dangerous than when he has a Bible in his hands. This is why Paul exhorts the believers at Colosse to have a faith fully grounded on Christ and His teachings: *"Beware lest anyone cheat you through philosophy and empty deceit, according to the tradition of men, according to the basic principles of the world, and not according to Christ"* (Col. 2:8). This is the only way not to be deceived by a wise and cunning enemy.

Satan rarely presents outright lies; rather, he depends upon a series of blurred deceptions to gain his footing and to wreak havoc within the Church. The Greek word rendered "deceive" in this verse literally means "to put something near or around." That is what Satan does: he puts what he wants us to believe near truth, and entices us to leave what God has affirmed as truth for what is not – that is deception.

God is a God of absolute truth; therefore, let our faith rest on the foundation of biblical truth. If so grounded, we will be less likely to fall prey to threatening accusations or the deceit of secular reasoning and philosophies. The value of our service relates directly with having fellowship with God in spirit and in truth. If we become satisfied with the goodness of God's blessings and yet lose sight of what He desires for us, we will become feeble and powerless – God strengthens those who want to be guided into the knowledge of Himself and the purposes of His grace. Let us not be tricked from the bedrock of God's Word.

October 12 – Beware of Legalism
Colossians 2:20-23

Therefore, if you died with Christ from the basic principles of the world, why, as though living in the world, do you subject yourselves to regulations – "Do not touch, do not taste, do not handle," which all concern things which perish with the using – according to the commandments and doctrines of men? These things indeed have an appearance of wisdom in self-imposed religion, false humility, and neglect of the body, but are of no value against the indulgence of the flesh.

Paul is confronting the legalistic Judaizers who wanted to pull the Colossian believers under the yoke of Law-keeping, after being liberated in grace by the gospel of Christ. We all have encountered those legalistic types who want to impose their stern lists of dos and don'ts upon us, which is nothing less than the world's religion of good works under a Christian disguise. We cannot earn God's love or increase His esteem for us by "doings"; the Christian is *"accepted in the Beloved"* (Eph. 1:6) – end of story. There is nothing that a believer can do to persuade God to love him or her more than He already does – His love is unchanging and has been fully displayed at Calvary (Rom. 5:8). Although Paul confronted legalism numerous times, his candid language to the saints at Colosse perhaps best captures his disgust for those promoting legalism. Let us beware of falling into the same pitfall!

Likewise, it is imperative to teach the *whys,* not just the *whats,* to our children and younger believers. Otherwise we will create hard-hearted miniaturized Pharisees instead of rearing up spiritually-minded children and saints who love the Lord. We must do more than simply legislate to our children what clothing they must wear, what activities they may or may not engage in, what friends they may associate with, what music they may listen to, and books that they may read, etc. If we decree all their doings without training and in honest reflection on the wisdom that Scripture affords, they will not learn to think and discern proper conduct for themselves. Such children will merely *"make a fair show of the flesh ... that they may glory in the flesh"* (Gal. 6:12-13). To offer one's self up as a living, holy sacrifice is pleasing to the Lord, but Christians glorying in their flesh is disgusting to Him.

October 13 – Seek Those Things Which Are Above
Colossians 3:1-3

If then you were raised with Christ, seek those things which are above, where Christ is, sitting at the right hand of God. Set your mind on things above, not on things on the earth. For you died, and your life is hidden with Christ in God.

Paul realized that the best means of preventing the Colossian believers from slipping into the deceit of intellectualism or the pitfalls of legalism was to set their minds upon the Lord Jesus. In the two previous chapters of His epistle to the Colossians, he affirmed Christ's supremacy over all creation, for He is the omnipotent Creator and Sustainer, the Savior of mankind, and Lord over all. Because all the fullness of the Godhead bodily dwells in Christ (Col. 2:9), Christ alone is the source of knowledge, wisdom, peace, grace, and access to the Father. Paul reminds the Colossians of their blessed union with Christ; because they were one "with Christ," they were complete "in Him." Next, he affirms that our identification with Christ should exhort us to holy living. Our *position* in Christ should motivate our *practice*.

The Holy Text intertwines what God has done in Christ and what we should do in Christ. Salvation is God's doing, but living out our salvation is our responsibility made possible by God's grace. Through spiritual birth, we are made one with Christ – an eternal union held together by God Himself. Notice the key to proper devotion on our part: "Set your affection on things above." Not affections, but affection. We are to only have one affection and that is to be for Christ. To please Him and exalt Him is our sole purpose in life. Yet, it is so easy to be distracted by things and allow this one affection to be displaced.

Sometimes believers can get so preoccupied with all the things in the world that oppose that they forget the importance of being occupied with Christ. Attacking atheists, agnostics, or the hordes of religious people in the world will not win them to Christ. Rather, we are to be caught up with Him and extol the glorious Savior through our preaching and testimonies. It is when we choose to exalt Christ, the altogether lovely One, before men, and not ourselves, that the lost will come to cherish Him also. The soul who is in love with Jesus Christ inescapably will be a good witness for Him!

October 14 – Put On Mercy, Kindness, Humility...
Colossians 3:12

Therefore, as the elect of God, holy and beloved, put on tender mercies, kindness, humility, meekness, longsuffering...

Those having salvation in Christ, the beloved of the Lord, are destined to spend a wonderful eternity with Him. Until our earthly sojourn is over, believers are to live holy lives and exhibit the captivating character of the altogether lovely Savior. His life within us must be demonstrated for others to experience and appreciate who He is, such that they would desire to know Him, too. Just as one might choose to put on an outer garment, Paul exhorts the believers at Colosse to put on the lovely character and disposition of Christ so that all can appreciate Him.

Tender mercies speaks of extending compassion to those who are undeserving. Generally speaking, *grace* is getting what we do not deserve and *mercy* is not getting what we do deserve. Showing compassion to those who are responsible for their own ruin and suffering is the heart of God. *"Mercies"* is grammatically plural to indicate that we should be well marked by this behavior.

Kindness speaks of a willing and selfless disposition to help others and show them goodwill. It is similar to grace in this respect – it longs to exhibit unmerited favor to others. *Humility* tramples down one's own pride and assumes the low ground in respect to others – esteeming them better than oneself. *Meekness* is power in control – the strength to allow oneself to experience injustice or hardship when it is not deserved without taking action. *Longsuffering* speaks of the ability to exhibit patience and not strike back when passions are provoked to do otherwise – it willingly and joyfully suffers long despite offenses.

Humility is perfect quietness of heart. It is to expect nothing, to wonder at nothing that is done to me, to feel nothing done against me. It is to be at rest when nobody praises me, and when I am blamed or despised. It is to have a blessed home in the Lord, where I can go in and shut the door, and kneel to my Father in secret, and am at peace as in a deep sea of calmness, when all around and above is trouble.

—Andrew Murray

October 15 – Put On Forbearance, Forgiveness, and Love
Colossians 3:12-14

"Bearing with one another, and forgiving one another, if anyone has a complaint against another; even as Christ forgave you, so you also must do. But above all these things put on love, which is the bond of perfection.

Paul provided a similar list of Christian virtues to be daily worn by the believers in Ephesus and then explained why they should: *"beseech you to walk worthy of the calling with which you were called ... endeavoring to keep the unity of the Spirit in the bond of peace"* (Eph. 4:2-3). Through the power of the Holy Spirit, Christ's love draws those who previously had nothing in common into intimate communion with each other. This is why believers are to behave *"with all lowliness and gentleness, with longsuffering, bearing with one another in love."*

What does it mean to be "bearing (or forbearing) with one another"? William MacDonald answers this question:

Bearing with one another describes the patience we should have with the failings and odd ways of our brethren. In living with others, it is inevitable that we will find out their failures. It often takes the grace of God for us to put up with the idiosyncrasies of others, as it must for them to put up with ours. But we must bear with one another.[37]

Next, Paul says that we are to have an unconditional releasing spirit even when there is an active offence that deserves a complaint. This does not mean that we tell the offender that we forgive him or her, but rather we release the matter to the Lord to deal with. That permits us to extinguish our anger over the issue and to think rationally about how to handle the situation. Could it be an edifying or corrective experience for the offender if I bring this to his or her attention, or should I just let it go and say nothing? The latter behavior is certainly wise if the offense is not a pattern of behavior, but an off-hand comment or random act. It is wrong to tell someone that you forgive them if they have not confessed their sin (Luke 17:3). While forbearance is slow to take offense, forgiveness is quick to let it go. Lastly, Paul says to put on love which is the bond of perfection. Just as wearing a belt holds things up or together – love binds all these Christlike virtues together to bless.

October 16 – Whatever You Do
Colossians 3:23-24

And whatever you do, do it heartily, as to the Lord and not to men, knowing that from the Lord you will receive the reward of the inheritance; for you serve the Lord Christ.

The devil's main ambition is to lead as many of those who were created in God's image away from Him and the salvation He offers. Satan knows his doom is sealed (Rev. 12:12, 20:10) and is determined to lead as many as possible into the eternal flames of hell (Rev. 13:15, 19:20-21). He does not want lost souls turning to Christ that they might be saved (1 Tim. 5:15; 2 Thess. 2:9-10). He is likely the most powerful being that God created and, thus, is a cunning and dangerous enemy, one that only God can control. Although believers are not commanded to confront Satan directly, we are to resist him by submitting to God in faith (Jas. 4:7) and to be knowledgeable of his tactics so that he does not gain an advantage over us through ignorance (2 Cor. 2:11).

If believers truly understand the real enemy and the real battle, they will be careful not to do the devil's bidding by engaging in disobedience, false accusations, slander, strife causing divisions, blasphemy, deception, lying, and gossip – these are devilish tools used to war against and harm Christ's Church. Rather, Paul affirms what the child of God's conduct should be: *"Whatever you do, do all to the glory of God. Give no offense, either to the Jews or to the Greeks or to the Church of God"* (1 Cor. 10:31-32). Let those who have experienced spiritual rebirth no more behave like children of the devil, but rather, let them walk in the newness of life as children of light!

At the Judgment Seat of Christ (2 Cor. 5:10; Rom 14:10-12), every believer will receive or lose rewards for those works done while on earth. Deeds which are done in Christ's strength and for His glory will be rewarded and that which is unprofitable for the kingdom of God will be burnt up (1 Cor. 3:11-15), and we, when in the presence of Christ, will be glad they were. Therefore, let us not be self-serving, self-exalting, and Church-harming children of God. But rather, may we remember Paul's exhortation: *"whatever you do, do it heartily, as to the Lord and not to men, knowing that from the Lord you will receive the reward of the inheritance; for you serve the Lord Christ."*

October 17 – With Grace and Seasoned With Salt
Colossians 4:6

Let your speech always be with grace, seasoned with salt, that you may know how you ought to answer each one.

Job's companions had begun well; they put aside their household affairs to silently identify with him and to console him. No doubt, seeing their loyalty after a week's time is what prompted Job to converse with them. However, in the course of time, Job's friends went from a ministry of comfort to one of accusations and rebuke; they suggested that Job was suffering for his own sin and that he needed to repent to receive God's forgiveness. Having repeatedly rejected their long-winded indictments, Job provided an overview of their assistance: *"Miserable comforters are you all"* (Job 16:2). His colleagues had only scorned and mocked him; they were not a solace to him (Job 16:20).

To be effective comforters and counselors, we must follow the Lord's example; otherwise, we will likely be "miserable comforters" to others also. John writes of the Lord: *"We beheld His glory, the glory as of the only begotten of the Father, full of grace and truth"* (John 1:14). The Lord Jesus was not just balanced, but all that He did and said was full of grace and truth. Just as grace and truth are inseparable aspects of the Lord's character, the believer should not invoke one quality over the other: our speech must be gracious and seasoned with salt. If it is not necessary to say, or cannot be said in love, or is not true, then the Lord would not have us say it. This is particularly important if the person you are speaking with is suffering.

Additionally, as we rely on the Lord to overcome various trials, we become better equipped to help others face the same challenges with confidence (2 Cor. 1:3-4). Why were Job's companions such miserable comforters? Because they failed to help Job; they opened their mouths without knowing the truth, with a lack of grace, and said what was not necessary. Because they had not experienced what Job had, they could not rightly empathize with him or know how to encourage him through the trial. Job states that if their roles were reversed, he would not do so, but instead would provide encouragement and comfort (Job 16:4-5). God's judgment of Job's friends affirms that it is better not to speak than to do so wrongly and needlessly hurt others.

October 18 – Turned to God From Idols
1 Thessalonians 1:9

For they themselves declare concerning us what manner of entry we had to you, and how you turned to God from idols to serve the living and true God.

The Lord Jesus told His disciples that He was the only means of obtaining eternal life: *"I am the way, the truth, and the life. No one comes to the Father except through Me"* (John 14:6). Peter declared the same truth, *"Nor is there salvation in any other, for there is no other name under heaven given among men by which we must be saved"* (Acts 4:12). The narrow way is God's way, and the only one that leads to salvation. Yes, God is a God of love (1 Jn. 4:8), but He could not justly save mankind by love alone – His sense of justice demanded that sin be condemned. Yet, it was God's love which supplied the solution by which mankind could be saved: *"But God demonstrates His own love toward us, in that while we were still sinners, Christ died for us"* (Rom. 5:8). Thus, God's love found a way to righteously offer salvation by judging His Son for human sin. He can legally offer the gift of eternal salvation to *"whosoever will"* (John 3:16). Those who reject His gracious offer will spend an eternity in the lake of fire, *"for the wages of sin is death"* (Rom. 6:23; Rev. 20:10-15).

The message of God's salvation is inclusive in its application; it is offered to anyone who will believe it (Rev. 22:17). However, it is exclusive in nature, for trusting in any other message brings eternal judgment (Gal. 1:6-9). God is *"not willing that any should perish but that all should come to repentance"* (2 Pet. 3:9), but a seeking sinner must trust Christ alone for his or her salvation; we must repent and receive Him as Savior (Luke 13:3; Rom. 10:9). Repentance means that we agree with God that we are sinners deserving His judgment and that we turn away from all that we ever thought would earn us heaven; such repentance indicates a deep grief over personal sin and a desire to turn from wickedness (Jer. 8:6). But we must turn to something also – that is, we must believe the gospel of Jesus Christ. This is what the Thessalonians did; they turned to God from idols. Their salvation was evident in that they diligently served the true God even while being persecuted for their faith (1 Thess. 1:5-9). They were the real deal!

October 19 – Waiting for His Son From Heaven
1 Thessalonians 1:10

To wait for His Son from heaven, whom He raised from the dead, even Jesus who delivers us from the wrath to come.

Christ will return from heaven to the air to remove His Church from the earth (1 Thess. 4:13-18). Seven years later, He will return to the earth with His saints to judge wickedness and establish His kingdom. Presently, Christ is seated on His Father's throne, but when He returns to the earth, He will establish His own throne and rule the nations.

The Old Testament saints may be raised up with the Church prior to the Tribulation Period (Heb. 11:40). This position may be represented in Revelation 4 by the appearance of twenty-four crowned elders on twenty-four thrones situated around Christ in heaven. The number twenty-four is used in Scripture to symbolically speak of the priesthood (1 Chron. 24). Thus, it is possible that the twenty-four elders, who are priests (Rev. 5:10), are associated with the twelve tribes of Israel and the twelve apostles of the Church, the gates and the foundations of the New Jerusalem, respectively (Rev. 21:12-14). Or, the Old Testament saints may be raised up with the tribulation saints at the end of the Tribulation Period, along with the restoration of the Jewish nation.

Regardless, we do know that the Church is not exempt from suffering for Christ, but the Church is exempt from divine wrath:

Much more then, having now been justified by His blood, we shall be saved from wrath through Him (Rom. 5:9).

For God did not appoint us to wrath, but to obtain salvation through our Lord Jesus Christ (1 Thess. 5:9).

God's wrath is against wickedness, not against His redeemed (Zech. 12:8-9). Therefore the Church must be taken to heaven before Christ opens the first seal on the scroll (Rev. 6:1) to initiate the Tribulation Period. Paul taught the Thessalonians that the Church would not go through the Day of the Lord, the Tribulation Period (1 Thess. 5:2-9). He spoke of non-believers as "they" and believers as "brethren," "you," "us," and "we." He then declared that the "brethren" would not be in the darkness of the Tribulation Period, but that non-believers would be.

October 20 – Mind Your Own Business
1 Thessalonians 4:11-12

That you also aspire to lead a quiet life, to mind your own business, and to work with your own hands, as we commanded you, that you may walk properly toward those who are outside, and that you may lack nothing.

In these verses of his first Epistle to the Thessalonians, Paul exhorted the believers concerning three matters of proper behavior: First, they were not to seek fame and fortune, but live a quiet life. Second, they were to keep their noses out of other people's business. Third, they were to labor with their own hands to support their needs and not expect to sponge off the goodwill of good-natured people. He wrote a second epistle (probably from Corinth) to them shortly after the first to correct misunderstandings and problems in the assembly.

Paul had taught the believers extensively concerning the Day of Christ in his first Epistle. This no doubt excited the believers to look each and every day for the coming of Christ for the Church, but apparently, some thought the Lord's return was so near that they did not need to labor any longer. "Why slave away on earth, when heaven is so nigh?" The situation was causing disunity in the assembly. Indeed, Paul had a forthright message for these lazy freeloaders:

If anyone will not work, neither shall he eat. For we hear that there are some who walk among you in a disorderly manner, not working at all, but are busybodies. Now those who are such we command and exhort through our Lord Jesus Christ that they work in quietness and eat their own bread (2 Thess. 3:10-12).

Christ is displeased by strife and division in His Church because it is associated with the work of the devil (Jas. 3:16), while the unity of God's people is precious to Him: *"Behold, how good and how pleasant it is for brethren to dwell together in unity!"* (Ps. 133:1). A busybody inserts his or her interests into the affairs of others, but a Christ-minded believer puts the welfare of others above his or her own interests – this type of attitude ends strife. Having the mind of Christ ensures His people are unified and doing *"all to the glory of God"* (1 Cor. 10:31).

October 21 – Waiting for His Son From Heaven
1 Thessalonians 4:13-18

But I do not want you to be ignorant, brethren, concerning those who have fallen asleep, lest you sorrow as others who have no hope. For if we believe that Jesus died and rose again, even so God will bring with Him those who sleep in Jesus. For this we say to you by the word of the Lord, that we who are alive and remain until the coming of the Lord will by no means precede those who are asleep. For the Lord Himself will descend from heaven with a shout, with the voice of an archangel, and with the trumpet of God. And the dead in Christ will rise first. Then we who are alive and remain shall be caught up together with them in the clouds to meet the Lord in the air. And thus we shall always be with the Lord. Therefore comfort one another with these words.

Believers in the Church Age are sealed by the Holy Spirit (Eph. 1:13) and are thus exempt from divine wrath forever. Having responded to the gospel message, believers in the Church Age will be removed from the earth before God refines and restores His covenant people to Himself during the Tribulation Period (Rom. 11:25). Hence, Christians are commanded to wait for Christ's imminent return to the clouds, at which time they will be suddenly translated from the earth, will receive glorified bodies (1 Cor. 15:51-51), and then will be escorted to heaven to be examined at the Judgment Seat of Christ (Rom. 14:10-12). The Church will not suffer God's wrath during the Tribulation Period, but rather will be kept out of it: *"Having now been justified by His blood, we shall be saved from wrath through Him"* (Rom. 5:9). *"I also will keep you from the hour of trial which shall come upon the whole world, to test those who dwell on the earth"* (Rev. 3:10).

Because Christ has suffered God's full wrath over human sin, those who have received His pardon through Christ will never come under His judicial wrath – ever! This is the same pattern for other saints also. Therefore the Church must be taken from the earth to Heaven before Christ opens the first seal on the scroll initiating the Tribulation Period (Rev. 6:1). Likewise, surviving tribulation saints and those Jews of spiritual Israel will be spared death when God judges the nations at the end of the Tribulation Period. God's wrath is against wickedness, not against His redeemed – those who are His (Zech. 12:8-9).

October 22 – Esteem Them Very Highly in Love
1 Thessalonians 5:12-13

And we urge you, brethren, to recognize those who labor among you, and are over you in the Lord and admonish you, and to esteem them very highly in love for their work's sake. Be at peace among yourselves.

Paul told the Thessalonians to put on love (1 Thess. 5:8) and then he spoke of two ways that they could practically demonstrate love to others. First, those elders laboring among them were to be highly appreciated, respected, and loved for the important shepherding work they do. Some within the church had apparently quit working and had become busybodies and freeloaders in the church (1 Thess. 4:11; 2 Thess. 3:10). Why work if the Lord's return is near? But Paul never told them that Christ's coming for His Bride was immediate, but rather imminent. No doubt the elders of the Church had rebuked these unruly saints and it had not been received well. Shepherding God's people is an arduous ministry, with much heartache, and opposition. Those church elders representing the Lord's character and care should be encouraged and loved by all whom they serve (Heb. 13:7, 17, 24).

Second, Paul writes: *"See that no one renders evil for evil to anyone, but always pursue what is good both for yourselves and for all"* (1 Thess. 5:15). Indeed, it is important to rejoice in the Lord and to pray for help during difficult situations, but if you are being overwhelmed with "people troubles," resort to the weapon of love. The more you are hated – the more you should love. Usually, in God's time, the oppressor will break down – because God's love is irresistible.

We once had an unsaved neighbor whose demeanor towards our family was unjustly harsh. We bore this plight and returned many acts of kindness to our rude neighbor for seven years without a favorable response. Then, on one frigid morning after a significant snowfall, our grumpy neighbor surprised us by arriving with his tractor and clearing away the snow from our long driveway. Our family watched from the living room picture window in disbelief. I turned to the children and said, "See guys, love really does work." When he was finished, I ventured outdoors to thank him. He responded, "I just wanted to say thank you for being nice neighbors." God's love in action is a wonderful resource to bring even the vilest sinners to their knees.

October 23 – Comfort the Fainthearted
1 Thessalonians 5:14

Now we exhort you, brethren, warn those who are unruly, comfort the fainthearted, uphold the weak, be patient with all.

Paul encouraged the Thessalonians to *"comfort the feebleminded, support the weak."* Often the faith of others is needed to strengthen the fainthearted (Heb. 11). Consequently, not only is the "shield of faith" a necessary part of a believer's spiritual armor, but it can also be used to assist other believers to stand fast in the faith (Eph. 6:16). As previously mentioned Roman soldiers used a leather-covered wooden shield which could be overlapped with the shields of other soldiers to create an impenetrable wall and ceiling against incoming fiery darts and arrows. There is strength in numbers, and the faith of the many can "pull up" those wobbly-kneed believers who tend to be weak in faith or those suddenly overloaded with crushing circumstances (Gal. 6:2).

Christians need each other, and we need each other's faith to carry on boldly for the Lord. We all suffer at times with mental weakness. Doubts pour over us like a flood. But praise God for those who will come alongside and lift up our heads heavenward. Paul was such a person. He was put behind prison bars, but his faith could not be constrained. As a result, others were *"much more bold to speak the word without fear"* (Phil. 1:14). May our faith be focused on Christ and be a benefit to His Body – the Church.

Remembering God's promises will be a rich source of encouragement to all those burdened by their circumstances. Especially during strenuous times, let us not neglect reminding each other of what God has pledged to do. One of these promises is that the Lord will never leave nor forsake the believer (Heb. 13:5). He also will not allow us more testing than we can bear without providing grace to continue in it or a way of escape (1 Cor. 10:13).

Paul understood this promise to be true and sought to remind others of it. To the suffering Christians at Thessalonica he wrote, *"He who calls you is faithful, who also will do it"* (1 Thess. 5:24), and to Timothy he said, *"If we are faithless, He remains faithful; He cannot deny Himself"* (2 Tim. 2:13). This type of true and living trust in God repels doubt and is the best way of assisting the fainthearted.

October 24 – Rejoice Always
1 Thessalonians 5:16

Rejoice always.

This is the shortest verse in the Greek New Testament, but one of the most important. Joy removes the burden. God's family should be a cheerful family, meaning we all must contribute to the atmosphere of joy. There is no room for a "doom and gloom" attitude. *"Yet if anyone suffers as a Christian, let him not be ashamed, but let him glorify God in this matter"* (1 Pet. 4:16). As a believer chooses to rejoice in the Lord while in the midst of a dire situation, God often glorifies Himself by working a miraculous solution to end the trial.

For example, pagans at Philippi accused Paul and Silas of wrongdoing. They were not extended the right of a fair trial, but instead were beaten, chained, and put into prison. How did these two servants of the Lord respond to this cruel situation? *"But at midnight Paul and Silas were praying and singing hymns to God, and the prisoners were listening to them"* (Acts 16:25). They prayed, which is the proper recourse for gospel expansion, and they rejoiced in their God through singing. How did the Lord respond to their praying and rejoicing? He brought a great earthquake, which released them from their captivity and then provided an opportunity for the jailer and his whole family to hear and believe the gospel of Jesus Christ.

The church at Philippi began when suffering for Christ was replaced with rejoicing in Christ. By doing so, Paul and Silas were showing the Lord that they were yielding to His sovereign will to achieve the best outcome of their situation, despite the hardship. Rejoicing during times of adversity declares one's faith in a special way that God appreciates, for this was the example of the Lord Jesus, *"who for the joy that was set before Him endured the cross, despising the shame"* (Heb. 12:2). The Lord was not delivered from the cross, but still had joy in enduring its horrors. Paul and Silas were not immediately released from prison and they rejoiced despite being severely beaten. Yet, in contrast, God did send an angel on two separate occasions to deliver Peter from prison (Acts 4, 12). Despite what God does, we can rejoice in Him, because He is in perfect control of every situation and desires to show His grace to the widest extent possible.

October 25 – Pray Without Ceasing
1 Thessalonians 5:17

Pray without ceasing.

"Pray without ceasing" does not mean we must constantly be uttering prayers. The Greek word *adialeiptos* is used here which means "constantly recurring," not "continuously occurring." It would be impossible to pray twenty-four hours a day, seven days a week. But it is possible to have an active recurring prayer life. Perhaps the following illustration will help. Have you ever heard someone say after returning from a long road trip in which they were traveling with another person, "We talked the whole way home?" There were likely pauses in the conversation, yet the dialogue was so enriching that no sense of diminished fellowship was noticed. To "pray without ceasing" means to stay in contact with God in such a way that our praying is like a long conversation with short pauses; we never sense a break in conversation. The believer should pray at regular times and as exercised when needs arise (to confess sin, to make intercession, to seek grace in a time of need). The Lord should never be far from your thoughts at any time during the day: *"Lord, You have heard the desire of the humble; You will prepare their heart; You will cause Your ear to hear"* (Ps. 10:17).

The Lord knows the desire of our hearts and grants the humble those desires. For what desire did the heart of the early church beat? Paul prayed for the souls of the nation of Israel – that they might be saved (Rom. 9:1-3, 10:1)! Paul also informed the Gentiles that they came to Christ as a result of God answering the prayers of Jewish Christians (2 Cor. 9:14). The early church prayed for boldness to spread the gospel message and God powerfully answered their request (Acts 4:24-30). As a result, many souls were saved and added to the Church.

The longest prayer in the New Testament, the Lord's prayer of John 17, reveals the heart of God for lost souls, for the preservation of the saved, and for unity of the Church. It would seem that these matters ought to be at the forefront of our praying as well. Often we use prayer in a *defensive posture* – responding to personal needs, sickness, and the loss of a job. We certainly ought to solicit God on such matters, but let us not neglect the Great Commission – like the early Church we need to charge forward against the gates of hell with *offensive boldness.*

October 26 – In Everything Give Thanks
1 Thessalonians 5:18

In everything give thanks; for this is the will of God in Christ Jesus for you.

Why are we to give thanks in all things? Because *"we know that all things work together for good to them that love God, to them who are the called according to His purpose"* (Rom. 8:28). This means that we have exactly what the Lord has for us. Does a critical spirit keep you from thinking positive? Do you tend to see a half-empty glass of water or a half-full glass? The reality has not changed, but your perception of it has. A thankful spirit and critical mind cannot exist together.

There is always something to be thankful for if one is in a frame of mind to look for it. When the antique vase accidentally slips from your hands and shatters into a thousand pieces upon impact with the floor, praise the Lord it did not hit your foot. If you are involved with a traffic accident in which your vehicle is ruled a total wreck, praise the Lord you were kept safe. A thankful mind frame will always find something to praise God about, no matter how mentally stretching the trial is.

Hudson Taylor devoted his life to being a missionary in China through the heart of the 19th century. His vision for evangelism established the China Inland Mission, which successfully solicited thousands of missionaries to venture to China while he coordinated their activities. Tens of thousands of souls professed Christ as Savior.

The years in China were difficult for Taylor, but the fruitfulness of his labor is evident to this day. Diseases had claimed the lives of two of the Taylors' children. Hudson and his wife Maria sent their remaining four children back to England with a trusted friend to be schooled and kept safe. Shortly after this, Maria Taylor gave birth to a fifth son, but within a week, cholera took this child's life also. Soon after this, his 33-year-old beloved wife became very ill and died. Mrs. Duncan, an eyewitness of Mrs. Taylor's homegoing, later wrote of the event: "As dear Mrs. Taylor was breathing her last, Mr. Taylor knelt down – his heart so full – and committed her to the Lord; *thanking Him* for having given her and for the twelve and a half years of happiness they had had together; *thanking Him*, too, for taking her to His own blessed presence, and solemnly dedicating himself anew to His service."[38]

302

October 27 – Do Not Quench the Spirit
1 Thessalonians 5:19

Do not quench the Spirit.

Sin quenches and grieves the Holy Spirit (Eph. 4:30). Because the verb is in the present tense and imperative mood, the phrase could easily be translated "stop quenching the Spirit." *Wuest's Expanded Translation* reads, "Stop stifling and suppressing the Spirit"! The Holy Spirit is likened to a flame (Isa. 4:4; Rev. 4:5). He warms our hearts, enlightens our minds, and empowers the believer's spirit, but He can be resisted. It is the effectual working of the Holy Spirit that Paul warned against hindering or even snuffing out. Although the Holy Spirit is always present in the believer, when the believer chooses to sin, it is as if he or she had thrown a wet blanket over His energizing capacity.

When an individual trusts Christ as his or her personal Savior, the Holy Spirit responds by regenerating that person (Tit. 3:5). That new believer becomes an available vessel in the hands of God to fill and pour out of as He chooses. But the extent that this is possible depends on personal sanctification. When we elect to flee ungodliness, we become vessels of honor available for God's sovereign use (2 Tim. 2:20-22).

As the believer submits to the known will of God, the Holy Spirit responds by filling that individual and equipping him or her for service with divine power. This can be clearly seen from the dawning days of the Church Age (Acts 1:4 with 1:12 and 2:1-4; Acts 4:23-32; Acts 6:9-10 with 7:55; Acts 9:6 with 9:17). Submission leads to Spirit filling, which results in usefulness and fruitfulness. Thus, the believer is commanded to *"be filled with the Holy Spirit"* (Eph. 5:18).

Paul informs us in Romans 6 that as we *know* and personally *yield* to truth, we *present* our bodies to God as a living sacrifice. We enable the Holy Spirit by losing ourselves through submission and yielding ourselves to God's revealed truth. According to God's foreknowledge of both our failures and our obedience, He has preordained us to specific works for us to accomplish for Him. We must truly lose our life to gain the vitality God desires for our spiritual life in Him (Luke 9:24). Only the Holy Spirit can empower us to live for Christ.

October 28 – Test All Things
1 Thessalonians 5:20-21

Do not despise prophecies. Test all things; hold fast what is good.

These two verses cannot be separated from each other: To despise prophecy (God's declared Word) would prevent spirit-filling by the Holy Spirit and squelch our overall spiritual growth. Before the Scripture was supplied to the Church by the apostles, there were prophets who immediately declared the Word of God in the local assembly and also tested the validity of what was said (1 Cor. 14:26-32). Paul was telling the believers at Thessalonica not to neglect studying, understanding, meditating on, and memorizing God's Word. Feeding on the Scripture in this way is what is necessary for spiritual growth. Peter writes: *"As newborn babes, desire the pure milk of the word, that you may grow thereby"* (1 Pet. 2:2). Both Paul (1 Cor. 3:2) and the writer of Hebrews (Heb. 5:12-13) acknowledge the need to study the foundational truths of the Christian faith (the milk of the Word), but also the necessity to move on to "meatier" topics.

We cannot test all things, to prove what is truth and deception, without first knowing what God's Word says. In the present culture, blatant wickedness besieges the heart of the rebel, and subtle deception snares the complacent believer. Deceit is often thoroughly forged with something acceptable. Consequently, much discernment is required in daily conduct, or the believer will certainly fall prey to the enemy's trickery and craftiness.

New Age propaganda has infiltrated corporate training, the medical profession, government-operated schools, and the entertainment industry. Many self-promoting preachers today are using the gospel for profit. The cults are advertising strong pro-family and pro-morality themes. They often ensnare individuals into their ranks by promoting good intentions at the cost of sound doctrine. Modern children's programming often disguises pantheism, animism, reincarnation, and necromancy within carefully arranged humor, special effects, and exhilarating music to create a more palatable message for children to digest under the eye of undiscerning parents. It is important that every believer test the validity of every aspect of their lives against God's Word. There is no reason to be deceived, so leave nothing to chance.

October 29 – Abstain From Every Form of Evil
1 Thessalonians 5:22

Abstain from every form of evil.

The KJV renders this verse, *"Abstain from the appearance of evil."* As we read in the following verse, the believer's spirit, soul and body should be fully consecrated to God. This means that we must abhor evil in thought and deed. The matter hinges on the believer's understanding that who and what he or she was positionally in Adam is dead – it died on the cross when Christ suffered and died on our behalf (Eph. 4:22; Rom. 6:6). All that we were before Christ is no more – we died with Him at Calvary. Because we have been legally declared dead, we may receive a new life – His life. We must now endeavor to live His life in practice and not follow our own ambitions (2 Cor. 5:14-17).

Being blameless is mentioned first in both lists of appointment criteria for church elders in 1 Timothy 3 and Titus 1. Blameless means "one's conduct is above reproach." It is a lifestyle that is so centered in holy living that no legitimate accusation of wrongdoing can be asserted. Being blameless means living a lifestyle that will not stumble a weaker brother in his faith (1 Cor. 8:9), or hinder the unsaved from hearing the gospel (1 Cor. 9:12), or bring reproach on the name of Christ (1 Tim. 3:7). Besides being blameless in conduct, God demands that our thought-life be consecrated to Him also. This is not possible until we realize that there is absolutely nothing in our flesh that can please God. Only when a believer's spirit, soul and body are yielded unto righteousness and the Holy Spirit's control can he or she be useful for the kingdom of God (Rom. 7:18-19). Oswald Chambers writes:

> It is the great moment of our lives when we decide that sin must die right out, not be curbed or suppressed or counteracted, but crucified. There is no room in our minds to think the way we did before coming to Christ. The consecrated mind frame does not allow the mind to pursue its own inherent vanity and lusts. It does not allow the mind to drift into the land of imagination to indulge the fallen nature. The believer must **remove** all unholy thinking, **renew** his or her mind to approve what is good and acceptable (this requires replacing what was removed), and **resist** the temptation to return to "stinking thinking."[39]

October 30 – Sanctify You Completely
1 Thessalonians 5:23-24

Now may the God of peace Himself sanctify you completely; and may your whole spirit, soul, and body be preserved blameless at the coming of our Lord Jesus Christ. He who calls you is faithful, who also will do it.

The Holy Spirit acknowledges man's physiological design of spirit, soul, and body. The spirit is *God-conscious* and refers to the innermost area of our being – the "inner man." The body is *flesh- and world-conscious*. It is the lowest portion of our existence, and forms the outermost being. Between these two components dwells the soul. The soul is *self-conscious* and comprises our intellect, our emotions, our personality, and our will. Through the five senses the soul links with the physical realm and through the spirit the soul connects with God. The soul is a bridge, a window, a medium set between the body and the spirit. When a believer is in fellowship with God, the Holy Spirit has freedom to commune with man's spirit, which transmits godly thoughts to the soul. This in turn exercises the body to conform to the Spirit's rule and thus be a vessel of honor for God's use.

But the spirit cannot act directly upon the body without the medium of the soul. Thus, the will of man can choose to ignore his spirit and follow the baser desires of the body. God created the soul of man to stand between and exercise power over the whole of man to discern and to determine to pursue the spiritual rather than the natural world. The soul of man includes his heart, will, and mind. The mind is the intellectual and cognitive center of the soul and, thus, ultimately decides the direction the soul will follow. The mind is, therefore, a frame that constrains the soul in the same manner that a window frame constrains the glass – an entrance between two realities is formed.

The bulk of scriptural exhortation is not focused on the soul, or the heart, but on the mind. The mind must be "transformed" (Rom. 12:2) in order to "form" a pure heart (Ps. 51:10). A pure heart serves to "conform" (Eph. 6:5-8) the will to God's will. The mind is the locale between the physical and spiritual realms where spiritual battles are won or lost. The mind frames the soul's will and emotions. If a believer truly desires the Holy Spirit to have free access through his or her soul window, the mind must be properly framed.

October 31 – Greet All the Brethren
1 Thessalonians 5:26

Greet all the brethren with a holy kiss.

Paul often concludes his epistles with this exhortation to those he has been instructing:

Greet one another with a holy kiss (Rom. 16:16).

Greet one another with a holy kiss (1 Cor. 16:20).

Greet one another with a holy kiss (2 Cor. 13:12).

What does Paul mean by this instruction to greet fellow believers with a "holy kiss"? "Holy" is translated from the Greek adjective *hagios*, which is normally translated "holy" or "saint(s)." The Greek noun *philema*, which is derived from the verb *phileo* which means "a brotherly love," is translated "kiss." *Philema* can be any personal greeting which is used to express genuine brotherly love with a wholesome overtone; it does not necessarily mean a literal "kiss." The idea is to convey warmth and Christian affection to any and all male and female believers without any kind of lustful ploy.

The manner in which genuine friendless is expressed will vary significantly from culture to culture. Some societies are less expressive and reserved than others, so the actual means of showing brotherly love will vary also: a facial kiss, a hug, a pat, a handshake, a nod, etc. It is also recognized that within each culture you have a range of expressive people. If you're a brother who wants to limit a sister that is just a little too hug-happy, try sticking your hand out as she is coming towards you, as if you were going to shake her hand. It is natural to return the gesture and then you will at least have your arms between you both when she arrives. I personally favor side hugs for sisters just so they or anyone watching has no misunderstandings. This is especially wise if either party is married. Regardless, whatever is expressed should be pure and blameless and should be available for all saints you associate with, not just the ones you enjoy the most (Jas. 2:1-4). Also, remember that encouragement cards, letters, and a host of electronic means are available to confirm love and appreciation to other believers.

November 1 – You Are Not in the Day of the Lord
2 Thessalonians 2:3-4

Let no one deceive you by any means; for that Day will not come unless the falling away comes first, and the man of sin is revealed, the son of perdition, who opposes and exalts himself above all that is called God or that is worshiped, so that he sits as God in the temple of God, showing himself that he is God.

Sunrises occur so frequently that we often do not appreciate their beauty. Yet, if you were waiting out the night in a dark jungle alone, you would have a much deeper appreciation for those first hues of morning bliss in the eastern horizon. This is why Christ, in the closing passage of Scripture, likens Himself to *"the bright and morning star"* (Rev. 22:16) which is most noticeable in the eastern sky just before dawn. Focusing on Christ instead of the spiritual darkness we are living in inspires hope for the glorious day which is to come. Bible prophecy is centered in the person of Jesus Christ (Rev. 19:10), the Bright and Morning Star. Scripture contains predawn events of His coming in order to encourage those who are watching and waiting for Him.

In his first epistle, Paul had spoken of Christ's imminent coming for His Church (1 Thess. 4:13-18) and also of the Day of the Lord which would follow (1 Thess. 5:1-5). Shortly after receiving Paul's first Epistle, someone, apparently posing as Paul, wrote a letter to discourage the church at Thessalonica (2 Thess. 2:2). These new and persecuted believers were wrongly informed by this counterfeit letter that they had missed the coming of Christ and were now in the Day of the Lord. Paul then wrote to them to correct the erroneous teaching.

Paul's main emphasis was to affirm that they were not in the Tribulation Period, since Christ had not yet returned to remove the Church from the earth. He then described two things that must happen prior to the commencement of the Day of the Lord: the professing Church will become apostate and the Man of Sin, the Antichrist, will be revealed (2 Thess. 2:3-6). Dark times will precede the curtain call of the Church Age, yet believers are promised that their *Bright and Morning Star* shall appear. He shall come for His beloved Bride at the dawning of the Day of the Lord, and then the *Sun of Righteousness* (Mal. 4:2) shall rise in His full fury and flood the earth with His glory!

November 2 – Dealing With the Unruly and Busybodies
2 Thessalonians 3:3-9

But we command you, brethren, in the name of our Lord Jesus Christ, that you withdraw from every brother who walks disorderly and not according to the tradition which he received from us. For you yourselves know how you ought to follow us, for we were not disorderly among you; nor did we eat anyone's bread free of charge, but worked with labor and toil night and day, that we might not be a burden to any of you, not because we do not have authority, but to make ourselves an example of how you should follow us.

A busybody is someone who injects their own interests, not the Lord's concerns, into your affairs. Such unruly behavior within a local church harms body-life and leads to disunity, division, and often corruption of what is important to the Lord. At such times a purifying action is needful to remedy the problem. Paul acknowledges this mysterious truth of Church body-life: *"For none of us lives to himself, and no one dies to himself"* (Rom. 14:7). *"And if one member suffers, all the members suffer with it; or if one member is honored, all the members rejoice with it"* (1 Cor. 12:26). Hence, we should never think that our personal sins do not have ramifications for others. The choices we make today affect our family members, our local churches, and indeed all the brethren. When the Body suffers, Christ suffers, and that is why this subject matter is important to Him – He loves His Church!

When a believer continues in willful sin, he or she should be rebuked (1 Tim. 5:20). A rebuke is a stern warning to the offending party to repent; it should carry the threat of punishment for continued wrong behavior (Rev. 3:19). If people, even elders, continue in sin, they must be stopped. Strong measures are warranted. This disgraceful conduct cannot be tolerated in the Church. As a sanctified Body gathered to the Lord, the local assembly should completely avoid those who have been warned but continue to be disorderly (2 Thess. 3:11-15), divisive (Rom. 16:17), or factious (Titus 3:10-11). The purpose of this shunning is to help another person see that he or she is out of fellowship with God, and therefore out of fellowship with His people. This action is motivated by love and not pity; that is, we want to do what is best for the unrepentant individual, not what will ease his or her sorrow.

November 3 – Admonish Him as a Brother
2 Thessalonians 3:13-15

But as for you, brethren, do not grow weary in doing good. And if anyone does not obey our word in this epistle, note that person and do not keep company with him, that he may be ashamed. Yet do not count him as an enemy, but admonish him as a brother.

Perhaps one of the best examples of not growing weary in doing good is Nathan's willingness to admonish David concerning his adultery with Bathsheba and the murder of her husband to conceal the matter (2 Sam. 12). Nathan's sudden arrival at the palace was unsolicited, unannounced, and probably unwelcomed by David, but God's servant did what was needed to restore his brother regardless. Both Lord and Nathan loved David, who was away from the Lord and consequently utterly miserable. In obedience to God's command, Nathan sought to restore David to God by confronting him over his sin.

Might there be more Nathan-like believers in the Church today who will not ignore those believers spiritually suffocating in sin. It takes real courage to lovingly rebuke those we love despite their social or religious rank. May we recall that David was the king of Israel and could have effortlessly ordered Nathan's execution. It takes real courage to stand in the light of God's truth and *"have no fellowship with the unfruitful works of darkness, but rather expose them,"* even when the person we are confronting has high status (Eph. 5:11). Nathan practiced what Paul exhorted the Christians in Thessalonica to do.

Only those who are walking close to the Lord will be able to discern issues of sin clearly and be able to have the mind of the Lord to handle such loathsome situations (Gal. 6:1). We must have a spirit of meekness and humility to restore those in sin, but without condoning what is wrong or being adversely influenced by those in the wrong. Peter reminds us that God has not changed since the days of the Old Testament, nor has His expectation for His people been altered: *"But as He who called you is holy, you also be holy in all your conduct, because it is written, 'Be holy, for I am holy'"* (1 Pet. 1:15-16). As believers, we need each other to be walking with the Lord. So thank the Lord when someone has both the spiritual sense and courage to tell you when you have gone your own way. Otherwise, how would you know?

November 4 – Order for the Genders
1 Timothy 2:9-12

In like manner also, that the women adorn themselves in modest apparel, with propriety and moderation, not with braided hair or gold or pearls or costly clothing, but, which is proper for women professing godliness, with good works. Let a woman learn in silence with all submission. And I do not permit a woman to teach or to have authority over a man, but to be in silence.

As previously mentioned, we live in days in which the devil is relentlessly trying to undermine the rudiments of God's creation order in Genesis 1, including, What is gender? and What is marriage? Unfortunately, many identifying with Christ today are falling prey to the undercurrent of humanism which attempts to erode God's purposes. As previously mentioned, Paul explains that what is created by another becomes the glory of the originator in *Creation Order*: God created man from the dust of the ground, thus man represents God's glory. God created the woman (the gender) from the side of the first man, thus the woman symbolizes man's glory. And the woman's long hair originates from her and is hence her glory (1 Cor. 11:7). What originates from another should not rule over the originator (1 Tim. 2:13-14).

Some have wrongly linked male headship to marriage only (e.g., 1 Cor. 11:3, ESV), but Eve was created as a woman; she later became Adam's wife. Rather, Paul is referring to God's design for each gender when He created male (to lead) and female (to help). Humanity will naturally devalue God and His purposes, but He has given believers a visible salute to His order, to preclude us from doing so (1 Cor. 11:3-7).

The Greek word *hesuchia,* is rendered "silence" twice in this passage and conveys the thought of "being settled down." It is not the stricter word for silence (*sigao*) used to speak of silence of women in the church meetings (1 Cor. 14:33). Hence, when men and women are gathered for spiritual exercise, the women were to receive instruction from male leaders with quiet subjection, but they were not forbidden to speak altogether, yet men were to be the ones leading them in prayer (1 Tim. 2:8). Rather than leading, the sisters were to dress modestly, as not to stumble their brothers, and to adorn themselves with good works as helpers submitting to God's order for the genders.

311

November 5 – Using Hospitality to Shepherd
1 Timothy 3:2

A bishop [overseer] *then must be blameless, the husband of one wife, temperate, sober-minded, of good behavior, hospitable, able to teach.*

Although all saints should practice hospitality (Rom. 12:13), those in spiritual leadership must *"be given to hospitality"* (1 Tim. 3:2). Church elders (overseers) are the ones held accountable for the proper functioning of the local assembly (Heb. 13:17). Elders are raised up from among the sheep (Acts 20:28) and are to remain among the sheep (1 Pet. 5:2-3). This availability enhances two important aspects of the shepherding work. First, it allows the shepherd to observe the attitudes and the behavior of believers and to provide timely exhortation, encouragement, and, as necessary, reproof. Second, this transparent relationship allows the sheep to observe the elder's godly character, selfless motives, and ability to properly teach the Scripture. Hospitality provides an excellent opportunity to shepherd God's people; accordingly, elders must *"be given to hospitality."*

The following practical guidelines will assist shepherds in exercising hospitality, which ought to be often, but not...

- "strictly" scheduled, lest the sheep assume they are just lined up in a chute for examination.
- just exhortative; otherwise hospitality will be interpreted as the dreaded "elders' visit."
- mechanical; hospitality has no fixed agenda or fixed format to be applied to everyone.
- respecting persons; include everyone to prevent the damaging effect of perceived favoritism.

It is suggested that the elders connect regularly with their sheep in the informality of a home; the shepherding benefits are immense. It is much easier to promote fire prevention than to be constantly responding to smoke. A proactive leadership given to hospitality will alleviate many difficulties in the local assembly before the problems are ever realized. Hospitality demonstrates Christian love to others in your home. Whether restoring, refreshing, and shepherding the Lord's people, or serving strangers, hospitality is a huge blessing.

November 6 – Do Not Neglect the Gift
1 Timothy 4:14-16

Do not neglect the gift that is in you, which was given to you by prophecy with the laying on of the hands of the eldership. Meditate on these things; give yourself entirely to them, that your progress may be evident to all.

In both personal interaction and through his letters, Paul had prompted his spiritual son Timothy to progress in personal consecration and in faithfulness to his ministry. All believers are called to maturity and to service – the two cannot be separated. Believers will accomplish their ministry within the body as they continue to grow spiritually, and exercise and develop their spiritual gifts.

Paul reminded Timothy that his ministry had been identified by apostolic authority; hence, he was not to neglect it. As he progressed in holiness and exercised his spiritual gift, there would be greater ongoing benefit to the Church and also to Timothy personally. Later, Paul exhorted, *"I remind you to stir up the gift of God which is in you through the laying on of my hands. For God has not given us a spirit of fear, but of power and of love and of a sound mind"* (2 Tim. 1:6-7).

It is evident that Timothy answered the call to salvation, the call to sanctification, and the call to service. Paul told the church at Philippi that there was no other man as likeminded with him as Timothy; consequently, there was no question in Paul's mind that he would properly care for them when he arrived (Phil. 2:20). Timothy had learned that the greatest use of his life was to expend it for Christ; only then would he gain something that would outlast his own life and count for eternity. This realization is true for all of us and motivated Charles Spurgeon to write the following passionate letter to his son concerning the importance of missionary work:

> I should not like you, if meant by God to be a missionary, to die a millionaire. I should not like it, were you fitted to be a missionary, that you should drivel down to a king. What are all your kings, all your nobles, all your diadems, when you put them together, compared with the dignity of winning souls to Christ, with the special honor of building for Christ, not on another man's foundation, but preaching Christ's Gospel in regions far behind.[40]

313

November 7 – Do Not Receive an Accusation
1 Timothy 5:19-20

Do not receive an accusation against an elder except from two or three witnesses. Those who are sinning rebuke in the presence of all, that the rest also may fear.

If you are faithfully serving the Lord, expect to be criticized. Evaluate criticism for potential constructive benefits, especially when it comes from those who love you unquestionably, and then cast the rest aside and forget about it. If you are prompted to critique someone else, know that if it pains you to do so, then you have the right attitude, but if you have even a hint of pleasure in the matter, then it would be best to keep still. Why? Because our flesh naturally opposes the things of God (Gal. 5:17), and *"the wrath of man does not produce the righteousness of God"* (Jas. 1:20). A spiritual person wants to edify others, not hurt them for the sake of personal vindication or self-justification.

This is especially true for church elders. Elders must protect each other and not engage in slander or criticism of fellow-laborers, especially to those they oversee. Realizing that the devil hates the Lord Jesus, and that such a governing body represents His authority on earth, warrants special protection of it. Believers are not to even listen to an accusation about a church elder unless there is irrefutable evidence available (1 Tim. 5:19). To do so just permits the devil to mess with our minds and we do not need his help when it comes to thinking negatively about others. If there is a legitimate matter of sin, the matter is not to be hidden (even if there is repentance); it must be made public.

Let us remember that it is God and not our accusers who control the worth of our service! When accusations come, attend to your character and allow God to protect your reputation as He deems best: *"The Lord rewarded me according to my righteousness; according to the cleanness of my hands He has recompensed me"* (Ps. 18:20). Ability usually rises to prominence, but without good character all will be lost. These are school days and God must bring us to the end of ourselves before we can be fully profitable to Him. This means that our great God is able to use false accusations to bless and honor those who trust in Him. Perhaps A. W. Tozer expresses this point best: "It is doubtful whether God can bless a man greatly until He has hurt him deeply."

November 8 – Godliness With Contentment
1 Timothy 6:6-10

Now godliness with contentment is great gain. For we brought nothing into this world, and it is certain we can carry nothing out. And having food and clothing, with these we shall be content. But those who desire to be rich fall into temptation and a snare, and into many foolish and harmful lusts which drown men in destruction and perdition. For the love of money is a root of all kinds of evil, for which some have strayed from the faith in their greediness, and pierced themselves through with many sorrows.

The root of sin seems to be dissatisfaction, with selfishness and pride trailing close behind. When we are not content with what we have, we murmur against God. Murmuring is half-uttered complaints that God hears anyway. It results from looking backwards instead of Godward. The nation of Israel grumbled and complained the whole time they were in the Sinai Peninsula. Why? Because they were always comparing what they presently had to what they once had in Egypt (Ex. 16:2-3)! This shows the insanity of sin – they had been slaves in Egypt.

We complain and grumble today because our expectations were not met in comparison to what we had the month before. Last month we complained because our expectations were not satisfied as compared to the previous month. Looking backwards at what once was and comparing it to our wanton expectations leads to complaining. The spiritual response to all of our life's situations is to look up with anticipation as to what a good God will do, to be thankful in all things, and to cease comparing ourselves with others or to what we once had. Verse 10 speaks of those who were not content and thankful for what God had provided. They coveted wealth and erred from the faith. If God wanted us to have more than what we have, we would have more.

Being thankful not only defeats dissatisfaction, but it also shows that we have faith in God to handle our distressing situations and to provide for our needs. As our Father is seeking to develop the character of His children, a thankful spirit during adversity may end the trial more quickly. May we recall that, *"Every good gift and every perfect gift is from above, and comes down from the Father of lights, with whom there is no variation or shadow of turning"* (Jas. 1:17).

November 9 – The Soldier, the Athlete, and the Farmer
2 Timothy 2:3-6

You therefore must endure hardship as a good soldier of Jesus Christ. No one engaged in warfare entangles himself with the affairs of this life, that he may please him who enlisted him as a soldier. And also if anyone competes in athletics, he is not crowned unless he competes according to the rules. The hardworking farmer must be first to partake of the crops.

In the final days of his life, Paul, having run his race and finished his course, sought to inspire Timothy to do the same. Timothy was to be like a rule-abiding athlete in finishing his race, lest he be disqualified, and a hardworking farmer, who enjoys a good harvest later. Paul also reminded him to be a good soldier who does not become encumbered by worldly affairs in order to please his commander. Likewise, we, as soldiers of the cross, are to remain on active duty and not be entangled with the cares of this world. The Greek verb rendered "entangles" is *empleko* which means "to be entwined with." While its tense indicates an ongoing activity, its voice is passive, which means the affairs of life are acting on the soldier. This means that the Christian soldier is not the one pursuing worldly activities; rather, they are pursuing him with the intent of ensnaring and incapacitating him. An alert soldier defends against such attempts. This can be problematic, as what we engage in initially seems harmless, but in time can master us.

While some activities may be permissible, they may not be worth the risk of involvement. Believers are to use Scripture to determine what is, for them, wise and foolish behavior. Paul relates a number of good principles for working out questionable matters of behavior:

- Will this activity stumble a weaker brother in the Lord (Rom. 14:13)?
- Do I have perfect faith that this activity is right to do (Rom. 14:22-23)?
- Will this activity unrighteously cause a lack of peace (Rom. 14:19a)?
- Will this activity promote the spiritual growth of others (Rom. 14:19b)?
- Could this activity become habit-forming (1 Cor. 6:12)?
- Could this activity hinder the lost from hearing the gospel (1 Cor. 9:12)?
- Will this activity promote my own spiritual growth (1 Cor. 10:23)?
- Will this activity bring glory to God (1 Cor. 10:31)?

November 10 – God Remains Faithful
2 Timothy 2:11-13

This is a faithful saying: For if we died with Him, we shall also live with Him. If we endure, we shall also reign with Him. If we deny Him, He also will deny us. If we are faithless, He remains faithful; He cannot deny Himself.

The writer of Hebrews tells us that God's chastening of His children is proof of His love for them (Heb. 12:6). God loves us too much to leave us the way we are. Though the Jews had repeatedly failed God, He had not deserted them; He has a plan to refine them and restore them to Himself in a coming day (Rom. 11:25). Our God is a covenant-keeping God and He will honor every promise that He has made. His covenant with Abraham and his descendants is not yet complete. Seeing God's love and faithfulness through the centuries to an often unthankful and rebellious people should prompt our esteem.

Paul reminds Timothy of God's faithfulness to His character and Word: *"If we are faithless, He remains faithful; He cannot deny Himself"* (2 Tim. 2:13). We have the Lord's promise to bring us safely through to the conclusion of our salvation – glorification with Christ:

Being confident of this very thing, that He who has begun a good work in you will complete it until the day of Jesus Christ (Phil. 1:6).

For our citizenship is in heaven, from which we also eagerly wait for the Savior, the Lord Jesus Christ, who will transform our lowly body that it may be conformed to His glorious body, according to the working by which He is able even to subdue all things to Himself (Phil. 3:20-21).

As Scripture affirms, the Lord is always faithful to keep His Word. Dear believer, the Lord will get you home with Christ-likeness one way or another, but the route you take to get there is largely up to you. Let us not be like the stiff-necked nation of Israel, whom God has had to repeatedly rebuke and chasten to remind them who He is and who they are. Such a life-style is painful for God's people and heartbreaking to God. Our identification with Christ, our hope and inheritance in Him, should cause us to be yielded and loyal to the One who is faithful.

November 11 – Vessels of Honor
2 Timothy 2:20-22

But in a great house there are not only vessels of gold and silver, but also of wood and clay, some for honor and some for dishonor. Therefore if anyone cleanses himself from the latter, he will be a vessel for honor, sanctified and useful for the Master, prepared for every good work. Flee also youthful lusts; but pursue righteousness, faith, love, peace with those who call on the Lord out of a pure heart.

Because Paul has been addressing two men (professing Christians) that were teaching false doctrine, the "great house" he mentions may refer to *Christendom*, which is not the same as *the Church* – "the house of God" (1 Tim 3:15). If there were an article before *megalei*, then we would read *"the great house"* and assume that Christendom was in view. Regardless, if Paul is using a great house in Ephesus containing many vessels as a simple object lesson or figuratively speaking of Christendom, the application is really the same. Vessels are articles available for service, but Paul refers to them as *people* in his analogy. This great household includes vessels of gold, silver, wood, and clay which are used for various tasks, some were for honorable functions and others, more abhorrent (v. 20). Some commentators associate the gold and silver vessels as being believers, and the wood and clay with mere professors in Christendom, but that is not Paul's point. It is not the material of the vessel or how it is used that is critical; the Master will determine that part. What is crucial is that the vessel be clean and available to be used now, when and where the Master determines.

To be a vessel of honor, then, one must shun false teachers and doctrines, and consecrate oneself to studying and following the Word of God. The error of Hymenaeus and Philetus (2 Tim. 2:8, 17) was teaching that the resurrection was past, and that there was now no hope for the believer; this teaching would have an adverse effect on a younger Christian. Believers should associate with those who are following truth, and purifying themselves from sin, thus showing love for the Lord. We are to avoid having close fellowship with those with a rebel spirit or who promote heresy. Paul informs Timothy that when believers make the choice to flee ungodliness, they become vessels of honor available for God's sovereign use.

November 12 – A Servant of the Lord Must Not...
2 Timothy 2:23-26

But avoid foolish and ignorant disputes, knowing that they generate strife. And a servant of the Lord must not quarrel but be gentle to all, able to teach, patient, in humility correcting those who are in opposition, if God perhaps will grant them repentance, so that they may know the truth, and that they may come to their senses and escape the snare of the devil, having been taken captive by him to do his will.

Not only did Paul want Timothy to be a vessel of honor fit for the Master's use, but he also wanted his spiritual son to be wise and effective as *a servant of the Lord*. We must realize that the character of the servant of God is as important as what that servant does. The servant of the Lord represents Christ in character and conduct. This is why God will not use filthy vessels (speaking of believers in sin or spreading false doctrine) for doing good works that will honor His name. They must come to him first to be cleansed and sanctified again by the blood of Christ to be brought into His blessed purposes. Furthermore, as revealed in Romans 9, while God uses the rebellious unregenerate to accomplish His purposes also, these individuals cause themselves to be vessels of wrath prepared for destruction. In contrast, Paul states that God uses vessels of mercy (sanctified believers) to proclaim His glory. To be a living vessel glistening with Christ's grace and enabled by the Holy Spirit to serve God is a wonderful experience!

For a servant of the Lord to have an effective ministry, he or she must first personally know the Lord, and then yield to God's revealed Word. Whatever we pursue outside the will of God is meaningless to Him and usually results in the disdain of His name. Because a true servant of God knows and loves the Lord, he or she is determined to abide in His Word (John 8:31). By doing so, believers are continually drawn into deeper communion with God (John 14:21) and will better display the character of God in action, and to experience the goodness of God in new ways. This close interaction with the Lord permits the servant of the Lord to be effective in service. Therefore, if Timothy fled youthful lusts, maintained a pure heart, and acted with gentle patience, he would have good opportunities to recover those who had turned away and were caught in Satan's snare.

November 13 – Being Thoroughly Equipped (Part 1)
2 Timothy 3:16-17

All Scripture is given by inspiration of God, and is profitable for doctrine, for reproof, for correction, for instruction in righteousness, that the man of God may be complete, thoroughly equipped for every good work.

Paul tells us that all Scripture is literally God-breathed. The Holy Spirit has preserved what God wanted to be in our Bibles from His originally inspired words given to the original apostles long ago. In the next chapter, Paul writes, *"Preach the word! Be ready in season and out of season. Convince, rebuke, exhort, with all longsuffering and teaching"* (2 Tim. 4:2). Timothy must understand that teaching, reproof, instruction, and correction through the use of God's Word are absolutely necessary to refine believers' characters in such a way as to make them profitable unto good works.

Doctrine teaches us to understand the mind of God. Reproof speaks to our conscience and confronts wrong behavior. Correction means to straighten what is bent. We all have character bents that need to be corrected in order for one to stand morally upright. Instruction in righteousness refers to a wide range of training tools that reveals the gap between what I am and where I should be. Doctrine teaches sound thinking, while correction straightens erroneous thinking. Instruction approves holy behavior and reproof confronts wrong behavior. Knowing and obeying the Word of God saves us from being defiled and delivers us from the world's influence and deception.

The Greek work translated "instruction" in 2 Timothy 3:16 is *paideia*, which means "education or training; disciplinary correction." In the NASV, *paideia* is rendered as "training," while the NIV translates it as "being thoroughly equipped." *Paideia* is rendered "the training" in Ephesians 6:4, *"Fathers ... bring them up in the training and admonition of the Lord." Paideia*, therefore, means "education or training, which includes disciplinary correction." The latter aspect of this training is clearly brought out in Hebrews 12, where four times *paideia* is translated as "chastening." Just as parents are to train up their children in the way they should go (Prov. 22:6), Christians have the responsibility to train younger believers in the way of righteousness.

320

November 14 – Being Thoroughly Equipped (Part 2)
2 Timothy 3:16-17

All Scripture is given by inspiration of God, and is profitable for doctrine, for reproof, for correction, for instruction in righteousness, that the man of God may be complete, thoroughly equipped for every good work.

Biblically speaking, there are two main objectives in preparing the next generation to serve Christ: training in righteousness (2 Tim. 3:16-17) and training for ministry (Eph. 4:12-13). These two passages show us the inseparable link between godly character and God-honoring service. Ministry which does not reflect the character of Christ does more harm than good. This is why the work of mentoring must focus on both character development and preparation for ministry. The Lord Jesus made the character of His Father known to everyone He came in contact with through His life and His works. Likewise, the passion of every believer should be that Christ might be manifest to the world by our joyful disposition, steadfast morality, and genuine care for others.

As just mentioned, the Greek work translated "instruction" in 2 Timothy 3:16 is *paideia*, which means "education or training or correction." Scripture must be used to teach those younger in the Lord proper character and behavior such that they exhibit Christ's character in what they do. This will require exposure to God's Word, conviction and encouragement from the Holy Spirit, and godly believers who can render timely character instruction, correction, and encouragement.

The Greek word translated "equipping" in Ephesians 4:12 is the noun *oikodome*, which means "building" or "edifying." Paul explains that all Christians are called to edify other members of the Body by speaking the truth in love and by using their spiritual gift to fulfill their assigned role in the Body so it can edify itself in love (Eph. 4:16-17). God-empowered ministry of this type builds up the Church and all members are to edify each other in love! This edification ministry will center in two main objectives: equipping others in righteousness and equipping others for ministry. Christians will accomplish their ministry within the body as they continue to grow spiritually and develop their spiritual gifts. We are called to maturity and to service – the two cannot be separated. So let us grow and build for the glory of God.

November 15 – Preach the Word (Part 1)
2 Timothy 4:2-4

Preach the word! Be ready in season and out of season. Convince, rebuke, exhort, with all longsuffering and teaching. For the time will come when they will not endure sound doctrine, but according to their own desires, because they have itching ears, they will heap up for themselves teachers; and they will turn their ears away from the truth, and be turned aside to fables.

Paul foretold of a time in the Church Age in which Christendom would not hold to sound doctrine, but would seek teachers that would preach what they wanted to hear. Just as false prophets plagued Israel throughout their history, false teachers have been harming the Church since Pentecost. Paul did not know when the rapture of the Church would be, but he did know that this apostasy would crescendo just prior to that event, just before the Tribulation Period (2 Thess. 2:3).

This meant that Timothy would need to be ready to confront such deception, so Paul equips his spiritual son with the tools to do so: First, Timothy was to use God's Word and not high-minded humanized arguments to confront false teaching. Scripture was to be at the center of his ministry. Second, he was to be diligent. This conveys the thought of urgency, preparedness, and continued diligence in season, out of season (i.e., whether there were opportunities or afflictions, he was to fulfill his calling). Third, those in doctrinal error were to be rebuked and corrected. Fourth, Timothy was to exhort with all longsuffering and doctrine: Those who were doing well were to be encouraged to continue to do so. All reproving, rebuking, correction, and exhortation was to be done with patience and per divine instruction.

Paul then explained why Timothy was to preach the Word. In the last days of the Church Age many professing Christians will not endure sound doctrine, but will follow silly fables and doctrines of demons, seeking teachers who will preach what they want to hear, pursue lusts with a dull and seared conscience, and follow legalism (touch not, taste not, marry not, etc.) to be esteemed holy. Hence, Timothy was to be alert, to keep a cool head during turbulent times, to do the work of an evangelist and to stay the course and fulfill his calling. Given the wicked days in which we live, this is good counsel for all of us.

November 16 – Preach the Word (Part 2)
2 Timothy 4:2-4

Preach the word! Be ready in season and out of season. Convince, rebuke, exhort, with all longsuffering and teaching. For the time will come when they will not endure sound doctrine, but according to their own desires, because they have itching ears, they will heap up for themselves teachers; and they will turn their ears away from the truth, and be turned aside to fables.

When preaching is necessary to rebuke God's people, the priest Ezra gives us a good pattern to follow (Ezra 9). Shortly after arriving at Jerusalem from Babylon, the scribe Ezra learned of the pitiful spiritual state of his countrymen. God wanted a "holy seed" that would represent Him among the nations – a pure people that would cleave to Him alone. Just as the wives of Solomon turned his heart after false gods, the foreign wives of the Jews in Ezra's time had corrupted their pureness and singleness of heart to follow Jehovah. This sinful practice must stop! The Jewish people could not afford to drift further away from the Lord; God had shown His faithfulness to chasten them if they did.

It was time to act, which meant God's Word must be declared with authority and power. He alone can revive what is near death. But before Ezra preached one word to the people, he first humbled himself before the Lord and continued in prayer with other like-minded believers throughout the day. Ezra identified with his sinning brethren and admitted to God that they had broken His law not to intermarry with pagans. Although not personally guilty of this sin, as a people they had failed to represent Jehovah and he took ownership in that offense.

Ezra then pleads for mercy on behalf of the people, though they are undeserving of it. Ezra's behavior is a sign of deep brokenness before the Lord. Then having completed the preparatory work of prayer with his companions and having entrusted God with the outcome, Ezra gathered the nation at Jerusalem. He is emboldened to preach the Word of God and to confront the sins of the people without regard to religious status or social rank. Sin is sin regardless of who the guilty party is, and it must be confronted with the authority of God's Word. But this must be done with God's Word and in humility! The result was that the people were swayed Godward and a great revival occurred (Ezra 10).

November 17 – The Crown of Righteousness
2 Timothy 4:6-8

For I am already being poured out as a drink offering, and the time of my departure is at hand. I have fought the good fight, I have finished the race, I have kept the faith. Finally, there is laid up for me the crown of righteousness, which the Lord, the righteous Judge, will give to me on that Day, and not to me only but also to all who have loved His appearing.

Christ is presently with all believers on earth; in the future, His Church will be with Him in heaven. His forever abiding presence with us is certain, though our intimacy with Him each day depends on our desire for it. With His exaltation looming, Christians are to live each day in the anticipation of Christ's coming. There is a reward for those who do, and their lives will be more joyful and fruitful in light of that imminent expectation. In a twinkling of an eye, what was corruptible will become incorruptible, and what was mortal will become immortal (1 Cor. 15:51-52), and we will be caught up into the air to be ever with the Lord (1 Thess. 4:13-18). At this event, often referred to as the Rapture of the Church, sin and pain will cease to exist within all believers in Christ. The believer's glorified body will be able to worship and to please God without any hindrance from the flesh or any ills of its previously fallen state.

Paul had one hope (Eph. 4:4), one earnest expectation, the *blessed hope*: *"Looking for the blessed hope and glorious appearing of our great God and Savior Jesus Christ"* (Tit. 2:13). While this may include aspects of Christ's future kingdom, the believer's faith and hope finish their course at Christ's coming for the Church (the rapture), yet love, as previously mentioned, continues forever (1 Cor. 13:8, 13). The Church is not to be waiting for the Antichrist to appear (his coming is a sign to the nation of Israel; Dan. 9:27), but for Christ Himself to translate them from the earth into heaven. The Church is not waiting for the inhabitants of earth to be slaughtered during the Tribulation Period, but rather longs to be removed from this wicked world to be with Christ. Those who truly have the hope of glory purify themselves now (1 Jn. 3:2-3). The Lord is pure and saints having the blessed hope will want to be found living purely when He suddenly returns from heaven.

November 18 – Plural Elders in Each Church
Titus 1:5

I left you in Crete, that you should set in order the things that are lacking, and appoint elders in every city as I commanded you.

Paul sent Titus to Crete to encourage the churches on that island to recognize the elders that the Holy Spirit appointed for each local church (Acts 20:28). There is no example (i.e., no God-honoring example) of one individual overseeing a local church in the New Testament. Rather, just the opposite was true; the oversight of each local gathering was to be plural in nature. God revealed a similar leadership structure for Israel to follow in Numbers 11:16-25; He was to rule over them as their God, and there were also to be seventy elders who would oversee His people by enforcing His written Law.

God's model for Church order is similar to the one given to Israel: Christ is head of the Church and elders are to oversee local churches. As with Israel, the men who led a local church were normally referred to as "elders." The New Testament clearly indicates that a plurality of qualified men was to share the spiritual leadership of a local church:

- There were elders in the church at Jerusalem (Acts 15:6, 22).
- The sick were instructed to call for the elders of the church (Jas. 5:14).
- Paul and Barnabas recognized "elders in every church" on their missionary journeys (Acts 14:23).
- Peter refers to the elders at particular local churches (1 Pet. 5:1).
- Paul instructed Titus to appoint elders in every city (i.e., every church).
- There were elders at the church at Ephesus (Acts 20:17, 28).
- Paul mentions that there were elders (overseers) and deacons in the church at Philippi (Phil. 1:1).

Elders (a plurality of godly men) are to govern each assembly; they are to pastor those whom God puts into their care, though they may not have received the pastoral spiritual gift (Eph. 4:11). All the elders of a meeting have equal authority, but they do not necessarily have equal gifting or the same spiritual gifts – this is what brings strength and balance to a plurality of church leadership. Elders serving in unity with the mind of Christ is a lovely picture of a triune God at work!

November 19 – The Renovation of the Holy Spirit
Titus 3:4-5

But when the kindness and the love of God our Savior toward man appeared, not by works of righteousness which we have done, but according to His mercy He saved us, through the washing of regeneration and renewing of the Holy Spirit.

Prior to trusting Christ as Lord and Savior, we do not have the ability to please God; in fact, our flesh nature directly opposes God in thought and in deed (Rom. 5:10, 8:7). The believer needs a new nature that longs to please God and perform His will (Rom. 8:5-6). This new nature is received from God at conversion through the acts of the Holy Spirit called cleansing and regeneration. This cleansing does not mean that new Christians had all their sinful bents, addictions, and bad character qualities removed at their conversion. But the purifying work of the Holy Spirit at that time will affect their thinking towards such things. They will not desire or be able to enjoy sin as they once did. In some cases, addictions will be overcome instantly, but in others, the believer will struggle to overcome what he or she now detests. The cleansing away of old attitudes and the implanting of new ones will prompt believers to learn to rely on the power of the Holy Spirit to overcome the conduct they now know displeases God. Regeneration is the implanting of a new life and a new order of living. David Gooding summarizes these works of the Holy Spirit at conversion:

The washing of regeneration is an initial experience of salvation which holds two ideas. First, it is a washing, a cleansing away of evil and polluted things. In the second place it is regeneration, the positive implanting of a new life, and order of living. The Holy Spirit washes us by bringing us to see the wrong and evil in our sinful attitudes and desires. He makes us feel their uncleanness, and leads us to repent of them and repudiate them. More deeply than that, He brings us to see that, in spite of all our efforts to improve ourselves, we cannot eradicate these evil powers within us: we need a Savior. We cry in the secret of our heart: O wretched man that I am! Who shall deliver me? For all too often the good things I want to do, I don't do; and the bad things I don't want to do, I do (Rom. 7:15-25). And He brings us to the point where we are prepared for all the changes of lifestyle that we must be willing to accept, if we receive Christ from now on as Savior and Lord of our lives.[41]

November 20 – Reject a Divisive Person
Titus 3:9-11

But avoid foolish disputes, genealogies, contentions, and strivings about the law; for they are unprofitable and useless. Reject a divisive man after the first and second admonition, knowing that such a person is warped and sinning, being self-condemned.

Many of the Lord's people tend to argue about things that have little or no bearing on eternal matters that are important to God. Paul tells Timothy to avoid such arguments because they tend to needlessly divide the Lord's people. How do Christians benefit by foolish disputes concerning genealogies, humanized traditions, or matters of Christian liberty? The Lord Jesus reproved the Pharisees for majoring on the minor aspects of the Law and neglecting the more important and profitable aspects (Matt. 23:23). We too must be careful not to seize on one aspect of truth from Scripture and push it at the expense of balance with the other truths of the Word of God. A heretic is often not a personal spreading false doctrine, but a teacher who is out of balance in what they preach. Preaching on one truth to the exclusion of others, or pushing political views instead of scriptural ones, or majoring on minors, or manipulatively painting over Scripture with the colors of his peculiar theory characterize a divisive person that should be admonished; otherwise the Body of Christ will suffer.

When someone becomes insubordinate or troublesome, they must be confronted personally by the Word of God. This should bring about conviction of wrong-doing and personal sin (Titus 1:9-11; Heb. 3:13). The Greek word *nouthesia* is rendered "admonish." Admonition literally means "to put in mind" and "calls attention to a subject matter by giving a mild rebuke or warning." A stern caution or forthright reproof is given by shepherds as they witness sheep meandering into forbidden territory. A divisive person is to be warned and if the pattern continues, he is to be rejected by the assembly so that he or she will understand the seriousness and feel the shame of their foolish disputing. Those who cause needless division among us must be admonished in order to curtail interpersonal arguments, laziness, unruly or rebellious conduct that threatens the peace and unity of the local assembly. If unresponsive, then punishment should occur.

November 21 – Do Not Drift Away!
Hebrews 2:1-3

Therefore we must give the more earnest heed to the things we have heard, lest we drift away. For if the word spoken through angels proved steadfast, and every transgression and disobedience received a just reward, how shall we escape if we neglect so great a salvation, which at the first began to be spoken by the Lord, and was confirmed to us by those who heard Him?

In reading the books of Exodus and Leviticus, it would appear that God had directly revealed the teaching of the Law to Moses at Mount Sinai. However, the writer of Hebrews informs us that much of this revelation was delivered to Moses through angelic messengers (Ps. 68:17). Moses, himself, acknowledges that hosts of angels were present with God on Sinai (Deut. 33:2). All that was delivered by these angels was from God and thus true and to be obeyed by Israel.

Yet, the writer has just finished asserting Christ's supremacy over all creation as the Son of God (Heb. 1). He also came to the earth to represent God and deliver His message of salvation to humanity. He was God's message and Messenger who would give His own life to secure God's offer of salvation. Christ, the Giver of this gift, is greater than the angels. Moreover, the gift He offers is more beneficial than the Law received by angels, because it actually secured forgiveness and restoration – the Law only condemned. The writer's point is that given the greatness of the gift and the Giver (above the Law and the angels), those who have received His salvation have a greater accountability to hold to the truth. He is speaking of neglecting, not rejecting salvation.

If we do not pay careful attention to the precious realities of blessing and responsibility that are associated with the gospel, we too can drift away from truth. We must continually keep in mind the things which are important to God. The addressees of this letter were marked by spiritual immaturity and sluggishness and the writer was implying that they were drifting from the important truths of the gospel (Heb. 5:11-14). If this behavior was not eliminated, they may have further slipped away from the truths of Christ's Supremacy and Headship in Hebrews 1. What often begins as a trickle of complacency swells to neglectful drifting in undertow of compromise. Let us not drift!

November 22 – Do Not Have an Evil Heart of Unbelief!
Hebrews 3:9-12

Where your fathers tested Me, tried Me, and saw My works forty years. Therefore I was angry with that generation, and said, "They always go astray in their heart, and they have not known My ways." So I swore in My wrath, "They shall not enter My rest." Beware, brethren, lest there be in any of you an evil heart of unbelief in departing from the living God.

The writer of Hebrews introduces the second of his five warnings to his Jewish audience: do not depart from the Living God in unbelief (v. 12). Naturally speaking, especially during times of testing and trials, we all tend to be like Thomas, "I will believe it when I see it." These warnings are primarily given to believers, as the writer includes himself in the warnings, "we" (e.g., Heb. 2:1), but there is also an application for those professing Christ, but were not actually saved. Concerning the message to believers, Warren Wiersbe writes:

The emphasis in Hebrews is that true believers have an eternal salvation because they trust in a living Savior who constantly intercedes for them. But the writer is careful to point out that this confidence is no excuse for sin. God disciplines His children. Remember that Canaan is not a picture of heaven, but the believer's present spiritual inheritance in Christ. Believers who doubt God's Word and rebel against Him do not miss heaven, but they do miss out on the blessings of their inheritance today, and they must suffer the chastening of God [and loss of reward at the judgment seat of Christ].[42]

During arduous seasons, every believer may be tempted to give up his or her confession of faith to go back into a corrupt world system – it will be easier for me to do so. It is not denying the faith, per se, but rather wondering if it is worth it. The warning from the writer is: "Yes, it is worth it and there is nothing for you from where you came." God has given you His best in Christ. To retreat will only cause you misery and pain – stay the course; it will be worth it when we are with Christ.

The message for the unregenerate listening to all this is: "What sin do you have in your life that is keeping you from coming to Christ?" Intellectual excuses are mere attempts to cover the sins of one's heart.

November 23 – Exhort One Another Daily
Hebrews 3:13

But exhort one another daily, while it is called "Today," lest any of you be hardened through the deceitfulness of sin.

It is evident, from the steady line of Old Testament prophets that God sent to His covenant people that He understands our constant need for encouragement, exhortation, and correction. This reality is still true today. In Acts 18:27 the Greek word *protrepomai* is rendered "encouraged" in the RV and NASV: *"The brethren encouraged him [Apollos]."* The meaning of this word is "to turn forward for oneself." The first portion of this word, *protrepo,* literally implies "to urge forward." The idea is to add energy to someone's good behavior so that they continue going on in the same direction. In Acts 18:27, the verb is in the middle voice which indicates the brethren's particular interest to propel Apollos forward in ministry at Corinth for the good of the Body. When God's people do well, especially in areas in which they tend to struggle, believers should add energy to the right behavior with praise and encouragement in order to reinforce it.

According to the writer of Hebrews, believers also need constant exhortation to serve the Lord properly: we are instructed, *"Exhort one another daily"* (Heb. 3:13). "To exhort" is translated from the Greek word *parakaleo,* which means "to call near and invoke." If a child of God has lost his or her direction, those with maturity are to draw near and direct his or her path. Perhaps someone who is lost has asked the reader for directions. Normally, you would draw near to the inquiring individual and then point out the way. Both encouragement and exhortation are necessary to assist God's people to live for Him.

Sadly, many of us get offended when we receive correction and reproof; we seem to forget that it is a normal part of Christian growth and something that we all need. Yet, it is important to remember that everything does not need to be addressed all at once, especially when discipling younger believers. It is best to prioritize and tackle the most important matters first and leave the lesser items for later. Before exhorting others (in person), it is good to examine ourselves for bents and to consider how to compensate for them when reproving others (e.g., if you tend to be critical of others; pray for grace not to be).

November 24 – Entering God's Rests
Hebrews 4:8-11

For if Joshua had given them rest, then He would not afterward have spoken of another day. There remains therefore a rest for the people of God. For he who has entered His rest has himself also ceased from his works as God did from His. Let us therefore be diligent to enter that rest, lest anyone fall according to the same example of disobedience.

The writer of Hebrews affirms that when men cease working to earn heaven and simply rest by faith in the finished work of Christ, they enter God's rest of salvation (Heb. 4:1-7, 10). This follows God's example of laboring six days in the work of creation to enter into His rest the seventh day – one must cease working to rest. The rest of the gospel secures peace with God, but not necessarily the peace of God. The latter is gained through the experience of going on with the Lord in faith. The Israelites did not keep going on with God after the initial Canaan conquest and over time many of them lost their rest because they failed to secure their God-given possession in faithful obedience.

Thus, the writer explains that Canaan, in present-day application, does not picture God's heavenly and peaceful abode, for the Israelites had to engage in hard fighting for years to conquer their enemies and lay hold of their God-given possession (Josh. 11:23, 13:1; Heb. 4:8, 11). Joshua understood that Canaan was not to be the final resting place for God's people (Heb. 4:8-9). The Greek word translated "rest" in verse 9 is *sabbatismos*, and is only found here in the New Testament. *Sabbatismos* literally means "a keeping of the Sabbath" and speaks of the future "battle-free" rest believers will enjoy with God in heaven forever. But as in the days of Joshua, the earthly sojourn of faithful believers today will undoubtedly be fraught with conflict (2 Tim. 3:12).

For earth-bound believers, heaven is still future, which means the battle against spiritual wickedness in high places is still ongoing (Eph. 6:12). Engaging in spiritual warfare is the believer's great opportunity to learn of and lay hold of all his or her spiritual blessings in heavenly places in Christ (Eph. 1:3). When at last the Bright and Morning Star standing alone in the dreary predawn hue becomes the rising sun in its full glory, then all of our earthly school days will be done. On that day, while basking in the inconceivable bliss of God's glory, rest indeed!

November 25 – Do Not Be Dull of Hearing!
Hebrews 5:11-14

Of whom we have much to say, and hard to explain, since you have become dull of hearing. For though by this time you ought to be teachers, you need someone to teach you again the first principles of the oracles of God; and you have come to need milk and not solid food. For everyone who partakes only of milk is unskilled in the word of righteousness, for he is a babe. But solid food belongs to those who are of full age, that is, those who by reason of use have their senses exercised to discern both good and evil.

The writer reminded his readers that the good things of Judaism had been replaced by "better" things in Christ. Christ was superior to the angels, to Moses, to the Levitical priesthood, to the Old Testament sacrifices and Covenant, and as a superior High Priest, Christ served before the living God in a better sanctuary in heaven! For this reason, five warnings are issued in the Epistle: Do not drift from the truth (Heb. 2:1). Unbelief precludes receiving God's rest (Heb. 3:7-12). Do not become dull of hearing (Heb. 5:11). Do not waver, but hold fast to the confession of our hope (Heb. 10:23). Look ahead; do not turn away from Christ (Heb. 12:25). The Jewish Christians had already received the best God could offer them – Christ; they were not to go back to what was inferior and offered them no hope!

This text presents the third warning: Do not become dull of hearing; it does not say that these people were dead in trespasses and sins (Eph. 2:1). The issue was not that they were apostates, but rather, they were not progressing in growth. They still wanted milk because they were babes, instead of the solid food adults eat. An unsaved person does not need milk; he or she needs life – to be born again.

These believers had chosen to keep feeding on the fundamental rudiments of Christian Faith (e.g., gospel truth, water baptism, resurrections, hell, etc.; Heb. 6:1-2) instead of learning the deeper things of the Faith, subjects like the priesthood of Christ (Heb. 5:5-10). Enough time had transpired since their conversions that they should have understood the more profound truths of Christianity and be teaching others, instead of being satisfied with baby food. The result of being dull of hearing is spiritual fruitlessness, not spiritual death.

November 26 – The Sacrifice of Praise to God
Hebrews 13:15-16

Therefore by Him let us continually offer the sacrifice of praise to God, that is, the fruit of our lips, giving thanks to His name. But do not forget to do good and to share, for with such sacrifices God is well pleased.

As previously stated, the Church is to be occupied with three main ministries in Christ's absence: the upward ministry of *Exalting God*, the inward ministry of *Edifying the Body*, and the outward ministry of *Evangelizing the Lost*. A stool which can safely support a person's weight must have at least three legs. Just as a stool is not stable unless each leg is bearing its share of weight, a local assembly will suffer if any of these three ministries are neglected. If an assembly has great worship, but no evangelism, in time they will die out. If a church engages in evangelism, but neglects discipleship, the babes in Christ will tend to be blown to and fro with every wind of doctrine. Many will eventually leave the church to find one better suited to their comfort level. If a local church has tremendous teaching, but fails to stimulate new believers to love and honor the Lord, those being discipled will not have the right motive for service, nor will they be inclined to flee sin.

The upward ministry relates to the worship of God. The scriptural imagery associated with a believer engaging in this ministry is that of a priest (Heb. 13:15; 1 Pet. 2:5, 9; Rev. 1:6). The Lord commanded His disciples to regularly remember Him and to proclaim the value of His death through the keeping of the Lord's Supper (Luke 22:10-20). The Lord's Supper, also called *"the breaking of bread,"* was a regular practice of the early Church each Sunday (Acts 20:7). It was also important to remember the Lord in the way He commanded and not to partake of it in an unworthy manner (1 Cor. 11:23-32).

Just as Levitical priests offered worship on behalf of Israel in the Old Testament, each believer-priest is to have an offering of praise and worship prepared each time their local church gathers to remember the Lord through the breaking of the bread. Though not all believers will share their worship audibly, all pure offerings rising from full and pure hearts mingle together to refresh the Lord. Praising and giving thanks to God in our speech and in our singing also exalts the Lord, as does sharing with others the goodness of God that we have received.

November 27 – Obey Those Who Rule Over You
Hebrews 13:17

Obey those who rule over you, and be submissive, for they watch out for your souls, as those who must give account. Let them do so with joy and not with grief, for that would be unprofitable for you.

The "those" and "they" in this passage refer to local church elders. Believers in their care were to obey their direction and respect their authority, which had come down from God to bless them. Whenever God bestows authority (e.g., in human government, the home, or in the local church), there is always accountability – how did those in authority reflect God's character while executing their office. The writer mentions that because the elders will have to give an account to the Lord for their shepherding work, the sheep should make it as easy as possible for them to do so with joy.

With this said, it is understood that it is appropriate for God's people to reject leadership that is not in the will of God (1 Sam. 14:45; Acts 5:29). Obedience and submission are not blind. If church elders make a directive that is clearly against Scripture, then the flock is not accountable to obey it. It is important to discern between what is merely a church practice in Scripture versus a direct command. For example, if for some reason the elders decided to have the Lord's Supper weekly on Saturday instead of Sunday, there is nothing scripturally wrong with doing so. The Lord's command is being obeyed (Luke 22:19-20); however, the practice of the early church is not being followed (Acts 20:7). The former is non-negotiable; the latter is simply not the practice of the early church, which is probably safe and wise.

Peter affirms how elders are to behave: *"Shepherd the flock of God which is among you, serving as overseers, not by compulsion but willingly, not for dishonest gain but eagerly; nor as being lords over those entrusted to you, but being examples to the flock"* (1 Pet. 5:2-3). Elders are to lead and be paradigms to those entrusted into their care. Biblical shepherding is not about *the need* of control, but rather, it is a selfless, gentle, humble, serving leadership that uplifts the sheep to thrive, which then makes them want to follow good shepherds (2 Tim. 2:24). If shepherds love those in their care as Christ loves them, generally speaking, sheep will not resist, but rather obey their elders.

November 28 – Testing of Your Faith Produces Patience
James 1:2-4

My brethren, count it all joy when you fall into various trials, knowing that the testing of your faith produces patience. But let patience have its perfect work, that you may be perfect and complete, lacking nothing.

Years ago, a faithful brother, a longstanding church elder, shared with me some helpful advice: "when you start meeting with the elders – you get a target on your back; when you are recognized as an elder – you get a target on your front." This beloved brother was kindly informing me, as a newly appointed elder, of the harsh reality of being a faithful shepherd. As God's people, we must realize that the devil will oppose every true work of God and the servants of God. If you are rightly laboring for the Lord in your calling, you will be criticized and accused of wrongdoing; it is part of the faith-building exercise which God permits to develop His people – so expect it! James tells us that there is a quality of patience that cannot be incorporated into our faith without experiencing God's deliverance through such painful trials.

The Lord Jesus was often criticized by the same pharisaical spirit at work in the world today. This self-exalting spirit morphs moral absolutes, the truth, and sound logic into a virtual reality which only suits its master, or those under its influence. The Lord did not waste time defending Himself against this hypocritical influence, but He did, on rare occasions, attempt to reason with those under its power (e.g., Luke 22:52-53; John 18:22-23). There is no suitable defense against someone controlled by a critical spirit – even the glory of God is transformed into evil.

Those who struggle with envy and pride are usually the first in line to speak their mind and the last to change it when the truth is known. Just expect such irritations in the Lord's work and keep serving the One who knows all about false accusations. Time will prove out the truth, but our exhibited humility during such times will speak louder than any evidence of the truth could. It is not our defense which is needful at such times, but rather our surrender to God in the situation. Also, remember to thank the Lord for those who loved you enough to contact you and hear the whole matter out before foolishly receiving gossip or a one-sided story as fact (Prov. 18:13; 1 Cor. 13:5).

November 29 – The Test of Obedience
James 1:22-25

But be doers of the word, and not hearers only, deceiving yourselves. For if anyone is a hearer of the word and not a doer, he is like a man observing his natural face in a mirror; for he observes himself, goes away, and immediately forgets what kind of man he was. But he who looks into the perfect law of liberty and continues in it, and is not a forgetful hearer but a doer of the work, this one will be blessed in what he does.

James tells us that one who hears God's Word without considering what it says is like a man who wakes up each morning, taking a fleeting glance at a mirror, and then quickly forgets what he saw. He receives no benefit from looking at the mirror although the mirror showed the man what needed to be corrected (i.e., shave, comb, wash, etc.). In fact, the mirror had no benefit to the man because he ignored it; likewise, if we casually read God's Word without introspection and a sense of duty, Scripture does not benefit us. Scripture is living and powerful and will change us if we have an openness to listen to the Lord and a willingness to obey Him: *"For the word of God is living and powerful, and sharper than any two-edged sword, piercing even to the division of soul and spirit, and of joints and marrow, and is a Discerner of the thoughts and intents of the heart"* (Heb. 4:12). Those who peer into God's Word and allow it to speak to their hearts and consciences will be marked by holy living – God's Word is God's way.

The Jews thought that they were a special people because they had God's Law; however, it was not merely having the Law that would mark them as a peculiar people in the world, but keeping it (Rom. 2:23-25). Because they taught the tenets of the Law, but then broke the Law in practice, the testimony of God was blasphemed among the Gentiles. James tells us that true children of God listen to and do what God's Word commands. To name Christ as Savior and then to reject His call to holy living effectively blasphemes the name of Christ in the world. Paul exhorts believers more than once to put away all blasphemies (Eph. 4:31; Col. 3:8). When God's people hear God's Word, but choose to ignore it, they minimize the legitimacy of the name of Christ and hence cause others to blaspheme God. Let us be hearers and doers.

November 30 – The Test of True Religion
James 1:26-27

If anyone among you thinks he is religious, and does not bridle his tongue but deceives his own heart, this one's religion is useless. Pure and undefiled religion before God and the Father is this: to visit orphans and widows in their trouble, and to keep oneself unspotted from the world.

Many of the contemporary terms and ideologies associated with "religion" and "worship" we commonly use today have no biblical basis. For example, in the New Testament the word "worship" is rendered from five Greek verbs some 91 times and three Greek nouns seven times. Interestingly, when rendered as a noun, it speaks of a test (Jas. 1:26-27) or has a negative meaning (i.e., speaks of false worship or man's religious rote; Acts 7:23, 26:5; Col. 2:18, 23). Since there are no adjectives, and the nouns do not relate directly to the believer's worship, we are left with an abundance of verbs confirming that "worship" is something that we do; it does not describe what we have done for God, nor does it describe who we are! As believer priests, all saints are to worship God and the Holy Spirit will lead this activity.

Introducing worship as an adjective or to formulate a title for men is opposed to the clear usage of the word in Scripture. If there is any "Worship Leader" in the local assembly, it is the Holy Spirit. His role is to guide believers into a deeper understanding of truth concerning the Lord Jesus and the overall greatness of God (John 4:22-24, 16:13-14).

With this understanding, we conclude that Christianity is not a religion, but Christian doctrine lived out produces the right kind of religion that pleases God. When one comes into a right relationship with God through the Lord Jesus Christ, then, and only then, is he or she able to please God by doing sincere and God-enabled deeds. World religion is an exhaustive system of *doings* apart from God's truth and God's enablement. The doing of good things does not define what true Christianity is, but Spirit-filled Christians do prove that Christianity is real. God is not impressed by religious ritual, humanized traditions, sanctimonious form, and sectarian smugness, but rather with personal living that conforms to divine truth (Col. 2:20-23). James says that taking care of the poor and having an unspotted life is proof of true religion.

December 1 – The Test of Brotherly Love
James 2:8-9

If you really fulfill the royal law according to the Scripture, "You shall love your neighbor as yourself," you do well; but if you show partiality, you commit sin, and are convicted by the law as transgressors.

On the eve of Calvary, the Lord Jesus told His disciples that their love for each other would mark them as His true followers in the world (John 13:35). Genuine, selfless love without partiality comes from God alone (1 Jn. 4:19). Because pure love is rarely witnessed in the world, the disciples were to love each other so that the unregenerate would notice and be drawn to God's love. This kind of love esteems others' interests higher than our own; this is the mind of Christ (Phil. 2:2-3). True love ensures that humility and self-sacrifice work in tandem.

The Lord told His disciples that *"he who is greatest among you shall be your servant. And whoever exalts himself will be humbled, and he who humbles himself will be exalted"* (Matt. 23:12). Greatness is demonstrated by serving others: Do we willingly serve others before ourselves? Do we quickly sacrifice our rights for the good of others (1 Cor. 9:19)? Do we serve to insert our personal opinions? Do we desire visibility or recognition for serving? How do we respond when treated like a servant (John 3:29-30)? Do we complain while serving? Do we gloat over our doings? Do we listen or seek to promote ourselves?

In Matthew 18:4, the Lord says that greatness in His kingdom would be achieved by humbling oneself, but in Luke 9, He adds the necessity of demonstrating His love and humility to the lowliest believer. Our esteem for the lowliest believer in the Church shows our true love for the Lord Jesus (Matt. 25:40). Sadly, because the disciples had been thinking of their own greatness (Luke 9:46), they lacked power in the Lord's work, and they lacked wisdom and commitment to properly do what the Lord tasked them to do (Luke 9:40, 54-56).

The book of Hebrews suggests a practical way to show love: *"Let brotherly love continue. Do not forget to entertain strangers, for by so doing some have unwittingly entertained angels"* (Heb. 13:1-2). Gaius entertained both the brethren and strangers in his home (3 Jn. 5). Our homes are great places to show the love of Christ to each other.

December 2 – The Test of Good Works
James 2:17-18

Thus also faith by itself, if it does not have works, is dead. But someone will say, "You have faith, and I have works." Show me your faith without your works, and I will show you my faith by my works.

The key words in James 2 are "see," "show," and "works" as related to the Old Testament characters of Rahab and Abraham. James' point is that true faith can be seen in God-honoring works. Accordingly, Scripture does not rebuke Rahab for deceiving the local authorities, but rather commends her faith as demonstrated by her care for the Jewish spies. It was not a blind or misplaced faith, but an act of her heart founded in truth. She made a proclamation to the spies, using the term *"we have heard"* which is securely connected by faith to the words *"I know"* (Josh. 2:9-11). Rahab had heard the stories of how the Israelites were delivered from Egypt, and how Jehovah had parted the Red Sea. She too had learned of their victories over the Amorites on the eastern side of the Jordan, a fact that caused great fear in Jericho.

But instead of surrendering, the inhabitants of Jericho fortified themselves against the Israelites; they were putting their faith in their constructed bulwarks. Rahab humbled herself and took a different approach – she sided with God and asked for mercy. James reminds us that God's extension of mercy has not changed: *"God resists the proud, but gives grace to the humble"* (Jas. 4:6). *"Humble yourselves in the sight of the Lord, and He will lift you up"* (Jas. 4:10). Rahab and her family received God's grace; the others in Jericho perished. Her conclusion was that the God of the Israelites must be the *"God in heaven above and in the earth beneath"* (Josh. 2:11). It is for this reason she harbored the spies and asked for mercy, and was saved.

James confirms that Rahab's act of kindness to the Jewish spies demonstrated the validity of her faith (Jas. 2:25-26), in the same way that Abraham's offering of Isaac proved Abraham's faith (Jas. 2:21-25). Abraham had been previously justified by faith (Gen. 15:6; Rom. 4:2-3), but true faith never stands alone – it has works of righteousness also. When sinners act in faith to what God reveals to them, they are accredited a divine standing of righteousness, but such a reality will be evidenced by good works. Faith without works is dead!

December 3 – The Test of Tongue Control (Part 1)
James 3:3-5

Indeed, we put bits in horses' mouths that they may obey us, and we turn their whole body. Look also at ships: although they are so large and are driven by fierce winds, they are turned by a very small rudder wherever the pilot desires. Even so the tongue is a little member and boasts great things.

James employs five word pictures in describing the destructive nature of the tongue and why it must be brought under control: a bridle in a horse's mouth, a ship's rudder, a raging fire, an untamed beast, and a deadly poison. The Greek word *chalinos* is used twice in James 3:2-3 and means "to curb the spirit." It pictures controlling a horse in a head stall. The Greek word *chalinagogeo* is employed in James 1:26. It is derived from *chalinos*, but includes the additional thought of "leading by a bridle or to hold in check, or to restrain." James instructs us to restrain our tongues and to hold them in check.

"For out of the abundance of the heart the mouth speaks" (Matt. 12:34). The tongue is the tail of the heart that wags out of the mouth and thus the tongue is a good barometer for gauging the spirituality of a person. Some people can fake spirituality a long time until some trial besets them or a derogatory comment is directed at them – then their tongue gives evidence to what is really within the heart. Those who are dead to men's praise will bear their contempt – those who are not will strike back. The spiritual man is like a worm (Ps. 22:6) – he absorbs ridicule – while the carnal man better resembles a serpent (Gen. 3:15), striking when his ego feels threatened.

How do we control ourselves under stress and when spoken ill of? Do we tease, jab, or use sarcasm to promote ourselves and put down others? This type of conduct must be avoided; it is destructive to church body-life and to home-life. Or do we set a guard about our lips to ensure we utter only wholesome and edifying speech? Do we speak what is necessary and then in love and grace (Eph. 4:15)? Understanding that the tongue is a powerful tool to render good or bad, let us heed Paul's exhortation: *"Let no corrupt communication proceed out of your mouth, but that which is good to the use of edifying, that it may minister grace unto the hearers"* (Eph. 4:29).

December 4 – The Test of Tongue Control (Part 2)
James 3:6-8

See how great a forest a little fire kindles! And the tongue is a fire, a world of iniquity. The tongue is so set among our members that it defiles the whole body, and sets on fire the course of nature; and it is set on fire by hell. For every kind of beast and bird, of reptile and creature of the sea, is tamed and has been tamed by mankind. But no man can tame the tongue. It is an unruly evil, full of deadly poison.

The prophet Isaiah notes that Messiah's ministry would be marked by learning through experience and teaching by example. God the Father instructed His lowly Servant daily how to care for the weary:

The Lord God has given Me the tongue of the learned, that I should know how to speak a word in season to him who is weary. He awakens Me morning by morning, He awakens My ear to hear as the learned. The Lord God has opened My ear; and I was not rebellious, nor did I turn away (Isa. 50:4-5).

Messiah would diligently listen with the intent to obey what was heard. This is why the Lord Jesus' ministry was so effective – He knew and always did the Father's will. When one speaks only the words God would want him to speak, then the greatest benefit of those words is enjoyed. Words fitly spoken are powerful to heal, to sooth, to correct, to exhort, and to do all that God desires His Word to accomplish. When we speak our own words, our troubles begin. Job challenged his three companions to abandon vague insinuations and to supply detailed allegations that he could consider; to this end he noted, *"How forceful are right words!"* (Job 6:25). Right words have force, but inappropriate words dig a pit for the innocent. It is our nature to jump to conclusions without all the facts and then to deliberately and ungraciously share these presumptuous verdicts with others. Such behavior distorts the truth concerning the guilty and even worse, defames and defrauds the innocent. God is not honored in either case. Solomon reminds us that *"there is one who speaks like the piercings of a sword, but the tongue of the wise promotes health"* (Prov. 12:18). This was Christ's example: All His words were "right words" to encourage, to strengthen, or to convict. Words can heal or hurt; let us be wise in how we use them.

December 5 – An Enriched Pray-Life
James 5:16

Confess your trespasses to one another, and pray for one another, that you may be healed. The effective, fervent prayer of a righteous man avails much.

When believers walk in integrity with God and are burdened over what concerns Him, God is inclined to honor their prayers for the honor of His own name: *"Now this is the confidence that we have in Him, that if we ask anything according to His will, He hears us"* (1 Jn. 5:14). Believers today can have this same assurance in the Lord. Not only does James tell us about effectual praying, but he also informs us of what type of wrong attitudes concerning prayer hinder God's blessings:

If any of you lacks wisdom, let him ask of God, who gives to all liberally and without reproach, and it will be given to him. But let him ask in faith, with no doubting (Jas. 1:5-6).

You do not have because you do not ask. You ask and do not receive, because you ask amiss, that you may spend it on your pleasures (Jas. 4:2-3).

The reason many of God's people today do not see the hand of God moving in their lives is that they are not dependent on Him. Either they do not pray, or they cannot do so in genuine faith, or they do so with impure motives (i.e., they lust for what is outside of God's will).

Speaking to His disciples shortly before His death, the Lord Jesus promised them: *"And whatever things you ask in prayer, believing, you will receive"* (Matt. 21:22). This is not a "blab it and grab it" reality, but rather affords assurance that our prayers offered in faith and in the will of God will be answered for the glory of God (John 14:13; 1 Jn. 5:14). Hence, we can confidently conclude with an "amen" – "so be it."

The Father desires to honor His Son through answering our prayers. Thankfully, there are still a few today with clean hands and pure hearts that regularly beseech the Lord to revive His Church and to show Himself strong in a world that desperately needs to see Christ. He is the ultimate solution to all of our problems, and thus, in Him, we find the answers to all our effective, fervent prayers.

December 6 – Christ's Example of Suffering
1 Peter 2:19-23

For this is commendable, if because of conscience toward God one endures grief, suffering wrongfully. For what credit is it if, when you are beaten for your faults, you take it patiently? But when you do good and suffer, if you take it patiently, this is commendable before God. For to this you were called, because Christ also suffered for us, leaving us an example, that you should follow His steps: "Who committed no sin, nor was deceit found in His mouth"; who, when He was reviled, did not revile in return; when He suffered, He did not threaten, but committed Himself to Him who judges righteously.

Peter was writing to the widely persecuted believers throughout Asia Minor. Before exhorting the saints as to how they should behave, Peter first notes Christ's selfless example of suffering patiently, even though He had not done anything wrong. To suffer patiently for God takes real courage! Nowhere in Scripture is this truth more evident than in the example of our Lord Jesus Christ at Calvary.

Matthew tells us that at the beginning of that day both thieves blasphemed the Lord (Matt. 27:44); however, Luke informs us that one thief had a change of heart. Sometime within those three morning hours this thief came to understand that he was a sinner, that he was rightly being punished for his crimes, and that Jesus Christ was the only means of saving his soul. What sign, what message, what miracle caused this thief to be converted? It was the patient suffering of an innocent Savior who never reviled His oppressors but rather demonstrated love for them through this intercession for them. The repentant thief knew that this was a supernatural feat, an authentic display of divine grace at work.

In the same way, as a believer suffers patiently for the Lord, a sweet savor of Christ is provided to a lost world; it is a savor of life unto life for those who repent, but it is a savor of death unto death to those who perish (2 Cor. 2:14-16). The knowledge of Christ in the believer's life, therefore, is to be an unavoidable fragrance to the lost.

May each believer live to please Christ, understanding that this will result in suffering, but also knowing that perseverance is pleasing to the Lord, strengthens our resolve to live for Christ, and is a testimony of the power of the gospel. Are you suffering patiently for Christ?

December 7 – Following Christ's Example of Suffering
1 Peter 2:19-23

For it is better, if it is the will of God, to suffer for doing good than for doing evil. For Christ also suffered once for sins, the just for the unjust, that He might bring us to God, being put to death in the flesh but made alive by the Spirit.

Napoleon Bonaparte once said, "It requires more courage to suffer than to die."[43] He also noted that, "It is the cause, and not the death, that makes the martyr."[44] After a heart-wrenching denial, Peter found the first statement to be true: he learned that it requires more courage to suffer daily for the Lord than to die once for Him. Ultimately, after finishing his course in life, Peter would die for the Lord. Though Peter was crucified upside down (he thought himself unworthy of being crucified the same way his Lord was), he understood that it was not the details of his death that were important, but rather the cause for which he had lived and for which he was ready to die – the cause of Christ.

Simply put, it is easier to die for the Lord than it is to live for Him by dying daily to self. There is no room for self-will, self-ambition, or self-exaltation in a life lived for Christ, and all those who lose their life for Christ's sake *"shall suffer persecution"* (2 Tim. 3:12). Given that we cannot escape suffering, how can we still joyfully live for Christ?

Here are some practical points to consider in regard to this question: First, Christ has waited 2,000 plus years to vindicate His name; can we not wait a little while with Him for all to be set right? Second, what you do when wronged is more important than asserting the facts (1 Cor. 11:19). Third, we expect opposition from the lost, but often the most grievous wounds are from other believers. Do not jump on the devil's side to get even; it is not the Lord's way. Fourth, stubborn sheep under conviction will bite rather than yield to truth and many will resort to fault-finding to justify their carnality – do not go wrong with them. Fifth, those who do the least have more time on their hands to criticize those doing the most – keep busy in the Lord's work and be given to prayer. Sixth, remember that God uses incredible pressure and heat to take a base element like carbon and fashion it into a beautiful diamond. Likewise, He uses "affliction" (derived from *thlipsis*, which means "pressure") to fashion believers into priceless trophies of grace.

December 8 – Elders Who Are Among You
1 Peter 5:1-4

The elders who are among you I exhort, I who am a fellow elder and a witness of the sufferings of Christ, and also a partaker of the glory that will be revealed: Shepherd the flock of God which is among you, serving as overseers, not by compulsion but willingly, not for dishonest gain but eagerly; nor as being lords over those entrusted to you, but being examples to the flock; and when the Chief Shepherd appears, you will receive the crown of glory that does not fade away.

Verse 3 is much debated: *"Neither as being lords over God's **heritage**, but being examples to the flock"* (KJV). The Greek word *kleros* is translated as "heritage" in this verse. Since Peter was speaking to fellow elders (*presbuteros*), some have argued that spiritual leaders have a rightful church position as "clergy." However, other Bible translations of this verse more clearly specify who the "heritage" is, where the term is translated: *"those entrusted to you" (NKJV)*, *"those allotted to your charge" (NASV)*, *"the charge allotted to you" (RV)*; Wuest's Expanded Translation renders it: *"the portions of the flock assigned to you."* *Vine's Expository Dictionary* states that *kleros* in 1 Peter 5:3 speaks of those assigned by God into the spiritual care of elders; the dictionary then notes, "From *kleros* the word 'clergy' is derived (a transposition in the application of the term)."[45] Clearly, the *kleros* of 1 Peter 5:3 is not those who shepherd God's flock, but rather the portion of the flock which is in their care. Harry A. Ironside comments on this verse:

> Note the expression, "the elders which are among you." There is no suggestion here of a clerical order ruling arbitrarily over the laity. These elders were mature, godly men, upon whom rested the responsibility of watching over the souls of believers, as those for whom they must give an account (see Heb. 13:17).[46]

For approximately the first 150 years of the Church Age, the New Testament model of Church leadership was generally followed, but then men created positions and hierarchies which squelched Body-life. The clerical system since that time has oppressed the ministry of believer-priests, and the Church seems to be satisfied to let it be so.

December 9 – Submit to God, Resist the Devil
1 Peter 5:5-9

"God resists the proud, but gives grace to the humble." Therefore humble yourselves under the mighty hand of God, that He may exalt you in due time, casting all your care upon Him, for He cares for you. Be sober, be vigilant; because your adversary the devil walks about like a roaring lion, seeking whom he may devour. Resist him, steadfast in the faith, knowing that the same sufferings are experienced by your brotherhood in the world.

From God's perspective, a believer commits spiritual adultery when he or she lives a carnal life in lieu of a crucified life. It angers the Lord and summons His chastening hand to discipline the believer. The Lord knows that we will be most joyful and fruitful while remaining on the "straight and narrow" way. James also reminds us that *"a double-minded man* [is] *unstable in all his ways"* (Jas. 1:8). When God's people venture away from Him, it always results in an unstable life that is marked by failure; it can be no other way.

Once we are mentally resolved to do what God says, then we will be able to resist the devil. With God's help we stand by faith on the truth and will not budge from it no matter what the cost. As seen by the satanic attack on Ananias and Sapphira (Acts 5), evil can take shape in our minds in various ways, but we are to resist it by drawing near to God and hold to His truth. Matthew Henry comments on this subject:

> We are taught to submit ourselves entirely to God. … Now, as this subjection and submission to God are what the devil most industriously strives to hinder, so we ought with great care and steadiness to resist his suggestions. If he would represent a tame yielding to the will and providence of God as what will bring calamities, and expose to contempt and misery, we must resist these suggestions of fear. If he would represent submission to God as a hindrance to our outward ease, or worldly preferments, we must resist these suggestions of pride and sloth. If he would tempt us to lay any of our miseries, and crosses, and afflictions, to the charge of Providence, so that we might avoid them by following his directions instead of God's, we must resist these provocations to anger, not fretting ourselves in any wise to do evil. "Let not the devil, in these or the like attempts, prevail upon you; but resist him and he will flee from you."[47]

December 10 – Beware of False Teachers
2 Peter 2:1-3

But there were also false prophets among the people, even as there will be false teachers among you, who will secretly bring in destructive heresies, even denying the Lord who bought them, and bring on themselves swift destruction. And many will follow their destructive ways, because of whom the way of truth will be blasphemed. By covetousness they will exploit you with deceptive words; for a long time their judgment has not been idle, and their destruction does not slumber.

A true teacher of God's Word will always lead His people into repentance and humility before God, never away from the Lord. This is why Moses prescribed such a stern punishment for false prophets in His day: *"But that prophet or that dreamer of dreams shall be put to death, because he has spoken in order to turn you away from the Lord"* (Deut. 13:5). False teachers/prophets may for a time feign humility and morality, but they are inherently self-exalting (i.e., they compete for God's honor) and are self-gratifying (2 Pet. 2:10-18). Peter states that these false teachers are prone to sexual immorality, to despise authority, to be animalistic, to be deceitful, and for financial reasons utter swelling words that appeal to the flesh but have no spiritual content. Such individuals will eventually lead the Lord's people away from Him. Accordingly, such individuals were to be exposed and slain in the Old Testament, and rejected and avoided in the New Testament.

Peter warned believers in the Church Age not to listen to false teachers and he also predicted their doom (2 Pet. 2:1-2). In responding to His disciples' question about things to come, the Lord confirmed that in the latter days of the Church Age many false doctrines would be spread. Besides mass deception, many would come claiming to be the Christ (Matt. 24:5). With the coming of the Lord nearing, His warning 2,000 years ago, *"Take heed that no one deceives you"* (Matt. 24:4), could never be more critical to obey. "No one" means well-meaning preachers and authors, too. Paul exhorted the believers at Thessalonica to *"Test all things; hold fast what is good"* (1 Thess. 5:21). Dear believer, avoid anyone who tries to lead you away from Christ by displacing Him, or by corrupting His Word or degrading His person!

December 11 – The Day of God
2 Peter 3:10-12

But the day of the Lord will come as a thief in the night, in which the heavens will pass away with a great noise, and the elements will melt with fervent heat; both the earth and the works that are in it will be burned up. Therefore, since all these things will be dissolved, what manner of persons ought you to be in holy conduct and godliness, looking for and hastening the coming of the day of God, because of which the heavens will be dissolved, being on fire, and the elements will melt with fervent heat?

The Day of the Lord is an Old Testament term that speaks of times when Jehovah visibly and powerfully judged the wicked on earth. This meaning continues into the New Testament and speaks of the Tribulation Period, the Millennial Kingdom of Christ, the destruction of the earth, and the Great White Throne Judgment (1 Thess. 5:1-11; 2 Pet. 3:10). "The Day of Christ" should not be confused with "the Day of the Lord," as the former day is connected with the rapture of the Church and the Judgment Seat of Christ prior to the Day of the Lord. This *day* is to be longed for by believers (1 Cor. 1:8, 5:5; Phil 1:6, 10).

Peter tells us that *the Day of the Lord* (speaking of the Millennial Kingdom) concludes with destruction of the earth and will be followed by *the Day of God*, often called *the Eternal State* (2 Pet. 3:12). Isaiah states that *"all the host of heaven shall be dissolved, and the heavens shall be rolled up like a scroll"* (Isa. 34:4). Isaiah then foretold that God would create a perfect new heaven and new earth (Isa. 65:17) – a matter which John says occurs right after Christ's 1,000-year reign and the Great White Throne judgment of the wicked (Rev. 20:7-21:1).

The Bible begins and ends with a wedding. Both weddings occur in a beautiful garden and in the presence of God. The first wedding is of Adam and Eve in the Garden of Eden. The last wedding in the Bible is the marriage of the Lamb and His Bride before the tree of life and God's throne (Rev. 21-22). As in Eden, the Creator is in fellowship with man in paradise (Rev. 22:1-6). Yet, the journey man travels between these two gardens is problematic, but thankfully this journey is bridged by a third garden – Golgotha where the Lamb gave His life for His Bride (John 19:41). Oh, to be with the Lover of our souls forever!

December 12 – Walking With God in the Light
1 John 1:6-9

If we say that we have fellowship with Him, and walk in darkness, we lie and do not practice the truth. But if we walk in the light as He is in the light, we have fellowship with one another, and the blood of Jesus Christ His Son cleanses us from all sin. If we say that we have no sin, we deceive ourselves, and the truth is not in us. If we confess our sins, He is faithful and just to forgive us our sins and to cleanse us from all unrighteousness.

Having already borne our sins, Christ has secured our *peace with God*; this opens the way for us to enjoy the *peace of God* while in happy fellowship with Him. And we are encouraged to do so, but God cannot come into the darkness to have fellowship with us; we must walk with Him in the light of divine truth. Thankfully, when we do sin, there is a provision for cleansing through the effectual power of Christ's blood. As we confess sin to the Lord, His blood has the power to repeatedly wash and cleanse us from all the stain of sin. Having God's forgiveness for sin and our consciences cleansed from guilt are wonderful blessings of our salvation in Christ: *"How much more shall the blood of Christ ... cleanse your conscience from dead works to serve the living God?"* (Heb. 9:14). Judicially speaking, all was forgiven when we were justified in Christ at conversion, but practically speaking, sins committed since conversion must be continually confessed and repented of to enjoy fellowship with God again.

Notice that John does *not* say that God cleanses our unrighteousness when we ask Him for forgiveness. Rather, it is when we "confess" our sins to Him that we are purified and are returned to fellowship with God again. The act of confessing means that we stand with God against ourselves, that is, we agree with Him that our wrong behavior was sinful and we are truly sorry for offending Him.

Confession is the responsibility of the believer, and cleansing is what only God can do. Both acts must be performed on an ongoing basis as we have a constant need for *"the blood of Jesus Christ His Son* [which] *cleanses us from all sin"* (1 Jn. 1:7). John's focus is how the believer can maintain fellowship with God. We are to walk in the light with God and confess to Him when we have strayed into the darkness.

December 13 – If You Do Sin

1 John 1:10-2:2

If we say that we have not sinned, we make Him a liar, and His word is not in us. My little children, these things I write to you, so that you may not sin. And if anyone sins, we have an Advocate with the Father, Jesus Christ the righteous. And He Himself is the propitiation for our sins, and not for ours only but also for the whole world.

We understand that Christians should sin less because of their sinless position in Christ (Rom. 6:1); however, sinless perfection is not possible until glorification occurs (1 Jn. 3:2-3). By drawing near to and being sustained by Christ, we will be conformed to His image and thus sin less (Rom. 8:29). Children of God are marked by righteous living (i.e., they do not practice sin; 1 Jn. 3:8-9). Those who have not been born again habitually practice sin without remorse – the fallen nature within them rules their behavior (1 Jn. 3:10).

Besides being our heavenly High Priest (Heb. 4:14), Christ is also our legal representative or "advocate" before the Father. This is a special comfort to every believer, especially knowing that Satan slanders us before God's throne day and night (Rev. 12:10). The English term "advocate" is only translated once from the Greek word *parakletos*, which is translated as "comforter" four times in John's gospel account in reference to the Holy Spirit. The role of advocate (or comforter) is to legally plead a case or to speak on the behalf of another in a court of law – a legal intercessor. When does Christ plead our case? Is it when we acknowledge and confess our sins? First John 2:1 states that Christ is our advocate when we sin, not when we confess our sins, though we certainly should repent and confess our sins.

When a believer sins, Satan may abruptly call God's attention to the despicable deed, but Christ, being on the throne with His Father, immediately addresses the offense. He concedes the ungodly behavior of the believer but then asserts that the penalty for that lawless deed has already been paid by Himself at Calvary. In this way, all the heavenly hosts see that God is righteous and that He has accounted justly for every sin that His children have done. God hates sin, but because He judged Christ for sin, He can extend the repentant sinner a full pardon and family status as His adopted child with full privileges (Rom. 8:15).

December 14 – You Have an Anointing
1 John 2:20-21

But you have an anointing from the Holy One, and you know all things. I have not written to you because you do not know the truth, but because you know it, and that no lie is of the truth.

Priests, prophets, and kings were often anointed with oil when consecrated to serve the Lord. The Lord Jesus was anointed by the Holy Spirit at the commencement of His ministry (Matt. 3:16; Acts 10:38). Similarly, each believer is anointed and called to serve according to God's will (Eph. 2:10). *"Now He who establishes us with you in Christ and has anointed us is God, who also has sealed us and given us the Spirit in our hearts as a guarantee"* (2 Cor. 1:21-22).

Not only does this anointing separate out the believer for God's purpose, but the anointing actually provides divine discernment of the truth, which enables the believer to follow after God's will in his or her ministry. John instructed the believers, *"Beloved, do not believe every spirit* [teacher], *but test the spirits, whether they are of God; because many false prophets have gone out into the world"* (1 Jn. 4:1). He also informed them of an anointing that they had received at spiritual rebirth from the Holy Spirit. There is no need to pray for this anointing as some do; every believer already has it. It is always spoken of in the past tense and has the purpose of giving spiritual discernment as to what is true and what is false.

These things I have written to you concerning those who try to deceive you. ***But the anointing which you have received from Him abides in you, and you do not need that anyone teach you; but as the same anointing teaches you concerning all things, and is true,*** *and is not a lie, and just as it has taught you, you will abide in Him* (1 Jn. 2:26-27).

With this spiritual resource each believer can validate what is truth and what is deception by the illumination of God's Word: *"Your word is a lamp to my feet and a light to my path"* (Ps. 119:105). As believers, we have what we need to learn the truth about Christ and His will for our lives. Thankfully, godly teachers will aid us also. But we must remember that slothfulness will either lead us into spiritual despondency or deception.

351

December 15 – The Antichrist Test
1 John 2:22-23

Who is a liar but he who denies that Jesus is the Christ? He is antichrist who denies the Father and the Son. Whoever denies the Son does not have the Father either; he who acknowledges the Son has the Father also.

The Lord Jesus has a specific message for those who deny that He is the incarnate Son of God: *"You are from beneath; I am from above. You are of this world; I am not of this world. Therefore I said to you that you will die in your sins; for if you do not believe that I Am [He], you will die in your sins"* (John 8:23-24). The "He" after the "I Am" affirmation is not in the Greek text. The Lord Jesus unequivocally stated that He is the great I AM of the Bible (i.e., the same one that Moses talked with at the burning bush). Anyone rejecting this truth cannot be forgiven of their sins, because they would, in effect, be calling Christ a liar. Accordingly, those who deny that Jesus Christ literally came down from heaven as the Son of God are governed by the spirit of Antichrist. God the Father cannot welcome anyone into heaven who rejects the teaching of Christ's deity!

Consequently, John tells us to identify the spirit of those teaching by this test, lest we be led astray by their doctrine: *"Every spirit that confesses that Jesus Christ has come in the flesh is of God, and every spirit that does not confess that Jesus Christ has come in the flesh is not of God. And this is the spirit of the Antichrist, which you have heard was coming, and is now already in the world* (1 Jn. 4:2-3). The apostles proclaim a unified message of Christ's deity in Scripture:

- Thomas declared that Jesus Christ was His Lord and God (John 20:28).
- Paul identified Jesus Christ as our Great God and Savior (Tit. 2:13).
- Paul and James stated that the Lord Jesus is the Lord of Glory (1 Cor. 2:8; Jas. 2:1).
- Referring to Christ, John and Paul said that God was made manifest in the flesh (John 1:14, 18; 1 Tim. 3:16).
- The apostles preached that Jesus Christ was the Son of God (Acts 9:20).
- Paul taught that God was in Christ reconciling the world (2 Cor. 5:19).
- Speaking of Christ, Paul states that *"in Him dwells the fullness of the Godhead bodily"* (Col. 2:9).

December 16 – Purified by Hope
1 John 3:2-3

Beloved, now we are children of God; and it has not yet been revealed what we shall be, but we know that when He is revealed, we shall be like Him, for we shall see Him as He is. And everyone who has this hope in Him purifies himself, just as He is pure.

Although Christ is in heaven presently, through our spiritual regeneration, He is able to reside within all believers on earth. In the future, His Church will be with Him in heaven. His forever abiding presence with us is certain, though our intimacy with Him each day depends on our desire for it. With His exaltation looming, Christians are to live each day in the anticipation of Christ's coming (2 Tim. 4:6-8). There is a reward for those who do, and their lives will be more joyful and fruitful in light of that imminent expectation.

In a twinkling of an eye, our mortal and corruptible bodies will become immortal and incorruptible (1 Cor. 15:51-52), and we will be instantaneously caught up into the air to be with Christ forevermore (1 Thess. 4:13-18). At this event, often referred to as the Rapture of the Church, sin and pain will cease to exist within all believers in Christ. The believer's glorified body will be able to worship and to please God without any hindrance from the flesh or any ills of its previously fallen state. Then, we will forever be with the Lord!

Accordingly, our blessed hope and earnest expectation is Christ's return: *"Looking for the blessed hope and glorious appearing of our great God and Savior Jesus Christ"* (Tit. 2:13). The believer's faith and hope finish their course at Christ's coming for His Church. The Church is not to be waiting for the Antichrist to appear (his coming is a sign to the nation of Israel; Dan. 9:27), but for Christ Himself to translate them from the earth into heaven. The Church is not waiting for the inhabitants of earth to be slaughtered during the Tribulation Period, but rather longs to be removed from this wicked world to be with Christ. John tells us that this disposition is a purifying hope. The Lord is pure and saints having the blessed hope will want to be found living purely when He suddenly returns from heaven. In the interim, believers are to abide in Christ and to look for His coming; otherwise, there is the possibility of feeling ashamed when He does appear (1 Jn. 2:28).

December 17 – Whosoever Is Born of God Loves
1 John 4:9

Beloved, let us love one another, for love is of God; and everyone who loves is born of God and knows God. He who does not love does not know God, for God is love.

Each of us was born after the flesh, but those born of God need not live after the flesh any longer (Rom. 6:2). It is God the Father's earnest desire that His children live up to His Son's moral likeness (1 Pet. 1:16) and also display His lovely character so others can appreciate Him. This is not possible if our allegiance is to other things, ideologies, and people. Accordingly, whatever prevents Christ from being first-place in our affections provokes Him to take corrective action (Rev. 2:4-5). In a practical sense, a believer who chooses to live after the flesh is daring God, "Do You still love me enough to correct me?" The answer is, "Yes, He does" (Heb. 12:6). For this reason, Paul exhorts those at Corinth: *"Therefore, having these promises, beloved, let us cleanse ourselves from all filthiness of the flesh and spirit, perfecting holiness in the fear of God"* (2 Cor. 7:1). To trust in one's flesh always disappoints the Lord and leads us into a chastening storm.

John tells us that instead of living for ourselves, whoever has been born of God has the ability to both experience and share God's love. God is love and those who have been united with Him receive His love and are enabled to love God and others in a way they never could previously. To exhibit this type of selfless, sacrificing love to others is a sure telltale sign that one is a child of God: *"If we love one another, God abides in us, and His love has been perfected in us. By this we know that we abide in Him, and He in us, because He has given us of His Spirit* (1 Jn. 4:12-13). God's holiness is reflected in us when we obey His Word and give Him first place in our lives, but His gracious character in us is revealed through sacrificial giving.

Through the power of the Holy Spirit, believers can convey the love of God to others in a supernatural way. It is not natural to love our enemies, to do good to those who persecute us, to bless those who curse us, or to withhold vengeance when it is just. The believer should never be satisfied with his or her outward projection of God's love. We can always love more because God's love is inexhaustible.

December 18 – No Fear in Love
1 John 4:18

There is no fear in love; but perfect love casts out fear, because fear involves torment. But he who fears has not been made perfect in love.

The Jewish nation today reveres Jehovah, but Israel is unfortunately estranged from Him and ignorant of His ways. As an example, orthodox Jews have a longstanding practice of not saying *Yahweh* (Jehovah) because of their fear of God and reverence for His name, yet they reject the Lord Jesus Christ – their only hope of salvation. Divine authority without a proper relationship prompts fear. The Jewish nation is presently out of touch with God; their spiritual state precludes them from knowing God intimately and experiencing His goodness.

Thankfully, love and not fear is to rule the believer's disposition towards God, though love does not displace proper awe and reverence for God. The Lord knows that love is a stronger motive for willful service, submitting to His commandments, and pursuing holy living than fear is. If one loves the Lord, yielding to His Word will be a delight. Love for the Lord is a stronger reason for obedience than is the fear of consequences. John says, *"There is no fear in love; but perfect love casts out fear, because fear involves torment. But he who fears has not been made perfect in love."* Because of Christ's finished work at Calvary, the judicial penalty for the believer's sin has been satisfied. This means that God is no longer angry with those He has forgiven.

As a result, believers are liberated to experience and share God's love: *"But if anyone loves God, this one is known by Him"* (1 Cor. 8:3). *"We love Him, because He first loved us"* (1 Jn. 4:19). The "Him" in this verse is not in the Greek text, but is implied. Literally, we are able to love as we should because we have received divine love. This means that we are no longer to be ruled by the fear we suffered from before becoming a child of God, but rather we are to revel in the love of God and to share with others and God what can only come from Him.

When an answer I did not expect comes to a prayer which I believed I truly meant, I shrink back from it; if the burden my Lord asks me to bear be not the burden of my heart's choice, and I fret inwardly and do not welcome His will, then I know nothing of Calvary love.

— Amy Carmichael

355

December 19 – Those Born of God, Love and Obey Him
1 John 5:1-3

Whoever believes that Jesus is the Christ is born of God, and everyone who loves Him who begot also loves him who is begotten of Him. By this we know that we love the children of God, when we love God and keep His commandments. For this is the love of God, that we keep His commandments. And His commandments are not burdensome.

When an individual believes and receives Christ for the forgiveness of his or her sins, he or she is then born again (spiritually; John 3:3; 1 Pet. 1:23) and becomes an adopted child of God (Rom. 8:15-16). Birth and adoption are acts which establish relationship; man's fellowship with God depends on him engaging in righteous behavior (1 Jn. 1:5-10). A continuation of godly behavior is now possible through the abiding presence and power of the Holy Spirit; if the believer chooses to walk according to revealed truth, his or her fellowship with God is unbroken. If one sins, fellowship is broken, but relationship is secured in Christ. As Christians confess their sins, they are restored to full communion with God (1 Jn. 1:9).

Before trusting in Christ for salvation, the believer was spiritually dead in trespasses and sins. But through the power of the Holy Spirit we have been made spiritually alive. He implants divine life within what was dead – this is called being "born again" or "born of God" and no one can enter heaven without being born again (John 1:12-13, 3:3). In time, as we choose to abide in Christ, this life implanted within us grows and enables us to be fruit-bearing branches (John 15:2-5).

John refers to the new nature as a righteous seed implanted within a new believer. This seed cannot invoke sin or lead the believer away from what pleases God (1 Jn. 3:9). Without being born again, a human soul will remain spiritually dead and without the capacity to please God. In this state, every individual will act as a child of the devil and be controlled by the lusts and desires of his or her flesh (Eph. 2:1-3). Consequently, if we are going to live for God, we must be born again and yield to that new and holy nature received from Him. God expects His children to live up to their divine family's reputation and resemblance – true children of God will seek to obey their Father's commandments and to live holy lives, for He is holy in all His ways.

December 20 – Those Born of God Overcome the World
1 John 5:4-5

For whatever is born of God overcomes the world. And this is the victory that has overcome the world – our faith. Who is he who overcomes the world, but he who believes that Jesus is the Son of God?

Those who have been born again overcome the world by faith, as they submit to God's Word and simply rest in Him to sustain the victory that Christ has already secured over the world. By faith we reject God-denying secular philosophies and human traditions, rather than be ruined by them (Col. 2:8). Because Christ was victorious over the devil and the world at Calvary, we can continue to proclaim that victory through faith and obedience to God's Word. We recognize who we are in Christ and continue to rely on Him alone to continue prevailing over the world, just as He did at the cross. This is the pathway to victorious Christian living in a Christ-denying world!

The Lord told His disciples that the world loves its own, hence, they would be hated by the world because the world hates Him (John 15:18-19). It is impossible to love the Lord as we should and also adore a satanic system which openly rejects Him: *"Friendship with the world is enmity with God?"* (Jas. 4:4). Worldliness is the love of passing things which have no eternal value. Worldliness opposes God, and God hates it. Whatever is born of God is destined to overcome the world because the Lord Jesus has already overcome the world: *"These things I have spoken to you, that in Me you may have peace. In the world you will have tribulation; but be of good cheer, I have overcome the world"* (John 16:33). It is natural for us to grow weary of confronting secular philosophies. But regardless, *"the just shall live by faith"* and *"This is the victory that has overcome the world – our faith!"* Happy is the believer who rests by faith in Christ above (Eph. 2:6), for He rules over all that happens below and we are to daily proclaim that reality.

In such a world as this, with such hearts as ours, weakness is wickedness in the long run. Whoever lets himself be shaped and guided by anything lower than an inflexible will, fixed in obedience to God, will in the end be shaped into a deformity, and guided to wreck and ruin.

— Alexander MacLaren

December 21 – Know That You Have Eternal Life
1 John 5:13

These things I have written to you who believe in the name of the Son of God, that you may know that you have eternal life, and that you may continue to believe in the name of the Son of God.

It is common to hear someone respond to the question, "Would you go to heaven if you died today?" with a squeamish "Well, I hope so." Whether or not such an individual is actually saved only the Lord knows, but what is evident is that the responder has no assurance of salvation. This is a matter that John wrote to alleviate. A true believer will gain understanding of the salvation that he or she possesses in Christ by studying and trusting in what Scripture proclaims about their security in Christ. This assurance of salvation guards the believer's mind against despair during strenuous times because his or her eternal future with Christ in heaven is secure, no matter what happens on earth.

Believers are therefore not hoping that they will be saved from God's judgment of their sin, for Christ has already been judged in their place. Rather, believers are to know that they are eternally secure in Christ (John 5:24) and long with anticipation for the conclusion of their salvation – glorification. Presently, they can rejoice that their souls are saved from the penalty of sin, that through the Holy Spirit they have power over sin, but are to continue to expect a future day when they will be saved from the presence of sin at Christ's coming.

Hope, in the biblical sense, is therefore defined as "having present joy in the future promises of God," a meaning borne out by the New Testament Greek words rendered as "hope." In the New Testament, *Elpis* is found eighty-six times and is translated "hope" all but once and its verb form *elpizo* occurs thirty-two times and is translated either "hope" or some form of "trusting." Only *elpis* and *elpizo* are translated "hope" in the portion of the New Testament pertaining to the Church Age (the books of Acts through Revelation). Therefore, when Christians "hope" in something, it means they are "anticipating something with confidence." The believer's hope is thus living, and allows him or her to have present joy in the future promises of God. The believer's calling in Christ is completely fostered in the assurance of His Word, especially the final call home.

December 22 – The Confidence That We Have in God
1 John 5:14-15

Now this is the confidence that we have in Him, that if we ask anything according to His will, He hears us. And if we know that He hears us, whatever we ask, we know that we have the petitions that we have asked of Him.

The prophet Samuel shows us that effective praying requires a genuine pursuit of God in righteousness and humility. In response to his wayward countrymen's request to pray for them, Samuel affirms that if they were sincerely repentant and continued to seek the Lord, then God would forgive them and they would have nothing to fear:

Do not fear. You have done all this wickedness; yet do not turn aside from following the Lord, but serve the Lord with all your heart. And do not turn aside; for then you would go after empty things which cannot profit or deliver, for they are nothing (1 Sam. 12:20-21).

The Lord loves His people in all ages, despite their failings and unfaithfulness. He cannot forsake them, though indeed He must chasten those who are His when necessary to restore them to Himself. We cannot change the past, but our future can be bright and blessed if we cling to the Lord and remain devoted to Him.

Samuel promised to faithfully pray for his brethren – that they would cling to the Lord and remain in *"the good and the right way."* Indeed, he wanted to pray for them and even felt that it would be sin not to pray for them. Samuel, being a man of integrity, epitomizes what James would later write: *"The effective, fervent prayer of a righteous man avails much"* (Jas. 5:16). Because he was a righteous man and knew the will of God, he had great confidence that his prayers would be answered. *"Now this is the confidence that we have in Him, that if we ask anything according to His will, He hears us."*

Believers with clean hands and pure hearts can have this same assurance in the Lord today. Beloved of the Lord, we likewise should be willing to pray that God will do whatever it takes to show the Church her sin and complacency. We, too, should consider it a sin not to pray for our brethren to know the truth, and then to fearfully and to faithfully walk in the good and the right way.

December 23 – True Hospitality (Part 1)
3 John 5-8

Beloved, you do faithfully whatever you do for the brethren and for strangers, who have borne witness of your love before the church. If you send them forward on their journey in a manner worthy of God, you will do well, because they went forth for His name's sake, taking nothing from the Gentiles. We therefore ought to receive such, that we may become fellow workers for the truth.

Gaius provides a good pattern to follow in the care of the Lord's servants. He extended hospitality to itinerant church workers and then did not send them away empty-handed (see Tit. 3:14). Commended workers serve the Lord (Acts 14:26), and thus the Lord wants His people to freely and amply provide for them in His name.

Our English word "hospitality" is translated from the Greek noun *philoxenos* or verb *philoxenia*, which together only occur five times in the New Testament. Hospitality literally means to be "fond of strangers (guests)." As full-time workers, we have often benefited from the saints' hospitality as we travel. Sometimes we stay with believers we have never met before, yet, after a few days together, a bond for life is formed. We have found the Lord's words in Matthew 19:29 to be true: for each one who rejects us because of Christ, there are another hundred believers who are ready to confirm the love of God.

Personally speaking, we enjoy hospitality the most when the host creates a relaxed atmosphere. That means we can enjoy Christian fellowship without the undue stress of unnecessary extras. Examples: a simple meal vs. a fourteen-course extravaganza; regular tableware vs. the best china, fancy napkins and placemats, and more silverware than one knows what to do with; the freedom to get what I need vs. being asked a hundred questions as to what I want. In other words, you can give your guests your best, without displaying your best. The tension of having someone in your home is reduced for both you and your guests by keeping hospitality simple and low-key, but adequate.

Hospitality demonstrates Christian love to others in your home. Whether ministering, restoring, refreshing, or shepherding the Lord's people or serving strangers unawares, hospitality is a huge blessing. All believers are to be given to hospitality; do not neglect this ministry.

360

December 24 – True Hospitality (Part 2)
3 John 5-8

Beloved, you do faithfully whatever you do for the brethren and for strangers, who have borne witness of your love before the church. If you send them forward on their journey in a manner worthy of God, you will do well, because they went forth for His name's sake, taking nothing from the Gentiles. We therefore ought to receive such, that we may become fellow workers for the truth.

"Let brotherly love continue ... entertain strangers" (Heb. 13:1-2). Gaius is praised because he entertained both the brethren and strangers in his home (3 Jn. 5). Peter preached the gospel in the home of Cornelius and then remained there many days to disciple those who put their trust in Christ (Acts 10). The home is a non-threatening location to visit with the lost about spiritual things. Often the unregenerate have nagging questions, but will not initiate a public conversation to get their inquiries answered. A home in which Christ is Lord demonstrates the validity of the gospel message. As your guests observe the peacefulness of your family life, they may be prompted to ask questions, which will then provide opportunities for sharing the gospel message.

Although all saints should practice hospitality, those in spiritual leadership must *"be given to hospitality"* (1 Tim. 3:2). Church elders are the ones held accountable for the proper functioning of the local assembly (Heb. 13:17). Elders are raised up from among the sheep (Acts 20:28) and are to remain among the sheep (1 Pet. 5:2-3). This availability enhances two important aspects of the shepherding work.

First, it allows the shepherd to observe the attitudes and the behavior of believers and to provide timely exhortation, encouragement, and, as necessary, reproof. Second, this transparent relationship allows the sheep to observe the elder's godly character, selfless motives, and ability to properly teach the Scripture. Hospitality provides an excellent opportunity to shepherd God's people; accordingly, elders must *"be given to hospitality."* Those elders who use their homes regularly to connect with those in their care (without favoritism) will enjoy immense benefits in shepherding the flock that God has put into their care. As mentioned previously, it is much easier to promote fire prevention than to be constantly responding to smoke!

December 25 – Beware of Cain, Balaam, and Korah
Jude 10-11

But these speak evil of whatever they do not know; and whatever they know naturally, like brute beasts, in these things they corrupt themselves. Woe to them! For they have gone in the way of Cain, have run greedily in the error of Balaam for profit, and perished in the rebellion of Korah.

The Lord's half-brother Jude warned believers of false teachers that were trying to lead them away from Christ. He wrote: *"Woe to them! For they have gone in the way of Cain"* (Jude 11). Cain's brother, Abel, was a keeper of sheep and gave the best of his flock and approached God by a burnt offering. God had respect for Abel's offering because it pictured the future death of His beloved Son, the Lord Jesus. Abel did not know about His future Savior or how He would be judged for his sins, but in faith he simply did what pleased God. Cain, however, was a "tiller of the ground" and brought to God what he had labored for – the fruit from a cursed ground. Cain offered to God his accomplishments (good works) and not an innocent substitute to bear judgment in his place – there was no life in the fruit. Cain chose to worship God his way!

The *"way of Balaam"* was an indictment against the false teachers in Peter's day who pursued the *"wages of unrighteousness"* (2 Pet. 2:15). Like covetous Balaam, these false teachers were attempting to represent God for financial profit. But Jude highlights *"the error of Balaam,"* which wrongly assumed that God had to judicially curse His people on the basis of their spiritual and moral failure. Balaam, a false prophet looking for riches, did not appreciate God's merciful character, or His means of righteously judging sin through a substitute.

Jude completes his trilogy of woes against false teachers by noting their end…they will perish in God's judgment just as rebellious Korah and his followers did in Numbers 16. Korah was called into Levitical ministry, but not to the Levitical priesthood. Korah did not want to minister in his God-given calling, but sought what he could not be, a priest. Korah led a rebellion against God's appointed leadership and priesthood to change this. God responded by causing the earth to swallow the rebels where they stood. Woe to those who intrude on Christ's priesthood and assume a position before men that is not theirs.

December 26 – Beware of the Nicolaitans
Revelation 2:15

Thus you also have those who hold the doctrine of the Nicolaitans, which thing I hate.

The truth that all believers are to be active priests within the Church is distorted by many practices in Christendom: clergy-led services, ministry by "professionals," church traditions and empty rotes, to name a few. Nowhere in Scripture do we read of a clerical position over the people, except for when the Word rebukes those who had wrongly assumed one, such as Diotrephes in 3 Jn. 9, and the Nicolaitans in Rev. 2:6, 15. The term "Nicolaitans," which is derived from the Greek word *Nikolaos*, means "victorious over the people," and referred to those individuals who ruled the laity.[48] *Thayer's Greek Lexicon* provides the literal meaning of the Greek word *Nikolaites*: "the destruction of the people."[49] At the time Revelation was written, a ruling body of clergy had evidently conquered the people and assumed rule over them. The Lord Himself used strong language against those who seized the rule over His people, saying He *hated* both the deeds (Rev. 2:6) and the doctrine of the Nicolaitans (Rev. 2:15). The only one who should be in a position of hierarchy in the Church is its Head – Christ. All those in the Body formed one class of people called "brethren" (Matt. 23:8).

As before noted, the Church generally held to the New Testament model of Church leadership for about the first 150 years of the Church Age. However, in time men created positions and spheres of control that suppressed the priesthood of the saints. The same stifling spirit of control can be witnessed today when church leaders try to control the ministries of the saints. Diotrephes seized control of his assembly and drove saints out of the assembly. He decided what was to be taught in the assembly; he even intercepted and prevented John's letter from being read to the saints. Elders are responsible to guide, to put into order (1 Cor. 14:23-35) and to test (Tit. 1:19) what ministry occurs in the assembly, but they are not to inhibit the exercise of the Holy Spirit in believers. To do so is to act like a Nicolaitan and the Lord hates it.

Our whole vocabulary of church activity will change if we really begin to take seriously the NT pattern.

— Layton Ford

December 27 – Do Not Let Anyone Take Your Crown
Revelation 3:11

Behold, I am coming quickly! Hold fast what you have, that no one may take your crown.

In heaven, believers will appreciate the Lord Jesus to the extent we have practically experienced Him in this life. This may explain why each saint in glory will receive a white stone with a special name (presumably of the Lord Jesus) written on it – a name that no one else is aware of (Rev. 2:17). Among the throngs of heaven, each person is guaranteed a special intimacy with the Lord Jesus which no one else can enjoy. Our lives are diverse, which means the Lord means something different to each of us. To the widow, He is "the Faithful Husband." To the orphan, He is "the Caring Father." To the abused, He is "the Comforter of Sorrows." Thus, we want to serve and experience the Lord now in the best way possible so that we can have the greatest means of honoring Christ throughout eternity.

The rewards for faithfulness that He gives to us at the Judgment Seat of Christ enable us to achieve this goal. This is why the Lord Jesus told the Church at Philadelphia, *"Hold fast what you have, that no one may take your crown."* His reward will be with Him when He comes to the clouds to snatch away His Church from the earth (1 Thess. 4:13-18; Rev. 22:12). In light of the Lord's imminent return, the saints at Philadelphia were to be attentive and faithful, lest they lose their reward (crown); this would allow someone else to earn it. This dynamic is what happened to Moses and Barak in the Old Testament: God had given them both service opportunities, but they complained and wavered, so the Lord transferred part of the prospect of service, and the accompanying honor, to Aaron and to Jael, Heber's wife, respectively. God has a work to do and it will be accomplished by those who are willing to serve Him, and God shall recompense them accordingly.

Like Moses and Barak, we too, when facing a daunting situation, are prone to rely on that which is visibly tangible rather than on the vast resources of an infinite God. Such situations serve as a reality check as to the quality of our faith. It is good to remember at such times that God can use our weak faith to affect His glory, but the honor we acquire in doing so will be of the same diminished quality.

December 28 – Do Not Be Lukewarm
Revelation 3:16-19

So then, because you are lukewarm, and neither cold nor hot, I will vomit you out of My mouth. Because you say, 'I am rich, have become wealthy, and have need of nothing' – and do not know that you are wretched, miserable, poor, blind, and naked – I counsel you to buy from Me gold refined in the fire, that you may be rich; and white garments, that you may be clothed, that the shame of your nakedness may not be revealed; and anoint your eyes with eye salve, that you may see. As many as I love, I rebuke and chasten. Therefore be zealous and repent.

John recorded the messages from the Lord to seven literal churches in Asia Minor (Rev. 2 and 3). The Lord sent a messenger to each of these churches with an assessment of their conduct, doctrine, and deeds. The encouragement and warnings to these churches is timeless and was preserved that believers down through the ages might avoid the pitfalls of the past and live to be praised by Christ. Ephesus was sound in doctrine and works, but did not love the Lord as they once did. Smyrna was a faithful church despite harsh persecution. Pergamos suffered from worldliness and permitted the Nicolatians (a developing clergy system) to conquer them. Thyatira was controlled by a prophetess named Jezebel; her followers were idolatrous and immoral. Sardis had a lifeless profession. Philadelphia was experiencing revival and had an evangelical focus. Laodicea was materialistic and suffered from a lukewarm commitment to Christ. While the Lord found something praiseworthy in most of these churches, He did rebuke five of the seven churches and called on those churches to repent.

His words to the church at Laodicea are sharp, *"As many as I love, I rebuke and chasten. Therefore be zealous and repent."* They deserved the rebuke of the Lord: their affection for the Lord and their love for their fellow man were lukewarm. Christ warns them that they were spiritually naked; they had not adorned themselves with the clothing of heaven – righteous deeds (Rev. 19:8). He candidly describes how He felt about their lethargy: "I am disgusted with you; you make me sick to my stomach!" Beloved, it is hard to imagine a harsher charge by Christ against those who are His; may we be sold out for the Lord Jesus!

365

December 29 – I Am Knocking on Your Heart's Door
Revelation 3:20

Behold, I stand at the door and knock. If anyone hears My voice and opens the door, I will come in to him and dine with him, and he with Me.

The Lord concludes His letters to the seven churches with this invitation. The Lord was knocking on the door of believers' hearts who were a part of the lukewarm, materialistic church at Laodicea. He is a perfect gentleman and will not force Himself upon those who would rather live without Him, that is, who would rather live for themselves. Yet, His love is patient and He continues knocking and asking for access so that He might enjoy full communion with those He loves. Those who open the door of their hearts to Him eagerly receive His rule, and will enjoy His peace and blessing also. Unfortunately, there is much lethargy in the Church today, and few permit the Savior in to dine with them. Thankfully, the Lord will always be found in the midst of His people attending to their needs (Matt. 18:20) – this is what the Great Shepherd does (Heb. 13:20-21). Those who willingly gather to Him instead of venturing into the world to find answers and gratification will never suffer the frantic anxiety of not knowing where their Beloved is.

Much of the modern Church is stranded in the spiritual doldrums of complacency or being comfortably pampered. Those who have been redeemed and cleansed by the blood of Christ must venture out into the world and tell others of their wonderful Savior. To be witnesses for Christ, we must demonstrate His goodness and holy character through selfless deeds; this is how others will become familiar with our Beloved. Everything about the Lord Jesus is wonderful, which means others, if given the opportunity, will find Him lovely too. Being self-focused and spiritually despondent has a tremendous cost – communion with the Beloved is lost. May every believer reckon himself or herself dead to self and alive in Christ (Gal. 2:20). Then we too will have the right realization of our relationship: *"I am my beloved's, and my beloved is mine"* (Song 6:3). We are Christ's before all else. Moreover, He is ours; there is no possibility of disappointment on our part. So when He comes knocking to possess more of us, we must let Him in.

366

December 30 – Worshiping at God's Throne
Revelation 4:2-5

Immediately I was in the Spirit; and behold, a throne set in heaven, and one sat on the throne. And He who sat there was like a jasper and a sardius stone in appearance; and there was a rainbow around the throne, in appearance like an emerald. Around the throne were twenty-four thrones, and on the thrones I saw twenty-four elders sitting, clothed in white robes; and they had crowns of gold on their heads.

John was permitted to see God's throne in heaven and records what he saw in this chapter. He mentions the throne of God twelve times and is careful not to describe anything else he saw except in its relationship to the throne. To emphasize this connection, Jim Flanigan observes John's use of five prepositional clauses:

Upon the Throne – Deity sitting in inscrutable splendor.
Round about the Throne – a rainbow, and twenty-four crowned elders, and four strange living creatures.
Out of the Throne – lightning, and thundering, and voices.
Before the Throne – seven lamps of fire, a sea of glass, and the proffered crowns of the elders.
In the midst of the Throne – the four living ones, who also surround the Throne; and ... the Lamb (Rev. 5).[50]

Nothing is described in this heavenly scene apart from its connection with God's throne. Why? Because God is sovereign over all things and is accountable to none – everything which exists is dependent upon Him. Without God upon His throne, nothing else would matter. This is why the first sight that John describes after being caught up into heaven by the Holy Spirit was God upon His throne. John describes the outshining of God's holy essence – His spectacular glory. The prophet relates this visible manifestation of God's essence to the colors reflected from a jasper and a sardius stone. The priority of what John describes is important. Some think that it will be streets of gold, foundations of precious stones, and pearly gates that will make heaven special; yet, heaven would not be a spectacular domain at all if God were not there. John, thus, begins his revelation with the most spectacular sight in heaven – God with His Lamb on His throne.

December 31 – Forever With God
Revelation 22:1-5

And he showed me a pure river of water of life, clear as crystal, proceeding from the throne of God and of the Lamb. In the middle of its street, and on either side of the river, was the tree of life, which bore twelve fruits, each tree yielding its fruit every month. The leaves of the tree were for the healing of the nations. And there shall be no more curse, but the throne of God and of the Lamb shall be in it, and His servants shall serve Him. They shall see His face, and His name shall be on their foreheads. There shall be no night there: They need no lamp nor light of the sun, for the Lord God gives them light. And they shall reign forever and ever.

Conditions on the earth during Christ's Millennial Kingdom will be wonderful, but this era should not be confused with the Eternal State, which includes a new heaven and earth with no evil present (Isa. 65:17). The heavens and the earth as we know them shall pass away with a great noise and their elements shall melt with fervent heat and be burned up (2 Pet. 3:10). Isaiah states that *"all the host of heaven shall be dissolved, and the heavens shall be rolled up like a scroll"* (Isa. 34:4), then God will create a new heaven and new earth (Isa. 65:17). This will occur after Satan's last rebellion is quelled at the conclusion of the Kingdom Age (Rev. 20:7-10). A divine audit will then be conducted to confirm that Christ has completely dealt with all sin and has restored creation to perfection and to its proper association with God. All the damage caused by sin will be corrected (1 Cor. 15:26-28).

Besides drinking from the pure river of water, the inhabitants of heaven are also invited to eat from the tree of life. The redeemed will be able to enter into God's city and reside with Him forever. Believers will enjoy unbroken communion with God for eternity. Scripture closes with this invitation: *"And let him who thirsts come. Whoever desires, let him take the water of life freely"* (Rev. 22:17). All those who do come will agree with David's assessment, *"Oh, taste and see that the Lord is good; blessed is the man who trusts in Him!"* (Ps. 34:8).

The Bible closes with this promise from the Lord Jesus to all believers, *"Surely I am coming quickly"* (Rev. 22:20). And we happily agree with John's response, *"Amen. Even so, come, Lord Jesus!"*

Endnotes

1. W. T. P. Wolston, Chapter 22: *The Beatitudes* (STEM Publishing); https://www.stempublishing.com/authors/wolston/HAND322.html

2. H. A. Ironside, *Isaiah* – Revised Edition (Loizeaux, Neptune, NJ; 2000), p. 255

3. William MacDonald, *Believer's Bible Commentary* (Thomas Nelson Publishers, Nashville, TN: 1989), p. 1217

4. Lawrence O. Richards, *The Teacher's Commentary* (Victor Books, Wheaton, IL; 1987), p 547

5. C. H. Mackintosh, *Genesis to Deuteronomy* (Loizeaux Brothers, Inc., Neptune, NJ; 1972), p. 458

6. William MacDonald, op. cit., p. 1229

7. Edythe Draper, *Draper's Quotations From the Christian World* (Tyndale House Pub. Inc., Wheaton, IL – electronic copy)

8. Warren Wiersbe, *Be Joyful: A New Testament Study – Philippians* (Victor Books, Wheaton, Il; 1996 – electronic copy)

9. Edythe Draper, op. cit.

10. Ibid.

11. Ibid.

12. Ibid.

13. Arthur Pink, *Why Four Gospels?* (Scripture Truth Book Co., Fincastle, VA; no date), p. 75

14. *The Expositor*, Vol. XXI No. 241 (Westminster Press, Chicago, IL: Oct. 1919), pp. 77

15. Warren Wiersbe, *Be Complete: A New Testament Study - Colossians* (Victor Books, Wheaton, Il; 1996 – electronic copy)

16. A. P. Gibbs, *Scriptural Principles of Gathering* (Walterick Publishers; 1935): *www.votbg.org/apg_spog.htm*

17. William MacDonald, op. cit., p. 1732

18. R. P. Amos, *The Church* (Henrietta. NY); no date

19. C. H. Mackintosh, *The Mackintosh Treasury* (Loizeaux Brothers, Inc., Neptune, NJ 1976; reprint by Believers Bookshelf Inc.; 1999), p. 794

20. Warren Wiersbe, *The Bible Exposition Commentary* (Victor Books, Wheaton, IL; 1989), 1 Cor. 9:24-27

21. C. H. Mackintosh, op. cit., Num. 8

22. William MacDonald, op. cit., p. 2083

23. H. A. Ironside, *Notes on the Book of Ezra* (Shiloh Christian Library, no date); pp. 5-6

24. H. A. Ironside, *Holiness – The False and the True* (Loizeaux, Neptune, NJ: 1912), p. 33

25. H. L. Rossier, *Meditations on the Book of Judges*, STEM Publishing (chp. 20): http://stempublishing.com/authors/rossier/JUDGES.html

26   Matthew Henry, *Matthew Henry's Concise Commentary on the Whole Bible* (e-Sword, electronic version), 2 Sam. 11:1-5

27   William Kelly, *1 Peter*, STEM Publishing: 1 Peter 2:11-12
      https://stempublishing.com/authors/kelly/2Newtest/1peter.html#a2

28   William MacDonald, op cit., p. 852

29   F. B. Hole, *Leviticus*, STEM Publishing: Leviticus 10
      F. B. Hole, http://stempublishing.com/authors/hole/Pent/LEVITICUS.html

30   Warren Wiersbe, *The Bible Exposition Commentary,* op. cit., Vol. 2, p. 142

31   Watchman Nee, *Sit Walk Stand* (Gospel Literature Service, Bombay, India; 1957), chp. 3

32   Ibid.

33   Ibid.

34   P. L. Tan, *Encyclopedia of 7700 illustrations* (Bible Communications, Garland TX; 1996, c1979)

35   R. C. Chapman, *Robert Cleaver Chapman of Barnstaple*, by W. H. Bennet (Pickering & Inglis, Glasgow, Scotland; no date – 1st ed.), pp. 125-126

36   William Kelly, *Isaiah - Exposition*, Part 2, STEM Publishing; chp. 26:
      http://stempublishing.com/authors/kelly/1Oldtest/ISA_PT2.html#a1

37   William MacDonald, op. cit., p. 2011

38   Dr. Howard Taylor, *Spiritual Secret of Hudson Taylor* (Whitaker House, New Kensington, PA: 1996), p. 273

39   Oswald Chambers, *My Utmost for His Highest* (Discovery House; 2005), April 10th

40   William MacDonald, *True Discipleship* (Walterick Pub., Kansas City, KS; 1975), p. 56

41   David Gooding, *In the School of Christ* (Gospel Folio Press, Grand Rapids, MI; 1995), p. 30

42   Warren Wiersbe, op. cit., Vol. 2, pp. 288-289

43   Edythe Draper, op. cit.

44   Ibid.

45   W. E. Vine, *Vine's Expository Dictionary of Biblical Words* (Thomas Nelson Publishers; 1985 – electronic version), *Kleros*

46   Harry A. Ironside, *Commentary on 1 Peter* (Loizeaux Brothers, Inc., Neptune, NJ; 1985), p. 56

47   Matthew Henry, op. cit., Jas. 4:7

48   *New Exhaustive Strong's Numbers and Concordance With Expanded Greek-Hebrew Dictionary* (Biblesoft and International Bible Translators, Inc.; 1994)

49   J. H. Thayer, *Thayer's Greek Lexicon* (Biblesoft Electronic Database; 2000), *Nicolaitan*

50   Jim Flanigan, *Notes on Revelation* (Gospel Tract Publications; 1987), pp. 40-41

An Old Testament Journey

May We See Christ?

WARREN HENDERSON

May We See Christ – An Old Testament Journey is a sequential study of Scripture containing 366 two-page devotions (758 pages). Besides the plain language of the Old Testament, God has employed a variety of types, symbols, and allegories in a complementary fashion to teach us about His Son. With the light of New Testament truth and the illuminating assistance of the Holy Spirit, we are able to understand and appreciate these fascinating Old Testament pictures. All of God's written Word speaks of Christ to some degree as He is the main emphasis of Scripture. Accordingly, the best reason to embark on this one-year journey is to more clearly see, know, and love Christ. May the Lord richly bless your daily contemplations of the Savior as you expectantly peer into God's oracles and witness the glory of His Son. — Warren Henderson